STAR TREK

FANS AND

COSTUME

ART

Folk Art and Artists Series
Michael Owen Jones
General Editor

Books in this series focus on the work of informally trained or self-taught artists rooted in regional, occupational, ethnic, racial, or gender-specific traditions. Authors explore the influence of artists' experiences and aesthetic values upon the art they create, the process of creation, and the cultural traditions that served as inspiration or personal resource. The wide range of art forms featured in this series reveals the importance of aesthetic expression in our daily lives and gives striking testimony to the richness and vitality of art and tradition in the modern world.

STAR TREK FANS AND COSTUME ART

Heather R. Joseph-Witham

University Press of Mississippi   Jackson

Dedicated to Sheila and Eze Joseph, with whom I began watching Star Trek, *and to Jerry Joseph, Renah Wolzinger, and Nigel Witham, with whom I continue.*

Copyright © 1996 by the University Press of Mississippi
All rights reserved
Manufactured in Hong Kong

Library of Congress Cataloging-in-Publication Data

Joseph-Witham, Heather R.
    Star trek fans and costume art / Heather R. Joseph-Witham.
        p.   cm. — (Folk art and artists series)
    Includes bibliographical references.
    ISBN 0-87805-919-9 (cloth : alk. paper). —
ISBN 0-87805-920-2 (pbk. : alk. paper)
    1. Star Trek television programs.   2. Star Trek films.   3. Fans (Persons)   4. Costume.
I. Title. II. Series.
PN1992.8.S74J67   1996
791.45′75—dc20   96-20446
                                        CIP

British Library Cataloging-in-Publication data available

CONTENTS

I FIRST went to a *Star Trek* convention, in 1989, by accident. My family and I were heading to a wedding reception at a hotel in Anaheim, California, when we noticed someone dressed as a Vulcan entering another elevator. Such was our excitement that we, along with the bride and groom and many of the wedding guests, skipped much of the reception and went to the *Star Trek* convention being held in another part of the hotel. As a baby, I had been introduced to *Star Trek* by my parents. Along with my brother and sister, I am a lifelong fan who had never thought to take my enjoyment of the shows and movies beyond watching them. It wasn't until 1992 that I decided to attend another "con" in order to research it as a traditional festive event for a folklore class. I met Russel Noel and Douglas Gaines, die-hard fans who later introduced me to Mimi Gallandt-Oakes, the current captain of a fan-run "starship" called the Palavra. Mimi invited me to attend fan events and meetings, which, along with the cons, introduced me to a fascinating people and culture.

Since 1993 I have been attending *Star Trek* cons in Southern California and interviewing costumed fans there, as well as at community service events they host or attend, at fan club meetings and in fans' homes. I was and am intrigued by this group, by its ideals and its art forms. Costumes, above all other fan arts, set this community apart from the world of non-fans, and they speak volumes about the artists who create them.

Since I am a fan myself, I understand the in-group language that Trekkers speak. However, I am slightly removed from the situation in that I am not a member of any fan group and do not (yet) wear any *Star Trek* uniforms to cons or events. Nonetheless, I have been treated as a member of this fellowship by the many Trekkers whom I have met and interviewed. I hope that this work does justice to them and their art.

I am eternally grateful to the many fans who allowed me to look into their lives, particularly Mimi Gallandt-Oakes, Cat Ramos, and Mike Sandeffur. I also thank all the members of the Palavra and everyone who graciously allowed me to interview and take pictures of them, including Douglas Gaines, Max Mejias, Dave Bourne, Jason Jacobs, Shanna Hoskins, Russel Noel, Alesha Holder, Bill Phillips, Tiger Manning and her husband, John Bates, Robin Baker, Michael Oakes and Ariel, Wayne Wills (good luck with your new shuttle, Wayne), Majel Barrett Roddenberry, Joe Pincetich, John Abbott, Debbie and Denis Hanon, Susan Eastgate and her sons, Ryan and Tyler, Thomas Phillips, John D. Wright, Roy D. Henderson, Paul E. Pierce, Saul Del Toro, Herbie Garcia, Marci Mesnard, Joyce Herndon, Gloria Lamden, Bobbie Schafer, and Dana Ebright. Many thanks go to Sheila Joseph, Nigel Witham, and Michelle Kram for transcription and typing help. Without Michael Owen Jones, this work would never have been attempted. I am very grateful to him for his enthusiasm, ideas, persistence, patience, and invaluable aid in organizing and editing this volume.

DOUGLAS GAINES is an excellent example of a Trekker fan and costumer. His life and activities demonstrate many of the hobbies of Trek fans. Doug has been dressing in *Star Trek* costumes for nine years. For an Anaheim *Star Trek* convention in 1995, Doug, a part-time actor living in San Diego, attired himself in the full battle regalia of a Klingon warrior (plates 1 and 2). His mother, an accomplished seamstress, helped him, and he used a few items bought at conventions as well as a multitude of materials including fake fur, plastic and sweatsuit fabric. He created the look based on his knowledge of Klingons from *Star Trek* shows, movies, and magazine pictures. He also applied his own aesthetic ideas about how he would look best as a Klingon. Doug often attends conventions looking like Mr. Scott from the original *Star Trek* television show or like a Bajoran-Klingon fusion he invented who wears a Federation uniform. When appearing as Mr. Scott, Doug puts tire gauges in his vest pocket to simulate the character's engineering tools. He also can dress quickly. However, when appearing as Dellahan, a Bajoran-Klingon character, Doug spends three hours applying makeup. Doug most enjoys appearing as Dellahan, because he created the character and writes stories about him (plate 3). The Dellahan personality alters as Doug's own life changes; he sees his story as well as his costumes as a never-ending process of evolving. Dellahan

is an extension of Doug. And when he is in *Star Trek* costume, Doug is taken "out of depressions." He says that costuming "makes me forget things for a while. Be somewhere else for a while." Moreover, Doug sees his fan activities as a way to bring *Star Trek* ideals about a positive future into his life. Being a fan is an intensely social activity. Doug belongs to several *Star Trek* clubs. He often brings his fiancée and her son to events as well. Indeed, Doug views many of his fan friends as family. Most of all, Doug costumes because of the enjoyment, excitement, and social opportunities it affords. "Everybody knows what *Star Trek* is and being associated with a phenomenon like that—it's fun! It's something I never tire of. I think I'll be fifty-five or sixty years old, I'll still be doing this makeup. It'll just be easier 'cause I won't have to do the wrinkles anymore."

Doug is one of many thousands, possibly millions, of people around the world who call themselves *Star Trek* fans. *Star Trek* fandom has inspired many other types of media fandom such as *X-Files* fans, *Alien Nation* and even *Beauty and the Beast* fans, all of whom hold conventions similar to Trek cons. But Trekkers are unique in their devotion to this particular fandom and the many artistic enterprises it has inspired.

In this volume I will explore one form of fan art. I describe how individuals create costumes using guidelines from the *Star Trek* universe and applying aesthetic principles

STAR TREK FANS AND COSTUME ART

and symbols from their own lives. Questions that will be addressed include: what is *Star Trek* fandom? Why is a popular culture medium important in people's everyday lives? Why may we consider fan costuming as a folk art? What are the boundaries of authenticity and innovation in costuming? And what does costuming mean for the individuals who participate in it?

Star Trek Fandom

In order to understand why people produce art based on *Star Trek,* it is necessary to understand what fandom is, and how it led to the invention of such art. The term "fan" originally meant "fanatic" and referred to a religious devotee. The word became attached to sports followers during the nineteenth century and, later, to female theater goers who supposedly had become attached to stage actors (Jenkins 1992:12). The term came to describe followers of the literary science fiction genre, which formed the groundwork for media fandom of the twentieth century. These fans were drawn to each other and formed clubs. The first science fiction con was held in 1936 in Philadelphia, and, by 1939, science fiction fandom had grown large enough to host a world science fiction convention. Individuals dressed as science fiction characters came to these early cons, and a costume contest was organized at each event.

Star Trek fandom followed from science fiction fandom. Trekkers follow some sci-fi traditions, such as cons and costume contests.

The original *Star Trek* television series premiered in 1966 and immediately drew a following. Later, when ratings dipped and the network considered cancelling *Star Trek*, its fans emerged as a powerful force. One fan, Bjo Trimble, led a letter-writing campaign to save the show, and about one million letters were sent to the network. *Star Trek* was allowed a third and final season.

Star Trek fans became truly active several years after the cancellation of the series. Having been marginalized and only "tolerated" by the literary fans at science fiction cons, Trekkers held their own con in New York in 1972 (Lichtenberg 1975: 52). Thousands turned out, and this became an annual event. There are now hundreds of cons all over the world each year. Some are fan-run enterprises, while others are held by official convention organizations. Following the early cons, *Star Trek* fandom and the official *Star Trek* industry developed symbiotically. *Star Trek* reruns began, attracting new fans who became active. They sent four hundred thousand letters to NASA, urging that the space shuttle prototype be named Enterprise after the ship in *Star Trek*. Because of fan interest keeping the *Star Trek* series and concept alive, *Star Trek: The Motion Picture* was made and released in 1979. Since then, there have been six more films, a cartoon series and three new television series, beginning with *Star Trek: The Next Generation*, which debuted in 1987. There are now countless new fans from a new generation.

Conventions are very important for fans and fan art. They are meeting places where old and new friends get together, and where new members for Trekker clubs, such as Star Fleet International, are recruited. Cons also serve as a marketplace for costume books and magazines and for such items as communicator pins, Bajoran earrings, Federation outfits, various weapons and toys and even Vulcan ears. Cons also represent a stage opportunity for costumers, where garments can be compared or copied, and fans can get ideas from other fan artists. People who are attired in daily clothing attend cons and ask costumers for autographs and photos, thus providing positive reinforcement for those exhibiting their creativity. Lastly, cons are a type of fan newsroom where information about new series episodes, new films, show stars and gossip about other fans is exchanged. Fans are able to meet at cons to talk to one another. A frequent subject, of course, is themselves. Fans know who they are and are very conscious of being a part of *Star Trek* fandom and, thus, of popular culture.

The Palavra

Fan clubs often begin with several friends getting together in recognition of a common interest. But *Star Trek* fandom has grown to such a degree that there are now many clubs and organizations. Some are formal groups with rigid standards; others are fairly informal with loose sets of rules. A fan can choose from any number of different fan groups.

The Palavra is a *Star Trek* fan club based in San Diego, California. It started as an idea in the minds of several current members. One fan, Alesha Holder, belonged to another San Diego starship called the U. S. S. Miramar. She came into fandom through her mother, a leader of that ship. Alesha then met Mimi Gallandt-Oakes at a *Star Trek* convention. Mimi was there in deference to a friend who was dressed as a Klingon, which she thought at the time was very "bizarre," as she herself had never considered dressing as an alien. Nonetheless, Mimi soon changed her mind and found that fandom was something she had been looking for all of her life. She and Alesha, with a few others, decided to "shuttle" off the Miramar and form their own ship, which was called the Palavra.

The Palavra gained interested members who then registered with Star Fleet International, the overarching club whose officers supervise smaller club actions. This situation is inspired by the TV series, in which Star Fleet is in charge of all of its ships, including the *Enterprise*. One year after the Palavra had become a shuttle, gained more members, and organized and participated in dozens of charity and community service events, it was commissioned to become a starship by Star Fleet International.

The Palavra members, their families, and a few Klingon friends from Klingon ships in the area attended a formal public ceremony for the commissioning of the U. S. S. Palavra–NCC201, an excelsior class starship. The ceremony was held outside a movie theater where DeForrest Kelley (Dr. McCoy on the original series) had earlier been signing autographs for the premiere of *Star Trek*: *Generations*. The theater management had invited club members to hold their ceremony there because the fan presence in costume was good for business. The ceremony, however, had nothing to do with business promotion but instead was a formal, touching, and meaningful experience for members.

Admiral Max Mejias from Star Fleet International came from Fresno to give the Palavra its Star Fleet certificate of charter. Mejias promoted Mimi from commander to captain and gave her Star Fleet's first orders. He commanded the Palavra "to work for the good and enjoyment of all. Be prepared to defend the Federation in your sectors against apathy and depres-

sion. Fire all phasers and torpedos at self-doubt and lack of self-esteem. Find the shyest and most obscure members on your ship and groom them to be future captains."

These orders characterize the goals and suggest reasons for belonging to a *Star Trek* club. Admiral Mejias, who wore a formal, knee-length Star Fleet jacket at the ceremony, explains why he costumes in *Star Trek* uniforms and why he belongs to Star Fleet. "Money just doesn't matter. You're poor, you're rich, black, white, short, tall, heavy, brilliant, dumb. The concept that all races [are equal] . . . no matter who you are and what you look like is the foundation of this organization. . . . I'm here because this is where my heart is, this is the humanity of the race." Members of the

Palavra members and friends stand at attention during the commissioning ceremony that made the Palavra a starship.

10

Palavra would agree with this idealization of *Star Trek* and Trekker clubs.

During the latter months of 1995, there was dissension in the ranks of Star Fleet International. Some members left to create a new organization called the United Federation of Planets Internationale. The Palavra chose to join this new group, but not all members saw the move as positive and some quit the ship to stay with Star Fleet. Groups fall apart and reconnect in various ways in any community. This action by Trekkers demonstrates that there is variation within Trek clubs, and that such differences are necessary in order for these groups to remain relevant to members.

Mimi Gallandt-Oakes, the captain of the Palavra, keeps members active and involved, holds club meetings at her home, supervises a club newsletter, and plans events for the group. She joined the Palavra initially because "it looked like fun," but believes that the ideals of *Star Trek* and the fact that all members are "doers" holds them together. She states, "We're somebody who believes in the future . . . in a better future. We believe . . . you can't just sit here. . . . You have to work for it. You have to do things. If you sit on the fence and you don't do anything, you're just as bad as the people who are causing the trouble to begin with." Club members are aware of what is occurring in their communities and attempt to make things better

with various charitable projects and activities through the vehicle of *Star Trek* fandom.

While the Palavra does many things for others, its members have also benefitted. Mimi met her husband, Michael Oakes, through fandom. He often attends events dressed as Commander Data, an android from *Star Trek: The Next Generation*. Alesha Holder, who was formerly engaged to a Klingon, met her current boyfriend through the club. Others expect the same. Herbie Garcia dresses as a character he invented called Sabachi, who is meant to be a Native American Federation officer and the brother of Commander Chakotay in *Star Trek: Voyager*. Garcia views this character as his own alter ego. He grew up watching *Star Trek* with his family and joined the

Mimi Gallandt-Oakes, the Palavra's captain, and Alesha Holder, her first officer, stand with a security guard as they prepare to accept their ship's commission from Admiral Max Mejias of Star Fleet International.

11

Palavra a year ago. He believes that it has helped his social life and makes him a part of a community. At one convention he said that he fully expects to meet "Miss Right" at a *Star Trek* event, because she definitely will be a *Star Trek* fan.

Other Palavra members have gained social lives, family time and self-esteem from club membership and costuming. Susan Eastgate is a single mother and a professional who joined the Palavra over a year ago. She attributes her current active social life to signing up with the *Star Trek* club. She attends events with other area Trekker groups (such as Laser-tech), baseball game challenges between Federation members and a Klingon club, group meetings, community service events, and conventions. This contact has gained her a number of close friends. She will be moving to Washington soon for a new job and has already gotten in touch with Trekker clubs there, as she fully intends to continue this activity and hopes it will engage her family and establish a social life in a new area. She brings her two sons, Ryan and Tyler, to most events. She states, "Before I joined the Palavra we still did things as a family but not as much as we do now. I'm a lot more active now, my kids are a lot more active now." Susan dresses in Klingon costumes as well as the Federation outfit she has in common with her shipmates (plates 4 and 5). She brings her

sons dressed in Federation uniforms to conventions (plate 6). She says of the boys: "They like the role-playing and it helps them release a lot of energy. They love the attention. . . . Every time somebody wants to get their picture, they are absolutely eating the attention up. . . . I think they get noticed more. It's good for their self-esteem."

Susan's son Ryan agrees with his mother's positive characterization of his experience with costumes. He portrays the character Wesley Crusher, from *Star Trek: The Next Generation*. Part of the fun for Ryan is meeting TV stars at conventions. He enjoyed speaking with actor Leonard Nimoy, who portrayed Mr. Spock in the original series, the films, and *The Next Generation*, and he is extremely pleased that he has

Herbie Garcia, a Palavra member, drew the facial design that marks him as a character related to Commander Chakotay of *Star Trek: Voyager* (Anaheim convention 1995).

met Majel Barrett Roddenberry (actress and widow of *Star Trek*'s creator) six times. Further, he gets to "fit in." He says, "I want to be like one of the people who are into this stuff." There are many other young people who go to cons with older family members. Mimi Gallandt-Oakes's daughter Ariel often attends with her parents. She is the executive officer of a cadet group for children begun by the Palavra. She often portrays Guinan, a character created by actress Whoopi Goldberg, and occasionally she is a Klingon or a Federation officer. She says, "I like dressing up 'cause I win cool prizes and give them to my mom and she likes them." But Ariel also role-plays and has a great time at cons and other events.

Some Palavra members are perceived negatively by outsiders for their Trekker activities and costuming. Mimi says her teenage son "calls us a bunch of *Star Trek* nerds." Referring to her and her husband's extended family, she states, "Well, they all think we're really weird." Alesha Holder has also found people who do not approve of her pastime. She says, "They think of us as a bunch of weirdos and lunatics dressing up in outfits that only actors should be wearing." For the most part, however, Palavra members' hobbies and costume wearing have been accepted by their mundane (mundane meaning all nonfans) friends and family.

Star Trek Federation outfits that Palavra members wear are called costumes by most outsiders (including myself), but members themselves refer to the outfits as "uniforms." This implies that, like other uniforms, whether those of Girl Scouts, the military or the police, the clothing serves to draw a line between members who belong to the group and those who do not. Indeed, at conventions, which are often held in hotels, costumes define the Trekkers' space, separating fans from the public while at the same time serving as an identifying marker of pride for fans.

Many believe the uniform should be complete and perfect. While some fans may wear a Star Fleet shirt with jeans, Mimi Gallandt-Oakes says, "I don't wear partial uniforms. It would be disrespectful to the uniform" (plate 7). This is because of the meaning behind the uniform, which is, Mimi says, "Everything that Star Fleet stands for. I suppose that Star Fleet is the future of the military and all of the respect that goes behind the military. There's a certain amount of dignity that goes along with it. I put the uniform on and I'm not Mimi anymore, I'm a commander. I have an attitude that I adopt out of respect to the uniform. The uniform's respect comes from Gene Roddenberry's dream and the respect that all of us, the Klingons, the Romulans, the Ferengi, we all respect Gene's dream and . . . we're working to make [it] a reality. Just because Gene isn't here anymore doesn't mean his dream isn't."

13

Gene's Dream

Many fans who wear *Star Trek* apparel to public events attempt to actualize the ideals of the show's creator, Gene Roddenberry, and the *Star Trek* universe. The program's visions and values are thus represented by the Trekker uniforms. Majel Barrett Roddenberry, Gene's widow and an actress who appears as Nurse Chapel on the original TV series and in the films, and as Lwaxana Troy and the computer voice on *Star Trek: The Next Generation,* agrees that the fan uniforms help to keep Gene's dreams alive. She adds that "Gene always insisted on the first series upon passing on all the costumes. Especially on all the women's costumes. That's why they were so scarce. So, costuming was always very important to Gene and to Bob [Bob Black—the costume designer for *The Next Generation, Deep Space Nine* and *Voyager*] it is too." Further, Majel, as fans adoringly refer to her, sells a line of Federation uniform patterns. She completely approves of fan costuming in public. "Oh, I think it's wonderful. It's very innovative of them. And they follow the patterns extremely well and they get terribly creative. Which means it lends itself a lot to art. I think these people [and] . . . the things they make are remarkable!" Fans appreciate that Majel gives her approval of fan art. They admire her and value her frequent presence at cons. They believe that she,

too, helps uphold the ideals of the *Star Trek* universe.

Dave Bourne, who appears as a Klingon, also connects Gene's dreams, fan ideals and fan apparel. "When I met Gene Roddenberry about a year before he died, he had commented on how nice my outfit was. And I was very touched because to me he's the father of *Star Trek* and if it wasn't for him we would not have been created. And so I want to be able to continue his thought. His dream was that there is a plausible future for us, where there won't be racism and . . . hunger, and we won't place the same value on money any more, and human life will mean something." Dave has worked very hard on his Klingon garment, and he uses his knowledge of sewing and Klingon fashion to help others create uniforms that suit them.

Many fans cite Gene's dream of a better universe as a major reason they are a part of *Star Trek* fandom and wear fan uniforms. Max Mejias, a Star Fleet admiral, discusses some of these hopes and values. "There are many faces, many costumes, but we're all friends. And we all love each other. And that was what Gene was trying to say. With his very first episode, he did something that shook the world. He put a black person, an oriental person, and white people all together on the bridge of the *Enterprise* for the first time ever. . . . And he was able to make it work. He put a Vulcan on there to symbolize and represent all the different races of the world. And, he made them all work together. . . . They were willing to give their lives for one another. It's an incredible dream. We're far from it. [The fans] are the dreamers and the hopefuls . . . that this world is going to make it." John D. Wright, who appears as a Klingon, agrees with this characterization. The people in *Star Trek*, he says, "believe in everybody as an equal. No matter if you're from another universe or from another planet. Everybody's an equal. I treat people with respect and I feel like you should treat everybody with respect. If everybody here did that we wouldn't be killing each other every day."

According to fans, peace, multiculturalism and the space program are visions of an imaginary world that Trekkers work toward in their regular lives as well as when they are in uniforms. Russel Noel of the Palavra states, "When we're here [in costume] we get to be in an imaginary time, which may still be possible. We have to think positively. A good working social system, where there's no homelessness, there's no racism. Where everybody can accomplish their goals in life." Russ has been a fan of *Star Trek* since childhood. He grew up watching his father work in the aerospace industry, which he feels complements the ideals in *Star Trek*. He sees fandom as important "to keep the space station alive." He believes that fans can accomplish much in the real world. Mimi

Gallandt-Oakes agrees. She says that wearing uniforms at conventions is "the fun, that's the play. The work is—Gene dreamed of a future when there wasn't any more poverty and . . . prejudice, and there wasn't any more upper class and lower class. And people didn't need anything. If you needed it, you could get it. . . . Of all the things that Gene dreamed of, he dreamed of peace. . . . So what we as twentieth-century Trekkers have to do is, rather than sit around going '*Star Trek* is so cool,' we have to work towards that goal." One way that Mimi and the Palavra work for Gene's values is through community service.

Indeed, all of the Trekker clubs focus on charity. Douglas Gaines belongs to Star Fleet International, the Klingon Assault Group and the Bajoran Tactical Strikeforce. He states that "the basic premise . . . is they are all community service clubs that do things to better the community through community service and in the guise of *Star Trek*." Roy Henderson leads a Klingon ship. "When I started my ship, it was done for the children. Last year we raised over twenty-three hundred dollars for charities. We did charity for abused children and we went to an elementary school [in Klingon garments]. We did a benefit for the adult special ed of Redlands, California. It's something we can do for others. And *Star Trek* has given us a way to do it. Gene Roddenberry had the idea when he gave people the

15

idea of a future world where all worked together." His Klingon group also enters costume contests at conventions. When they win they receive toys as prizes; then, dressed in full Klingon battle regalia, they give these to children at Christmas. Roy quips, "Have you ever seen a Klingon with a Santa hat on?"

Some fans join Trekker clubs and begin wearing uniforms because of fan club involvement in community service. John Bates was a passive fan with no intention of becoming a full-fledged Trekker. When he met Palavra members he was attracted by the fact that they do charity work. He now appears regularly in a Federation security uniform at events. The wearing of Trek garments is a key to the success of many community service events. For example, Trekkers wear their futuristic outfits to elementary schools to discuss science with the children. The unusual apparel gets students' attention and becomes a teaching device. Hospital visits from those in uniform are exciting for children as well. Indeed, the outfits allow fans to actualize some of their peaceful and charitable goals. Dave Bourne, captain of a Klingon ship, puts it this way: "We do a lot of charity events. And if it takes wearing a weird outfit like this and drawing attention to a problem that is going on on this earth, I'm willing to do it any day." For Trekkers, the wearing of these garments is an excellent way to actualize Gene Roddenberry's

dreams and fans' visions. When fans wear uniforms, they are viewed by other fans as supporting these principles and goals.

The Boundaries of Authenticity

There is a continuous dialectic among costume artists about how strictly they should adhere to the specifications of a uniform as it is seen in a *Star Trek* show, and how much of their own tastes can be used in costume making. The debate and discussion among fans is whether to maintain the tradition of "authentic" uniforms or to allow for personal aesthetics and "innovative" outfits.

The general view among fans is that the more a clothing item looks like one in the shows, the more authentic it is, and the more authentic, the better. J. A. is an entrepreneur. He has been a *Star Trek* fan since the 1960s and turned his fandom into a business. He sets up a table at conventions and sells souvenirs and Federation uniforms (plates 8 and 9). He sews each piece himself, using the Majel Barrett Roddenberry patterns, and wears his uniform while selling, saying, "If you're wearing a costume, the fans relate to you and they realize you're a fan." Of the items he makes, he says, "Everything on it is as authentic as possible." J. A. dislikes seeing people dressed in some of the more idiosyncratic outfits. He believes that Trekker uniforms

16

should be as similar to those in the TV shows and movies as possible. Many fans concur. There may be some pressure on fan costumers to maintain "authentic" standards in garment creation. As fans work within a community of other fans, certain standards exist that are considered "normal."

Folklorists use the term "normalform" to describe a basic, recognizable, or standard form of a folklore item (Georges and Jones 1995:128–32). The normative or normalform uniform for a fan artist is one that imitates precisely what is seen in a magazine, TV show, or movie. However, when a uniform is different from the normalform but is still recognizable as being, say, a Federation uniform, it is called a version of that original garment. There are many variants of any uniform seen on the screen in fan costuming. Fans do not have to adhere to on-screen standards. While Paramount Pictures owns the rights to official *Star Trek* uniforms, no one stops the fans from bringing their own personalities into their creations. The tradition of fan costuming is not static. People make outfits that have meaning for them, thus keeping the tradition alive and exciting. Variation in garment creation allows individuals to bring their personal lives into their hobbies. They can establish an intimate connection to the figures and characters they use as their inspiration.

Some fans utilize uniforms and makeup to depict a specific character from the *Trek* shows and therefore have little latitude in costume creation. Saul Del Toro portrays Commander Chakotay from the newest *Star Trek* show, *Voyager* (plate 10). He dresses as this character because he relates to Chakotay, who is an American Indian. Saul is part Indian and part Spanish. He comes in uniform to cons because it makes him feel that he is a part of the *Trek* world. He says, "You get away from reality and you're in a better universe. Where it's more peaceful than having all these racial things." Michael Oakes and Wayne Wills of the Palavra imitate the characters of Commander Data (a golden-skinned android) and Chief Miles O'Brien, respectively. They do this largely because each bears a remarkable likeness to the figure he represents. Thomas Phillips portrays Commander Geordi La Forge (plate 11). He carries a visor that flashes a red light like the one the character wears. The visor gets hot so he has to use it without the battery except when he goes on stage during costume contests.

The creative choices of many fans who wear Federation uniforms are particularly evident when they select a specific type of uniform or determine the accessories to be added (plate 12). Palavra member John Bates states, "For Star Fleet there is very little leeway we can do with our uniforms other than putting an insignia on or something like that, because every time you see a Federation [character] in a movie or a TV show, they are all the same." Mimi Gallandt-Oakes qualifies this, saying, "There is also freedom, because there's the original series, the first movies, the next movies. That's three uniforms. *The Next Generation, Deep Space Nine,* and there was a sixth uniform that didn't actually make it into the movies." Mimi chose the uniforms that suited her tastes. She says of the first movie costumes, "Those white things had to go. I have all the uniforms except for the original series and the disco pajama uniform, because they both look like pajamas." Mimi, however, has added to her uniforms and at times has dyed her hair pink and cut it to make it look like a Vulcan hairdo; she also wears Vulcan pointed ear pieces with her Federation uniform.

The Palavra struggled with different costume ideas that would identify it as a group. Members toyed with berets and various hats. They decided to use black turtleneck shirts beneath their uniforms because the purple and grey ones worn on the show are difficult to locate. Also, some in the Palavra wear the *Star Trek II* movie uniform, which is quite recognizable; because it is not sold at cons it must be made at home, and very few fans have it (refer to plate 4).

Russel Noel attires himself as a Federation member who does a great impression of Captain Kirk. He views costume authen- ticity as important, yet he has created some astounding props to accompany his uniform. Russ's garment is a near-replica of one used in the movies *Star Trek II* through *Star Trek VI* (plate 13). He made it before a pattern was released by starting and stopping his VCR while watching the movies. He says that the color and material of his uniform are wrong. He couldn't locate the exact color, and the wool gabardine used in the films is too expensive. He found his "genuine 1970 style double knit flair pants" at a Salvation Army store, bought a leather belt and then made a Star Fleet logo as a belt-clatch. Russ also wears a suede jacket uniform similar to one worn by Kirk in a film (plate 14). Russ's decision about which uniform to wear at a given occasion may reflect his mood of the moment. He appeared in his dark suit after undergoing chemotherapy for cancer.

Russ learned to sew and to create props from his years of theater experience both on and off the stage. His real training and artistry emerge in the props he made to accompany his costume. Although one can buy metal pins at conventions, Russ opted to use plastic for the pins and insignias he attaches to his jacket. He also made a hand-held phaser weapon out of different materials. Russ explains, "This particular design is called [the] Type IIB phaser pistol. It was used in *Star Trek: The Search For Spock.* Now using one of the textbooks available . . . [with] engineering drawings in it, I was able to use those drawings and make this full-scale replica. I made it out of balsa [wood]. Basically, I wanted something light that I could carry around all day so I used balsa. . . . It's customized slightly." Russ updated the style of the phaser from the original show and can attach it to the Type IIB phaser. He also used balsa wood to create a future version of the original show's flip-top communicator. One company is marketing its own plastic communicator that has a sound chip in it with the voices of some of the original *Star Trek* cast. Russ is considering playing on this theme. "As a joke I wanted to make one where you flip the thing open and it goes 'AT&T.'"

Fans in Federation costumes must often adhere to a limited range of costume possibilities, but those portraying aliens enjoy greater freedom. There are no patterns for Borg, Ferengi or Romulan uniforms and only a few for Klingons. Most fans make garments that adhere to the basic form of the alien they are using as a model, but create the rest the way they like. Doug Gaines says, "There aren't really any rules to it. Every time you see a different group of Klingons on the series they are always slightly different." Michael Oakes adds, "So there's an individuality that's allowed in the Klingon uniforms. . . . There is a basis that

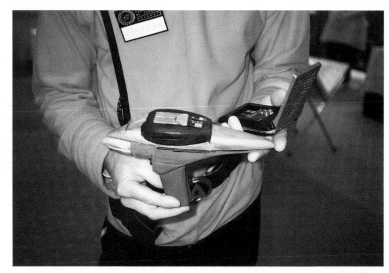

you follow . . . like the shoulder pieces [and the battle armor]. . . . But as far as color and individuality, what are you going to put on the trophy sash?"

Klingons and other aliens sometimes feel pressure to create costumes that appeal both to themselves and to other fans. Roy Henderson says of Klingon uniforms, "Each one of them is a piece of art. If you look at all the different Klingons, they look similar, but you'll notice that each one of them varies just slightly." Roy notes that Klingon ships, houses or groups differ from each other because effort is taken for a Klingon club to have some unifying marks. He also acknowledges that his "own aesthetics" went into the creation of his costume through his stylistic choices (plates

Russel Noel holds phaser and communicator that he made. The phaser consists of two separable parts. The black portion on the top center can be removed from the larger gray phaser, and both can then be used separately.

15 and 16). Yet, he states, "The closer I can get it to the ones on the TV or the movies it seems the better the people like it. Authenticity has a lot to do with it. If it's not exactly what they've seen, or close to the TV series, they tend to [say], 'Well that's nice, but. . . .' This is what they want to see, more like the stars."

Some fans care little about authenticity and create what they want. They usually learn from fellow fans and are more concerned with what their fellow aliens think of their uniforms than with what noncostumed fans think, or what is occurring on the TV shows. Dave Bourne says of Klingons, "We don't have standards. We would like to just have the general look of the Imperial [Klingon Division]." He continues, "There's panels that we hold at conventions, plus we have fellow Klingons that help us design things, give us ideas, and we put it on paper and we put it in our minds and develop it." Fellow Klingon Shanna Hoskins adds, "Yeah, we feed off of each other as far as costume ideas go." Indeed, alien portrayers often stretch the boundaries of the *Star Trek* costume tradition.

Alien Invasion

Star Trek writers have invented many different types of aliens, including the Ferengi,

Russel Noel holds phaser made from balsa wood.

who are a group of greedy capitalists, and the Romulans, who are humanoids with a slightly xenophobic twist. There is the honorable warrior race of Klingons, and the part-machine Borg. The Bajorans are religious zealots who just ended a war with the Cardassians, a physically ugly and warlike people. There are also the Q, omnipotent but selfish beings, the Ocampa, who have nine-year life spans, the Trill, beings with immortal slugs inside of them, the logical-minded Vulcans and a multitude of other aliens that are less defined or explored.

Fans invest an immense amount of creativity in making alien costumes. Joe Pincetich is a high school band director, father and husband who attends conventions as a Romulan (plate 17) with his wife who appears as a Bajoran. A science fiction buff, Pincetich likes the "consistent" and "fairly good stories" on *Star Trek*. He is not a member of a fan club, but comes to cons because for him "it's fun" and "recreational." He decided to be a Romulan partly because few fans appear as Romulans at cons—probably because there are not many Romulan fan clubs, and group reinforcement is important in costuming. Pincetich explains that "Romulans are more fun. They're just as warlike as everybody, but they just have a little bit more panache." When he shows up dressed at cons the experience is enjoyable because "people come up and talk to you [when costumed]," and ask for information about Romulans or for photos and autographs. "I like to meet the people, they're always friendly and supportive." The reasons that Pincetich has for costuming also inspire him to make an excellent, and, he hopes, an "accurate" uniform.

Pincetich attempted to make his garment look similar to those on the show, but he had to approximate most elements, because no patterns exist for Romulans, and different materials are available. To make his uniform, he first laid newspaper down and cut out his own pattern. He bought quilted silver lamé and, using a colored marker, put black markings in each quilt square. Then he cut some dry deck of the sort that is used for car floormats and added bias tape to make the cross piece on

his chest. He added a few pins and purchased a foam headpiece, which he painted to match his skin tone, and then glued on eyebrows. When Joe wears his uniform at conventions, he attracts dozens of admirers.

One group usually in evidence at cons is Bajorans. As a sympathetic alien people extensively shown on *Star Trek: Deep Space Nine,* they are popular and often portrayed. Marci Mesnard and Joyce Herndon appeared at a con as Bajoran Kais—religious and political leaders of the planet Bajor (plates 18 and 19). Their hats and robes, which are particularly complex, were made without patterns and with colors and materials that appealed to the wearers (plate 20). The only Bajoran costume items that are available for purchase are the unusual Bajoran two-piece earrings. Many fans wear the earrings in daily life with ordinary clothes (plate 21). Debbie Hanon, a member of the U. S. S. Miramar, appears as a specific Bajoran, Ensign Ro Laren from *Star Trek: The Next Generation* (plate 22). She does this because she likes the character and enjoys portraying her. Debbie, who has been sewing since she was ten years old, says, "I just always felt it was the only art I could do." Debbie expresses her artistry through the sewing of costumes for herself and for her children, whom she sometimes brings to events. She also has created a *Voyager* outfit and portrays B'ellanna Torres, a half-Klingon, half-human from that show (plate 23). For her, being an alien is a family affair which she shares with her husband, Dennis Hanon, an accountant and cartoonist who makes a distinctive Klingon (plate 24). Dennis designed his uniform by watching the shows and then drawing the picture he wanted for an outfit. He sewed about a yard of vinyl material onto an existing shirt to make his tunic. He affixed fur arms and foam for the trim and then attached a headpiece, wig and makeup (plate 25). It took him two weeks to make the costume, and, he says, it continues to undergo "subtle changes." For example, he added a sash on which he has placed pins representing the Klingon "house" of which he is a member, pins showing events and places where he has been and a Klingon wedding band pin. He enjoys being a Klingon, saying that "they're very popular."

Klingons are by far the best-known and most numerous aliens portrayed by fans. This is due in part to the large amount of screen time given to these characters. They are shown as honorable yet warlike people who have fascinating personalities and aggressive, gruff demeanors. Marc Okrand's publishing of *The Klingon Dictionary* in 1985 sparked a Klingon Language Institute, on-line computer Klingon newsletters and a Klingon summer language camp (Gorman 1993:57). There are recognized Klingon foods, a language, clothing, customs, music, religion and mythology. In-

deed, between the official *Star Trek* outpourings and the many Klingon fan groups, a real Klingon culture has developed, one to which fans continue to contribute with their costumes and Klingon hobbies.

Klingons insist that to be a part of their culture you must be ready for fun and adventure, the occasional Klingon exotic dance and perhaps some living Klingon food. Roy D. Henderson is a fifty-one-year-old draftsman for Riverside County who is also an admiral in the Imperial Klingon Armada (refer to plates 15 and 16). He became interested in Klingon uniforms because, he says, "I came down here [to a con] and I saw that people have more fun when they're in costume." Those who wear Klingon fur pay a price, however. Roy lost seven pounds from sweating at a three-day convention this year. Also, he has spent about twelve hundred dollars so far on his uniform. He views his costume as perpetually unfinished, because he is always seeing a new pin or piece he likes enough to add to his outfit.

Roy and his shipmate, Paul E. Pierce, believe that a certain type of personality is attracted to the idea of portraying a Klingon. Klingons are almost like a fraternity, but, as Paul states, "without the initiation and without the hazing." Paul says that to be a Klingon, "You have to be bigger than life. . . . You have to look a certain way. If you look nasty we don't accept you. Because to be a Klingon you have to have honor and dig-

22

nity, and we are loyal to each other. Outside of these uniforms we are as close [as] friends . . . could possibly get." Paul views *Star Trek* as a metaphor for our world and aliens as a symbol for a certain type of human being. "Klingons are like bikers. I've been a biker for years. Bikers are very honorable people. They're very family oriented, they take care of their own. We would never put anyone else down because of their race, creed, color, or because they were from another galaxy." Indeed, at public events, Klingons appear to be the "cool" club of which everyone wants to be a part.

The feeling of being Klingon occurs when a person is costumed. Fans enjoy wearing the uniform whether they are at a con, a Klingon feast or a community service event. Paul states, "When I'm in a Klingon uniform I rule the school. I'm the king, that's it. We sign autographs, we have pictures. We've made personal appearances at the request of people at parties. It's like being an actor without all the fame and glory. But when we come here [to a con] everybody knows who we are." Roy agrees and states, "People here know me in this costume. But if I take all the makeup off they don't know me until I say something." Klingons are indeed quite conspicuous in public, and Roy's wife says she is going to forego her Federation uniform for a Klingon one, because "Klingons have more fun!"

Another well-dressed Klingon is John D. Wright (plate 26). He is a diesel mechanic who is also the man-at-arms on an otherwise all-female Klingon ship called the Valkyrie. John likes *Star Trek*'s ideals and identifies most with the Klingons. So he bought a book of costumes at a con, and made garment pieces similar to pictures he liked in the book. Most of his uniform is made with "household items." He added vinyl shoulders and used stuffed animal fur from a fabric store for his cloak (plate 27). He has spent about five hundred dollars on his uniform. His coworkers think he's "a little bit nuts" (fortunately his fiancée is Klingon), but he says that wonderful things occur when he is in his Klingon apparel. "At the last convention in Vegas I dressed up in a Federation uniform with the Klingon headpiece. A little kid comes up to me and he hands me a note and it said 'Worf' [a Klingon character from *Star Trek: The Next Generation*] on it. His mom came up and she said it was a secret message from the Klingon High Command. I opened it up and this kid had drawn a bunch of little circles. I did the Qapla' [a Klingon salute] to him and he had this big smile. His mom said, 'You just made his life.' That made up for everything."

For some Klingon portrayers, uniforms help to bring out different aspects of their personalities. Dave Bourne, a deputy sheriff, has made some unique apparel items such as a plastic canvas bag with a Klingon symbol on it (plate 28). He is part of the Klingon Honor Division, a club he started two and a half years ago. He goes by the Klingon name Ta'KorG epetai-Bok'Turas. Creating his Klingon garment, he says, "helps me bring out a part of me that if I wasn't wearing this stuff I wouldn't have out. I'm very timid at times." Dave's friend and fellow Klingon Shanna Hoskins, who goes by the name Lady Kona Kahoshka KaSara, says of Dave, "It gives him an excuse to be crazy!" As for herself, Shanna says, "I explain myself as being an introvert with extrovert tendencies. And costuming helps me bring that side of myself out and feel justified in doing it. I've got the outfit on, I can be silly and crazy now" (plate 29). Shanna has learned to make her own uniforms. "I like it. It brings something into my personal life because I'm really creative. I like working with my hands, making something 'neat.' And getting attention because of it. It's a high." Costuming allows Shanna and Dave a creative outlet and the personal freedom to change character for a while.

Another Klingon, Tiger Manning, feels that when she wears a uniform she is very different from how she is in real life. She has an assortment of garments, but in all of them she presents an alluring and unusual figure (plate 30). However, she says, "I'm just the young Republican type. I'm not really this outgoing looking." Tiger further explains the lifestyle of the Klingon female:

"You can wear push-up bras and fishnets and you're not like a slut. You're a Klingon. Klingon women . . . have power over themselves. Dressing like this isn't dressing for men. . . . It's your own thing. I couldn't go out on the street dressed like this and feel like I was actually in charge of myself. . . . In here when men look at me, it's not a big deal. I'm a mean Klingon woman." Self-empowerment is a part of the Klingon philosophy. Tiger's friend Gloria Lamden says that costuming shows "self-control." Gloria adores the attention she gets in uniform. "Klingons have a big kinship. . . . They take me . . . with open arms." Since Tiger and Gloria enjoy wearing Klingon apparel, it is fortunate that they have backgrounds in creating garments to call upon when inventing their uniforms (plate 31).

Becoming a fan artist often has much to do with personal background. In Tiger's case, her entire family is involved in fandom, including her husband and her mother, Cat Ramos. Tiger states, "I kind of got into it through osmosis." Her own talents serve her well in this hobby. Tiger explains, "When I was a kid my parents gave me things like a Barbie with no clothes and I would have to make the clothes. . . . I never had store-bought costumes. . . . I've always just kind of whipped them together out of whatever I could find. It's more fun that way." Tiger won an award for costume design in high school. She is proud of her talents and feels no compunction to look like an "authentic" Klingon, but creates uniforms that have never been seen on *Star Trek* and that suit her own sense of aesthetics.

Outstanding Artists

Within the fan community a few people are well known for the artistry of their uniforms. Two of these people are Cat Ramos and Mike Sandeffur, who appear as Klingons. They are popular with other fans, who consider them interesting and excellent costumers. The lives of both individuals will be discussed in order to discover how and why they create and wear these outfits, and what meaning they find in their hobby.

When Cat Ramos arrives at a con, people immediately crowd around her (plate 32). She has the sort of rare magnetic personality that draws young and old alike. She is well known in fan circles across the country because of the many different fan activities, including writing and costuming, in which she is involved.

Cat came into the Klingon world for reasons other than the wearing of uniforms. In her daily life she is a mother and an environmental engineer who does water pollution abatement studies throughout the United States. Previously, Cat had substance-abuse problems. About twelve years ago, she became attracted to the Klingon way of life and their code of honor, and she became a Klingon. She says, "It's like my way of staying clean and sober. The worst possible insult you can give a Klingon is 'toke strav,' which is 'willing slave.' And you know, when you do drugs or alcohol and you can't control yourself, you are a willing slave to that substance. A Klingon would rather die than be a willing slave to anything or anybody."

Klingonness became Cat's empowerment, although at first she didn't attire herself as a Klingon, explaining that "for a little while I really didn't want to dress up because I thought it would sort of ridicule the essence of the power of the principles of Klingon, which is what a Klingon embodies. So, it took a little while. But now I know how to separate it, so it's just fun when you wear costumes and it's empowering for the rest of my normal life." Now, when Cat is in uniform, she is able to relax and have a good time (plates 33 and 34). She lets anyone approach her for pictures and conversation and to squeeze her large biceps. Sometimes, she says, "I've got Klingon music on tape and I like to get together a whole group of people and everybody sings in Klingon."

Cat's Klingon activities go beyond making Klingon uniforms. She has an affinity for languages and taught herself to speak Klingon from *The Klingon Dictionary* and a correspondence course. She says, "I claim to be one of the ten most fluent speakers, readers and writers in the known galaxy." She now teaches the language at an annual summer camp in Redlake Falls, Minnesota. Cat is also a member of several fan groups, including the Fallout Sisterhood, the Klingon Assault Group and a ship called the Iron Pride. An indication of how personal fandom can be, the ship's name refers to the fact that all members work with iron. Some "pump iron"; others work with it professionally, make things with it, or enjoy swordplay. The term "pride" is used because group members see themselves as having an affinity with cats.

Cat writes *Star Trek* novels for which she does extensive research. For example, she will read a technical novel if she is going to include subspace communications in her own writing. "The reason for that is that Trek people—I like to say Trek enthusiasts—are really knowledgeable," she says. "There is also this continuity to it. If you kind of deviate from that they catch you on it right away and they don't like it. You can do just about anything you want, but if you miss the continuity, you're history." People rarely receive payment for writing fan novels and stories. However, other fans have given Cat some costume pieces, such as a dagger pin to put on her Klingon sash, in appreciation for her work.

While Cat is careful to maintain Trek traditions in her writing, her uniforms indicate an emphasis on personal aesthetic choices. Her creation of a twenty-third-century Klingon looks a lot rougher than the current Klingons. Also her leather and iron-studded halter top are pieces that no Klingon has worn before (plate 35). One reason she adorns herself with these accoutrements is that "it's really sometimes difficult for people to tell I'm a female, even from a distance. I guess because I'm tattooed, and the headpiece and all that." On one occasion she had a Beavis and Butt-Head pin on her Klingon uniform. Other unusual items include her gloves; they are workout gloves to which she added deer antler at the knuckles and attached stiff leather gauntlets to reach up her arm. Cat rarely looks the same way twice. Changes to her costume include, for instance, the addition of little copper beads to the braids on her wig; sometimes she wears fur sleeves and arm bands, sometimes not. There is astonishing detail on Cat's costume, from the tiny knife stuck in her custom-made boots to the functional spring-loaded tribladed knife she carries. She gun-blacked the knife, had her name inscribed on the blade and had a Klingon sheath made for it. She also wears a pin that indicates her first sapient kill as a Klingon while role-playing. Her victim, of course, was a Star Fleet member.

Cat takes pride in her costume and those she has created for others. One of these is an outfit for her son-in-law, Tiger's husband. She got him a Ninja outfit at a marshal arts supply store and Klingonized it by adding an honor sash with pins that she sewed. Once the headpiece, wig and makeup are applied, he becomes a Klingon. Cat's creations for herself and others garner her a lot of attention.

Sometimes complete strangers approach Cat and give her pictures they took of her at previous cons. She often tells a story about when she was driving in her car with her daughter Tiger and Tiger's baby, and all were in their Klingon clothing. "I was coming into San Diego when I came back past the immigration checkpoint at San Onofre. They just looked at me and said, 'We can see that you're aliens, but are you legal aliens?' They made us get off at the side of the road where they're searching through everybody's trucks. They had us step out and show our weapons and stuff like that. They were all Trek fanatics except for one and he had no clue what we were doing."

Not all of the attention Cat gets for being a Klingon is positive. She says, "This sort of thing you gotta downplay a little bit around my company, because there is a tendency for people to think you are a bunch of goons." People often think that "that's not a real professional thing to do." Cat explains that occasionally someone asks why she doesn't "get a life." She counters, "Well, I have a job and I travel all over the country and I've been sober for about eleven and a half years and I'm a power

Cat Ramos's functional Klingon weapon. The two side blades retract, and Cat's name is engraved on the hilt.

lifter and I ride a Harley. Is that a life? . . . I write novels about the Klingon Marine Corps in the twenty-third century. I teach the Klingon language and stuff. You know, this *is* a life!" The many fans of Cat's costume artistry and writing would agree.

Mike Sandeffur is also acknowledged by fans for his outstanding costuming. Mike is an ex-navy man who teaches computer skills at a private San Diego business college. He is fifty-two years old and has a wife, children and grandchildren. With the heeled boots he wears, he is six feet four inches tall—an imposing Klingon!

Mike has been a *Star Trek* fan since the original TV show but didn't become interested in fandom until *The Next Generation* went on the air. He attended a convention, signed up with the Klingon Assault Group

27

and joined a local ship called the Stranglehold. He was attracted to Klingons for many reasons. "Klingons are more of a warrior race. I was always fascinated with ancient Egyptians, the knights, battle armor. I hate to use the word, but it's more machismo than Federation people. They [the Klingons] have more personality." And Mike enjoys the adventurism and honor of being a Klingon. "I don't think there is anything more proud than a Klingon warrior."

Mike has converted his garage into his own fan room to house his growing collection of Klingon items. He built a doorway to the room that looks exactly like the door on the *Enterprise* on *The Next Generation*. Inside the room he has satellite antennae on the walls to approximate the feel of a Klingon bridge. He has erected Klingon ship models, character figurines, photographs of himself and *Star Trek* stars, a map showing the location of Klingon clubs in the United States and his Klingon weaponry and armor. Some of Mike's costume pieces are in evidence among the collection.

When Mike is costumed he feels some aspects of his personality are enhanced and some change. "I am an arrogant type of person. Very sure of myself. And so the Klingon mentality kind of fits my personality somewhat. It allows me to role-play a

little bit." He feels more comfortable and incognito in group settings when in uniform. Furthermore, he says, "I can do a lot of things that I probably wouldn't normally do." Mike's college students believe that the Klingon is his normal self and that he's actually dressing up during the week.

Indeed, Mike puts a lot of himself into his Klingon garment. He is a perfectionist who does not consider his uniform to be completely finished despite the fact that he receives unending compliments both from costumed and noncostumed fans. Mike began creating his outfit by observing Klingons on television. Then, he says, "I just started watching the movies, playing them over and over again. I made some mental notes, found my wife's sewing machine.

Mike Sandeffur before costuming. He sits in his converted garage room, which is filled with Klingon collectibles. He added the vent above the computer for its Klingon look.

28

Got some Naugahyde and leather and some different materials and just started sewing. That was my first attempt at even making any kind of clothing. I got along just fine." Mike "played with" the garments until he felt that he had it right.

Mike used various materials and techniques in the creation of his uniform. For example, he Klingonized a pair of leather work gloves. He "cut the fingers out, stitched up grooves, added a couple pieces of chrome and eagle claws and a leather gauntlet with the tubing around the outside . . . painted black." The claws on the gloves, he insists, are for back scratching (plate 36). The main vest is made from linoleum flooring, Naugahyde, velour, some brass, chains from a woman's purse and a few more baubles and bangles (plate 38). He used leather cut from his mother-in-law's old purse to make his chest plate (plate 37). His boots are basic motorcycle boots, but "with Naugahyde added to the top and then my floor tile tip and a casting of a sperm-whale tooth for the hook." Mike also carries a Klingon knife and a disruptor weapon. The disruptor is a replica of the weapon used by official Klingons and had to be bought. Mike affixed various pieces like a pin from Norway that his wife had given to him. He felt that, since it looked Klingonish, why not attach it to a sleeve?

Finally, Mike adds a foam headpiece which he dyed and to which he adjoined hair and eyebrows (plates 39, 40, and 41). He experimented with different makeup techniques, colors and shading methods to discover the tones that made him look like a proper Klingon. When Mike is fully costumed and his artistry is displayed on his own body, well, he *is* a Klingon (plate 42)!

The Meaning of Costuming

Fan costumers come from many demographic categories and often have little in common except that they like *Star Trek*. While there are as many different motives

Part of Mike's collection. A Klingon bird of prey flies above a picture drawn by a fan friend. A photograph of Mike in Klingon gear is placed below one of the character Worf from *Star Trek: The Next Generation.*

for costuming as there are fans, some common reasons can be found by addressing the meaning of uniforms at the individual level, the group and community level and the global level of fandom.

For some individuals, costuming is an enjoyable pastime as well as a means to an end. When suitably attired, fans are transported to another world at convention or Trekker events. This provides the same type of escapism that can be found at various Renaissance faires or even on Halloween. Fans know that they are in a certain reality, but they suspend the rules of everyday life for a little while and enter a forum for play. When fans are in uniform at a convention or community service event, they have the time and space to be with friends or family, to role-play, to shop or to entertain and be entertained. While all of these activities can be available to the noncostumed, uniformed fans are able to enter an alternate reality as characters who belong in that reality, and thus to feel more fully a part of the events occurring around them.

For many fans, costuming is a very personal art that fulfills deep psychological needs. Some, like Mimi, take pride in wearing a uniform that is imbued with positive meaning and hope for a better future; others find satisfaction in the creation of the uniform. Finishing and publicly wearing an outfit made by one's own hands gives a feeling of accomplishment and fulfills the need for a creative outlet. Folklorist Michael Owen Jones notes that "[p]eople make art because of the quality of specialness . . . inherent in the process and in the form created." Further, artists embellish everyday reality by creating items they view as being extraordinary (Jones 1995). Fans see themselves as participating in a very special phenomenon, and the uniforms they invent can aid them in feeling that they are outside of time and in a fascinating realm.

Costuming is quite public, and some fans are motivated to create uniforms because of the consequences of wearing them. Those who are attired in interesting or well-made garments attract much attention at events. They are photographed, asked for autographs and queried about how to make a costume like theirs. At fan events, costumers are celebrities, and this manner of observation brings positive reinforcement for fan artists.

Some costumers have individual motives for their hobby. Cat Ramos found personal empowerment in becoming a Klingon. Mike Sandeffur is able to be involved in what he views as something ancient and honorable, being reminded by his Klingon uniform of chivalrous knights. Other fans associate their outfits with the Trek shows, science fiction or various values and objectives. For Palavra members, costumes represent high moral principles. These motives were likely lacking elsewhere in fans' lives, but they found a space and a stage for them in fandom. Fans, like other people, look for a place or a group in which they can express ideas that are important to them. What some may find in belonging to a religious group or a body-piercing club, fans find in fandom and in costuming.

Fans in clubs are part of a larger community that provides a place for learning about making and wearing costumes as well as reinforcement to continue. Group members distribute knowledge of a shared historical tradition, which has certain ideas and values and some explicit behavioral and material manifestations. *Star Trek* fandom provides stimuli not available in mundane life. Costuming is one aspect of this fan culture that upholds and enhances fandom and presents a public face to the everyday world.

A third level of meaning for fan costumers is found in the global arena. Fans can be found in all walks of life. They are scientists, laborers and teachers. They believe that they are a part of the creation of a positive future for the human race. The physical "icons" of this hope are found in the Smithsonian Institution, at conventions and community service events, and on television. Fans feel part of a global effort to actualize a positive future. Thus far, fans have used their costumes on a personal level for themselves and their clubs and on a social and charitable level at community service events. It would not be surprising if fans become more political as a global group in the future.

Conclusion: Popular Culture and Folklore

A study of the costume art of *Star Trek* fans raises questions about the nature of popular culture and folklore. It also poses interesting challenges to our understanding of the interrelationship of these phenomena.

Narvaez and Laba (1988: 1) define popular culture as "cultural events which are transmitted by technological media and communicated in mass societal contexts. Accordingly, the performance contexts of popular culture are usually characterized by significant spatial and social distances between performers and audiences." The authors emphasize mass production and distribution of objects and performances, that is, through television, feature films, popular magazines, radio programs, commercial recordings, and manufactured items. The *Star Trek* shows and films, as well as the factory-made uniforms, model kits, souvenir cups, posters and jewelry, epitomize this. When Narvaez and Laba write that the performance contexts of popular culture involve social and spatial distances between audiences and performers, they mean that shows are scripted, acted and edited and *then* presented to an audience; objects are designed and mass-produced for, rather than with, the consumers; and the officially sponsored conventions are organized by a few for attendance by the many. This contrasts with folkloric performances in which narrating, **31** for example, occurs among people who interact with one another so that reactions of listeners directly affect the storytelling process (Georges 1969; 1979; 1981). It differs, too, from the creation of folk art in which the unique qualities of the handmade objects reflect the individuality of the maker and his or her interaction with friends, family or customers. The official outputs bear little resemblance to the local clubs and grassroots events that small groups of fans organize for their own participation.

The term "folklore" refers to expressive or symbolic behavior "(1) that we customarily learn, teach, and utilize or display during face-to-face interactions, and (2) that we judge to be traditional." For a behavior to be considered "traditional" it need not be ancient, only based on known precedents or models and therefore exhibiting a degree of continuity and consistency with the behavior of other people (Georges and Jones 1995:1).

Star Trek fans have created an extensive body of lore. It includes the stories they tell, songs, special gestures and greetings, even the name they give themselves (Trekkers) and, of course, their clubs, customs and homemade costumes. When Dave Bourne (plate 28) taught Shanna Hoskins (plate 29) how to make Klingon apparel, the two of them engaged in face-to-face interaction during which skills and designs were taught, learned and displayed. When Tiger Manning (plate 30) began to costume

as a Klingon like her mother, Cat Ramos, she modeled her behavior after Cat's (plate 32), thus perpetuating knowledge, ideas and ways of doing things that she had seen and learned firsthand. That these costumes are also art is apparent in their being considered "special" because of the skill and technical excellence evident, and their generating an appreciative, contemplative response in the creators and others (Jones 1989; 1995). The makers have transformed the ordinary—an old pair of work gloves, a piece of fabric, cardboard tubing, fake fur, linoleum flooring—into something extraordinary. The products embody both individual choices and "a communal aesthetic shared by a group of artists and their audience and shaped and reshaped by them over time" (Teske 1983:35; see also Vlach 1986).

Theories about the relationships among folklore, popular culture and the mass media often differ and sometimes conflict. Disagreements occur partly because theorists define the phenomena differently. For instance, contrary to what many folklorists believe, some writers on popular culture assume that folklore is the same thing as folk culture, and that the latter consists of the beliefs, activities and products of an illiterate peasant class or lower stratum of society of an earlier age. Theories also clash because their proponents bring different social agendas or political perspectives to their arguments. John Fiske believes that "people in industrial societies are not the folk," and that there is no "authentic" folk culture any longer; hence, there is no folklore in the modern world (Fiske 1989: 169, 15). He views popular culture as the culture of the subordinated and disempowered which, he contends, opposes the mass media—the dominant culture or "the Hegemony." But as we've seen, Trekkers, who have generated a large body of lore inspired by *Star Trek*, are not opposing official Trek culture as represented by mass media. Rather, they use it, add to it and sometimes redefine it through their customs and costumes. They would not be happy if their activities caused the overthrow of the official culture from which they draw and to which they contribute.

Other scholars have posited more integrative relationships than Fiske proposes. Janice Radway, in *Reading the Romance*, describes how some women who read romances discuss and find meaning in them, relating these novels to their personal lives and interactions with others. In *Enterprising Women*, Camille Bacon-Smith analyzes ways in which a group of female *Star Trek* fans manipulate narratives based on mass media productions to express their own beliefs, needs and discontent. Henry Jenkins in *Textual Poachers* discusses how fans adopt themes and stories from the mass media and popular culture, relating these to their social experiences and adapting them for use in their daily lives. Although the authors are not always discussing folklore per se, the term is appropriate to many of the customs and activities that they describe.

Data on *Star Trek* lore—including the costumes made by fans—indicates that Trekkers do not passively watch television or films but actively use the ideas, symbols and products of mass media and popular culture as personal resources for their own ends as they communicate and interact with one another. In addition, as I noted early in this volume, fans affected the dominant culture by mounting a letter-writing campaign forcing the television network to continue *Star Trek* for another season, and causing NASA to name the space shuttle prototype Enterprise; and, marginalized by organizers of science fiction conventions, the Trekkers started their own grassroots clubs and activities. There is, then, a dialectic at work between folklore and popular culture. The *Star Trek* shows and movies inspired fandom (and served as sources for the creation of folklore), but the movies and TV series after the first one would not have been made without popular fan response.

This dialectic is evident in other ways. William Shatner, who played Captain Kirk on the original *Star Trek*, appeared on *Saturday Night Live* in a now-famous skit in which he told Trekkies to "get a life!" Although he was acting, fans took his words seriously; they have become defensive about having "a life." The term "Trekkie," used in this skit and in newspaper and magazine articles, came to be equated with "nerd" or "geek." Fans responded by calling themselves and one another Trekkers rather than Trekkies. Mimi Gallandt-Oakes says, "Trekkie is like the computer nerd with the pencils." Trekkers, however, have a "life beyond Trek." Moreover, says Mimi, "We're not defined by Trek; Trek is defined by us." Had fandom not developed with its body of lore and folk art that integrates popular culture into people's everyday lives, *Star Trek* would have existed only for two seasons as a television series and then disappeared from the scene. Fans co-opted the concept of Klingons and their way of life from media productions, but then created a fan-Klingon culture (with distinctive dress, language, songs and tales) not in evidence on screen. Fan Klingons challenge Federation members to food fights for charity food drives and do an immense amount of community service, neither of which is a Klingon activity depicted in the mass media or sanctioned by official conventions and organizations. In their turn, the media draw from the fans' activities. In 1995, Hallmark advertised a Christmas ornament depicting a Romulan ship. In the commercial a woman is surrounded by Romulans. Rather than cowering in fear, she asks the aliens if they came from a *Star Trek* convention!

To conclude, folklore and the mass media and popular culture enjoy a symbiotic relationship. Folklorists have discussed how traditional proverbs, folk speech and fairy tales are used in advertising (e.g., Burns 1969; Degh 1994; Falassi and Kligman 1976; Georges and Jones 1995:2–10; Mieder and Mieder 1977) as well as how advertising jingles appear in folklore (Dundes 1963). They have remarked on the "folklure" of traditional costumes and body adornments which are quickly commodified, mass-produced and sold as high fashion (Denby 1971; Wojcik 1994). Apparent in the activities of *Star Trek* fans is the fact that many individuals deftly appropriate and utilize elements of popular culture for their own creations, including costumes. People display their designs in firsthand interaction, learning their skills and gaining ideas from one another as well as modeling their costumes on precedents they have examined. Employing their own aesthetics and those of their interactional networks (Blumenreich and Polansky 1974), individuals make garments for many reasons, from the sensory pleasures involved in sewing and working with fabric to expressing their personalities or alter egos, conveying values and socializing with others. As long as fans find beauty, importance and meaning in homemade costume art inspired by *Star Trek* as a product of mass media and an element of popular culture, then this example of folklore will—as Mr. Spock would say— "live long and prosper."

References

Amesley, Cassandra. 1989. "How to Watch *Star Trek.*" *Cultural Studies* 3.

Bacon-Smith, Camille. 1992. *Enterprising Women: Television Fandom and the Creation of Popular Myth.* Philadelphia: The University of Pennsylvania Press.

Blumenreich, Beth, and Bari Lynn Polansky. 1974. "Re-evaluating the Concept of Group: ICEN as an Alternative." In *Conceptual Problems in Contemporary Folklore Studies*, edited by Gerald Cashion, pp. 12–17. Bloomington, Ind.: Folklore Forum Bibliographic and Special Series, no. 12.

Burns, Tom. 1969. "Folklore in the Mass Media: Television." *Folklore Forum* 2:90–106.

Davis, Erik. 1995. "True Believers." *TV Guide—Collectors Edition*, pp. 78–82.

Degh, Linda. 1994. *American Folklore and the Mass Media.* Bloomington: Indiana University Press.

Denby, Priscilla. 1971. "Folklore in the Mass Media." *Folklore Forum* 4:113–25.

Dundes, Alan. 1963. "Advertising and Folklore." *New York Folklore Quarterly* 19:143–51.

Falassi, Alessandro, and Gail Kligman. 1976. "Folk-Wagen: Folklore and the Volkswagen Ads." *New York Folklore* 2:79–86.

Fiske, John. 1989. *Understanding Popular Culture.* Boston: Unwin Hyman.

Georges, Robert A. 1969. "Toward an Understanding of Storytelling Events." *Journal of American Folklore* 82:313–28.

———. 1979. "Feedback and Response in Storytelling." *Western Folklore* 38:104–10.

———. 1981. "Do Narrators Really Digress? A Reconsideration of 'Audience Asides' in Narrating." *Western Folklore* 40:245–52.

Georges, Robert A., and Michael Owen Jones. 1995. *Folkloristics: An Introduction.* Bloomington: Indiana University Press.

Gerrold, David. 1984. *The World of Star Trek.* New York: Bluejay Books, Inc.

Gorman, James. 1993. "Klingon: The Final Frontier." *Time* 141, no. 14 (April 5): 57.

Jenkins, Henry. 1992. *Textual Poachers. Television Fans and Participatory Culture.* New York: Routledge.

Jones, Michael Owen. 1989. *Craftsman of the Cumberlands: Tradition and Creativity.* Lexington: University Press of Kentucky.

———. 1995. "The 1995 Archer Taylor Memorial Lecture: Why Make (Folk) Art?" *Western Folklore* 54:253–76.

Laba, Martin. 1988. "Popular Culture and Folklore: The Social Dimension." In *Media Sense: The Folklore-Popular Culture Continuum*, edited by Peter Narvaez and Martin Laba, pp. 9–18. Bowling Green: Bowling Green University Press.

Larsen, Elizabeth. 1993. "A Galaxy Of Trekkies." *UTNE Reader* 57 (May-June): 41–42.

Lichtenberg, Jacqueline. 1975. *Star Trek Lives.* New York: Bantam Books.

Mieder, Barbara, and Wolfgang Mieder. 1977. "Tradition and Innovation: Proverbs in Advertising." *Journal of Popular Culture* 11:308–19.

Moskowitz, Sam. 1954. *The Immortal Storm. A History of Science Fiction Fandom.* Atlanta: The Atlanta Science Fiction Organization Press.

Narvaez, Peter, and Martin Laba. 1988. "Introduction: The Folklore-Popular Culture Continuum." In *Media Sense: The Folklore-Popular Culture Continuum,* edited by Peter Narvaez and Martin Laba, pp. 1–8. Bowling Green: Bowling Green University Press.

Radway, Janice A. 1991. *Reading the Romance: Women, Patriarchy, and Popular Literature.* Chapel Hill: University of North Carolina Press.

Teske, Robert T. 1983. "What Is Folk Art? An Opinion on the Controversy." *El Palacio* 88: 34–38.

Turnbull, Gerry. 1979. *A Star Trek Catalog.* New York: Grosset and Dunlap.

Vlach, John Michael. 1986. "'Properly Speaking': The Need for Plain Talk about Folk Art." In *Folk Art and Art Worlds,* edited by John Michael Vlach and Simon J. Bronner, pp. 13–26. Ann Arbor: UMI Research Press.

Warner, Harry, Jr. 1969. *All Our Yesterdays. An Informal History of Science Fiction Fandom in the Forties.* Chicago: Advent Publishers, Inc.

Winston, Joan. 1977. *The Making of the Trek Conventions.* Garden City, N.Y.: Doubleday and Co., Inc.

Wojcik, Daniel. 1994. *Punk and Neo-Tribal Body Art.* Jackson: University Press of Mississippi.

Zoglin, Richard. 1994. "Trekking Onward." *Time* 144, no. 28 (Nov. 28): 72–79.

PLATE 1
Douglas Gaines appearing
as a Klingon-Bajoran
fusion character called
Dellahan, which he
created. His costume is
Klingon battle gear
(Anaheim convention
1995).

PLATE 2
Douglas Gaines in full
Klingon battle regalia with
Klingon weapons drawn.

PLATE 3
Douglas Gaines showing
an earlier incarnation of
his Dellahan character. He
is wearing a Federation
costume and role-plays
with a friend (Los Angeles
convention 1993).

P L A T E 4
Susan Eastgate as a
Federation officer. She
holds a phaser weapon
made by Russel Noel
(San Diego 1994).

P L A T E 5
Susan Eastgate as a
Klingon warrior firing a
Klingon disruptor weapon
(Anaheim convention
1995).

P L A T E   6
Susan's sons, Ryan and Tyler Eastgate, wear Federation uniforms bought by their mother and play with plastic weapons (Anaheim convention 1995).

P L A T E   7
Mimi Gallandt-Oakes,
captain of the Palavra,
sells merchandise at a
convention. She wears a
Star Trek: Deep Space Nine
Federation uniform.

P L A T E 8
J. A. sells at a convention.

P L A T E 9
Each uniform is handmade by J. A. He makes more red uniforms than other colors because they sell the best.

P L A T E   1 0
Saul Del Toro portrays
Commander Chakotay
(Anaheim convention
1995).

43

PLATE 11
Thomas Phillips as
Commander Geordi
La Forge (Anaheim
convention 1995).

45

PLATE 13
Russel Noel in his
Captain Kirk pose. He
wears a costume that
he constructed after
watching the Trek films
and holds a phaser
weapon that he made
from balsa wood (Los
Angeles convention
1993).

P L A T E   1 4
Russel Noel in another
outfit that imitates a
movie costume. Russ was
in a difficult period in his
life as he struggled with
cancer. His choice of dark
colors indicates his mood
at the time (San Diego
1994).

PLATE 16
Roy Henderson applies a
headpiece and makeup to
enhance his Klingon
appearance.

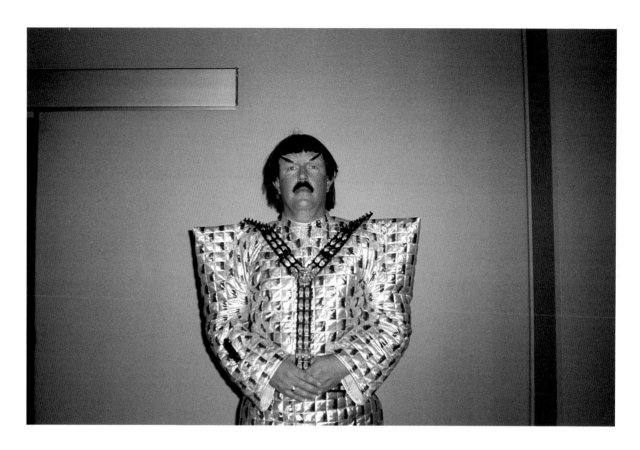

PLATE 17
Joe Pincetich as a
Romulan. He made his
costume without any
patterns or guidelines.

Marci Mesnard created
this costume of a Bajoran
Kai. She used fabric paint
to make the lined pattern
(Anaheim convention
1995).

PLATE 19
Joyce Herndon is
costumed as a Bajoran
Kai. She chose fabric and
colors that appealed to
her (Anaheim convention
1995).

PLATE 20
Joyce Herndon's complex
Bajoran hat had to be
made without a pattern.

PLATE 21
Bajoran-style earrings like
this one can be bought at
conventions and are often
worn to non-Trek affairs.

53

PLATE 22
Debbie Hanon appears as
a Bajoran character called
Ro Laren (San Diego
convention 1994).

PLATE 23
Debbie Hanon as a half-
Klingon, half-human
character called B'ellana
Torres (Anaheim
convention 1995).

54

PLATE 24
Dennis Hanon as a
Klingon. Note the battle
sash with various Klingon
letters and pins.

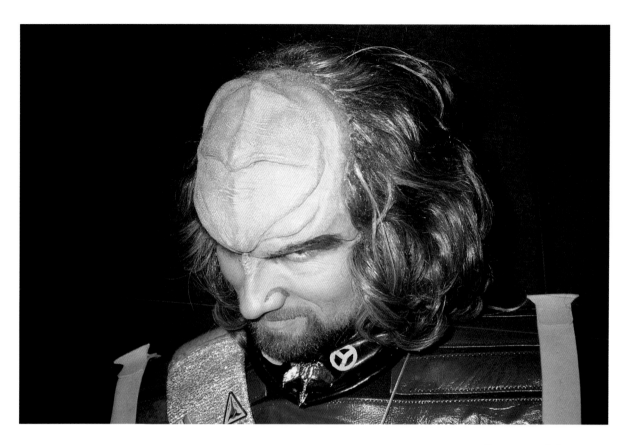

PLATE 25
Dennis Hanon chose a
headpiece and soft wavy
hair that appealed to his
sense of aesthetics.

56

P L A T E 2 6
John Wright as a Klingon.
Note the heavy makeup
he chose and how his
hair, headpiece, and
costume differ from those
of other Klingons.

PLATE 27
John Wright made this cloak with the Klingon symbol from fake fur commonly used to make stuffed animals.

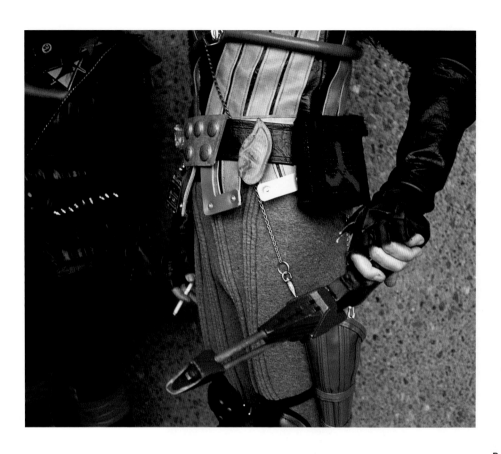

PLATE 28
Dave Bourne as a
Klingon. At his belt is
a black bag with a red
Klingon symbol he made
from plastic canvas. He
also holds a Klingon dis-
ruptor weapon, and an
ear from an earlier "kill"
is at his belt (Anaheim
convention 1994).

59

PLATE 29
Shanna Hoskins as a
female Klingon. Note the
distinctive headpiece and
tunic she has created
(Anaheim convention
1994).

PLATE 30
Tiger Manning as a half-
Klingon human. While
she bought the Klingon
battle axe, she designed
and made this unique
Klingon costume
(Anaheim convention
1994).

PLATE 32
Cat Ramos as a Klingon.
Note the copper beads
on her braids and what
she calls her "more
gnarly" headpiece. She
also has added vampire
teeth to her look.

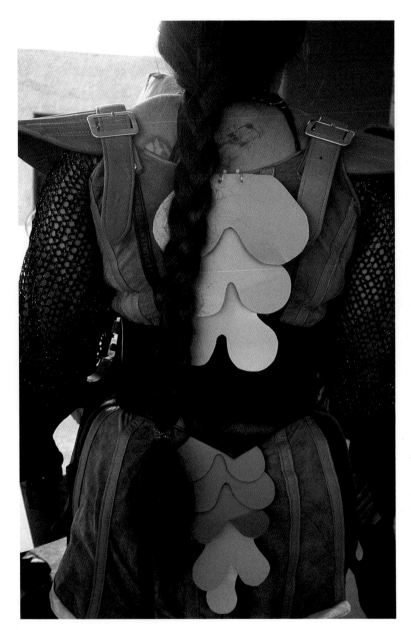

P L A T E   3 4
The rear of this costume
has a more extreme
spinal cover than do
other costumes.

PLATE 35
Cat's unique halter. Much
of her Klingon jewelry
was given her by fan
friends and artists.

P L A T E   3 6
Mike holds his functional
knife. Note the chrome
and eagle claws he affixed
to his gloves.

PLATE 37
After putting on a fur
undershirt, Mike follows
with his black Klingon
pants, his vinyl armor and
his headpiece, to which
the hair and eyebrows
are already attached.

PLATE 38
The rear of Mike's
costume.

69

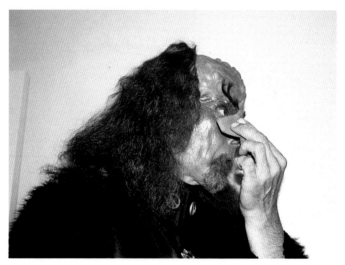

PLATE 39
The makeup and shading
Mike applies to his face
match his headpiece color
and make him appear
rough.

PLATE 40
Mike shows the contrast
between his own skin and
the makeup color.

PLATE 41
When he is fully attired, it is easy to see the clear and precise lines of the tunic Mike has made. The pins and gold pieces on his costume are well placed and attest to Mike's perfectionism when it comes to costume creation.

PLATE 42
Mike points his pain stick.
His boots, which have
claw tips at the toes, add
inches to his already
formidable height.

CONNEMARA PONY BREEDERS' SOCIETY 1923-1998

Elizabeth Petch

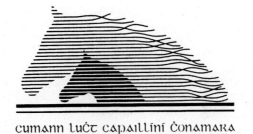

cumann luċt capaillíní ċonamara

Published by
CONNEMARA PONY BREEDERS' SOCIETY
Clifden,
Co. Galway,
Ireland.

Design & Layout: Stephen O'Connell

Front Cover Photograph: Con Doyle
Back Cover Photograph: J. Petch

ISBN 0 9502358 1 4

Printed by Litho Press Co., Midleton, Co. Cork, Ireland.

CONTENTS

PREFACE

The Connemara Pony Breeders' Society was founded in 1923 to foster and develop our native breed which was threatened with extinction, and as the Society reaches its 75th Anniversary it is time to remember those who founded the Society and gave many years of dedicated service to the Connemara pony and its breeders. In this history I have endeavoured to trace the progress of the Society and its work in developing the pony from its original use as a working pony to the all-round performance pony which is acclaimed all over the world today. It has not been possible to name every breeder and every pony throughout the seventy-five years of the life of the Society, but this book has been written as a tribute to all those who have contributed to the work of the Connemara Pony Breeders' Society and are part of its history.

Elizabeth Petch 1998

ACKNOWLEDGEMENTS

My thanks to the many people who have helped me with the research for this book and who have allowed me to use their photographs. Connacht Tribune, Irish Times, Irish Independent, Irish Farmers Journal, Equestrian Photo Services, National Library of Ireland, Dúchas, the C.P. Societies, and photographers Michael Connaughton, Ruth Rogers, Maymes Ansell, Mary Tarry, Con Brogan, Liz Harries and the late Jimmy Walshe.

I am grateful to Garnet Irwin for her photographs of the early stallions and to John Petch, Beatrice Milleder, Bob Blackburn, Eithne MacDermott, Thomas Bachmann, for their photographs, and for photographs from the private collections of Tadhg O'Sullivan, Frank O'Malley, Tom Killeen, Mary Treacy, Mairtin Mylotte, Margaret Moran, Maeve Kelly, Kathleen Villiers Tuthill, Donal Kenny, Margaret Lynch, Col. A. Morris, Stephanie Brooks, Anne Hemphill, Deirdre Romanes, Mary Kelleher, Murty McGrath, Pat Lyne, Mary McGuire, Bobby Bolger, Josie Joyce, Ciaran Curran, Vincent Joyce, Johnny Brennan, Joan Hawkins, Jean Santry, Padraig Hynes, Henry O'Toole and the late Tommy McDonagh. My grateful thanks also to Dan-Axel Danielsson for his computer programme which was invaluable in researching the Stud Books, to Bay Goodwin for her help with the RDS Show results, to Carole Seigne for her encouragement and proof reading, to many other friends who have helped me gather material for the book, and finally to my long-suffering husband John and my family who have all supported me throughout the writing of the book. I am greatly indebted to Stephen O'Connell for his patience and long hours of work on the design and layout of the book, and my thanks also to Tom MacLochlainn for his contribution in Irish, and to Tadhg O'Sullivan for kindly agreeing to write the introduction to this book.

INTRODUCTION

To all of us who love Connemara, Elizabeth Petch has done an immense service in researching and presenting in such a readable manner the origins and unique character of this region, its people and above all its rare breed of small horses which for some reason we call ponies, and which are as much a part of the landscape as the black-faced sheep, the dry-stone walls, the turf ricks and the heather. Her task was to write the offical history of Connemara Pony Breeders' Society over its first 75 years, and this, in as much as a lay reader can judge, she has done supremely well. What is perhaps not sufficiently realised is how close the breed came to extinction, beginning with the post-famine period, a process of decline which was not eased in any way by the various misguided government schemes intended to improve the breed, some of them quite egregious, like the introduction of thoroughbred, half-bred and even Hackney blood. That the Connemara Pony has nevertheless reached the quality it possesses today is tribute to those who have patiently worked to improve its characteristics since the Society was founded.

One of the great strengths of this book is that it communicates with ease to the general reader, unfamiliar with breeding techniques, pedigrees and so on. The casual visitor can become bored at a horse show, and the casual reader can be wearied by pages of data about animals whose names he has never or at best rarely heard of previously. But here the story is told in such a way that the reader develops an interest in the human effort that went into the development of the Society and the improvement of the breed, rather than being confronted with the kind of developments which are of interest mainly to the professional breeder. The fact that such-and-such a horse was bought by an American buyer is just a fact, but if one reads that the buyer went on to become President of the American Connemara Pony Breeders' Society, that already is a story.

We are thus in good hands; the hands of someone who not only knows her horses but understands them in their relationship with human beings. The horse, after all, would probably be extinct in large areas of the world but for the interest which men and women have shown in it, and it is virtually certain that this fate would have overtaken the Connemara pony but for the vision of Michael O'Malley and the devoted work of many other enthusiasts, all of whom receive not merely fair but generous treatment in this very important work. Mrs Petch is a strict historian, in the sense that she seems to me to regard her task as to set down accurately what occurred over these last 75 years, rather than to advance opinions or initiatives, whether her own or those of others. She uses a light touch in describing, for instance, Bartley O'Sullivan's proposal in his well-known 1939 paper, for a cross between the Irish Draught and the Connemara; though Bartley, I might remark in passing is probably treated with greater respect and referred to more often than anyone else in this history. As the eldest of his children I can sincerely place on record the gratitude of his family for this generous recognition of his life's work.

One could perhaps debate the wisdom of the decision taken about 1965 to confine certain show trophies to breeders resident in Connemara, though the objective reasons for it were clear enough. Ironically, viewed from the perspective of 1998, it was a good omen, in as much as it was a sign that the Connemara Pony had "arrived" and was attracting the attention of better off buyers and breeders from outside Connemara. It was also the lift-off point in the fortunes of the breed. At that time, Connemara ponies were exhibited in Montreal;

the Swedish Connemara Pony Society was formed and there were good portents for a worthwhile surge in exports. Since then Connemara Pony Societies have been formed all round the world, this brave little animal is eagerly sought after for shows, riding, hunting and other sports; it is one of the most popular breeds on the equestrian scene. Breeders in Connemara have proved that they can successfully compete with the best anywhere. The Connemara Pony no longer belongs exclusively to the West of Ireland. It belongs to the world. And this book is a fit tribute to that great achievement.

T.F. O'Sullivan
Dublin 1998

AN CAPAILLÍN

Bhí uair ann agus thug capaillíní beaga gioballacha an fheamainn abhaile as an gclimín le cur ar na fataí. Thug siad clocha agus gaineamh le bealaí nua a dhéanamh. Thug siad an mhóin thar chis go teallach. Threabh siad, tharraing agus d'iompar.

Ach ní capaillín oibre feasta é. Ní ar na portaigh ná ar na cladaigh a bhíonn a thriall anois ach ar na teaspeántaisí móra. Seilgeann, léimeann agus siúlann sé timpeall go huaibhreach. Agus an domhan anois i ngrá leis.

Mar a deir an seanfhocal "Nach minic a rinne bromach gioballach capaillín cumasach."

Tomás MacLochlainn

OFFICERS OF THE CONNEMARA PONY BREEDERS' SOCIETY
1923-1998

Presidents

1923-1927 Rev. C.J. White P.P. Roundstone.
1927-1932 Rt. Rev. Monsignor McAlpine P.P. V.G. Clifden.
1933-1952 Very Rev. Canon Cunningham P.P. V.G. Clifden.
1953-1972 Lord Killanin, Spiddal.
1973-1978 Mr Sean Keane, Galway.
1978   Mr Martin Treacy, Spiddal.
1979-1990 Mr Donal Kenny, Dublin.
1990-1998 Mr Eamonn Hannan, Moycullen.
1998-   Mr John Luskin, Cong.

Vice Presidents

1930-1942 Rev. T.H. McCullagh P.P., Oughterard.
1930-1933 Rev. C. Cunningham P.P., Roundstone.
1933-1955 Mr C.J. Kerin, Oranmore.
1934-1935 Very Rev. Canon Patterson P.P., Clifden.
1943-1945 Rev. Matthew Kenny P.P. Clifden.
1947-1953 Lord Killanin, Spiddal.
1953-1959 Very Rev. Canon Corcoran P.P., Clifden.
1953-1997 Very Rev. Canon Moran P.P., Oranmore.
1959-1976 Mr T. McD. Kelly MRCVS, Athenry.
1990-1994 Mr T.J. McDonagh, Roundstone.
1990-1998 Mr Dermot Power, B. Agr. Sc., Galway.
1995-   Mr Peadar O'Scannaill MRCVS, Clifden.
1998-   Mr William Diamond, Tully.

Secretaries

1923-1960 Mr Michael O'Malley, Rosmuck (Joint Sec).
1924-1960 Mr Bartley O'Sullivan, Galway (Joint Sec).
1960-1961 Miss Alice Burke, Galway (Acting Sec).
1960-1963 Mr Sean Keane, Galway (Acting Sec).
1961-1963 Mrs Phil MacDermott, Galway (Asst. Sec).
1963-1979 Mr John Killeen, Galway.
1963-1979 Mrs Phil MacDermott, Galway (Asst. Sec).
1979-1990 Mrs Phil MacDermott, Galway.
1990-   Ms Marian Turléy B.Sc.H.Dip.Eq.Sc. Clifden.

High Cross, Clonmacnoise.

CHAPTER 1

ORIGINS

• Irish Hobbies • Influence from Spain • Decline following the Famine •
• Galway to Clifden Railway • Congested District Board • Ewart Report •
• Michael O'Malley's Journey to Olympia • The O'Malley Booklet •

The *Conmaicne* were a tribe of people who claimed to be descendants of Conmac, son of the legendary Maeve, Queen of Connaught. They settled in several districts in Connaught, and those who lived west of Lough Corrib were known as the *Conmaicne Mara*, the Comaince of the Sea, to distinguish them from other branches of the Conmaicne tribe living further east. The district they occupied was in the north west region of West Galway, and as was the custom then, the leading local tribe gave its name to the place. Thus the region became known as Conmaicne-Mara, or Connemara as we know it today. They were finally overrun by the O'Flahertys, a powerful clan who had lands east of Galway, until they were driven out of them by the Normans led by de Burgo, and were forced into Connemara in 1225, and the O'Flahertys continued to rule the region until the 17th Century when their lands were confiscated.

Today the name Connemara refers to the larger area stretching west from the city of Galway with Lough Corrib and Lough Mask and the Twelve Bens and Maamturk Mountains to the east and bounded to the west by the Atlantic Ocean. It is a wild and beautiful land of mountains, bogs and lakes, with its rugged and deeply indented coastline lashed by Atlantic gales. There is little arable land, and the small fields are strewn with rocks and boulders. For countless generations a breed of ponies has existed in this remote area, living on the sparse grazing of bog and mountain and enduring the harsh winter conditions with little shelter from the rain and gales blown in from the Atlantic. This rugged environment produced, through natural selection, a breed of tough hardy ponies living out in all weather, who were renowned for their strong constitutions, as only the strongest could survive. From birth they learned to pick their way through bogs and boulders, across rock and seaweed on the seashore, or down steep mountain tracks, and they developed a surefootedness for which they have become renowned.

The history of ponies in Connemara goes back to the arrival of the Celts in the 4th Century BC. The Celts came with their herds of horses across northern Europe, extending through England, Scotland, Wales and finally to Ireland, and it is believed that the old dun ponies of Connemara, especially prized for their hardiness and endurance, were the most typical of their Celtic ancestors. The Celts drove chariots, and the first real proof of the existence of ponies in Ireland was found at Tara in Co. Meath, where archaeologists discovered the remains of ponies and chariots. Chariot races were also held at Loughrea in Co. Galway during the summer harvest festivals. Evidence of the use of ponies in early Christian Ireland is found at the ancient monastic site at Clonmacnoise on the eastern shores of the river Shannon where the High Cross has illustrations of ponies and chariots at its base.

Irish Hobbies

In the Middle Ages ponies were referred to in Ireland as Hobbies, and were much prized because they were able to amble and this made for a much more comfortable ride when travelling long distances. The amble is a special gait in which the animal moves both legs on one side forward and then the legs on the other side, causing a slightly rocking motion which is much more comfortable than the trot.

There are several references to the Irish Hobby in early manuscripts, and in all cases they remark on its "easy paces", the same term also used at a later date to describe the Connemara Pony, and implying that the pony could amble.

Written in 1565, Blundeville's description of the Irish Hobby is interesting and he says,

"If any man seek to have a race of fine ambling horses to travel by the way, then I would wish his stallion to be either a fayre Jennet from Spayne, or else a fayre Irish ambling Hobby. The Irish Hobby is a pretty fine horse, having a good head, and a body indifferently well proporcioned, saving that many of them be slender and thin buttocked; they be tender mouthed, nimble, light, pleasant and apt to be taught, and for the most part they be amblers, and therefore very meet for both saddle and to travel by the way".

In 1633 Edmund Campion writes about the Irish Hobbies in *Historie of Ireland*, and as well as noting their easy paces, he suggests they may have come from Spain,

"Horses they have of pace easie, of running wonderfully swift. Therefore they make of them great store, and wherein at times of need they repose a great piece of safetie. This breed Rafael Volateranus says to have first come from Asturia, the part of Spain between Galicia and Portugal, whereof they were called Asturcones, a name now properly applied to the Spanish Jennet."

Later still, in 1771, Richard Berenger, Gentleman of the Horse to King George III writes,

"Ireland has for many centuries boasted a race of horses called Hobbies, valued for their easy paces, of middling size, strong, nimble well moulded and hardy".

Influence from Spain

It is evident that there was trading by sea between Spain and Ireland from the earliest times, and the similarity between the Irish Hobby and Asturian small horse or pony (also called the Spanish Jennet) is obvious. The fact that the Asturian comes from the north west corner of Spain which was close to the trade route from La Coruna to Ireland adds weight to the belief that these ponies were imported into Ireland as early as the 12th century. During the 16th century when Galway became a major port trading mainly with Spain and Portugal there is again evidence of Barb and Andalusian stallions being imported from Spain by wealthy merchants in Galway city, and these we are told, were the best that money could buy.

There is a well-known and romantic story that when the ships of the Spanish Armada were wrecked along the west coast of Ireland in 1588, Andalusian stallions swam ashore, and mixed with the herds of Connemara mares running wild on the hills. This may only be a delightful myth, but perhaps it can also be interpreted as the storyteller's way of explaining the obvious Arab characteristics to be detected in the Connemara pony.

In the paper on the Connemara pony written by Bartley O'Sullivan in 1939, he states,

"Coming down to more recent times, we have reasonably reliable accounts of the importation of Arab horses by certain estate owners in Connemara, and mating of these with the native breed, as late as the middle of the last century. Taking all the stories of the importation of horses for mating with the native animals in those far-off days, they have this in common, the source was Spain, Morocco or Arabia, and the type Andalusian, Spanish and African Barb, or Arab. On this evidence alone we are justified in accepting that Spanish and African Barb or Arab horses were crossed with the native Connemara, but we have more conclusive evidence still in the distinctive Arab characteristics discernible in many of the present day Connemara ponies... It is highly probable, however, that centuries before the introduction of foreign blood, a race of hardy ponies, or small horses existed in the West of Ireland. The changing conditions down the ages affected the characteristics of the breed and in time shaped it into the type of pony which roamed the hills of West Connaught when the first Arabs made their appearance."

Prior to 1800, Connemara was considered to be a lawless place and smuggling and poteen making were widespread. It was a hiding place for outlaws and deserters, and travellers were warned not to venture into such a wild country. However, all that was to change in the 1820s and 1830s when a network of roads, designed by the engineer Alexander Nimmo, was built through Connemara, and the region was opened up to travellers, speculators and people in search of land. Many came seeking work building the new roads, the population of the region increased rapidly, and the town of Clifden and the village of Roundstone were developed. Some local landlords who had previously lived outside the area, took up residence in their estates in Connemara, notably the Blakes at Renvyle, the Martins at Ballynahinch, and the D'Arcys at Clifden.

In the years that followed, the small coastal strips of arable land became densely populated, as seaweed was used to fertilise the land, and more mountain and bogland came under cultivation to grow potatoes for the increasing population. Even today, the ridges or "lazy beds" used for growing the potatoes in those days can still be seen on the hillsides which have long since reverted to their wild state. However, the practice of sub-dividing small holdings of land by the tenants meant that too many people were trying to eke out an existence from too small a piece of land, and overcrowding and poverty was the result.

Decline following The Famine

In Connemara, as in many other parts of Ireland, much of the population was entirely dependent on the potato as the only food, and when the potato blight struck in 1845, and continued through 1846 and 1847, the result was a famine of the most catastrophic proportions. The population of Connemara was decimated, thousands

Pony with seaweed (lazy beds in background).

of people died of starvation or famine related diseases, thousands more emigrated to escape the misery and poverty, and most of the large estates were made bankrupt. The population of Ireland was reduced by two million in those three disastrous years, and the pattern of emigration began which was to continue for many generations following the famine.

Life in Connemara was a struggle for those who survived the famine years, and extreme poverty meant that many people were forced to sell their pony mares, and the numbers were greatly reduced. There was also indiscriminate breeding in some districts with poor quality colts being allowed to run out on the hills and breed with the mares.

The influence of the Arab and Barb sires imported by the big landowners was also declining, as many of the large estates were bankrupt, and there was a general feeling of hopelessness and despair.

Galway to Clifden Railway

The Government in London did little to alleviate the misery until 1890 when Mr Arthur Balfour the Chief Secretary for Ireland visited the West of Ireland to judge for himself the condition of the people in the distressed districts. Following this visit he allocated a grant towards the building of a railway line between Galway and Clifden which would provide employment for the many people living along its route. The work was hard and the men worked for very little pay, but the line which was forty-eight miles long was finally opened in 1895.

Congested Districts Board

Mr Balfour was also responsible for setting up the Congested Districts Board in 1891, which was to try to encourage the people living in the over-populated areas of the western seaboard to improve their way of life, and all sorts of schemes were set up to develop their farming skills and their livestock. The Congested Districts were mostly in the West of Ireland, and included Counties Donegal, Leitrim, Mayo, Galway, Clare, Kerry and

Cork. One of the responsibilities of the board was to improve the breeds of livestock, which included providing stallions for the various Congested Districts.

From 1891 to 1903 the Congested District Board introduced a variety of different stallions into Connemara including Barbs, Thoroughbreds, Half-breds, Hackneys and Welsh Cobs. However well-intentioned these schemes may have been, many of the stallions introduced by the Board during those years were considered to be very unsuitable for crossing with the Connemara pony, and in particular, the results from crossing the Hackney with the native mares were most unsatisfactory.

Among the sires which the Congested Districts Board placed in Connemara was a chestnut Welsh Cob called Prince Llewellyn, who was offered to Mr William Lyons and located with his kinsman Mr Thomas Lyons, Tullaboy. This sire was to influence the Connemara pony breed in the years to come through two of his sons, Dynamite and Powder, who were both bred by Mr Lyons from good Connemara mares. They proved to be successful sires, and their progeny were among the best mares in the Maam Cross district. Dynamite was a famous trotting pony, and his son Cannon Ball, foaled in 1904, became the first stallion to be registered in the Connemara Pony Stud Book.

If the crossing with Welsh cobs had continued, many of the qualities and characteristics of the Connemara pony would eventually have be lost, however the first crossings seem to have been successful where the sires were of the right stamp, and were mated with good pony mares.

In 1897 a Royal Commission was appointed to report on the state of horse breeding in Ireland, and it paid particular attention to the work of the Congested Districts Board. One of the men who gave evidence to the Commission was Mr Samuel Ussher Roberts, who had lived in the west of Galway for twenty five years. He stated that the ponies in Connemara were *"the best animals he ever knew, with good shoulders, good hard legs, good action, and great stamina. "* He never knew one of them to have a *"spavin or a splint, or to be in any respect unsound in his wind"*, while Mr R. Begley described the old stamp of Connemara pony as *"long and low with good rein, good back, and well coupled"*.

Most of the men from Galway reporting to the Commission had a personal knowledge of the Connemara breed, and they agreed that it had greatly deteriorated in the years following the famine, but Mr John Purdon reported that there were still some good specimens of the breed, and he described a drove of about 20 mares and foals he had seen in Connemara recently, and said they were the loveliest mares he had ever seen, with beautiful heads and clean limbs. They belonged to Mr William Lyons of Bunakill, who had kept a special breed for generations, and was well known as a successful breeder of the purest Connemara ponies.

The Ewart Report

In 1900 the Department of Agriculture and Technical Instruction came into being, and Professor Ewart, M. D. F. R. S. of Edinburgh University was Commissioned by the Department to go to the West of Ireland, and in consultation with some local experts, make a study of the actual condition and possibilities of the Connemara pony. It was the first time a serious study of the Connemara pony had been made, and a report on his findings was published in November 1900 in Volume I of the Department's Journal.

In this report, Professor Ewart states that soon after reaching Connemara, he was struck with *"the strength, endurance and easy paces of the ponies, with their intelligence and docility, and with the capacity to work under conditions which would speedily prove disastrous to horses reared under less natural conditions."*

He also thought there was a complete lack of uniformity in the ponies he saw between Maam Cross and Leenane, Cashel, Carna, Clifden and other centres, and concluded that instead of forming one breed, Connemara ponies belonged to five fairly distinct types which he called:

- The Andalusian Type
- The Eastern Type
- The Cashel Type
- The Clydesdale Type
- The Clifden Type

The first part of his report contained a detailed study of the ponies he selected from these groups, and the following is a brief summary of how he described the different types in his report.

The Andalusian Type: This group included what might be called the original or old Connemara type, and resembled ponies still seen in Andalusia. They varied from 12 to 13 hands, some were black, grey or chestnut, but the most characteristic were a yellow-dun colour. They seemed slightly roach-backed, a tendency in the Barb, and these Andalusian-like ponies of Connemara were probably the result of a more or less perfect blending of the aboriginal West of Ireland ponies with horses introduced from the East during medieval times, or from Spain during the 16th or 17th centuries. Ewart noted

National Library

Andalusian Type

that the yellow dun-coloured Connemara ponies were highly prized in some districts, not only because they were hardy and easily kept, but also because in staying power and vitality they were more like mules than horses.

The Eastern Type: While the Andalusian type resembled the Barb, the ponies which Ewart described as the Eastern type showed a marked similarity to the Arab, and Arabs were probably introduced into Connemara at the end of the 18th century. In former generations most of the ponies in Connemara may have been chestnut, but in 1900 the most common colour was grey, and it is widely recognised that the colour grey tends to persist, once it has been introduced, especially when it is the flea-bitten grey of an Arab.

A three year old light grey filly seen at the market in Clifden was taken as an example of this group. In the ears, width between the eyes, length of head, girth, the tail, and the mane, which was lank and clung closely to the neck, she closely resembled an Arab, but with a shorter neck. She showed the intelligence of an Arab, and was extremely gentle and good tempered, although she had never been handled before her arrival in Clifden. This filly showed a marked influence of Arab blood in her ancestry.

The Cashel Type: These ponies were descendants of an old grey stallion living in Cashel who was more like an Irish hunter than an Arab, and he was noted for his strength, speed, and great staying power. The typical members of this group were characterised by a long head, high withers, and long forelegs, and the gelding in the illustration was a son of the Cashel stallion. He might have been thought by some to be the best and most typical Connemara pony, but was quite unlike the old dun-coloured ponies of the Andalusian type, or the Eastern type with its Arab influence, or the short-legged Clifden type.

National Library

Eastern Type

The Clydesdale Type: Ponies belonging to this group were seen at rare intervals through Connemara and were described as stout, cob-like ponies, capable of carrying heavy loads, and when required, covering great distances at a fair speed. Their strong limbs, great girth, and powerful loins were said to be inherited from Clydesdale sires which were believed to have been introduced some thirty or forty years earlier. The three examples seen of this type were nearly black, and measured 14 hands with a girth of 70 inches.

The Clifden Type: The ponies in this group although only a little larger than the old Andalusian-type Connemara were very different in build. They had beautifully moulded intelligent heads, well arched ribs, good shoulders, with well developed loins and hind quarters, and short legs made to withstand an enormous amount of hard work. These short-legged ponies of the Clifden group probably would be regarded as representing the best kind of Connemara pony, and undoubtedly belong to an old strain. The grey mare whose photograph illustrated the Clifden type was an excellent pony, capable of carrying enormous weight, and was endowed with considerable speed and stamina, and it seemed likely that there was considerable blending of

7

types in the Clifden breed.

This type was the one which Professor Ewart suggested was the most valuable and worth preserving, not only because it was well adapted for the country, and would prove invaluable for crossing with other breeds, but also because he knew of no other ponies in the British Isles with so much stamina as those included in the Clifden section.

Clifden Type

When reviewing the Ewart report some forty years later in his paper on the Connemara Pony, Bartley O'Sullivan maintained most emphatically that *"There is nothing that could be described as a Clydesdale type, apart from a few cross-bred horses, to be met with near Galway city, there is no Clydesdale blood west of the Corrib and certainly no ponies with points even remotely resembling those of the Clydesdale".*

He also states in his paper that *"the Cashel Type is not known today. Cashel is in the heart of the pony country, producing some of the best ponies available, and animals such as those described by Professor Ewart as belonging to the Andalusian type, are quite common there today."*

Bartley continues, *"with the exceptions mentioned in the preceding two paragraphs, the characteristics and types enumerated by Professor Ewart are all represented in the ponies of today, (1939) although there is a tendency towards a blending of these, leading to an evolution of a more uniform breed".*

Cashel Type

The second part of the Ewart report was published in May 1901, in the Department's Journal, and covered the environment of the ponies, their work, and how to improve the breed.

Environment: Ewart described the old dun Connemara ponies as being capable of living where all but wild ponies would starve, and that they owed their hardiness and freedom from disease largely to their feeding on the wild herbs and dwarf shrubs that grew plentifully on the moors and uplands. *"When climate, physical features and geological formation of the West of Ireland are taken into consideration, there was no escape from the conclusion that Connemara is in many respects well adapted for the breeding and rearing of stout, active, hardy ponies."* Ponies reared under natural conditions in Connemara had been sold all over Ireland, and they had *"helped to gain for Irish horses their widespread reputation for vigour, hardiness and intelligence."*

Work: The ponies were essential to the small farmer in Connemara, owing to the rugged nature of the country, and the inaccessible position of some of the homesteads, and the pack-saddle and pillion were in everyday use. In describing the work of the ponies, Ewart wrote,

National Library

Boy on pony with creels.

"A two year old filly having been purchased - a bridle is soon woven out of horsehair, and a primitive pack saddle constructed out of four pieces of wood. The only additional pieces of furniture needed are mats or sacks to place under the saddle, and a cushion or pillion for the hindquarters, on which the owner at times sits when on the way to market, horsehair or ordinary ropes hold the various trappings in position.

The work of the ponies varies with the season of the year. At one time they may be seen climbing steep hillsides heavily laden with seaweed, seed corn, or potatoes, at another they convey the produce to market. Sometimes it is a load of turf, oats, or barley, at other times creels crowded with a lively family of young pigs.

During the summer and autumn the ponies are often seen trudging unsteadily along all but buried in a huge pile of hay or oats, each with a puzzled foal thoughtfully bringing up the rear.

Returning from market each pony generally carries two men, one in front and the other on the pillion behind. A good pony can easily carry two men thus disposed for a considerable distance at the rate of ten miles an hour. The women seem to be quite as much at home on the pillion as the men."

How to improve the Connemara Ponies
Ewart suggested that it might still be possible, out of native material, to produce a breed of ponies fairly uniform in make, size and colour, capable not only of performing the arduous work of a small upland farm,

but also, under favourable conditions, of developing into hunters. Many excellent light hunters, and riding and driving ponies had been bred in Connemara, and this was partly because the ponies as a rule were non-impressive, and partly because many of the mares, although unshapely and deficient in bone, belonged to good stock and seldom lacked stamina.

On the majority of small farms it was almost impossible to keep a foal as well as a mare through the winter, with the result that nearly all the foals were sold long before they reach maturity. The demand for the half-bred foals had attracted buyers from outside Ireland, and some of the best mares and foals had been carried off, and unless the leakage was checked, both Connemara and the rest of Ireland would suffer.

If an attempt was to be made to regain the reputation the ponies of Connemara enjoyed up to the middle of the 19th century, something more was needed than sending high class sires into the district.

Recognising the need to have good broodmares as well as good sires, some form of stud farms should be established for breeding pure stock in order to perpetuate the best characteristics of this once famous breed of Connemara Ponies.

In order to improve the Connemara pony, two things seemed imperative:-
(1)   to increase the bone, and
(2)   to improve the make without destroying the hardiness, vigour, stamina, and docility.

Ewart suggested that the best mares might be selected to start a new and improved strain of Connemara ponies, and that sturdy active pony sires should be chosen to breed with the mares.

In conclusion he said *"Connemara is in a sense already a huge stud farm which produces annually a large crop of foals With a little organisation, the number might be considerably increased. "*

However he warned that *"the Connemara breed is so valuable and fertile and free from hereditary disease that their extinction would be a national loss,"* and added that *"unless steps are taken soon, they will be numbered with the past."*

Despite this warning, no action seems to have been taken in response to it, even though the reports to the Royal Commission on Horse Breeding in Ireland in 1897 had also stated how much the breed had deteriorated in recent years.

The Ewart report was a lengthy document of thirty-four pages with twenty one photographs, but much of the report is irrelevant today, and his "five types" tend to be confusing for contemporary breeders of Connemara ponies. Bartley O'Sullivan was convinced that Professor Ewart may have seriously under-estimated the number of Connemara ponies running out on the mountains, and suggested that the report was based on only a small portion of the native breeding herd, and that there were hundreds of ponies in the remote valleys of Connemara who were never seen by Ewart during his visit.

The report lay unheeded for many years, but when the Connemara Pony Breeders' Society was formed in 1923, one of Ewart's suggestions for the improvement of the breed was acted upon by the new committee when they decided to select the best mares and stallions from within the breed to form the foundation stock for the Stud Book.

In 1901, the Congested Districts Board admitted in an annual report that the old type of Connemara pony had become very scarce, and in an attempt to preserve it, a stud of fifteen Connemara mares and two Erris ponies was established at Lough Glynn, Co. Roscommon. Nine of the Connemara mares were put in foal to an Arab stallion, two to a Connemara pony stallion, and the two Erris ponies to a Thoroughbred.

It was planned that ten of the mares would be covered by the Arab in the 1902 season, and seven by a young and very promising Connemara pony stallion, and all the results were to be watched and carefully noted. Unfortunately no records can be found of this breeding programme, and further efforts were not made to improve the situation.

The Congested District Board during the twelve years it had been responsible for the provision of stallions in Connemara, had done little to improve the Connemara pony, even admitting in the annual report in 1902 that there were very few good ponies left in districts where they had once been plentiful, and Bartley O'Sullivan wrote in his paper in 1939 that *"the result of this haphazard breeding was at its best unsatisfactory, and at its worst well-nigh disastrous"*

In 1903 the Congested Districts Board's work in connection with Agriculture and Livestock was transferred to the Department of Agriculture and Technical Instruction of Ireland.

Michael O'Malley's Journey to Olympia

Finally, the plight of the Connemara pony was brought to the notice of a wider public by a young man called Michael O'Malley, whose untiring efforts on behalf of his native breed eventually led to the formation of the Connemara Pony Breeders' Society.

Born in Rosmuck in 1884, he went to Glasnevin Agricultural College in Dublin as a young man to study veterinary science, but due to his father's failing health and early death, he returned home to help in his family business, and never completed his studies. He had a great love of the Irish language and was a personal friend of Padraig Pearse, who owned a cottage near Michael's home, and in later years he founded an Irish college in Rosmuck in 1933 in order to encourage the revival of the Irish language and the speaking of Irish in the district.

Michael O'Malley had known the old breed of Connemara ponies all his life, and was appalled at the awful change from the old type of pony which had been brought about by the horse-breeding schemes, and the apathy and indifference of the Connemara breeder. He took great pride in his native Connemara and its ponies, and was among those present at a meeting of the Connemara Pony Committee which was held in Clifden on 15th November 1911, when a description and definition of the Connemara Pony was drawn up.

An attempt to form a society seems to have failed through lack of funds, but Michael O'Malley was determined to promote his native pony in which he believed so passionately, and so he decided to take two ponies to

Michael O'Malley

Olympia in London in June 1912 to take part in a parade of Types of British and Continental Horses and Ponies. The two ponies he chose to represent the Connemara breed were his four year old steel grey stallion Irish Dragoon, and a six year old cream mare Eileen Alanna, and he was awarded a Diploma from the International Horse Show for taking part in the display with his ponies. Thirty-six different breeds were represented in the parade, and it must have been a proud day for Michael and his groom Joe Walsh to show their Connemara ponies in the Grand Hall at Olympia, having travelled such a long and arduous journey from Rosmuck to London. His efforts were well rewarded as his ponies were much admired, and the hardships of the long journey had been worthwhile.

Following his return from Olympia he wrote a letter to the Irish Farming World, headed "A Plea For The Connemara Pony", in which he deplored the deterioration of the Connemara pony, due to the introduction of unsuitable sires, and urged that steps should be taken to revive the old breed. He describes the old type of pony who used to be seen on the hills and mountains of Connemara as *"that pleasant looking animal with the short stout legs, the strong thick neck and wide chest, the powerful back and deep barrel, and the full and intelligent looking eye. "* These ponies were bred to survive the winter on the mountains, but the new improved type, with *" their shaggy wet coats of hair, their tottering long legs, and the shivering of their lanky bodies"* would make the owner *"uncertain as to their safety on the mountains. "* He concludes his letter by saying he would like to see the Department of Agriculture start a scheme on behalf of the Connemara breed similar to one started on behalf of the Irish Draught the previous year, and if that step was taken, *"the revival of and proper recognition of the Connemara pony would be sure, quick, and lasting."*

In response to his letter a number of correspondents from all over Ireland wrote to the Irish Farming World in support of his views, giving examples of the exceptional Connemara ponies they had owned, and regretting the decline of the breed.

In all twenty letters were published between November 1912 and July 1913, and in one letter William O'Malley M. P. wrote from the House of Commons, London, expressing his admiration for the patriotic efforts Michael O'Malley was making to revive the Connemara pony, and wishing him God-speed.

Michael O'Malley Booklet

Having had such a positive response to his letters, Michael O'Malley then decided to compile a booklet of all the letters which had been written to the Irish Farming World, and had it printed by the Connacht Tribune at his own expense. His aim in compiling the booklet was to *"show people, but especially Connemara Pony Breeders, in a handy form what others think of our ponies, with a view, and an ardent hope, that they (Connemara Pony Breeders) will, even at the eleventh hour, make an effort to save the breed. "* Michael O'Malley was a keen amateur photographer, and all the photographs in the booklet were taken by him. He also included a list of names and addresses of gentlemen *"who will be glad to give... their sound and mature views on pony breeding in the West".*

Many of those whose names he listed attended the meeting at which the Connemara Pony Breeders' Society was formed ten years later, and some of them became members of the first Council.

The intervening years were ones of great turmoil in Ireland's history, when the struggle for independence became a reality, with guerilla warfare against the military and the Royal Irish Constabulary bringing dreadful reprisals by the Black and Tans, including the burning of fourteen houses in Clifden on St Patricks night 1921. The signing of the Treaty in December 1921 gave birth to the Irish Free State, but was followed by the outbreak of Civil War in June 1922 which continued until the spring of 1923 when the Government of the emerging Irish Free State was faced with the task of rebuilding a badly damaged society and economy.

Despite these disturbed times, Michael O'Malley continued his campaign for the Connemara Pony, and found a friend in Mr F. Prendergast who was Chief Agricultural Inspector for the Western Region at the time. He was head of the Agricultural College at Athenry and was sympathetic to Michael's pleas for the rescue of the Connemara Pony. He helped him to gain the support of Mr Fogarty, the Secretary of the County Committee of Agriculture in Galway, and they also enlisted the help of Father C. J. White P. P. from Roundstone who was more than willing to support any cause which would be of benefit to the people of Connemara.

Tourist Coach, Leenane, 1890-1910

CHAPTER 2

1923 - 1931

• Formation of the Connemara Pony Breeders' Society • Inspections • First Council • Early Shows •
• Nomination Scheme • Cannon Ball • President Resigns • Foal Subsidies • New President •
• Volumes I and II Stud Book published • Two Stallion Lines Established •

On December 12th 1923, Mr W. G. Fogarty, Secretary of the Galway County Committee of Agriculture, called a meeting of Connemara pony breeders and others at Sweeneys Hotel in Oughterard, for the purpose of taking steps that would lead to the preservation and improvement of the Connemara Pony.

The meeting was attended by a large number of breeders and other people interested in the project, and included the following: The Very Rev. C. J. White P. P. Roundstone, R. J. Peacocke,Maam Cross, C. J. Kerin, Oranmore, Michael McDonagh, Letterfive, Thomas Lyons, Tullaboy, George Lyons, Bunakill, P. H. Joyce, Rahoon, William Roe, Oughterard, E. A. Sweeney, Oughterard, W. F. Prendergast, Athenry, T. McD. Kelly MRCVS, Athenry, W. G. Fogarty, Galway, B. O'Sullivan, Clifden, James McDonnell,Oughterard, Michael O'Malley, Rosmuck, Joseph Mongan, Carna.

The object of the meeting having been fully and ably explained by Mr Fogarty, the Secretary of the Co. Committee of Agriculture, and Mr Prendergast, Agricultural Inspector for the Western Region, the Rev. C. J. White was then moved to the chair, when most interesting views were given by several present as to the merits and value of the Connemara Pony.

In his opening address Father White made an impassioned plea for the Connemara Pony and stated that: *"Everything in Connemara has a distinctive feature that marks it out. The men were men of grit, the women were charming and beautiful. As for the ponies, they could go anywhere, live anywhere, did not require luxurious food, had remarkable staying power, and were much better value than bigger horses. On the mountainside, in the valleys, or on the hard rocky surface they were equally effective. He urged that in the efforts made to revive them, there should be no such word as failure!"* (Connacht Tribune 15th December 1923)

A long and lively discussion followed when various breeders put forward different views as to how best to improve the breed. Thomas Lyons said that the introduction of Hackney blood by the Congested Districts Board had been a mistake, and he advocated the use of Welsh Cobs, citing the example of a remarkable pony he owned who was a Connemara/Welsh Cob cross, the chestnut cob Dynamite, who had won everywhere. He also said that action was lost through inbreeding, but that the the use of an Arab stallion imported by the Martins of Ross had been successful. C. J. Kerin felt the Welsh Cob cross had done the breed no good, and they had the best saddle ponies in Connemara before the Welsh Cob came in. He told the meeting that *"it is up to everyone of us as far as we can to develop our distinctive type of stock and put our distinctive nationality on them before they leave our country. "*

It was felt that there was still plenty of the "old breed" to be found in the heart of the pony districts of Connemara, and it was the opinion of the meeting that the best results were likely to be obtained by breeding only from carefully selected native stock.

Formation of the Connemara Pony Breeders' Society

A decision was taken unanimously by the meeting to form The Connemara Pony Breeders' Society then and there, and a provisional committee was appointed, with Rev. Father C. J. White as President, and Mr Michael O'Malley as Hon Secretary.

The provisional committee consisted of: Messrs C. J. Kerin, Thomas Lyons, George Lyons, William Roe, William Duffy, Patrick Joyce, Joseph Mongan, Richard Kearney, T. McD. Kelly, W. F. Prendergast.

These men went to work straight away, and decided to approach the Galway County Committee of Agriculture for a grant of £100 to enable them to offer free nominations to 100 mare owners, and the Department of Agriculture was to be asked to complete their list of existing pony stallions in Connemara.

A sub-committee of C. J. Kerin, George Lyons and Michael O'Malley were then given the task of drawing up a scheme to be submitted to the next meeting of the Society on 2nd Jan 1924.

The scheme which was approved and adopted at the next meeting was a simple one.
1. That the improvement of the Connemara Pony should come from within, i. e. the best of the available native blood to be selected and mated in a proper manner.
2. Up to 100 mares of the right type to be selected for a foundation stock, as well as the necessary number of stallions.
3. That the Galway County Committee of Agriculture be asked to give a grant of £100 and also the Department of Agriculture be asked for another £100. The former to enable the Society to offer free nominations to mare owners, and the latter for purchasing the necessary number of stallions and for the organising and giving of prizes at a local show during 1924.

The Objects of the Connemara Pony Breeders' Society
(a) The encouragement of the breeding of Connemara ponies and their development and maintenance as a pure breed.
(b) The publication of a Stud Book for animals which have been passed as eligible for registration.
(c) To arrange for the purchase of suitable registered stallions of the Connemara pony breed and for their location at approved centres.
(d) To hold an Annual Show and arrange for classes and prizes at selected shows.
(e) To make arrangements for exhibitions and for special sales of registered ponies, with a view to encourage home and foreign trade.

(f) To co-operate with the Department of Agriculture, the County Committee of Agriculture, and the Royal Dublin Society, with a view of more effectively promoting the work of the Society.

The business of the new Society moved swiftly, and by 16th January grants had been secured from the Co Committees of Agriculture of Galway and Mayo totalling £125 so that the committee was able to set the dates for the first inspection shows in April 1924 and offer 125 free nominations of £1 to brood mares of suitable type to be selected at the following inspection centres: Galway, Oughterard, Spiddal, Maam Cross, Derrynea, Cashel, Clifden, Letterfrack, Leenane, Clonbur.

The Inspection Team

The men chosen to act as Inspectors for the Society were:

- Mr Dan Twomey, Chief Livestock Inspector, Dept. of Agriculture, Dublin.
- Mr C. J. Kerin, Oranmore, a well-known judge of horses.
- Mr. T. McD. Kelly MRCVS, Athenry, a well respected horse vet and judge.
- Mr. Tim Cotter, Tuam, Department of Agriculture Inspector.

These four men were well chosen, they were all from outside Connemara, with no vested interests in the Connemara pony, but had the knowledge and the integrity required to provide continuity and consistency in the selection of foundation stock for the Stud Book. They served as an inspection team and as judges at the Annual Show for more than thirty years, and up to the year before his death in 1955, Christy Kerin only missed one Show. The breeders of today owe them a great debt of gratitude for their long and unstinting service to the breed. The inspections were central to the foundation of the stud book, and have continued to be an essential part of the monitoring and safe-guarding of the breed up to the present day.

Attry Maid (25)

17

First Inspections

The inspectors' first report to the Council was printed in Volume I of the Connemara Pony Stud Book which was published in 1926 with entries for 9 stallions and 93 mares. It reads as follows.

To the Council.   *April 1924.*

Gentlemen,

We beg to report that we carried out the inspections of Connemara Ponies from the 15th to 19th April, 1924. The results of the inspections may be summarised as follows:-

Centre	Mares		Stallions	
	Presented	Passed	Presented	Passed
Galway	20	5	8	1
Oughterard	30	3	4	1
Spiddal	4	1	-	-
Maam Cross	50	17	4	-
Derrynea	17	7	3	-
Cashel	65	18	9	2
Clifden	23	1	5	-
Letterfrack	20	3	-	-
Leenane	5	1	-	-
Clonbur	15	4	2	1
	249	60	35	5
Roundstone Show	90	15	15	1
Total 1924	339	75	50	6

In making our selections we endeavoured to adhere to the type of pony which made the breed famous in the past, that is a compact deep-bodied animal, short-backed and well ribbed up, standing on short legs, having good bone, sloping shoulders with well balanced neck and head. The ideal height we regard as ranging from 13 to 14 hands and the average height of the selected ponies is about 13 hands 2 inches.

We paid particular attention to action, and selected ponies of free, easy and true movement. In this connection it may be well to mention that a number of ponies which might have been regarded as otherwise suitable, were rejected owing to action which was seriously faulty.

We are pleased to be able to report that the selected mares conformed to the ideal standard and that a large proportion of them were excellent in type and quality. It was very noticeable, however, that the best mares were for the most part over ten years old and that taken as a whole the younger mares were somewhat disappointing.

We are of the opinion that the majority of the selected mares are as true to type and fully as good as the best which have been bred in Connemara in the past. After careful consideration we have come to the conclusion that these will form an excellent foundation stock, which properly utilised, will become the basis of an improved breed of ponies that will prove admirably suited to local requirements and command a ready market further afield.

It is clear that the good old native type has been disappearing in recent years from many districts and it is essential that an earnest and sustained effort should now be made to foster and develop the breed.

Insofar as the mares are concerned at all events, we are quite satisfied that there is still sufficient good material available. With regard to the stallions, however, we regret that we are not in a position to report so favourably. It will be observed from the figures quoted above, that we inspected in all 35 stallions and of these there were only 5 which could be regarded as approximating to the desired type. The majority of the stallions presented for inspection were of a nondescript type and wholly unsuitable for the purposes of the Scheme. It appears to us that the breeders have not exercised the same care and judgement in the selection of their stallions as they did in the case of brood mares.

While we are satisfied that the stallions now recommended are of fair average quality and may, with advantage, be used for mating with the selected mares, we feel that an effort must be made to find better class sires for use in future years. We believe it may be possible to find such stallions in Connemara, or at least to breed a number of really high class sires by mating the best selected mares with the stallions we now recommend for approval. From the detailed lists which accompany this report the present location of both the selected mares and stallions can be ascertained and we desire to submit for consideration of the Council the necessity for making a more equitable distribution of the available stallions so that a registered stallion may be within reasonable distance of all selected mares.

All mares and stallions were submitted to a strict veterinary examination and those recommended for registration were passed sound and free from hereditary disease.

Signed,

C. J. Kerin, D. Twomey, T. McD. Kelly, MRCVS. T. Cotter.

First Stallions Purchased

In May 1924 the Council purchased their first two stallions, for £20 each.
- *Gold Digger (5)* five year old dun with small star standing 13.2hh, registered at Cashel in 1924, bought from Joe Molloy, Lettershana, Cashel, placed with George Lyons, Bunakill.

- *Connemara Dan (3)* two year old black with star, height 13.1hh purchased from P. H. Conroy, Kylemore, and located with Val Keaney, Gowla, Cashel.

It was also planned to purchase Rebel for that season, but the Council had to wait until 1927 before they succeeded in buying him and he could be put on the list of stallions owned by the Society.

The other stallions approved for the 1924 season, but in private ownership were:
- *Cannon Ball (1)* twenty year old grey, 13. 3hh, owned by Henri Toole, Leam, Oughterard.
- *Rebel (7)* two year old grey, 13. 2hh sire Cannon Ball (1), owned by Gilbert Ryan, Rosshill, Galway.
- *Mount Gabel (6)* seven year old bay, 13. 2hh owned by Martin Walsh, Finney, Clonbur.

The First Council

At a General meeting of the Society held in Galway on 31st May 1924 the First Council for the Connemara Pony Breeders' Society was formally elected and consisted of the following:

President
Rev. C. J. White, PP Roundstone.

Vice President
Joseph W. Mongan, Carna

Hon. Secretaries
M. J. O'Malley, Rosmuck
B. O'Sullivan, Clifden

Council Members

C. J. Kerin, Oranmore.	T. Cotter, Tuam
W. F. Prendergast, Athenry	T. McD. Kelly MRCVS, Athenry
D. Twomey, Dublin	William Roe, Oughterard
Michael B. Wallace, Tully	George Lyons, Bunakill
Thomas Lyons, Tullyboy	Ambrose Lee, Clifden
H. G. Connolly, Clifden	Thomas McDonagh, Galway
Michael Crowley, Galway	Thomas Ruane, Oranmore
R. E. Willis, Oughterard	

Stud Book Editing Committee
W. F. Prendergast, T. McD. Kelly. T. Cotter, C. J. Kerin, the Secretaries.

The first Council was composed of a good cross section of people who were all committed to the preservation and improvement of the Connemara pony. There was also an underlying purpose to the scheme in that by helping to improve the pony, this would in turn benefit the people of Connemara who bred the ponies, many of whom were very poor in those days.

The greatest strength in the Council was the enormous dedication and length of service to the Society that was given by many of its founder members, and there was surely no finer example of this than the man who became Joint Secretary with Michael O'Malley at that meeting, Bartley O'Sullivan. The two men served as Joint Secretaries for the next thirty-six years, but it was Bartley O'Sullivan who in time became the man responsible for running the Society.

The First Council
Back row (L to R): Bartley O'Sullivan, Michael O'Malley, Willie Roe. ***Middle row:*** Michael Wallace, Josie Mongan, Tim Cotter, T. McD. Kelly. ***Front row:*** Tom Lyons, W.F. Prendergast, Father C.J. White, Christy Kerin.

21

Bartley O'Sullivan

Bartley O'Sullivan was born near Caherciveen in Co. Kerry in 1889, and was educated at the National School in Fylemore. He was a bright pupil, and was encouraged by his teacher to go to the Albert Agricultural College in Glasnevin, Dublin, where he gained a first class certificate, and in 1909 the Department of Agriculture and Technical Instruction offered him the post of Assistant Agricultural Overseer in Clifden at a salary of £65 per annum.

In his early days in Connemara he travelled the district on a bicycle, but by the early twenties he had acquired a Triumph motor-cycle, Regisration No. C. J. 1927 and for this vehicle he carried several permits, one issued by the Crown Forces, another by the IRA and another by the Free State. For those were disturbed times and he needed to be prepared to negotiate the road blocks of one or other faction along his route, often having to manhandle his motor bike over a trench or a felled tree laid across the road by the insurgents.

His lodgings in Clifden were a bit too close to the RIC. Barracks for comfort, especially when the barracks came under fire from the Republicans, so being a resourceful young man, he acquired an iron shutter which had been blown off a barrack window, and lashed it securely to the bottom rail of his bed.

Bartley was captivated by Connemara and settled happily in Clifden, where he met and married his wife May. She was born on the tiny island of Inishshark off the

Bartley O'Sullivan

Cleggan coast where her mother was National School teacher, and her father was a police constable on the island of Inishbofin. Bartley and May had six children, and they remained in Clifden until 1929 when his job took him to Galway.

By 1923, Bartley had been working as an Agricultural Overseer in Connemara for fourteen years, and his job helping the small farmers in the district had given him a thorough knowledge of the area and the people he worked with. He already knew Michael O'Malley well, and shared his enthusiasm and love for the Connemara pony, and he was present at the public meeting in Oughterard when the Connemara Pony Breeders' Society was formed. He also assisted in the organisation of the first tour of inspection held in April 1924, and when he became Joint Honorary Secretary with Michael O'Malley, his administrative skills and his experience in working for the Department of Agriculture were of great value to the Council.

The Connemara Pony Breeders' Society had already come a long way in just six months of its existence, and plans were now made for the first Connemara Pony Show to be held at Roundstone on 15th August 1924. The judges appointed were: Messrs D. Twomey, C. J. Kerin, and T. McD. Kelly. MRCVS.

A show committee was nominated, and the offer from the Royal Dublin Society of silver medals as prizes for the Show was accepted with gratitude. These medals are still presented every year for the Annual Show, and are much coveted prizes, and the support for the Connemara Pony Breeders' Society by the Royal Dublin Society has continued without a break for seventy-five years.

First Connemara Pony Show, Roundstone – 15th August 1924

The First Connemara Agricultural and Home Industries Show was held at Roundstone in the grounds of the Monastery by courtesy of the Franciscan Brothers. It must have been a colourful occasion with 2000 people attending the Show, many of whom had travelled more than twenty miles on foot from all parts of Connemara. There were 500 entries overall, with all kinds of home industries and farm skills being catered for, as well as 150 entries in the Connemara Pony section. The attendance at the Show also included many visitors from all over Ireland, Waterford, Kilkenny, Dublin, Athlone etc.

The opening ceremony was performed by The Maharajah Jam Sahib of Nawanjar, (Prince Ranjitsinjhi), one of the greatest cricket players of all time, who had recently come to live at Ballynahinch Castle, and he was accompanied by his nieces, Princess Baba and Princess Bjaniba and a considerable retinue. He was received by a guard of honour of the National army and the Civic Guard.

Ranji (as he came to be known) was a keen fisherman, and usually arrived in Connemara for the fishing season in mid-June and stayed until October. Every year when he arrived in Galway he bought five cars, two sedans for himself and his guests, and three model T Fords to be used by his aides while he was at Ballynahinch.

In those days motor cars were a rare sight in Connemara, and people used to run to the roadside to watch whenever one drove past. Before leaving Connemara each autumn to return to India he would give the cars to his friends, often the local school teacher, superintendent of the Gardai or the local priest.

He was a colourful character and was very popular with the local community. Father White was a close personal friend, and in his opening address to introduce the Prince and welcome him to the Show, he stressed that the people of Connemara were anxious to develop their land, their fisheries, and their home industries. In his reply the Prince thanked the people for their welcome and kindness since he had come to live at Ballynahinch, and when he was taken on a tour of the Show, he admired the cottage industries section, bought some Connemara rugs, and gave orders for some Roundstone lace. He was also introduced to some of the owners of the prizewinning ponies, and admired the legendary *Cannon Ball (1)* shown by his owner Henri Toole.

The Connemara Pony Stallion Class and RDS Silver Medal was won by the Society's new purchase, *Gold Digger (5)* shown by George Lyons, with the famous old pony *Cannon Ball (1)*, now perhaps past his prime aged 20, taking 2nd place for Henri Toole, and *Connemara Dan (3)* 3rd for Val Keaney.

First place and RDS Silver Medal for the best Registered Connemara Mare with foal at foot went to Cannon Belle (47) a ten year old mare, who is thought to have been sired by Cannon Ball, and owned by James Mullane, Camus, Costello. Bayleek Polly (33) was 2nd for James O'Toole, Faulkerra, Clifden.

The winner of the class for mares without foal and RDS Silver Medal was Renvyle Katie (34) owned by Peter Flaherty, Cloonlane, Renvyle, and she was one of the three mares selected at the first inspections in Letterfrack in April 1924. Martin Coyne, Renvyle owned another of the mares selected that day, but was unable to take his mare to Roundstone. When Peter Flaherty returned home after the show he gave the RDS Silver Medal he had won to his friend, as he maintained that Martin's mare was the better pony and would have won the Medal if she had gone to the Show. The RDS Medal remains with Martin's son Pakie Coyne at Ardnagreevagh, Renvyle as a little bit of history from the first Connemara Pony Show.

There were 108 entries in the class for non-registered mares, with 90 shown on the day, and from that number fifteen were selected for registration. The winner was Bunowen Beauty (37) owned by John Sweeney, Bunowen, Ballyconneely. In the non-registered stallion class the inspectors were again strict, and only selected one out of the fifteen entries.

In paying tribute to the Society's President at the end of the day, Mr Prendergast stated that the huge success of the day was due in no small measure to the wonderful energy and enthusiasm of Father White, who had worked tirelessly to make the show a day to be enjoyed by everyone who attended. In reply Father White said:

"Gentlemen, let me assure you that while I am in Connemara, and in fact alive, I shall always support your Society, and do what I can to further the interests of Connemara and its people. This has been one of the happiest days of my life, and well may I call this moment the end of a perfect day. Because of the enthusiasm and earnestness shown by everybody who has helped me to make our show what it has been, I find it hard to make special mention of anybody, but I feel that Mr O'Sullivan deserves special thanks for the manner in which he has worked, and therefore I have great pleasure in thanking him sincerely on behalf of you all. " (Taken from minutes of CPBS)

Nomination Scheme

The breeding programme for 1925 got underway with the decision to offer all mares already on the register a free nomination to a registered stallion without further inspection, and the nomination fee was fixed at ten shillings.

Inspection centres for non-registered stock were reduced to five and were arranged for Oughterard, Maam Bridge, Recess, Kilkerrin and Galway to be held on 15th and 16th April. There was a big drop in the number of ponies brought out at the inspection centres compared to 1924, and the greatest number were presented at the Annual Show at Recess. The inspectors were again very strict and only selected the best type of ponies, so that only 18 more mares and 3 stallions were added to the register.

Centre	Mares		Stallions	
	Presented	Passed	Presented	Passed
Oughterard	9	1	2	-
Maam	2	1	2	-
Recess	10	5	1	-
Kilkerrin	3	-	-	-
Galway	3	3	-	1
Recess Show	70	8	9	2
	97	18	15	3

Shortly after the inspection tour, the three year old stallion *Charlie (2)*, a roan pony standing 13. 2hh, who had been inspected and passed at Galway, was purchased by the Connemara Pony Breeders' Society from Mr C. Costelloe, Galway. He was located for the 1925 season with Val Keaney, Gowla, Carna, while *Connemara Dan (3)* was moved to James O'Toole, Faulkeera, Clifden. *Galway Grey (4)* who had been passed at Roundstone Show in 1924, stood with his owner Colman Conneely at Ballinahown, and they brought up to seven the list of registered stallions available to registered mares for the 1925 season.

Garnet Irwin

Charlie (2)

At a general meeting of the Society held in Recess in May, Bartley O'Sullivan, who was already Joint Secretary, was asked to take over all the practical work in the running of the Society, and this included the writing of the minutes which up to then had been kept by Michael O'Malley. From this time onward Bartley O'Sullivan was the man who became responsible for a great deal more than keeping the minutes, and it was his job to arrange the purchase and sale of stallions, the placement of stallions with custodians, the organising of the Show, the publishing of the Stud Book, and all the day to day decisions for the Society. He remained Joint Secretary with Michael O'Malley for the next thirty-five years, but as time went on, Michael O'Malley became less involved in the administration side, and the bulk of that responsibility fell on Bartley O'Sullivan's shoulders. The Connemara Pony Breeders' Society is very fortunate indeed that such a dedicated man should have devoted so much of his life to the running of the Society's affairs, and without his enormous contribution, it is doubtful that the Connemara Pony Breeders' Society could have achieved so much.

In making the arrangements for the 2nd Annual Connemara Pony Show it was agreed that it would be confined to ponies, and would be held at Recess on 29th June. Also it was agreed that in future there would be no expenditure on *"free entertainment at shows."* Maybe entertaining the Prince Ranji had proved a costly affair the previous year!

Prizewinners at Recess Show, 1925.

2nd Annual Pony Show, Recess – 29th June 1925

The earlier date for the Annual Show proved to be a good choice, and the Show was held in beautiful weather with an increased entry of 170 ponies. It was held in a field just opposite the ruins of the Recess Hotel, and a large number of people visited the Show on the special excursion train. Exhibitors came from all over Connemara, some on horseback, and again many had travelled more than twenty miles with their ponies.

The judges were Mr C. J. Kerin, Mr D. Twomey, and Mr T. McD. Kelly MRCVS, and for the second year the prize for the best registered stallion and the RDS Silver Medal went to *Gold Digger (5)* shown by George Lyons, Bunakill. The new young stallion *Charlie (2)* took second place for Val Keaney, Gowla, Cashel, and in 3rd place was Colman Conneely's *Galway Grey (3)*

In the non-registered stallion class the winner was a three year old grey stallion owned by Michael O'Neill, Clifden, who was accepted for the register and named *Connemara Boy (9)*. The second pony in this class was a nine year old black stallion 13.1hh who also belonged to M. J. O'Neill, and he too was accepted for the register, and named *Black Paddy (8)*. The other seven entries in the class were not registered as stallions.

In the following years both these stallions were purchased by the Connemara Pony Breeders Society, *Black Paddy (8)* in the spring of 1926 and *Connemara Boy (9)* in 1928, and *Connemara Boy* was to become the founder of one of the famous stallion lines of the breed.

The class for registered mares was won by Bayleek Polly (33) for James O'Toole, Faulkeera, Clifden and second place went to Cannon Belle (47) James Mullane, Camus, and this mare also took the RDS Silver Medal for best mare with foal at foot.

In the class for non-registered mares eight were accepted for the register out of an entry of 70, and the winner of the class was an eight year old mare, Jessie Grey (86) owned by Michael O'Brien, Toombeola.

It was the practice in the early days of the Society to hold a General Meeting at the end of Show day, which must have been quite demanding for the secretaries and everyone involved in running the Show.

At the meeting in Recess, the 1925 Show was considered to have been an even greater success than the previous year, and Mr Dan Twomey stated that he was pleased with the very marked improvement in the type of pony on show, and felt that there were fewer of the nondescript type, and that the people of Connemara had grasped the correct idea as to the type that was required. The next and most important step was to ensure that only registered stallions were used for service on the registered mares. He stressed that although a market for the ponies would not be difficult to find, it was too soon yet to think of selling any ponies, and it was essential that the good breeding mares were kept in the Connemara district until stocks had built up.

Mr Prendergast also expressed great satisfaction at the remarkable progress which had been made by the Society in such a short time, and congratulated all those who had put so much effort into it. He said that the Stud Book should be produced at the expense of the Society, and that it should be done well. This was agreed, and it was decided that the printing of the first Connemara Pony Stud Book should go ahead, and it could be printed at the cost of approximately £30.

It was agreed unanimously that a presentation should be made by the members of the Council to Michael O'Malley on the occasion of his marriage to Miss B. Quinn, of Tubbercurry, Co. Sligo which was to take place the following day. It seems typical of the energy and enthusiasm of Michael O'Malley that he should spend the eve of his wedding helping in the running of the Connemara Pony Show!

During the 1926 season the work of the Society suffered rather a setback in that the number of stallions on the list was reduced from seven down to four. Firstly Mr George Lyons reported that *Gold Digger (5)* was not proving to be a satisfactory sire, despite having won 1st prize at both the Society's first two shows, and he requested that he should be placed elsewhere or sold. The second stallion owned by the Society, *Connemara Dan (3)* was not breeding well and was castrated, and none of his progeny were registered subsequently. The privately owned *Galway Grey (4)* was also removed from the list, and *Mount Gabel (6)*, also in private ownership, died during the year.

The final blow was that the legendary *Cannon Ball*, No 1 in the first Volume of the Stud Book, died in March 1926, at the age of 22, and his loss was mourned throughout Connemara. He was already an old pony when he was registered by the Society in 1924 at their first inspections, but he was acknowledged as having been a very successful sire, and many of the best ponies in the Maam district were said to have descended from him.

Cannon Ball, No. 1 in Stud Book

In a paper on the Connemara Pony written by Bartley O'Sullivan in 1939 he gives details of *Cannon Ball's* breeding and states that:

Cannon Ball (1)

"Early in the 1890's, the Congested Districts Board, having decided to locate Welsh Stallions in Connemara, approached Mr William Lyons of Bunakill near Maam Cross, who in those days kept on an average about thirty Connemara pony mares, and offered him a stallion. Mr Lyons chose the Welsh Cob, Prince Llewellyn, which was located with his kinsman, Mr. Tom Lyons... Cannon Ball was by Dynamite out of a native mare, and Dynamite, also out of a native mare, was by Prince Llewellyn."

Dynamite won local distinction in trotting matches, which were a feature of life in Connemara in those days, and his reputation brought a rich American buyer, who bought him for £100, and took him to the USA where he won many more races in New York and other American centres.

However it was his son *Cannon Ball* who became a legend in his own lifetime in Connemara, and regularly won the Farmers' Race at the Oughterard Pony Races. He lived all his life at Leam, near Oughterard with his owner Harry Toole (known as Henri to his friends). They travelled to Athenry Market every Saturday a distance of some 60 miles round trip, and often would stop along the way if a mare was found waiting for *Cannon Ball's* services. This was common practice for most of the stallions in those days as they were working ponies too. His owner Henri was fond of the odd pint along the way, and often on the way home after a long session in the pub, it was left to *Cannon Ball* to find his own way home, while Henri lay snoring in the bottom of the cart.

The two had a very special understanding, but on the racecourse, Henri always got a jockey to ride *Cannon Ball*, sometimes it was Mark Geoghegan or Jack Bolger who rode him but John Connolly from Galway was his most regular partner. He was never beaten in all the years he raced at Oughterard and other racecourses, and often won more than one race in a day. He always carried top weight and usually won comfortably but at short odds. Once he raced the train from Oughterard to Leam for a bet, a distance of about four miles, and won easily and was waiting at Leam for the train to pass.

The fame of this very special Connemara pony was such that a report of his death and "wake" was written in the Connaught Sentinel entitled *A Connemara Wake*. When news of *Cannon Ball's* death became known, large numbers of people came to the house to sympathise with Henri. They brought *Cannon Ball's* body into the kitchen where it was laid out on a canvas, and the old pony was "waked" as if he was a human being.

Soon after midnight he was placed on an stable door, and ten strong men carried him to the hay-lined grave where he was buried standing up and looking towards the Oughterard Racecourse. At dead of night as the interment took place, the following verse was read by the light of a flickering candle:

Sleep, brave old pony, sleep; thy race is run;
No more with earthly kin you'll mingle;
Dream of racecourse tracks you've won-
And bookies left without a jingle.

Cannon Ball was aged twenty by the time the Connemara Pony Breeders' Society was formed, and it was acknowledged that there were many good ponies descended from him already in the district. But in the early days of registration, no breeding was entered into the Stud Book unless it could be proved beyond doubt, and so there are only two ponies entered in the Stud Book with *Cannon Ball* as their sire. However, in the Stallion files kept by Bartley O'Sullivan with records of all the details of the stallions owned by the Society, there is an entry stating that *Rebel (7)* was sired by *Cannon Ball*. This fact may not have been proved until after the Volume I of the Stud Book was published, but as *Rebel (7)* was to become the foundation sire of the most prolific stallion line in the breed, it is very satisfactory to know that he was the son of a great pony who showed all the best attributes of the breed – Courage, Endurance and Intelligence.

In order to increase the stallion list for 1926, the Council then purchased *Black Paddy (8)* from M. J. O'Neill, one of the stallions registered at Recess Show, and placed him with Mark Geoghegan, in Oughterard. Michael O'Neill's second stallion, *Connemara Boy (9)* was also added to the list but remained in his ownership, and covered the Clifden area.

Colt Foal Subsidies

There were still many unlicenced stallions in Connemara, some of them running uncontrolled on the hills during the season, and they posed a very great problem for the Society, as a number of pony owners did not avail of the Society's sires, and so a lot of indiscriminate breeding was still taking place. It was also of great concern that the standard of colts being put forward for inspection was not nearly good enough, and in an effort to improve this, a scheme was devised to subsidise breeders in respect of good colt foals likely to make sires. 5 colt foals were to be selected for the scheme at the Annual Show at Carna, and a sum of £5 to be paid to the owner to keep the colt for 12 months when he would be inspected again. Then if the colt was considered good enough the owner would be paid a further £5 to keep him for another year. The subsidy could be renewed for a further period of 12 months and finally the Society had the option to purchase the colt. Many of the mare owners could not afford to keep an extra pony, particularly a colt, through the winter, and most of the foals were sold at weaning time, so how to safeguard promising youngstock was a big problem for the Society.

The 1926 inspection tour saw even fewer ponies being presented for registration, and so it was decided that in future the inspections would only take place at the Annual Show.

Centre	Mares		Stallions	
	Presented	Passed	Presented	Passed
Derrynea	16	2	1	-
Cashel	12	-	2	-
Clifden	7	1	1	-
Maam Cross	6	2	2	-
Carna Show	70	18	9	1
Total	111	23	15	1

3rd Annual Pony Show, Carna – 16th September 1926

The third Annual Show was held at Carna, and again there was an increased entry in the pony section. Despite the day starting off in a thick blanket of Connemara mist, the enthusiasm and hard work of the Vice President Josie Mongan, proprietor of the local hotel at Carna, and his hardworking Show Committee ensured that the Show was a great success, and attracted a large crowd of people from all over Connemara. The judges were Mr D. Twomey and Mr C. J. Kerin, and the winner of the Registered Connemara Pony Stallion was *Connemara Boy (9)* the four year old grey owned by Michael O'Neill, Clifden, with *Charlie (2)* also a four year old, being placed second for Val Keaney, Cashel.

Cannon Belle (47) once again took the RDS Silver Medal for the best mare with foal at foot for James Mullane, and White Lily (98) a 15 year old mare was placed 2nd for W. Roe, Oughterard.

In the non-registered mare class there were 70 entries, with 18 being accepted for registration, and the winner was a two year old, Calla Grey (99), owned by Mark Keaney, Callancruick.

First President Resigns

At the meeting following the Show it was announced that the Council was unfortunately to be deprived of two of its most valued members due to promotion. Firstly Father White, their first President, had been transferred to another parish outside Connemara, and secondly Mr W. F. Prendergast was being transferred to the Department of Agriculture in Dublin.

Father White, during his three years in office, had been a most hard working and energetic President, and since its formation in 1923, his enthusiasm and support for the work of the new Society, his organising abilities and his help in raising funds had been an inspiration to everyone. He had a great love of Connemara and had worked tirelessly for the betterment of its people, and he would be greatly missed. Rev. Father Cunningham PP was his successor as Parish priest at Roundstone, and he was co-opted to the Council.

Mr Prendergast had spent many years in the Western region as a Department Inspector, and took a great interest in the Connemara pony. Together with Michael O'Malley, he had been one of those chiefly responsible for organising the public meeting at which the Connemara Pony Breeders' Society was formed, and since then he had been involved in the work of the Society at every level. It had given him great satisfaction to see the progress that had been made in such a short time to improve the breed, and as a member of the editing committee he was pleased that Volume I of the Connemara Pony Stud Book had been produced in such an excellent manner.

Warm tributes were paid to both men for their encouragement and work for the Society and for the people of Connemara.

Volume I of the Stud Book

Volume I of the Stud Book was a slim red book with a hard back cover and contained the details of nine stallions and ninety-three mares. It was printed at a cost of £45 and was priced at 1/-.

The introduction to Volume I outlines clearly the aims of the Connemara Pony Breeders' Society at the time of publication in 1926.

"The history of the development and improvement in all classes of livestock has shown; that the careful recording of pedigrees is the most effective way in which progress can be made. The Arab, the Thoroughbred and all the well known breeds of horses and ponies owe their pre-eminence and value to the fact that the history and breeding of each individual animal can be traced back for generations.

The publication of a Connemara Pony Stud Book is an attempt to foster and develop, on systematic lines, a native breed which has existed for centuries, the merits of which are recognised not only in Ireland but outside it.

In Connemara, unlike many other pony breeding localities, breeding mares work throughout the year; consequently a form of natural selection for utility purposes is continuously at work. Awkward, ill-tempered, or badly constituted animals are of little or no value to the Connemara farmer owing to the nature of the work which has to be done and the conditions under which it has to be carried out. It will be understood, therefore, that only the very best can be retained for breeding which accounts for the fact that although unsuitable foreign blood has been introduced from time to time, its influence on the permanent breeding stock has been slight.

Though the pony population of Connemara has decreased in recent years a large number of good typical ponies still remain, and most of the pony requirements of the country can be supplied from this area if immediate steps are taken to foster and develop the breed. . . .

Ponies vary slightly in size and character, according to the district in which they are bred, but it is generally admitted that a compact, short-legged pony, about 13.2 hh with good shoulders and true and easy movement is the most suitable type to develop. This class of animal, while eminently suitable for the work in Connemara is also the type which is likely to meet with the most demand from outside. The aim of the Society is to secure by continued selection and careful fostering a breed of ponies uniform in size and shape, suitable for general utility purposes and which, when bred from under favourable conditions, would be capable of producing high class riding animals.

Individual effort to improve a breed usually results in temporary benefit. The Society, therefore, looks to breeders throughout Ireland for support and co-operation. Good foundation stock is available. Careful selection and intelligent breeding are all that are needed to ensure success. "

In the spring of 1927 Christy Kerin succeeded in buying **Rebel (7)** for the Society for the sum of £25, and he was placed with Mark Geoghegan, Oughterard for the season. Mark was a skilled horseman and was often chosen by the Society to train their new stallions before they moved out to other parts of Connemara. From the time he was a young boy he had developed a special way with ponies and would break and train a young pony in a day.

Black Paddy (8) who had been with Mark in 1926 moved to a new location at Letterfrack. The custodian was Michael Diamond, whose cousin Willie Diamond has cause to remember **Black Paddy**, as his earliest memory of him as a small boy was the day the stallion bit his thumb!

Connemara Boy (9) had been bought by Val Mannion, Cloonisle, and remained on the list, and **Bryan (10)** a 10 year old black stallion owned by Owen Naughton, Inverin was added to it. These last two stallions were in private ownership.

Apart from the six stallions approved by the Society for service of registered mares, there were a further 26 unregistered stallions standing in Connemara during the 1927 season, many of whom were unlicenced and of a very unsuitable type. This situation was causing a very serious problem for the Society in its efforts to improve the type of pony being bred.

4th Annual Pony Show, Carna – 29th September 1927

The Show was again held at Carna, but at the later date of 29th September 1927 due to a General Election being called for the date originally chosen for the Show. No doubt the change of date was to accommodate the Society's Vice President, Josie Mongan, who was a candidate in the election, and it was Josie Mongan, the newly elected Cumann na nGaedheal T. D. who acted as host on Show day in his native Carna. The judges were Messrs. D. Twomey, C. J. Kerin, C. J. McCarthy and T. Mc. D. Kelly MRCVS.

The stallion class and RDS Silver Medal was won by Mark Geoghegan, Oughterard, with the lively *Rebel (7)* now aged five, who enjoyed showing off and standing on his hind legs, and Hugh King, Cashel, won the class for mare with foal at foot and RDS Silver Medal with his eight year old mare Bunahown (17).

A feature of the Show was the increased number of foals shown, many of whom were by *Charlie (2)*. This was due to the new subsidies being offered for the best foals, but in the event only three of the five colt foals availed of the subsidy, the owners of the remaining two selected having refused on the grounds that they had nowhere suitable to keep a colt through the winter. Subsidies were also offered for filly foals on similar lines to the colt foal scheme but with the subsidy of £2. 10/-.

The non-registered mare class was very disappointing with only four mares registered out of an entry of 55, and it was the opinion of the judges that most of the best mares from that district were already on the register.

New President Elected

The Annual General Meeting on 18th January 1928 saw the election of a new President, The Right Rev. Monsignor Mc Alpine PP VG, who had been Parish Priest at Clifden since 1898. Although he was an old man of 81 when he came into the Society, he was still a formidable character, and had a most profound influence on the town of Clifden during some of the most turbulent years in its history.

Born in Mayo into an evicted tenant family of 13 children, he became closely associated with the Land League and was a life long friend of Michael Davitt. He was a member of the Congested Districts Board from 1898 until its dissolution in 1923, and felt passionately about the land of Ireland. A fluent Irish speaker and a gifted orator, he used this to great advantage to further any cause he adopted, although he often became over zealous in his efforts to fight for a cause he believed in. In the first two years of his term in Clifden he completed the new spire on St Joseph's Church, built the clock tower, had a bell erected and a new organ installed. He worked tirelessly for his parish and in 1908 went to America to raise funds to build the Clifden Town Hall. When elected President of the Connemara Pony Breeders' Society, he pledged his full support to the Society, but in the event he became just a figurehead, and his Vice Presidents acted for him during his four years in office.

Monsignor McAlpine PP VG

Two new stallions were purchased by the Council in the spring of 1928. The first was the six year old *Connemara Boy (9)* who was bought from Val Mannion, Cloonisle for £25 and located with Thomas de Courcey at Errisbeg, Roundstone. The second stallion purchased, *Adventure (11)*, was a half-bred, an attractive three year old dark brown pony standing 14. 1hh, by the very well bred TB stallion Thistleton owned by C. J. Kerin, and out of a Registered Connemara mare Galway Rose (78) bred by John Fallon, a butcher in Galway. This was the first time that the inspection committee had decided to register a pony that was not bred from

Connemara Boy (9)

native stock, and perhaps it is an indication of their frustration in trying to find suitable sires to use on the registered mares.

Adventure (11) was placed with Mark Geoghegan, Oughterard, and *Rebel (7)* moved to Val Keaney, Cashel where he was to spend the next ten years of his working life, while *Charlie (2)* moved to a new custodian, Ed. Conneely, Glentrasna, Rosmuck.

5th Annual Pony Show, Clifden – 6th September 1928

The Show was held in the grounds of the old Clifden Workhouse, and the judges on the day were Messrs. C. J. Kerin, T. Cotter, C. J. McCarthy, J. Mahony, T. McD. Kelly MRCVS.

Rebel (7) took the RDS Silver Medal for the second year in the stallion class, this time for Val Keaney, and White Lily (98) won the registered mare with foal class and RDS Silver Medal for Willie Roe. It was disappointing that no awards were made in the class for two year old colts due to insufficient merit, but in the class for non-registered mares, nineteen were selected out of a total of sixty entries. The only stallion accepted for registration was a five year old grey belonging to M. J. O'Neill, Clifden, and he was given the name *John Quirke (13)*.

Bartley O'Sullivan Promoted

During 1928 Bartley O'Sullivan competed for and won promotion to the post of Secretary and Accounting Officer of the County Committee of Agriculture, succeeding Mr Fogarty who had died earlier in the year.

This was the first appointment of its kind awarded by merit under the Local Appointments Commission, rather than under the old system of political patronage, which made it somewhat of an innovation in Ireland at that time. The Committee had its own candidate, and a vigorous debate ensued, reported in detail in the local newspaper, the Connacht Tribune. But the Local Appointments Commission stuck to their guns, and though the Committee finally accepted the nomination "under duress", their new secretary was not long in convincing them of his suitability for the job. Four years later, the Minister for Agriculture, Dr Ryan declared that the appointment of Mr. O'Sullivan in Co. Galway had been intended "to lead to an improvement in the administration of the Agricultural and Livestock Schemes in that county. This expectation was realised".

His new appointment and move to Galway lead Bartley to tender his resignation to the AGM of the Connemara Pony Breeders' Society in January 1929, but the Council refused to accept it, and he was persuaded to carry on as Hon. Secretary despite the increased work-load it entailed. The work for the Society was unpaid, and he received £20 for his expenses for a whole year.

6th Annual Pony Show, Oughterard – 11th September 1929

The Show was held in the field next to the Oughterard railway station, and the judges were Mr C. J. Kerin, Mr T. Cotter, Mr T. McD. Kelly MRCVS. *Rebel (7)* won the stallion class and his 3rd RDS Silver Medal for Val Keaney, Cashel, while Gentle Annie (108) owned by Patrick Linnane, Cushatrower, Toombeola, took the class for mares with foal at foot and RDS Silver Medal. Her colt foal by *Connemara Boy (9)* won a subsidy, and two years later was registered as the stallion *Heather Bell (15)*. The other colt foal to win a subsidy that year was by Rebel (7) out of Fanny O'Brien (51) owned by Ml. O'Brien, Derrough, Maam Cross, and he became the registered sire *Heather Grey (16)*.

Garnet Irwin

Rebel (7) with Val Keaney.

For the first time there was a class for two year old colts or fillies, the progeny of a Registered Connemara Pony Mare and a Registered Connemara Pony Stallion, and from this class two fillies were registered. They were:

- Maid of Derrough (140) s. Gold Digger (5), d. Fanny O'Brien (51), breeder, Michael O'Brien, Derrough, Maam Cross.

- Winnie (141) s. Charlie (2) d. Cashel Dolly (13), breeder, Tom King, Cashel.

Neither of these two fillies are entered in the Stud Book with their pedigrees, but their breeding was shown in the catalogue, and they had both won subsidies as foals. This was the first small step towards creating a Stud Book of registered stock, bred from ponies already in the Stud Book, and it must have given some encouragement to the inspection committee, even though it was very limited progress.

Despite the offers of subsidies to retain the foals, most of them were still being sold at the Autumn foal fairs, due to the economic conditions in Connemara at the time, when the price of a foal was a valuable addition to the family income. As a general rule, the better the foal, the more likely it was that it would be sold out of the district.

Seven un-registered mares out of an entry of sixty-five were also accepted for the Stud Book, but none of the four stallions presented at the Show were passed.

In the spring of 1930 the Society purchased the seven year old stallion *John Quirke (13)* from M. J. O'Neill Clifden for £25, and located him with Michael Diamond at Letterfrack. He replaced *Black Paddy (8)* who was removed from the list, sold back to M. J. O'Neill for £7, and was subsequently castrated. *Black Paddy (8)* had not proved a successful sire and from the three seasons that he stood at Letterfrack with Michael Diamond, only two of his progeny were registered in the Stud Book, the stallion *Noble Star (17)* and one daughter Patricia (716).

7th Annual Pony Show, Oughterard – 10th September 1930

The Show was held once again at Oughterard, and the judges were Mr C. J. Kerin and Mr T. Cotter. *Connemara Boy (9)* won the stallion class for Thomas de Courcey, Roundstone, this time beating *Rebel (7)* into second place. The class for the best mare with foal at foot and RDS Medal was won by Rose (117) owned by Joseph Joyce, Derradda East, Recess and her filly foal by Rebel also won her class.

In the RDS Championship Class for young mares up to six years old, the winner and reserve were both to become foundation mares whose progeny can be traced right up to the present day. In first place was the three year old Winnie (141) daughter of Cashel Dolly (13) shown by her breeder Thomas King, the local postman in Cashel, who was a great supporter of the early shows, and in reserve was Mark Geoghegan's Silver Gray (143) whose daughter Irene (624) was to become one of the famous matriarchs of the breed.

Thirty mares were presented for registration at the Show, and nine were accepted, but only one out of the class of four two year old fillies was registered, she was Lizzie (149) by Rebel (7),owned by Thomas Holleran, Oughterard.

The only stallion accepted in 1930 was *Tommy (14)*, an eight year old grey who was 13.0hh, owned by Comyn Naughton, Glenicmurrin, Costello. He was believed to have been a son of *Cannon Ball*, but there is no written proof of it in the records. He was included on the list of approved stallions from 1931 to 1935, and travelled to Spiddal every week. He remained in private ownership during the five years he was in Connemara before being sold, but only left two registered mares in the Stud Book.

8th Annual Pony Show, Roundstone – 10th September 1931

The Show returned to Roundstone for the first time since the first Show in 1924, and again the Society welcomed a distinguished visitor to the Show, this time the guest was Mr William T. Cosgrave, the President of Fine Gael. In his speech he praised the people of Connemara for their great spirit and expressed his pleasure in being invited to spend his holidays in Connemara and to be a guest at their Show. He complimented the Society for the work being done to improve the Connemara Pony, and he was also particularly impressed with the display of cottage industries, especially the homespun tweed which he said was a truly Irish product.

The Show had the most successful inspection to date with eight two year old fillies from registered parents being passed, five of them by Rebel (7). They included Colleen Bawn (159) who was another of the early mares to become the foundation of a famous family. In all 70 mares were presented from which 21 were registered. The judges were Mr C. J. Kerin, Mr T. Cotter and Mr T. McD. Kelly.

A total of eight stallions were presented and from them one three year old colt and two two year old colts were registered. The two year olds were both subsidised as foals, one was *Heather Bell (15)* by Connemara Boy (9) dam Gentle Annie (108) owned by Patrick Linnane, Cushatrower, Toombeola, and the other was *Heather Grey (16)* by Rebel (7) dam Fanny O'Brien (51) owned by Michael O'Brien, Derrough, Maam Cross.

The three year old was another from M. J. O'Neill's herd, and he won the class for Colts of Connemara Type, the progeny of non-registered mares. He was registered as *Noble Star (17)*, and his sire was Black Paddy (8). Although his dam was not registered, her breeding was noted by Bartley in the Society's records stating that she was a grey mare bred by T. Adams, Moyard, and was by an unregistered pony stallion belonging to Michael McDonnell, Derryinver.

These three stallions were all purchased by the Society subsequently, and two of them, *Heather Bell (15)* and *Noble Star (17)* were to play a significant role in the development of the breed.

They were added to the Society's list in 1932, and *Noble Star (17)* was placed with Jack Bolger, Oughterard, *Heather Bell (15)* with Michael Nee Shinninagh, Clifden and *Heather Grey (16)* remained with his breeder, Michael O'Brien, Derrough, Maam Cross.

Volume II of the Stud Book

At the close of 1931, the second volume of the Stud Book was published at a cost of £30, there were 450 copies printed, and they sold for 1/-. It covered the period from January 1926 to September 1931 and included details of 86 mares and 8 stallions bringing the total number of registered ponies in Volume I and Volume II to 17 stallions and 179 mares.

In the introduction to Volume II it was stated that the mares selected were excellent in type and quality and should prove very suitable as foundation stock. However the stallions were not of the same uniform good quality, and there was a great need to retain the best foals to form the breeding stock of future years.

In reviewing the years from 1924 to 1931 which was the period covered by the first two volumes of the Stud Book, the Society had achieved all of the objects laid down at the foundation of the Society.

A Stud Book had been established, suitable stallions purchased and located at approved centres, an Annual Show had been held, and grants had been obtained from the Department of Agriculture, the County Galway Committee of Agriculture, and the Royal Dublin Society.

The Society had worked to encourage the breeding of Connemara ponies and to maintain them as a pure breed. Through the inspection of all ponies before registration the standard of the mares had seen a significant improvement, although the quality of the majority of the stallions inspected was unsatisfactory, and out of the 44 colts presented during the period, only four could be described as high class sires.

The fact that many of the early sires listed in this period left very few or in some cases no registered progeny, again underlined the problem of the foals leaving the district at weaning time, and this greatly hampered the work of the Society.

Two Stallion Lines Established

However despite these problems, by 1931 two stallion lines had been established. The first was to become the most prolific male blood line descending from *Cannon Ball (1)* through his son *Rebel (7)*, and in order to follow this line through succeeding generations, this line shall be called the Blue Line.

The second stallion line which can trace its roots right back to the first volume of the Stud Book was founded by the sire *Connemara Boy (9)* and it descended through his son *Heather Bell (15)* and this line shall be called the Red Line.

Two more stallions in this period had sons registered in the Stud Book, one was *Black Paddy (8)* whose son *Noble Star (17)* left eleven registered sons, but despite this, a male line was not established through the succeeding generations. However this line features in the back breeding of many good ponies, and is called the Yellow Line.

The other stallion with a registered son was *John Quirke (13)*, who replaced *Black Paddy (8)* on the stallion list in 1930, and was the sire of *Silver Pearl (18)*. Again this line was not to continue as a male line beyond the next generation, but a number of good mares trace back to this blood line which is called the Pink Line.

CHAPTER 3

1931-1939

In 1931 the scheme for subsidising the colt foals was dropped as it had not proved successful, because the majority of the pony breeders in Connemara occupied holdings so small that very often they could not find a place to keep a colt. The mares were kept on mountain commonage for the great part of the season, and there were obvious objections to running colts on commonage with other ponies. Even when a breeder did manage to find a place to keep a colt, the holding was usually so badly fenced it was impossible to keep him under proper control.

Colt Purchasing Scheme

The Society therefore decided that it was necessary to take steps to remedy this situation by buying some of the best colt foals each year, and holding them until they were old enough to be assessed, and in this way be able to provide a sufficient number of good stallions to stand in Connemara.

The new scheme for purchasing colt foals was not put into practice until 1934, because the Society found it very difficult to find good grazing land with adequate fencing to hold the colts. In future years it was to become one of Bartley O'Sullivan's biggest problems, as it fell to him to organise the grazing and manage a growing herd of young stallions. However the first group of eight colt foals was purchased in 1934 and taken out to Innishgoill Island in Lough Corrib, which had been leased for two years by the Society. The island of Innishgoill with some 300 acres is the largest island in Lough Corrib, and lies off the shore near Oughterard. It is an island of great historical interest, and there are the remains of two 12th century churches to be found there. The island can be visited by boat from either Cong or Oughterard, and many people have enjoyed a visit to it with John Luskin in his boat the Corrib Queen. The island is now covered in trees planted by the Forestry Commission, and so there is no longer any trace of the grazing lands where that first group of Society owned Connemara colts lived in 1934.

9th Annual Pony Show, Roundstone – 6th September 1932

The Show was smaller than in previous years with 114 entries in the Connemara pony classes. The newly acquired Society stallion *Noble Star (17)* won the stallion class for Jack Bolger for the first time, and Jack was to repeat it with *Noble Star* for the next three years and again in 1937. *Rebel (7)* was again in second place, and also stood second to *Noble Star* for the next three years, winning the class for the last time in 1936. However at the 1932 show, *Rebel* dominated the foal classes with all the prizewinners being sired by him. There were 39 mares presented for registration but only 10 were accepted, and neither of the two stallions put forward were passed. The judges were Mr C. J. Kerin, Mr T. Cotter, Mr T. McD. Kelly, MRCVS, Mr J. Kyne MRCVS.

Garnet Irwin

Noble Star (17)

At the meeting after the Show, it was decided that the 1933 show would be held in Clifden, and Father Cunningham explained to the press that *"This is a kind of nomadic show without either roof or tent, that is because its purpose is primarily educational, and we have to hold the show in different places each year so as to reach all Connemara, so that the work that is being done will help the greatest number of people. "*

Death of Monsignor McAlpine – Election of New President

In November 1932 Monsignor McAlpine PP VG, who had been President of the Connemara Pony Breeders' Society for four years, died at the age of 84, and at the Annual General Meeting held on 10th February 1933 the Rev Father Cunningham PP Roundstone was elected to become the third President of the Society.

Mr C. J. Kerin was elected Vice President and the other two Vice Presidents were Mr Josie Mongan TD and Rev Father McCullagh PP.

Rev Father Cunningham PP

At the end of the 1932 season, the privately owned stallion *Bryan (10)* was sold out of Connemara leaving no registered progeny, and the list of nine approved stallions standing for service in Connemara remained the same for the following two seasons with no new stallions being registered. The only changes made were that *Charlie (2)* moved to Michael Diamond at Letterfrack, and *John Quirke (13)* went to Ed Conneely at Glentrasna.

During the thirties there was a period of economic recession in Ireland which caused great hardship, especially to the people in Connemara when the prices for cattle, sheep and foals dropped disastrously. Despite this the work of the Society went on, although it was making very slow progress in the registration of two year olds bred from registered stock, as so many of the young ponies were sold out of Connemara before they reached registration age.

10th Annual Pony Show, Clifden – 7th September 1933

The RDS Silver Medal for best mare with foal at foot was won by Thomas Cloherty, Loughconeera, Kilkerrin with his mare Cashel Lass (11). Her filly foal by Connemara Boy (9) also won her class, and was registered two years later as Lougheera (228).

The best young mare up to six years old who also won a RDS Silver Medal was Derrada Fanny (182) owned by Patrick Flaherty, Ballinafad, and her claim to fame was that she was the dam of two stallions, both bought as foals by the Society, *Lavalley Rebel (24)* and *Clough Rebel (33)*, but it is sad to note that these were her only two registered progeny.

Entry for the riding class.

Riding Class Introduced

A new class was introduced in 1933 for ponies of Connemara type shown in saddle and ridden by boys not exceeding 16 years of age. There were 11 entries and it was won by Tom Folan (John) Callowfeenish with his mare Anne (163). The following year, girls were also included, but out of an entry of 23, only one girl was entered, and she was Anne Tulloch, Shanbolard, sister of Graham Tulloch and mother of Nicola Musgrave. In the subsequent years the class reverted to boys only, and girls were not included again until 1940.

At the AGM held in April 1934 a new Vice President was added to the officers of the Society when the Very Rev Canon Patterson PP. Clifden was elected. Two Council members Col. Joyce and Michael Wallace were dropped from the Council as they had not attended any meetings, and P. K. Joyce, Clifden was appointed a member of Council. At the same meeting Mr Dan Twomey was congratulated on his promotion to Secretary of the Department of Agriculture.

Closure of Galway to Clifden Railway

It was also stated at the meeting that *"the Council of the Connemara Pony Breeders' Society viewed with great alarm the suggestion to close the Railway line between Galway and Clifden, and that they considered the closure of the line would militate against the development of the turf and other industries in the district"*. The Council passed a resolution to call on the Minister of Industry and Commerce to take steps to prevent the closure of the line. The Council were not alone in voicing their concern at the proposed closure, and many other people in Connemara were also making protests at the decision of the Great Southern Railway Company. The line had been built just forty years previously, and was officially opened on New Years Day 1895.

It was built at a time when Clifden and the whole district of Connemara had seemed very remote, and the coming of the railway had provided a vital link with the rest of Ireland. It had brought many visitors into the district, and was used to carry turf, cattle, sheep, pigs and fish to the markets outside the district. On the day of the Annual Connemara Pony Show, there were special excursion rates to bring visitors and ponies to the Show, and it was also used by pony owners bringing their ponies to the Oughterard or Clifden Races.

However, all the protests were of no avail, and the decision to close the line went ahead the following year. The last passenger train pulled out of Clifden on Saturday 27th April 1935 at 5p.m. and made its way back to Galway blowing its whistle in farewell to the little groups of people who had gathered to wave goodbye to the train.

11th Annual Pony Show, Clifden – 6th September 1934

This was the last Show to have the benefit of the railway. There was an increased entry of 162, and the RDS Medal for the best mare with foal at foot went once more to Rose (117) owned by Joseph Joyce, Recess, with Thomas Cloherty's Cashel Lass (11) winning the young mare championship.

First Colt Foals Purchased for Stallion Scheme

In 1934 the Society bought in the first group of colt foals for the new scheme to raise colts as possible future stallions, and the winning colt foal at the Show was one of their first purchases. He was by Noble Star (17) d. Attry Maid (25)

Rose (117)

owned by Joseph Ridge, Recess, and was registered two years later as *Innishgoill Star (20)*. In all eight colt foals were bought by the Society for an average price of £4, and were put out on Innishgoill Island which was to be their home for the next two years.

Out of four stallions presented at the Show, only one three year old was registered for his breeder Stephen Walsh, Keelkyle, Letterfrack. His sire was John Quirke (13) and his dam, Stephen's roan mare Bess (201), who was by an unregistered Connemara pony stallion owned by Michael McDonnell, Derryinver. He was registered as *Silver Pearl (18)*, and remained in private ownership with Stephen Walsh, until Stephen's tragic

Silver Pearl (18) with Stephen Walsh.

and untimely death following an accident in the ring during the Stallion class at Carna Show in 1940.

Silver Pearl (18) was included on the Society's list in 1935, and *Heather Grey (16)* was removed, having left no registered progeny after three years on the Society list, he was sold at the end of the 1934 season.

Michael O'Neill, Clifden took over *Heather Bell (15)* and in August of that year *Charlie (2)* died of a colic at the age of thirteen. He left nine registered mares, and although he did not found a direct male line, two of his daughters became the dams of stallions, Winnie (141) the dam of *Cashel Star (39)*, and Calla Roan (196) dam of *Calla Rebel (38)* By the end of the 1935 season, *Tommy (14)* owned by Comyn Naughton was sold out of Connemara leaving only two registered progeny.

However, one of them, Small Change (701), through her daughters Small Change Miss (1329) and Ashe Grey (1673), became the foundation mare of a family which can be traced down through the female lines to the dams of today's stallions *Westside Mirah (892)* and *Garryhinch Finn (974)* and other well-known ponies.

12th Annual Pony Show, Carna – 12th September 1935

The Show returned to Carna in 1935, and the entries were increased to 192. The stallion class was once again won by *Noble Star (17)* for Jack Bolger, and the Champion brood mare class and RDS Medal went to Morgan Mulkerrin, Callowfeenish with Feenish Rose Anne (103), while the class for young mares was won by Michael O'Neill with Black Girl (206).

In the two year old filly class Thomas Cloherty, Loughconneera, took 1st prize with his filly Lougheera (228) sire Connemara Boy (9), dam Cashel Lass (11), and in 2nd place was Festy Folan, Ardmore, Carna, with another daughter of Connemara Boy (9), Sliabh na mBan (227). Both these mares were to become foundation mares of famous mare lines which are still intact today.

The non-registered mare class was very large, with an entry of 68, from which 17 were registered, and among them were Cuach na Coille (236) owned by Martin Walsh (Pat), Kylesalia, and Film Star (245) owned by Martin Walsh, Callowfeenish. The second group of colt foals was purchased by the Society at the Show, and five of them were registered under the Lavalley prefix two years later, including *Lavalley Rebel (24)* by Rebel (7) dam Derradda Fanny (182).

During 1936, inspections were held at Clonbur, Maam, Maam Cross and Oughterard with a total of twenty mares being passed from forty-three presented for inspection. In the Autumn of that year the first crop of Society-owned foals were assessed at the Oughterard centre as two year olds, and three out of the four shown were accepted into the Stud Book. They all took the name of their island home as a prefix and were:

- *Innishgoill Hero (19)* sire Rebel (7) dam Mynish Lass (101)
- *Innishgoill Star (20)* sire Noble Star (17) dam Attry Maid (25)
- *Innishgoill Laddie (21)* sire Rebel (7) dam Dooyher Lass (188).

13th Annual Show, Carna – 14th September 1936

For the first time two classes for geldings were included in the Show, as the Society had begun to receive enquiries for driving ponies from outside Connemara, and it was thought that a gelding class might produce suitable ponies for this market.

A new rule was also introduced which barred the winner of the class the previous year from entry to the class in which it had won first prize. This applied to the stallion class and all the classes for mares, and it prevented the classes from being dominated by one pony year after year. In the stallion class, without *Noble Star (17)* who had beaten him three years running, *Rebel (7)* emerged the winner, and took his last RDS Medal for Val Keaney.

Colleen Bawn (159)

Garnet Irwin

Buckna (TB)

The class for registered mares aged six or over with foal at foot by a registered Connemara pony stallion caused something of an upset that year, as the mare who originally won the class, Colleen Bawn (159) owned by Pat Mulkerrin (Tom) Callowfeenish, was later disqualified when it was discovered that she was not eligible to compete as her foal was not by a registered Connemara pony stallion. The foal in question was a filly and her sire was in fact a TB horse called Buckna, who was brought into Connemara to race in the pony races. She was a late foal and only three weeks old at the time of the Show, but two years later she came back to Carna Show, was placed 1st in the class for non-registered mares, and was accepted into the Stud Book, her name was Carna Dolly (442). Through her son Carna Bobby (79) she was to become one of the best-known mares in the Stud Book, and another mare who was also destined to become a famous foundation mare for the

44

breed, was Sliabh na mBan (227), owned by Festy Folan, Ardmore, Carna, and she won the young mare class and RDS Silver Medal at Carna Show in 1936.

In 1937 the Annual General Meeting was held at Maam Cross on 9th March and it was proposed that in future the Annual Connemara Pony Show should have a fixed venue and not be changed from year to year. After some discussion as to whether Clifden or Carna would be the more suitable venue, it was decided that Carna should become the permanent show centre. The Show date was fixed for 26th August.

By now the Society's new scheme for colts was beginning to show results, and the first three two year olds selected from the group raised on Innishgoill Island had entered the Stud Book. There were eight more yearling colts being run on for another year, and a third group of colt foals was purchased by the Society at the Show at Carna including one by *John Quirke (13)*, one by *Connemara Boy (9)* and two by *Noble Star (17)*.

The stallion list was reviewed for the season, and the three young Innishgoill stallions joined the approved list for 1937 bringing the list up to ten. *Adventure (11)* moved to Michael Conroy, Ballyconneely, and *Innishgoill Hero (19)* was placed with Tommy McDonagh, Derrylea.

Both of these men were new stallion custodians, and it was the first year that they stood a stallion for the Society. Michael Conroy continued to act as a stallion custodian for the next 27 years, and handed over to his son Josie in 1963, while Thomas McDonagh held Society stallions until 1943, and was a well known exhibitor at the Society shows for over forty years. He was a Vice-President of the Society from 1990 until his death in 1994.

Innishgoill Star (20) was placed with Michael Diamond, Letterfrack, and *Innishgoill Laddie (21)* began his stud duties with Jack Bolger at Oughterard, along with *Noble Star (17)*. Of the three Innishgoill stallions, *Innishgoill Laddie (21)* was by far the most successful in the years to come, and proved to be a worthy successor to *Rebel (7)*, carrying the Blue Line into the third generation.

During the Spring of 1937 inspections were held at Oughterard, Maam Cross, Recess, Clifden, Letterfrack, Leenane and Clonbur. A total of 95 mares were presented, out of which 55 were registered. There were no stallions presented at any of the centres.

Volume III of the Stud Book

Following the Inspection tour in 1937 the Council published Volume III of the Stud Book, in which there were details of the registrations from January 1932 to April 1937. It contained details of 4 stallions, *Silver Pearl (18)*, *Innishgoill Hero (19)*, *Innishgoill Star (20)* and *Innishgoill Laddie (21)*, and 159 mares.

In the introduction to Volume III the inspectors wrote the following remarks:

"The stallions recommended for registration in Volume III are of true pony type and of fair average quality, and are likely when mated with suitable pony mares to transmit the desirable characteristics of the breed. A large proportion of the selected mares are excellent in type and quality. Among them are some promising fillies, the produce of registered stock. The ponies selected for registration were examined by a Veterinary Surgeon and passed as sound and free from hereditary disease. "

Also included for the first time in the preface to the Stud Book was:

POINTS OF THE CONNEMARA PONY

Height: 13 to 14 hands.

Colour: Grey, black, bay, brown, dun, with occasional roans and chestnuts.

Type: Body compact, deep, standing on short legs and covering a lot of ground.

Shoulders: Riding.

Head: Well balanced head and neck.

Action: Free, easy and true movement.

Bone: Clean, hard and flat; measuring 7 to 8 inches below the knee.

CHARACTERISTICS

Hardiness of constitution, staying power, docility, intelligence and soundness.

14th Annual Pony Show, Carna – 12th September 1937

Once again the Show had an increased number of entries, with 210 in the pony classes, and an overall entry of more than 800 exhibits, ranging from cattle and sheep, poultry and butter, fruit and vegetables, knitted garments and embroidery, homespuns, Irish dancing, singing and story telling, and a farm prize competition. The Annual Inspections also took place at the Show, and 28 mares were registered out of a total of 42 presented, including six two year old fillies from registered parents.

Noble Star (17) won the stallion class for the 5th time for Jack Bolger and the winner of the Mare with foal class and RDS Silver Medal was Anne (163) owned by Tom Folan (John) Callowfeenish, while the young mare championship went to Thomas Conneely, Bontroughard, Carna with Goldfinch (276).

For the fourth year the Society bought a group of five of the best colt foals at the Show. There were two by Noble Star (17), one by Connemara Boy (9), one by Rebel (7) and one by John Quirke (13). When they were registered two years later they were given the prefix Clough.

In the autumn of 1937 the second group of two year old colts owned by the Society was presented for inspection at Oranmore. There were eight in the group and five were registered, all were given the Lavalley prefix, which was the name of the townland where they had been raised. Four of the Lavalley colts joined the stallion list in 1938, and one was sold to Athlone.

The spring inspections of 1938 were held at 15 different centres in Connemara with a record number of mares being accepted for registration, a total of 62 passed out of 129 presented and a further 21 were passed at the Show and at a later inspection, making a grand total of 83, the highest number in one year since the inspections were first held in 1924.

One stallion was registered in the spring of that year for Bartley Naughton, Glenicmurrin, Costello, a son of Comyn Naughton who had owned *Tommy (14)*. He was a dun five year old, 13. 3 h. h and was registered as *Paddy (28)* but had no recorded breeding. He was owned privately by Bartley Naughton, and covered the same district as *Tommy (14)* had before him. He was put on the approved list in 1938 and remained on it until 1946 when he was sold to Miss Spottiswoode, went to England, and was renamed Cama of Calla. The stallion list increased to 13 for the 1938 season and four of the Lavalley stallions were added.

Innishgoill Hero (19) had been removed from the list at the end of the 1937 season, and was sold out of Connemara in the Spring of 1938. He has three registered daughters in the Stud Book.

Founding the Green Line

Two other stallions were put on the approved list for 1938, both the property of Michael Wallace, Tully, Ballinahown, although neither were registered, they were approved for the service of Connemara Pony mares nominated for the 1938 season. They were:

- *Mountain Lad,* a grey pony 13. 3hh foaled 1928, standing with his owner Michael Wallace at Tully.
- *Finnane Hero,* a chestnut pony, 14. 3hh standing at Finnane, Oughterard.

Michael Wallace was one of the founder members of the Council and had a large herd of ponies running on the mountain at Tully. *Mountain Lad* ran with this herd, and remained privately owned. In the Spring of 1939 he was registered as No 32. in the Stud Book, at the age of eleven, but he was never owned by the Society, and he died in the winter of 1939, and left very few registered progeny.

His most important contribution to the breed was a son, *Tully Lad (48)* who was foaled in 1938, and was bred at Tully out of a little black mare called Tully Beauty (374). These two stallions, father and son, were to provide the foundation of the third stallion bloodline which can be traced down through the male line to the present day, and to follow its progress this line is called the Green Line. The ponies bred on the Tully mountain were reputed to be a very tough breed, and this valuable characteristic has been handed down through this line though succeeding generations.

Rebel (7) had left Val Keaney Gowla at the end of the 1937 season and was placed with Ed Conneely Glentrasna, and *John Quirke (13)* was moved to Val Keaney in his place. For ten years *Rebel* had been with Val and his brother Patrick (who often took over the job as custodian when Val went away to England), and they were very fond of the old pony. He had travelled his district throughout the season, and his route each week was Recess on Monday, Derryrush on Tuesday, Toombeola on Thursday, and Carna on Saturday. He won the stallion class four times and was second on six occasions. He was an attractive gay pony, who looked very like his sire Cannon Ball, and he enjoyed showing off in the ring. He used to stand on his hind legs and sometimes would put his fore-legs up on his handlers shoulders, but Patrick Keaney said he was as light as a feather and never hurt them. It must have been a sad day for them to hear that *Rebel* was put down in May 1938 on the advice of the vet Tommy Kelly, as his heart and lungs were in a bad state, and he would not have been able to work another season.

Rebel (7) was the last surviving stallion from the original list in 1924, and was only sixteen when he died. He was on the list during the very early years of the formation of the Society, when his progeny often dominated the foal classes at the Show, but many of them were sold as foals, and so his list of registered progeny is not large, with just 35 entered in the Stud Book. He was a worthy son of *Cannon Ball (1)* and handed down the most prolific stallion line in the breed through his sons *Innishgoill Laddie (21)*, *Lavalley Rebel (24)* and *Calla Rebel (38)*. Some of his best daughters were Colleen Bawn (159), Anne (163), Retreat (320), and Rusheens Pride (613).

15th Annual Pony Show, Carna – 25th August 1938

Jack Bolger brought out the new young stallion *Innishgoill Laddie (21)* to win the stallion class for the first time, while the RDS Silver Medal for the best registered mare over six with foal went to Golden Gleam (296) s. Adventure (11), owned by Dudley McDonagh, Maam Cross, with Cuach na Coille (236) in second place for Martin Walsh, Kylesalia. The young Mares class was won by Calla Belle (272) for Festy Mulkerrin, Callowfeenish.

A new class was introduced for yearling or two year old fillies of Connemara Pony type out of a non-registered mare, and the winner was a two year old filly shown by Festy Mulkerrin and registered that day as Callowfeenish

Golden Gleam (296)

Dolly (437). In the class for non-registered Connemara Pony mares another two year old filly won first prize for Pat Mulkerrin (Tom), Callowfeenish, and she was also accepted into the Stud Book and her name was Carna Dolly (442). These mares became two of the best-known foundation mares of the breed, and can be found in the bloodlines of many of today's successful ponies.

Three of the Society's two year old colts entered the Stud Book in September 1938, and for the first time they did not all carry the same prefix. *Curra Noble (29)* was another son of Noble Star (17) dam Curraduff (211), both the others were from the Red Line, *Derry Boy (30)* by Connemara Boy (9) dam Derry Grey (207), and *Dun Heath (31)* by Heather Bell (15) dam Winnie Nee (194).

Several changes were made in the stallion list for 1939, and the Council decided that *John Quirke (13)* should be taken off the register, but would remain with his custodian Val Keaney in lieu of £5 deposit paid by Val in 1924 for his original stallion *Connemara Dan (3)*.

Connemara Boy (9) was sold to Patrick McMahon, Cartron, Kinvara, and *Lavalley Con (26)* was sold to Jack Bolger but both remained on the list. With the three new young stallions also included on the list, there were 14 registered stallions for the service of nominated mares, and a further three non-registered stallions were also approved.

At the Annual General Meeting held at Maam Cross in March 1939 it was decided that Volume IV of the Stud Book would be published at the end of the year at the increased price of 2/6d. In future a registration fee of 2/6d would be charged for all ponies entering the Stud Book, but the owners would be entitled to a free copy of the volume concerned. It was also decided that mares over 20 years of age would not be eligible for a free nomination.

Two Patrons of the Society

On the proposal of Mr Josie Mongan T.D., The Most Rev. Dr Browne, Bishop of Galway was appointed Patron of the Society. The Most Rev. Dr Walsh, Archbishop of Tuam, was also appointed a Patron of the Society in 1940, and later he donated the Archbishop's Cup to the Society which was first presented in 1944 and has been competed for at the Annual Show every year since then.

For some time the Society had been receiving a growing number of enquiries about the Connemara pony, even from as far afield as the Government of Japan, and news of the work of the Society was spreading. Extracts from some of letters were read by the Secretary, including a letter to the "Horse and Hound" from Sir Alfred Pease, a well-known English horse breeding expert who had visited the Annual Show at Carna, and wrote to congratulate the Connemara Pony Breeders' Society in their efforts *"to preserve such a valuable and obviously hardy breed"*... he was struck with the substance, quality and beauty of this Connemara breed, and wondered how it had ever been evolved. He stated that *"it was surprising to me to see such numbers of ponies of outstanding excellence at a single show... I feel that you have in this breed a national asset of great value"*. He also added that he could detect strains of Arab, or Spanish or African Barb in some of the ponies.

Another record number of mares were registered during the 1939 spring inspections which were held at 28 centres throughout Connemara, and together with those inspected at the Annual show at Carna, 94 mares were entered in the Stud Book from a total of 169 presented.

16th Annual Pony Show, Carna – 31st August 1939

Noble Star (17) was again the winner of the Stallion class, this time for his new custodian, Tommy McDonagh, Derrylea, with Val Keaney in 2nd place with *Lavalley Rebel (24)*. Patrick Mulkerrin (Tom) won the Young Mares RDS Silver Medal with his three year old mare Carna Dolly (442).

The entries in the pony section were increased to 226, but the classes in the home industries section of the Show had exploded and the overall entries for the Show exceeded 1000.

At a meeting following the Show Bartley O'Sullivan stated that unless he could get more assistance and co-operation at the following year's Show, he would not undertake to organise a general show. He also brought

Adventure (11)

to the notice of the Council the increased number of young stallions owned by the Society, and he suggested someone should be employed to look after them.

Volume IV of the Stud Book

The fourth volume of the Stud Book was published at the end of 1939 and contained details of 10 stallions and 195 mares, and it covered the period from 1937 to 1939. It marked the end of the first part of the laying down of the foundation stock of the breed in the years from 1924 to 1939, when the Society sought to improve the breed from within by selecting the best of the native stock.

In the introduction to Volume IV it was noted that more fillies were being kept until registration age than had been the case before. While many foals were still sold at weaning, the wide distribution of Connemara pony foals throughout the country was acknowledged to have had a decidedly beneficial influence on the Irish horse breeding industry generally.

Society Stallions in Connemara

By now the Society had almost complete control of the stallions in Connemara, and this was largely due to the success of the colt foal scheme introduced in 1934 when the Council decided to buy in the best foals each year, and select from them the ones most likely to make useful stallions for the breed. Of the 14 registered stallions on the approved list in 1939, 10 were the property of the Society, and seven of the young stallions raised by the Society were at stud in Connemara.

This was a huge step forward from the situation in 1931 when the Council had great difficulty in finding any stallions of a suitable standard, and their initial scheme to subsidise colt foals had failed. Now at last some progress had been made, and although as yet the young stallions were not proven sires, there seemed to be hope for the future.

However there was also some cause for concern in that the gene pool was very small, and at the end of the 1939 season the stallion list was composed of six from the Red Line, three from the Blue Line, four from the Yellow Line, one Pink Line, one Green Line and two others, *Adventure (11)* and *Paddy (28)*.

STALLIONS ON APPROVED LIST 1939

Red Line

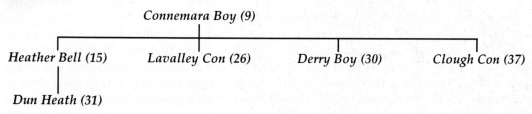

Connemara Boy (9)

Heather Bell (15)   *Lavalley Con (26)*   *Derry Boy (30)*   *Clough Con (37)*

Dun Heath (31)

Blue Line

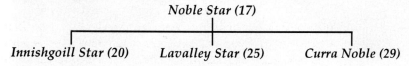

Innishgoill Laddie (21)   *Lavalley Rebel (24)*   *Clough Rebel (33)*

Yellow Line

Noble Star (17)

Innishgoill Star (20)   *Lavalley Star (25)*   *Curra Noble (29)*

Pink Line
Silver Pearl (18)

Green Line
Mountain Lad (18)

Adventure (11) was removed from the list at the end of 1939 after standing in Connemara for 12 seasons and was sold to Ballina at the end of the year. No son of his was registered, but he left 30 registered daughters, among them some well known names, including Golden Gleam (296), who was dam of the stallions *Gil (43)* and *Keehaune Laddie (52)*. Other were Speculation (295), Adventure's Own (569), and Truska Molly (774), also Camilla of Calla (1010) who was one of the first mares exported to England. Many of his progeny were good racing ponies, and he was raced regularly in Connemara and won on several occasions.

    Mountain Lad (32) died in the winter of 1939, leaving very few registered progeny, but the one yearling colt he left at Tully was in time to take his place on the stallion list, he was *Tully Lad (48)*.

Five more Society owned two year old colts were registered in the Stud Book in the autumn of 1939 and were given the prefix Clough. From this group two were selected to stand in Connemara on the approved list, for 1940. *Clough Rebel (33)* s. Rebel (7) d. Deradda Fanny (182) who was a full brother to *Lavalley Rebel (24)*, was placed with Michael Conroy, Bunowen, and *Clough Con (37)* s. Connemara Boy (9) d. Kilkerrin Beauty (246) joined *Noble Star (17)* with Tommy McDonagh, Derrylea, Clifden.

Tommy often used to tell the story of how he travelled these two stallions together leading them off his bicycle on his rounds. His route went to Toombeola, Cashel and Recess on Tuesdays, Ballyconneely and Clifden on Thursdays, Clifden and Cleggan on Saturdays. He kept the two stallions stabled beside each other with only a small partition between them, they were fed in the same trough, and they always got a slosh of porter added to their evening feed. When watering them he led them down to the lake together so they were well used to each other and never caused any problems. His stallion rounds must have kept him very fit, because he was a mile runner of some repute, and won almost every bicycle race in Connemara for eight years.

Noble Star (17) with Tommy McDonagh

CHAPTER 4

1939-1945

In 1939 Bartley O'Sullivan was asked by the Department of Agriculture to write an Article on the Connemara Pony for the Journal of the Department of Agriculture, and it was published in the Department's Journal Vol. XXXVI. No 2. This was a comprehensive paper on the origins of the breed and the work of the Society from its foundation in 1923 up to 1939, and, with the exception of the annual reports, it remains the only official paper written about the Connemara Pony by an officer of the Society. It has been invaluable in helping the research of the early days of the Society.

In this paper Bartley makes some interesting observations and suggests that to prevent staleness in the breed:

"It will be necessary in the near future to introduce fresh blood. Crossing with small Thoroughbreds, advocated by many, has not given encouraging results. Some valuable fillies have resulted from such crosses, but they are not ponies, and few of them could stand up to the conditions if turned out to fend for themselves on the mountain. The colts, mostly, have been very disappointing.

A small Irish Draught type stallion Lough Ennel, foaled 1905, by Prince Henry, located near Leenane about 1909, stood in that district until 1932 and got some very useful stock.

If a short-legged, strong-boned Irish Draught Stallion, not more than 15 hands high were available, and crossed with suitable pony mares, the progeny would be likely, I believe to command a ready sale to meet home requirements, as well as the demand from buyers attending local fairs.

No Arabs have been introduced in recent years. It appears that this cross, generally speaking, improved the style but tended to lighten the bone. "

It is apparent that the Council were aware of the problems, and were actively considering increasing the gene pool by introducing some fresh blood from outside the native stock in Connemara. During the following years various stallions were introduced, Irish Draught, Thoroughbred, and Arab, and a limited number of registered mares were permitted to be covered by these stallions. It was not expected that many of the foals produced from these crosses would be retained for breeding, but it was thought that useful information could be gained from this experimental scheme.

17th Annual Pony Show, Carna – 29th August 1940

The Show in 1940 saw a decrease in the number of entries in the pony classes, and the registrations at the Show were taken from the best of the two year old fillies bred from registered sire and dam. The class for non-registered mares was not of a sufficiently high standard to merit prizes, and none were accepted for registration.

The RDS Silver Medal and Championship for the best registered mare over six years went to Cuach na Coille (236) for Martin Walsh Kylesalia and her two year old filly Kylesalia Grey (611) was 2nd in her class. The stallion class was won by *Innishgoill Laddie (21)* for Jack Bolger, with Stephen Walsh taking 2nd place with his stallion *Silver Pearl (18)*. During the class Stephen was accidentally kicked by one of the other

Garnet Irwin

Innishgoill Laddie (21)

stallions in the ring, and sadly he died two days later from his injuries, leaving a wife and young family behind him. Following Stephen's death, *Silver Pearl* had to be sold, and he was bought by Jack Bolger who stood him at Oughterard for the next four seasons. He was sold to Wexford in the winter of 1944 leaving sixty registered daughters in the Stud Book. They included Ciro (551), Molly Conneely (562), Joyce Grey (933), Cluggan Dolly (978), Little Nell (988), Silver Dolly (1000), and Ballinafad Lass (1125).

He had only two registered sons, *Silver King (66)* dam Retreat (320) who was bought as a foal by the Society in 1944 and registered in 1946, but was sold to the Government of Mysore State, India in October of the same year. He was the first registered Connemara pony to travel so far away from his native home, and was the forerunner of the many thousands of ponies who have since found their way to distant lands.

Silver Pearl's second registered son was *Man of Barna (73)* who was privately owned by Joe Hoade of Barna. He was on the approved list for three seasons 1949 to 1951, but left no registered son. His best daughter was Rose of Barna (1337). It was a great pity that this good male line petered out after just two generations, but his daughters have ensured that *Silver Pearl* left his mark on the breed.

By now the Society had accumulated a large number of colts, and were able to sell off those they did not need for service in Connemara. The 1940 registration comprised of a group of five two year old colts who had been purchased by the Society as foals or yearlings, and from them one was selected for the approved list. He was *Calla Rebel (38)* s. Rebel (7) d. Calla Roan (196) by Charlie (2), bred by Val Keaney (Pat), Callancruick, and he was placed with John Fahy, Kilcolgan in 1941, and remained with him for six years.

Four more were registered and sold outside Connemara, and among this group was *Cashel Star (39)* s. Noble Star (17) d. Winnie (141) by Charlie (2) who went to Ted Carey, Tullaghansleek Stud, Castletown Geoghegan, Co. Westmeath, who has had a Connemara stallion in his yard ever since, standing alongside his Thoroughbred and Irish Draught stallions.

During 1940 *Connemara Boy (9)* died of tetanus at the age of eighteen with Patrick McMahon, Kinvara, having served for 14 years on the approved list, twelve of them in Connemara. He was the foundation stallion of the Red Line and had six stallion sons registered in the Stud Book. Of these all

Group of Society-owned colts.

but one of them were on the approved list for service in Connemara, but it was through his son *Heather Bell (15)* and his grandson *Dun Heath (31)* that the Red Line was to carry on into succeeding generations. He also left 32 registered daughters and among them there are such well known names as Sliabh na mBan (227), and Lougheera (228), who were the foundation mares of good mare lines. At the Show in 1940 the first three two year old fillies were all his daughters, with a granddaughter in fourth place, a nice tribute to the old stallion in his last year of life.

His grandson *Dun Heath (31)* was sold to Castlecomer Co. Kilkenny at the end of the 1940 season having only been two years in Connemara. He spent one year with Mortimer Davoren in Moycullen and one year with Val Keaney, Gowla, Cashel. He left only seven registered progeny but among them were two ponies who were to leave their mark on the breed. Both were foaled in 1941, one was Double Dun (803) who was the dam of *Carna Dun (89)* and the second was *Dun Lorenzo (55)* who was the stallion son who carried the Red Line into the next generation and had a huge influence on the breed during the years he served in Connemara from 1943 to 1959.

Death of Vice President – Lord Killanin Elected to Council

In 1941 there were a number of changes in the Council, with many of the original members no longer taking an active part in the running of the Society's affairs.

The Rev Canon Patterson V. F. Clifden who was one of the Vice-Presidents of the Society died, and in May of that year a good friend of the Society and founder member of the Council Mr W. F. Prendergast also died. The Rev Canon Cunningham P. P. V. F. moved from Roundstone to Clifden Parish, but remained as President of the Society, and three new Council members were elected, one of them being Lord Killanin, Spiddal.

18th Annual Pony Show, Carna – 28th August 1941

The Show had a smaller entry with just 162 in the pony classes. Jack Bolger showed Silver Pearl (18) who won the Stallion class, and Film Star (245) took the RDS Silver Medal and mare championship for Martin Walsh, Callowfeenish. Pat Sullivan's Lougheera (228) won the class for mares without foal at foot and her yearling filly also won her class. The riding class was once more open to girls as well as boys, and was won by Garnet Irwin's mare Ciro (551), and she won it again in 1942, 1943 and 1945.

At a meeting held in Mongan's Hotel Carna on Show Day a presentation was made on behalf of the Society to Mr Josie Mongan T. D. as a token of their esteem on the occasion of his marriage to Miss Maureen O'Neill of Clonmel. Josie was by then 61 years of age, but was still full of energy and enthusiasm and continued to work tirelessly for the people of Connemara and for the Connemara Pony Breeders' Society. He rarely missed a Council meeting and often took the chair. As the proprietor of Mongan's Hotel, he was the central figure at Carna on show days, and in a piece written in the Connacht Tribune, (8th Sept. 1945) Josie is described like this.

Josie Mongan T.D.

"He had a word of welcome for everybody, for there is nobody in the West whom he does not know or who does not know him, and he is supreme in his headquarters at Carna. To the outside world he may be known by the dignified title of Mr Joseph Mongan, T.D , but anywhere west of the Shannon he remains Josie. "

Irish Draught Stallion Purchased

It was also at this meeting that a decision was made to purchase an Irish Draught colt by Clonmult which had been offered to the Society by Mr Whooley, Skibbereen, Co. Cork. Mr Tommy Kelly MRCVS and Mr Tim Cotter were asked to go to see the colt and to buy him if he was found to be suitable. There is letter in the stallion records from Tim Cotter written from the Eldon Hotel Skibbereen just one month later recommending that the Society should buy this colt. He states that in his opinion *"he is a high class colt, and has good bone (approx. 9 inches). This colt shows a good deal of 'breeding'. He has a nice hard head which is not likely to affect the pony character of his produce when crossed with pony mares. "*

The colt was purchased for £30, and was the first Irish Draught sire bought in by the Society and approved for use on registered mares. He was named *Skibbereen* and was located with Jack Bolger in October 1941, where he remained for the following three seasons. He then moved to John Costello at Spiddal for 1945 and 1946, and at the end of the season he was removed from the list, later he was castrated and sold to Matt Healy, Oughterard for £25. He had eight fillies registered, but this first experiment of introducing Irish Draught blood was not considered to be a success, as the results were not promising, and *Skibbereen* left no lasting impression on the breed.

One non-registered stallion was put on the list of approved sires in 1941 and allowed to be used on registered mares. He was *Dynamite*, a grey cob whose sire was *Heather Grey (16)* by Rebel (7) out of a mare from Co. Mayo. He was an over-height strong cob and was never registered, but stood at Oughterard for his owner Pat Mogan until 1945 when he was removed from the list. His job during the war years was to pull the mail van between Oughterard and Clifden, and he was used mainly for breeding working cobs. He had one son who was purchased by the Society as a yearling and registered as *Midros Explosive (58)* in 1944 but who was sold to Co Roscommon the same year. Working cobs were needed during the war years, but there was also a steady demand for Connemara ponies from all over Ireland for use as harness ponies when petrol was strictly rationed and people once again turned back to horse transport.

Two three year old colts owned by the Society were registered in October 1941 and were added to the list for 1942. They were *Gil (43)* s. Innishgoill Laddie (21) d. Golden Gleam (296) by Adventure (11) bred by Dudley McDonagh, Maam Cross, who went to John Walsh, Kylesalia, and *Airgead (45)* s. Noble Star (17) d. Blooming Heather (304) by Rebel (7),who went to Ed Conneely, Glentrasna, replacing *Heather Bell (15)* who was sold to Co. Leitrim.

Heather Bell had been on the Society's list of approved stallions for nine years and left 30 registered progeny. He passed on the valuable tough Red Line to his son *Dun Heath (31)*, and among his daughters were Lucy Grey (567), Maam Belle (819), Dun Belle (779), Windy (782) and Noreen (867).

Gift of Thoroughbred Stallion Winter

The second introduction of outside blood also happened at the end of 1941, when the Society received a gift of a six year old Thoroughbred stallion *Winter*, a grey horse 15. 3 hh, by Manna out of Snowstorm. He was very well bred and his granddam Snow Maiden was full sister to Caligula who won the St Leger. He was presented to the Society by Mr H. J. Ussher, Brackenstown, Swords, Co. Dublin, and was kept during 1942 with Christy Kerin at Oranmore. He moved to Jack Bolger in Oughterard in the Spring of 1943 and was put on the Society's list of approved stallions for a limited number of registered mares.

Winter (TB)

Sadly this horse never really had time to prove himself as he died suddenly of a ruptured liver in November 1943, but he did leave one registered son *Creganna Winter (63). Winter* was the sire of the first twins recorded in Connemara when Clare Girl (422) owned by Nicholas Byrnes, Oughterard gave birth to twin foals in 1944, twins are still very rare in Connemara ponies.

Three of his daughters made their name in pony racing in Connemara, Nancy Winter (1003), (who raced under the name Migoli,) Rangoon (1063) and Rose of Killola (1365), and the *Winter* blood continues on today through the progeny of *Creganna Winter (63)* and Rose of Killola (1365), through her son *Dun Aengus (120).*

Clare Girl (422) with twin foals by Winter

At the AGM held in Clifden on 31st March 1942, Bartley O'Sullivan tendered his resignation from the office of Honorary Secretary, but stated that he had no intention of leaving the Society, which could always count on any assistance which he could reasonably give. However the Secretarial work had increased enormously and bore no resemblance to that of earlier years. There was also the considerable amount of work involved in the management of their stock of ponies. He suggested that the Council should endeavour to secure the services of a paid secretary who should also be capable of managing the stock.

The members of Council present spoke in appreciation of the work done by the Honorary Secretary and after some discussion it was decided that consideration of Mr O'Sullivan's resignation be adjourned to the next meeting of Council. The date of the Annual Show was to be 27th August and as the next meeting was likely to take place on Show Day, the Secretary was left with no choice but to continue his duties as usual.

19th Annual Pony Show, Carna – 27th August 1942

This year the Show was very successful, with entries increased on the previous two years. Carna Dolly (442) won the RDS Silver Medal for mares up to six years, and Cuach na Coille (236) was again the winner in the Senior Mare Championship, while *Noble Star (17)* took his sixth Silver Medal in the Stallion Class, this time with Tommy McDonagh.

The winner of the yearling colt class was a dun colt by *Dun Heath (31)* dam Droighneann Donn (280)

Carna Dolly (442)

exhibited by Josie Mongan's brother James Mongan, who had bought him as a foal from his breeder John Curran, Carna. He was sold again after the Show to Dick Curley, Galway who in turn sold him to Mr L. O'Dea, a solicitor in Galway. He was registered in September 1943 and given the name *Dun Lorenzo (55)* because Mr O'Dea lived at Fort Lorenzo, Taylors Hill, Galway, a place which in later years became the home of John Brennan, whose ponies carried the well-known Fort as their Prefix. *Dun Lorenzo* was bought by the Society when he was registered, and placed with John de Courcey Roundstone for his first year of service in Connemara 1944.

Bartley O'Sullivan's Resignation Resolved

A Council meeting was held in Mongan's Hotel on Show Day, and the matter of Bartley O'Sullivan's resignation which had been adjourned from the last meeting was addressed. Mr Christy Kerin was in the chair, and he paid tribute to the work which the Secretary had done for the Society, and added that his resignation would be a very serious blow to the Society. He proposed that Mr O'Sullivan would withdraw his notice of resignation, and also that he might consider the offer of remuneration of £100 per annum. Mr Michael O'Malley seconded and other members supported the tribute to the Secretary.

In reply Bartley O'Sullivan thanked the members of Council for the sincere expression of appreciation of his services which he valued highly. He wished that the Council could find someone suitable to appoint as Secretary and Manager, but he realised that there was little likelihood of getting a competent officer at the limited rate of remuneration which the Society could afford, and so in the circumstances he consented to continue his services as before.

Regarding their very generous offer, he suggested cutting the amount proposed by half so as not to put too much strain on the Society's funds, and it was finally agreed that he would accept £60 per annum, and that he could also pay a small honourarium to his clerical assistant out of Society funds. This was so typical of the man!

It was indeed fortunate for the Council that Bartley O'Sullivan agreed to continue to act as Honorary Secretary, and that he was prepared to put so much work into the running of the Society as well as his important job as Secretary of the County Committee of Agriculture.

New Vice President. Sean Keane Joins Council

At the next AGM held in Recess in March 1943, Father Kenny P. P. Rosmuck was appointed as a Vice-President of the Society replacing Father McCullagh who had left Connemara. A new member of Council was also elected, and he was Sean Keane, the recently appointed Agricultural Overseer for the Connemara District and the Western Islands.

Sean Keane came from a farming family at Kilworth, Fermoy Co. Cork and joined the Department of Agriculture in 1936. He spent his early years as a potato inspector in Co Offaly where he met and married Mary Lalor. He moved to Galway in 1941 and remained there for the rest of his life. He lived at Newcastle, Galway and had three daughters and one son. He was a keen fisherman, and there was plenty of opportunity to enjoy his sport in Connemara, but after he became a member of the Council of the Connemara Pony Breeders'

Society, it was the Connemara pony which became his life-long interest. He worked along side Bartley O'Sullivan for the next 18 years, and during those years he took on much of the field work for Bartley, as well as helping with the organisation of the Annual Show. After Bartley's death, Seane Keane became acting Secretary of the Council until the appointment of John Killeen in 1963, and he held the office of President of the Society from 1973 until his death in 1978.

The Spring inspections in 1943 were held in April, and four of the Society-owned 2 year old colts were registered. Two were sold out of the Connemara district, and two were retained by the Society. One was *Kylesalia Star (49)*, a son of Cuach na Coille (236) by Lavalley Star (25) the other was *Keehaune Laddie (52)*, by Innishgoill Laddie (21), dam Golden Gleam (296), a full brother to *Gil (43)*. They were both put on the approved list in 1944.

Two older stallions were also registered for Michael Wallace, Inverin, one was a son of Finnane Hero, the non-registered sire owned by Michael Wallace who was approved for service of registered Connemara mares and was on the list for one season. He was a six year old chestnut 13. 2hh, who was registered as *Finnane Rover (47)* and was bought by the Society at the inspections. He was included on the stallion list for five seasons before being sold in 1949. The second stallion owned by Michael Wallace was the five year old son of Mountain Lad (32) dam Tully Beauty (374), who was registered as *Tully Lad (48)*. He is described as bay, star, black points height 13. 3 hh, but he is remembered as being more black than bay.

He was put on the approved list in 1943, but remained with Michael Wallace at Tully to run with his herd on the mountain until June 1949 when he was bought by Jack Bolger, who then sold him to the Society in December 1949.

Tully Lad (48) was the one who carried the Green Line into the second generation, and he stood at Oughterard with Jack Bolger for his first season as a Society-owned stallion in 1950.

Volume V of the Stud Book

Forty-seven mares were registered during the 1943 Spring inspections, and during the year Volume V of the Stud Book was published. It cost 2/6, and for the first time included an index of the breeders. It covered the period from November 1939 to March 1943 and contained particulars of 20 stallions and 253 mares, bringing the total number of ponies registered since the Society was formed to 839.

Of the twenty stallions registered in Volume V seventeen were selected from the young stock bought by the Society as foals under the scheme introduced in 1934, and included five young stallions standing in Connemara in 1943. The surplus were sold outside Connemara to various parts of Ireland, and the Society had received favourable reports from their new owners. The number of registered mares receiving nominations for free service by a registered Connemara pony stallion exceeded 300 per annum and this did not include mares over fifteen years of age who were debarred from receiving a nomination, although the majority of the older mares were still breeding regularly.

20th Annual Pony Show, Carna – 26th August 1943

There were 214 entries in the Show and *Silver Pearl (18)* won the stallion class once more for Jack Bolger. In the young mares class, the RDS Silver Medal was won by the three year old Lily of the Valley (738) by Noble Star (17) who had also won her class the previous year, and Lougheera (228) won the senior mare championship. Eleven mares from the non registered class were entered in the Stud Book, and among the ten two year old fillies registered was a dun filly named Double Dun (803) s. Dun Heath (31) d. Carna Girl (525) who was to become the dam of *Carna Dun (89)*.

Three stallions were removed from the approved list at the end of the 1943 season and were sold out of the Connemara district. *Lavalley Star (25)* had been six years on the list, and was only eight years old when he was sold to Co. Offaly. He had carried the Yellow Line from *Black Paddy (8)* through *Noble Star (17)* into the third generation, and was the best of Noble Star's sons, leaving 44 registered progeny including four stallions.

Among his daughters were two mares who became the dams of future stallions, they were An tSailchuach (663) the dam of *Strongbow (90)* and Dolan Rose (1132) dam of *MacDara (91)*. Some other good mares by him were Bunreacht (735), Heather Black (798), Loughconeera Star (717), and Errisbeg Star (1054).

His son *Kylesalia Star (49)*, dam Cuach na Coille (236), replaced him on the list in 1944, but only remained in Connemara for one season before being sold to Northern Ireland, leaving no registered progeny.

Lavalley Star's second son to stand in Connemara was *Clough Droighneann (67)*, who was foaled in 1944, and his dam Droighnean Donn (280) was also the dam of *Dun Lorenzo (55)*. He was removed from the list after only two years of service, in 1947 and 1948. He had four registered daughters but left no stallion son to carry on the Yellow male line into future generations, and so another male blood line was lost. One of his daughters, Lehid Rose (1417), who was foaled in 1949, went down in history as one of the longest living ponies in Connemara, and lived until she was almost forty years of age.

Clough Rebel (33) was also sold at the end of the 1943 season having spent four years with Michael Conroy at Bunowen. He was a full brother to *Lavalley Rebel (24)* and there were some really good mares among his eighteen registered progeny. Six of his bestknown daughters were Silver Bridle (394), Calla Brown (922), Rebel Star (986), White Linnet (1060), Village Swallow (1061) and Gowlane Grey (1083). The last three all made their way to England where they were successful at early shows there, and became foundation mares for the breed in the UK.

Following the loss of the T. B. stallion *Winter* after only one season on the approved list, the Council were anxious to keep a son from this sire, and in 1944, on the recommendation of Christy Kerin, they bought a bay yearling colt from Edward McDonagh, Creganna, Oranmore, out of his mare Creganna Peggy (741). She was foaled in 1930, and was a chestnut with a white face, height 13. 2, and was registered in 1943. *Creganna Winter (63)* was registered in 1946 and put on the approved list of stallions the same year.

Irish Draught Sire Purchased

During 1944 the Society also bought an Irish Draught sire, a two year old bay with a star standing 15 hh named *Hillside Rover*. His sire Owenbeg (282) and dam Locan na Gleanna (2217) were both on the Irish Draught register, and he was bred by Anthony Kirby, Gortbawn, Ayle, Westport. He was inspected for the Society by Mr Tim Cotter, and he was purchased for £50. He was described as being of compact build, with very good bone, but he was also considered to be rather plain. He went onto the approved list of stallions in 1945 and spent his first year with John de Courcey, Roundstone.

He then moved to Michael Conroy in 1946 and remained with him for four seasons before being removed from the list and sold to Patrick Coyne, Mullaghgloss, Renvyle.

He made very little impact on the breed with only three daughters registered by him, but one mare whose breeding is not recorded, but who is believed to have been by him is Loobeen Queen (1499) owned by Pakie Coyne, of Ardnagreevagh, Renvyle. She was foaled in 1949, a bay with a white star, 14 hh, and through her daughters Loobeen Lily (2919) and Noreen Ban (2355) she features in the background of some of today's best known stallions, including *The Fugitive (368), Atlantic Cliff (663), Loobeen Larry (670), Abbeyleix Owen (496)* and *Mervyn Kingsmill (762)*.

In the summer of 1944, Bartley O'Sullivan suffered the tragic loss of his wife May at the early age of 42, leaving him with six children to bring up on his own. It was a devastating blow to him, but he was a very devout man, and no doubt his strongly-held religious beliefs were a consolation to him at that time. Bartley immersed himself in the work for the Connemara Pony Breeders' Society and continued as its Secretary until he died in 1960. His son Tadhg who was the eldest in the family, and later joined the diplomatic service, has given these memories of those early years.

> *"If you were a member of the O'Sullivan family, there was no escaping the Connemara Pony. The womenfolk found themselves roped in to sew colourful rosettes for the prizewinning exhibits at the Show; the boys, once their spelling was good enough, spent long hours helping with the proof-reading of the Show catalogue and (rare privilege) the Stud Book. One duty eagerly sought after was the selling of the catalogue on the great day. In the 1940's it cost a shilling a copy, and there was a commission of a penny per copy sold, so that the industrious salesperson could make quite a little profit from the day. It certainly beat sewing rosettes!"*

He also remembers Bartley as being an expert on bee keeping, who would gladly give lectures on the subject to groups all over the county. He was a keen gardener, and grew his own vegetables. He also loved to swim, whether it was at Salthill or his native Kerry, which he visited once a year and where he also indulged in a passion for hill walking.

He made his annual pilgrimage to St Patrick's Purgatory at Lough Derg on 27 occasions, and was involved in a number of charities including the Seamen's Institute. His job as Secretary to the County Committee of Agriculture took him to the annual agricultural Spring Shows at the Royal Dublin Society, where he bought premium breeding stock for Galway, and many of the contacts he made there became supporters of his work for the Connemara pony.

21st Annual Pony Show, Carna – 31st August 1944

The Show had an entry of 210 in the pony classes, and it was the first year that the Perpetual Silver Cup presented by His Grace the Most Rev. Dr Walsh, Archbishop of Tuam, Patron of the Connemara Pony Breeders' Society was awarded to the Best Broodmare in the Show. It was open to all broodmares including first prize-winners of classes at the previous year's Show. It was won by Cuach na Coille (236) for Martin Walsh, Kylesalia, and to confirm her supremacy in the Show ring during the 1940's, Cuach na Coille (236) won the *Archbishop's Cup* again in 1945, her last time to compete before she

Cuach Na Coille (236)

was sold to England. This beautiful cup has been competed for every year since, and bears many famous names on its plinth, it is now known as the Archbishop's Cup and goes to the winner of the four year old mare's class.

Cuach na Coille (236) was the outstanding mare of her era, winning her class and the RDS Silver Medal in 1940, 1942 and 1944, as in those days the winner of a class could not compete in the same class the following year. It was very fitting that her name should be the first on the Archbishop's Cup. She bred four registered stallion sons, two of which stood in Connemara, *Kylesalia Star (49)* and *Coill Ruadh (80)*. She had a foal every year, but only two of her daughters were registered. She was the model of her day and epitomised the type of mare the Connemara Pony Breeders'Society was trying to promote.

Lavalley Rebel (24) had been moved to Peter Connolly, Bealdangan, a new stallion custodian, in the spring of 1944, having been misused by his former handler, who had used him to pull a heavy side-car carrying immigrants from the Aran Islands with their possessions up the rough road from Costello to Moycullen, which was much too hard a job. However, with his new custodian, he soon regained his health, and went on to

Lavalley Rebel (24)

63

take first prize in the stallion class at the 1944 Carna Show. In second place was the new three year old stallion, *Dun Lorenzo (55)*, shown by John de Courcey.

Noble Star (17) was sold to Listowel Co. Kerry at the end of 1944 having been on the approved stallion list for twelve years. During that time he had eleven sons and seventy-four daughters registered in the Stud Book. He dominated the stallion class during the thirties and won it five times for Jack Bolger, 1932-35 and 1937, and twice for Tommy McDonagh 1939 and 1942.

Despite such an impressive record, *Noble Star (17)* failed to leave a strong male line, and from all his sons, only *Lavalley Star (25)* had any registered sons. Sadly they made no impact on the breed and left no heir to the Yellow line which then petered out on the male side after only three generations. However *Noble Star (17)* had some good daughters who have contributed much to the breed through their progeny, notably Dunroche (773), dam of Winter Roche (1495), Nora (682), dam of *Macnamara (175)*, Doon Lily (1259), dam of *Doon Paddy (95)*, and Lily of the Valley (738), dam of *Man of Barna (73)*.

Silver Pearl (18) was also sold by Jack Bolger during the winter of 1944 and he went to Co. Wexford. It is a lasting regret that this stallion left the district without leaving a good son to follow him, and so another male line was lost after only two generations. *Clough Con (37)* was sold to Castlerea, Co. Roscommon having spent five years on the list and he left six registered daughters.

A total of 103 ponies were registered in 1944 which was a record, and included three stallions reared by the Society, but only one of them, *Rusheen Heather (56)*, s. Heather Bell (56) was put onto the approved list, and placed with Frank McDonagh, Derrylea for the 1945 season before being sold to Donegal. He has two registered progeny in the Stud Book, a stallion *Dan McCann (76)* and a mare, Solus na Realta (1262). She was owned and bred by Mrs Yseult Cochrane, Stranorlar, Co. Donegal who was one of the first people from outside Connemara to exhibit ponies at the Clifden Show.

Third Irish Draught Stallion Approved

The third Irish Draught Stallion to be added to the list of approved stallions was *May Boy*, a grey horse standing 15 hands, who was bred in Co. Longford by Patrick O'Donohoe. He was by Irish Mail and his dam was by Lord Shannon, and he was bought by the Department of Agriculture in 1932 and placed on the Aran Islands. Some years later he came off the Islands and was sold to a man from Claregalway called Fox. He in turn sold him to Jack Bolger, who passed him on to John de Courcey, but then Jack re-purchased him, and in late 1944 *May Boy* was approved for use on Connemara mares, and went on the list in 1945. He remained in Jack's ownership and stood at Waterfield, Oughterard until the end of the 1950 season, when he was sold again to Athenry.

May Boy was considered to be the best of the Irish Draught stallions and left twenty-one registered progeny. He was described as *"a very good type of small (Draught) stallion, who brought some nice ponies"*.

Two of his daughters were out of the good mare Retreat (320), they were Ruby (1219), and May Retreat (1569), and the latter won her class in 1955. Another good daughter was Pollnaclough Grey (1518), bred by Michael Keady, Pollnaclough, Moycullen, and her progeny included *Ceileog (109)*, Juliet (3623) and Bealtaine (4491).

21st Annual Pony Show, Carna – 30th August 1945

There were 200 entries for the Show which was held on a beautiful fine day, and many people came to Carna from all over Ireland to visit the Show. Lord Killanin was particularly welcomed to the Show and thanked for the interest he showed in the Society since his recent return home after the war. Carna Dolly (442) won the RDS Medal, and Jack Bolger won the stallion class with the 4 year old *Dun Lorenzo (55)*.

The three Irish Draught Stallions had all been introduced during the war years when the trade was mainly for work ponies and driving ponies, and there was a need for good strong cobs. However after the war was over, there was a change in the market, and within a year, there began to be a growing demand from England for riding ponies. The Society realised that the results from the introduction of Irish Draught blood were not promising, and it was decided that no more Irish Draught sires should be used.

Skibbereen was the first to be removed from the list, and he was sold at the end of the 1946 season having been castrated. *Hillside Rover* remained with Michael Conroy for a further three seasons, and then he was sold, and *May Boy* stood at Oughterard with Jack Bolger until the end of the 1950 season when he too was sold.

Ponies arriving at Carna for the Show.

The Society decided to continue with the gradual introduction of Thoroughbred blood, through the mares, and considered that *"where carefully chosen Thoroughbred stallions of the correct type are crossed with pony mares of good substance and quality, it is more likely to produce beneficial results"*.

The three year old half-bred son of Winter (TB), *Creganna Winter (63)* who was registered in 1946, went on the approved list and was placed with John Walsh, Kylesalia for the season.

Little Heaven TB Sire Purchased

Then in December 1946 the Society purchased a small Thoroughbred stallion called *Little Heaven* from the Orchardstown Stud, Clonmel. He was foaled in 1942, a bay, standing 15 hands, his sire was Bala Hissar, by Blandford, and his dam was Outport by Portlaw. His price was £100, a much larger sum than was paid for any of the previous stallions bought by the Society. He was a horse of some quality, and although he appears to have been a bit light of bone and rather on the leg, he was considered to be very suitable for use on some of the heavier type of Connemara mares to produce a pony of quality with substance.

Garnet Irwin

Little Heaven (TB)

He was approved for service of registered Connemara pony mares, and placed with Jack Bolger at Oughterard for the 1947 season, and was limited to forty mares. His fee was Five Guineas, and nominated Connemara mares paid £1. 5s. 0. with their nomination ticket, fees to be paid before service. He remained with Jack Bolger for all the five seasons he was on the list until the end of the 1951, and travelled by lorry to Clifden, Cashel and Carna during his last three seasons.

His registered daughters were few in number, and they did not leave a lasting impression on the breed as most of them were either used for pony racing or sold out of the district. However one registered mare by him, Dancing Spanner (1750), was the dam of Roundstone River (4746) who won the Championship of the Show for Tommy MacDonagh in 1974 and was later sold to France. Her full brother, *Roundstone Oscar (337)* left 36 registered progeny before going to Canada, and one of Oscar's sons, Ballinaboy Barry (655) was owned by the Society and stood at Carna for two seasons with Festy Mulkerrin in 1978/79.

Famous Half-breds

Little Heaven was also the sire of several famous half-breds who were to do much to promote the Connemara pony during the 1960's. Little Model gained international fame as a dressage horse having been ridden in the Rome Olympics in 1960 by Mrs Brenda Williams, and placed third in the European Championships in 1963, while the most famous son of all was the brilliant showjumper Dundrum, who was the mount of Tommy Wade, and this little horse of just 15 hands thrilled the International show jumping world with his amazing ability.

Dundrum's dam was a registered Connemara pony mare called Evergood (1126) by Gil (43) out of Queen Maeve (795) by Lavalley Star (25), and she was bred by Joe Joyce, Derrada East, Recess. She was sold to Patrick Crowe, Goold's Cross, Co. Tipperary, and was in foal to *Little Heaven* when she left Connemara. Her colt foal was subsequently bought by the Wade family who lived in the village of Dundrum, Co. Tipperary, and the little bay horse was given the name Dundrum which later became a household name in the horse world.

His remarkable achievements in the International show jumping scene during the 1960's are legendary, and include such famous wins as the King George V Cup, the Puissance at RDS, the Dublin Grand Prix, and he was on the Irish team who won the Aga Khan Cup. His successes focussed attention on his pony background and also the fact that his dam was a registered Connemara pony mare.

Before she was sold out of Connemara, Evergood (1126) was placed 2nd in her class at the Connemara Pony Show at Clifden in 1950, and it was in that same year that *Little Heaven's* most famous son in Connemara won the two year old colt class for John Mylotte, Carna, and he was registered later that year and was named *Carna Dun (89)*. His dam was Double Dun (803) sire Dun Heath (31) dam Carna Girl (525) who was by Rebel (7), so that he had solid old Connemara breeding on his dam's side tracing back through the Blue and Red bloodlines to *Rebel (7)* and *Connemara Boy (9)*. She won her class as a foal in 1941 but was unplaced as a two year old.

Little Heaven may not have had as much influence in Connemara through his daughters as had been envisaged by the Council, but his greatest gift to the Connemara Pony Stud Book was his son *Carna Dun (89)* who in turn gave so many really outstanding mares to the breed. The other legacy which has been carried down through future generations is great jumping ability, which so many ponies from this blood-line have inherited.

The Council had also received letters from several people suggesting that an infusion of Arab blood might be considered. Mrs Nicholson of Kells Co. Meath wrote in 1945 inviting the Council to visit her to see ponies she had bred from crossing Connemara mares with her Arab stallion Naseel. Her stallion was the outstanding sire of children's riding ponies of the day, and his progeny were successful in the Show ring both in Ireland and England. Mrs Nicholson became a member of the Society and was invited to attend the Show, but although the Council agreed to see the results of her Arab x Connemara ponies, no further action was taken at that time.

Dundrum and Tommy Wade

68

CHAPTER 5

1946-1951

• Killanin Cup • Exports to England • ECPS formed 1947 • Show moved to Clifden 1947 •
• Carew Cup • Classes at Spring Show 1951 • Volumes VI & VII Stud Book published •
• Death of Josie Mongan TD •

23rd Annual Pony Show, Carna – 29th August 1946

A new cup had been presented by Lord Killanin for the best mare four years old or under, and the Killanin Cup was won for the first time by Tom Mulkerrin (Pat), Callowfeenish with his three year old mare Ocean Wave (949) by Gil (43). It must have been a very special day for the Mulkerrin family, as the dam of their winning three year old was Carna Dolly (442), and she won the Archbishop's Cup for the best broodmare at the Show. The stallion class was won by *Lavalley Rebel (24)* shown by Jack Bolger, and the two year old filly class was won by Festy Folan with a daughter of Sliabh na mBan (227) by Gil (43). She was registered at the Show in the name of her new owner Miss Spottiswoode, and was called Cornflower of Calla (1022).

Founding of English Connemara Pony Society 1947

1946 was a turning point in the history of the Connemara Pony Breeders' Society, when a number of visitors from England came to Ireland after the war, visited the Connemara Pony Show, and started buying ponies. It was the beginning of the export of Connemara ponies in large numbers to another country which was to lead to the formation of the first Overseas Society.

Miss Cynthia Spottiswoode recognised the potential of the Connemara pony as a riding pony, and began to promote the Connemara pony in England, and in Volume VI of the Connemara Pony Stud Book which was printed in 1947, she is listed as the owner of eleven registered mares, which was quite exceptional in those days. She used the suffix Calla for her ponies, and during the late forties and early fifties, she imported thirty-six Connemara

Miss Spottiswoode
with Camilla of Calla (1010))

69

ponies into England where she sold them to new owners, many of who became enthusiastic supporters of the breed.

She was sometimes based at Oughterard, but also in Ascot, Devon and Newmarket, and had many contacts in the horse and pony world in both countries. Through her dedication to the Connemara pony she became the driving force in forming a small group of enthusiasts who founded the English Connemara Pony Society in 1947, and she became its first Secretary.

Among the ponies she imported into England in 1947 was Cuach na Coille (236) who by now was 18 years old. Having been such a great prizewinning mare in Ireland, Miss Spottiswoode felt that Cuach na Coille would be a marvellous ambassador for the breed, and would do much to promote the Connemara pony in England. Her judgement was correct, and when the first Connemara Pony Show to be held in England took place at Ascot the following year, Cuach na Coille (236), with a filly foal at foot by Tiger Gill (68), won first prize in her class.

24th Annual Pony Show, Clifden – 18th August 1947

There were 186 entries at the Show, which moved to Clifden in 1947 and the stallion class was won for the third year by Jack Bolger, this time with *Tiger Gill (68)*. Martin McDonagh, Knock, Ballyconneely won the Killanin Cup with White Linnet (1060) s. Clough Rebel (33) d. White Star (466), and the Archbishop's Cup went to Rossleague Grey (637) s. Silver Pearl (18) owned by Mrs Charlotte Browne, Letterfrack.

Show Moves to Clifden Permanently in 1947

For twelve years the Annual Show had been held at Carna, but in 1947 the Council decided to move back to Clifden, and planned to return to the practice of moving the Show to different venues in Connemara. However, the 1947 Show at Clifden was so successful financially, it was felt that no other centre in Connemara could equal it, and from that year onwards the Annual Connemara Pony Show has always been held at Clifden in August every year up to the present day. The moving of the Show from Carna was very disappointing for the breeders in the Carna district, which was considered one of the best pony breeding districts in Connemara, and following the move to Clifden, the number of breeders in the area slowly decreased over the years.

During the early post-war years, there were many visitors to the Show from England and also from other parts of Ireland, and many of them bought ponies. The Council was pleased that there was such a good demand for Connemara ponies, and after the slow trade during the war years, it was encouraging that the prices were improving. However several Council members expressed their fears that the better prices would tempt breeders to sell their good young mares, and so deplete the breeding stock in Connemara which the Society had been striving to build up during the previous 25 years.

Lord Killanin Vice President

At the AGM in April 1947 Lord Killanin was made a Vice-President of the Society, and two new members of the Council, who were also to become future Vice Presidents, were Rev. Father W. Moran P. P. Rosmuck, (better known in later years as Canon Willie Moran), and Mr Peadar O'Scannaill MRCVS, who also joined the Inspection Committee. Mr Dick Curley was elected a member of the Council.

From the five 2 year old colts who were registered in 1946, two joined the list for the 1947 season in Connemara. *Clough Droighneann (67)* sire Lavalley Star (25) dam Droighnean Donn (280) was placed with John Kyne, Leagaun, Moycullen, while *Tiger Gill (68)* by Gil (43) dam Tiger Tank (908) joined *May Boy (ID)* and *Little Heaven (TB)* at Jack Bolger's yard in Oughterard.

Four more 2 year old colts were registered in 1947, but *Farravane Boy (71)*, sire May Boy (ID) dam Farravane (746) by Noble Star (17) was the only one selected for the approved list in 1948. He was the only son of an Irish Draught stallion to be retained by the Society and he remained on the list until 1953.

Volume VI of the Connemara Pony Stud Book

Volume VI was published at the end of 1947, covering the period from May 1943 to September 1947, and it cost 3/6.

Farravane Boy (71)

It included 20 stallions, all of which, with one exception, were selected from colts raised by the Society, and also included particulars of 320 mares, bringing the total number of registered ponies to 72 stallions and 1107 mares.

25th Annual Pony Show, Clifden – 18th August 1948

This year, for the first time, breeders from outside the Connemara district brought ponies to exhibit at the Show. Kevin McLoughlin, Portnoo, Co. Donegal brought his 3 year old colt *Kiltoorish Lad (74)*, a full brother to *Tiger Gill (68)*, to be registered at the Show, and he also showed two mares. The second breeder, also from Donegal, was Mrs Yseult Cochrane, Stranorlar, whose three year old mare Solus na Bhflaitheas (1090) sire Keehaune Laddie (52) dam Little Twin (563) won the RDS Medal for young mares and the Killanin Cup. Grey Granite (313) s. Rebel (7) won the RDS Medal for mares of 6 years and over, shown by Thomas Hynes, Canal Stage, and Orphan Maid (675) won the Archbishop's Cup for Laurence McDonagh, Maam Cross.

End of Colt Foal Purchasing Scheme

The problem of finding suitable grazing land for the young stallions was still causing much difficulty, and the Council was indebted to Father Heffernan and the African Missions Fathers at Kilcolgan who had kindly provided land for the Society. Because of the difficulty over grazing, and also because the Society had a number of colts already, it was decided not to buy any colt foals in 1948 or in 1949.

During 1948, nine colts were registered, and six of these young stallions joined the list in 1949, making a record number of 15 registered Connemara stallions standing in Connemara, as well as the two Irish Draughts and *Little Heaven*.

Three of the new young stallions were sired by Gil (43) who was also still on the list, and he won the stallion class at Clifden in 1948. *Cilciarain (78)* had been bought as a foal from his breeder Joseph Ridge, Rosdogan, Kilkerrin when he won his class, and his dam was Irish Beauty (669) by Rebel (7), so he carried the Blue Line on both sides of his pedigree. *Carna Bobby (79)* whose dam was Carna Dolly (442), and *Coill Ruadh (80)*, dam Cuach na Coille (236) were bred from two of the outstanding mares of the day who were both winners of the Archbishop's Cup.

Dun Orphan (77) represented the Red Line and was bred by Laurence McDonagh, Letterfore, Maam Cross. He was sired by Dun Lorenzo (55), and his dam was the 1948 winner of the Archbishop's Cup, Orphan Maid (675) by Innishgoill Laddie (21).

Garnet Irwin

Gil (43)

Tully Nigger (81) came from the very small Green Line founded by his grandsire *Mountain Lad (32)*, and was by Tully Lad (48) out of a mare called Irish Humour (699) who was a black mare registered without breeding. He had been bought by Michael O'Malley as a foal, and was sold to the Society as a yearling. He stood at Moycullen for the 1949 season with George Kyne, and was then taken off the list in December 1949 when the Society purchased his sire Tully Lad (48) from Jack Bolger. *Tully Nigger (81)* was then resold to Michael O'Malley who sold him to the USA in 1950.

The final young stallion to join the list in 1949 was a son of Silver Pearl (18) called *Man of Barna (73)* who was bred by Michael Joyce, Lehenagh, Cashel and owned by Joseph Hoade, Barna. He was the last representative of the Pink Line, and his dam Lily of the Valley (738) by Noble Star (17) won the RDS Medal for young mares in 1943. He was privately owned, and was on the approved list three seasons, but sadly he was castrated in 1951 leaving no registered son. There was a good colt by him out of White Nell (962) who won his class as a foal and also as a two year old, but he was never registered. A full sister to this colt was Rose of Barna (1337), a winner of many prizes including Best Broodmare with foal at foot in 1964, and she became a foundation mare for Miss Frances Lee Norman's Clonkeehan Stud. *Man of Barna (73)* went on to be a successful pony under saddle and won many prizes at the RDS Shows as a gelding.

The last group of Society-owned colts which had been bought in as foals were inspected for registration in 1949, and five out of the six were sired by *Creganna Winter (63)*. It seems that the Council was determined to keep the Winter line intact. However, it was not to be, as the best of these was *Creg Coneera (82)* whose dam was the good mare Lougheera (228), but sadly he did not make any lasting impression on the breed despite spending eight years on the list. The remaining four were either sold or left no progeny.

Tooreen Laddie (86) was also registered that year and was the last of Innishgoill Laddie's sons. He was bred by Luke Nee at Derryinver out of Grey Swan (475) who had no recorded breeding. He was on the list for four seasons before being sold to Col. Hume Dudgeon, in Stillorgan, Co. Dublin who in turn sold him to the USA in 1955 where he became the second stallion to be registered in the American Connemara Pony Stud Book. He left several useful daughters among his progeny including Fraoch Ban II (1542) and Leam Lassie (1838), and his son *Tooreen Ross*

Tooreen Laddie (86)

(99) inherited all his toughness and strength, which he passed on down this branch of the Blue Line.

26th Annual Pony Show, Clifden – 17th August 1949

In 1949 another silver cup was presented to the Society, this time by Lady Carew, Castletown House, Celbridge, Co. Kildare. It was to be awarded to the best Yearling or Two Year old pony at the Show, and was called the *Lady Carew Cup*. The first pony to win it was a yearling filly by Gil (43) dam Village Swallow (1061) bred by Paddy King, Lehid and exhibited by P. K. Joyce, Clifden, with the winning two year old filly Maumeen (1260) shown by Willie Diamond in Reserve, and the Killanin Cup went to White Linnet (1060) owned by Jack Bolger. Wireless Wave (477) owned by Mrs Kathleen Culley, Cleggan, won the Archbishop's Cup, and Jack Bolger once again won the Stallion Class with *Carna Bobby (79)*.

Wireless Wave (477)

Lavalley Rebel (24) was removed from the list at the end of the 1949 season, having served for 12 years in Connemara, and had 26 registered progeny born in Ireland. Among the best of his daughters were Rebel Kate

(736), Clare Dun (1266), Glen Belle (1342) and Windy Rebel (1473), and his only registered son Inver Rebel (93) was foaled after he had left Connemara.

Lavalley Rebel (24) was sold to John O'Mahony Meade, Chepstow, who with his wife Phyllis had been a regular visitors to Connemara and the Clifden Show since the end of the war. They had already bought a number of mares from Jack Bolger, and were among the earliest supporters of the breed in England. In Volume VII of the Stud Book which was published at the end of 1951, they are listed as the owners of five mares. They set up their successful Leam Stud at their home in Chepstow in Wales, and John O'Mahony Meade later became President of the English Connemara Pony Society.

There was still a steady demand for ponies, and they continued to be sold to England and to other parts of Ireland. There were good reports of Connemara ponies competing successfully in England, and at one important English show, ponies bred in Connemara filled the first five places in a class for all Mountain and Moorland breeds.

The first few ponies were exported to USA in 1950, sent out by Michael O'Malley, they included the black stallion *Tully Nigger (81)*, two mares, Winter Mollie (1323), and Victory Gill (1189), and a dun colt Lavalley Pride, but transport costs were so high to USA that it seemed unlikely that a trade could be opened up.

Three New Council Members, including First Lady Member

At the AGM held in April 1950 three new members were added to the Council, they were Miss E. B. Berridge, Screebe, who was the first woman to be appointed to the Council, Mr Roderic Kelly, MRCVS, a nephew of Mr T. McD. Kelly, MRCVS and Mr Paddy Daly, Lough Mask House, Ballinrobe. The Council had changed considerably since the formation of the Society in 1923, and only seven of the original founder members still remained. Mr R. Kelly and Mr Paddy Daly were both appointed to the Inspection Committee.

Mr Tim Cotter had moved to Dublin on his retirement from the Department of Agriculture, but he remained a member of the Inspection Committee and the Editing Committee, and continued to act as a judge at the Pony Show at Clifden every year until 1966. He was a familiar figure in the ring with his homburg hat and grey mackintosh, and he travelled to Galway twice a year for the Inspections and for the Show. He was a meticulous judge and paid great attention to detail, and he was invited to judge at the RDS Spring Show on many occasions when classes for Connemara ponies were first introduced there in the fifties.

Mr Dan Twomey also remained a member of the Inspection Committee, although he no longer acted as judge at the Annual Show, but he continued his interest in the Connemara pony, and as Secretary of the Department of Agriculture was able to be of considerable help the Society in their work.

Tim Cotter

The Connemara Pony Breeders' Society – 1950

Patrons
Most Rev. Dr Walsh, Archbishop of Tuam.
Most Rev. Dr Browne, Bishop of Galway.

President
V. Rev. C. Canon Cunningham, PP. VF. Clifden.

Vice Presidents
J. W. Mongan TD. Carna. *
C. J. Kerin,Oranmore. *
Lord Killanin, Spiddal.

Hon. Secretaries
Michael J. O'Malley, Rosmuck. *
Bartley O'Sullivan, County Buildings, Galway. *

Council
The President and Vice Presidents.
Timothy Cotter, 21 Woodlands Drive,Stillorgan. *
D. Twomey, 51 Landsdowne Road, Dublin. *
V. Rev. Fr. Hanrahan,PP. Letterfrack.
V. Rev. Fr. Heffernan, Blackrock Road, Cork.
V. Rev. Fr. Corcoran,PP. Carna.
P. D. Joyce, Seaview, Clifden.
V. Rev. Fr. W. Moran,PP. Rosmuck.
Frank McCabe, Dalysfort Road,Galway.
Comdt. Dan Corry, Palmerston, Dublin.
Roderic Kelly MRCVS. Galway.
P. Daly, Lough Mask House, Ballinrobe.

Henry G. Connolly, Solicitor, Clifden.
T. McD. Kelly MRCVS. Athenry. *
P. O'Droighnean, Moycullen.
Sean MacGiollarnaith. DJ. Fort Eyre,Galway.
V. Rev. Fr. Moran,PP. Carraroe.
Sean Keane, Newcastle, Galway.
Richard Curley, Prospect Hill, Galway.
Peadar O'Scannaill MRCVS. Clifden.
C. Howard,B. Agrl. Sc. Galway.
Peter Walsh, Inverin.
Miss E. B. Berridge, Screebe.

denotes founder member of the Council.

27th Annual Pony Show, Clifden – 16th August 1950

The Show in 1950 had increased entries of 213 ponies and the stallion class was won by *Man of Barna (73)* s. Silver Pearl (18) d. Lily of the Valley (738) for Joe Hoade, Barna, who also won the two year old filly class with Rose of Barna (1337) by *Man of Barna (73)* d. White Nell (962). Colman Griffin won the RDS Silver Medal for senior mares with Windy (782) s. Heather Bell (15) d. Furnace Lass (366), and the Archbishop's Cup for the best broodmare went to Orphan Maid (675) s. Innishgoill Laddie (21) owned by Major Crean, Portnoo.

An Auction Sale was held on the day of the Annual Show at the Showgrounds, and the particulars of the ponies for sale were given in the Show catalogue. It was conducted by P. K. Joyce, the auctioneer from Clifden, and almost all the Show entries were listed for sale. Six of the Society owned young stallions were entered, but only one was sold on the day, *Glentrasna (84)* and he was bought by Dick Curley, a member of the Council. There is no record of how many ponies were sold, but the Auction was held again in 1951 and 1952, and then dropped the following year, and so maybe it did not prove to be successful.

The winning two year old colt at the Show was *Carna Dun (89)* sire Little Heaven (TB) dam Double Dun (803), owned and bred by John Mylotte, Carna, and having won his class, he then went on to win the Carew Cup for the best yearling or two year old. He was purchased in September 1950 by the Society for £65, and was the only two year old colt registered that year. He was the third TB X Connemara stallion to be registered by the Society, the others being *Adventure (11)* and *Creganna Winter ((63)*, and of the three, he was to have by far the biggest impact on the breed. He entered the list of approved stallions for the 1951 season and spent his first year at stud with Brendan Burke, Claddaghduff, before moving to John de Courcey, Roundstone in 1952.

His sire *Little Heaven* spent his last year on the list in 1951, and when in 1952 he was found to have a cataract in his eye, the Dept. of Agriculture (who issued the stallion licenses) ordered that he should be castrated due to unsoundness. He was castrated and was subsequently sold at Athenry market, but sadly there is no further account of him.

Classes for Connemara Ponies at RDS Spring Show

In 1951 the Royal Dublin Society offered to arrange for classes for Connemara Ponies to be included in their Spring Show for the first time. The Show was held in May and was an Agricultural Show catering for all breeds of cattle, sheep, pigs, and the horse section included children's' riding ponies, hacks, polo ponies, and harness horses. The Council decided to draw up a list of suitable ponies, and invited their owners to exhibit them in Dublin. The ponies were inspected before they could be entered for the Show, and Sean Keane was put in charge of all the organisation, including the transport, selection of the best ponies, the provision of grooms to accompany the ponies and accommodation in Dublin.

The selection took place in early March, and was held at the Inspection centres. Three classes were included in the schedule:

(1) Registered Connemara Pony Mare 7 years old and over.
(2) Registered Connemara Pony Mare 3 to 7 years old.
(3) Two Year Old Filly, the progeny of Registered sire and dam.

Mr T. McD. Kelly was invited to judge at the Show, and there were 34 entries, 21 of them from Connemara. The senior mare class was won by Garnet Irwin with her good mare Ciro (551) by Silver Pearl (18), and in second place was a 19 year old mare by Rebel (7), Carna Rose (231), whose dam Rose (117) had won the RDS Silver

Garnet Irwin and Ciro (551) at Spring Show, 1951

76

Medal four times at the early shows in Connemara in late 20's and early 30's. Lorelie (1263) by Dun Lorenzo (55) bred by Mrs Anne Goodbody won the class for young mares, while Willie Diamond won the 2 year old class with a filly by Dun Lorenzo.

Some adverse criticism was voiced about the ponies, saying that they were in poor condition, but it was difficult to produce ponies from Connemara looking their best so early in the year, as they would not normally have shed their winter coats by early May, and in those days the ponies would not have been housed or given extra feeding to prepare them for a show. Despite these difficulties, the Council was anxious that the RDS would continue to provide classes for Connemara Ponies, as the Show was a good shop window for the breed, and several of the ponies exhibited at the Show had been sold for good prices.

Death of Josie Mongan TD

During 1951 the Society lost one of its outstanding founder members, Josie Mongan T. D. , who died on 12th March 1951, on the day after his 71st birthday. He became ill in the car on his way to Dail Eireann, and was taken to Clifden Hospital where he died later that evening. His good friend Canon Cunningham PP, President of the Connemara Pony Breeders' Society and his wife were with him when he died.

In the Connacht Tribune Josie was described as the *"greatest champion of the Connemara people that had ever arisen. Due to his untiring efforts, Connemara has received so much special treatment from successive governments over the past 25 years. Governments could come and go, but Josie, it seemed, went on for ever. "*

He was a founder member and the first Vice President of the Connemara Pony Breeders' Society and held that office from 1924 until his death. He was also a founder member and past President of the Irish Tourist Association, founder member and President of the Hotels Federation, and elected representative of the Irish Sea Fisheries Association. He had devoted all his public life to working for the good of Connemara and its people, and from the very beginning was a driving force in the work of the Connemara Pony Breeders' Society.

His hospitality as proprietor of Mongans Hotel in Carna was legendary, and it was largely thanks to his enthusiasm and hard work that the Annual Show at Carna survived through the difficult years of the war. He was

James Mongan, Canon Cunningham PP,
Josie Mongan TD, Michael O'Malley

first elected as Cumann na nGaedheal Member for West Galway in 1927, and remained a T. D. for the rest of his life. Coming from the Irish speaking district of Carna, he had a great love of the Irish language, and always spoke in Irish in Dail Eireann. He was a personal friend of Mr William T. Cosgrave, and invited him to attend the Annual Show at Roundstone in 1931. He was survived by his wife Maureen, his brother James, and his sisters, Mrs M. Mylotte, Carna, and Agnes and Monica Mongan who owned the Glendalough Hotel, Recess.

John Killeen Elected Member of the Council

Also in 1951 a new member was elected to the Council who was to devote much of the latter years of his life to the Connemara Pony Breeders' Society, he was John Killeen. He was born on a small farm in Knock, Co. Mayo in 1897, and was one of six children. His mother died when he was ten, and because of the poverty in Ireland, particularly in Co. Mayo during the 1920s, four of the family emigrated to the United States. John won a scholarship to Mountbellew Agricultural College, and later to Athenry Agricultural College, and joined the Department of Agriculture in 1920. He worked in Donegal and Mayo before coming to Galway in 1937 where he became Supervisory Inspector for the Congested Districts area of Connaught which also included Donegal, Clare, Kerry and West Cork. He knew both Bartley O'Sullivan and Sean Keane through his work, and it was through them that he became involved in the work of the Connemara Pony Breeders'Society. He retired from the Department in 1962, and succeeded Bartley O'Sullivan when he was appointed Secretary of the Society in 1963.

28th Annual Pony Show, Clifden – 16th August 1951

Lord Killanin joined Messrs C.J. Kerin, T. Cotter and T. McD. Kelly MrCVS to judge the 1951 Show and there were 173 entries. Jack Bolger won the stallion class with *Carna Bobby (79)* and Mrs K. Culley, Cleggan won the Archbishop's Cup for the best broodmare with Wireless Wave (477), and the Killanin Cup went to Clare Dun (1266) s. Lavalley Rebel (24) d. Miss McGauley(749) owned by Mrs Hall, Emlaghmore, Ballyconneely. Val Keaney (Pat) Callancruic, Cashel won the Carew Cup with his yearling filly by Tiger Gill (68) d. Calla Lass (433).

For the three years 1949 to 1951 the wording for the youngstock classes at the Annual Show was changed from, *"the progeny of Registered Connemara Pony sire and dam"* to *"the progeny of Registered Connemara Pony mare and an approved stallion."* This change was in order to accommodate the progeny of the Approved sires, the two Irish Draughts and the T. B. *Little Heaven*. However, following a complaint from an exhibitor who objected to the progeny of *Little Heaven* competing in the same class as purebred Connemara ponies, special classes were provided in 1952 and 1953 for progeny of the approved stallions.

This was in fact a short term measure, as the Council decided in 1951 that no further first-cross ponies should be registered. The two Irish Draught Stallions were both removed from the list in 1950, and *Little Heaven's* last season was 1951. However the decision was modified at a Council meeting the following year when it was felt that cutting out every first-cross pony was too drastic a measure to take at that stage of development, and that it should be at the discretion of the Inspection Committee to allow some first-cross ponies to be registered, but only if they considered the pony to be typical of the breed and to be of exceptional merit.

One of the ponies to benefit from this decision was May Retreat (1569) by *May Boy ID* who subsequently won her class in 1955 and later became a valued foundation mare for Miss Blanche Miller in England. Another was Pollnaclough Grey (1518) also by *May Boy ID* who was a good brood mare for Michael Keady, Pollnaclough, Moycullen and the dam of several successful ponies.

Two colts were registered in 1951, the first was *Strongbow (90)* who was black. Bought by the Society as a foal from Festy Folan, Kilkerrin, he was the only remaining son of *Calla Rebel (38)*, and his dam An tSailcuach (663) was by Lavalley Star (25). He was not kept for use in Connemara, and was sold to Cloghran Stud, Co. Dublin as a teaser the same year. However later on in his life he was bought by Miss Lee Norman, and stood at her Clonkeehan Stud in Slane for several years before being exported to Germany at the age of twenty.

The second colt registered that year was *MacDara (91)*, who had been bought by the Society after winning the yearling colt class in 1950. He was bred by John McCahill, Roundstone, and was by Dun Lorenzo (55) dam Dolan Rose (1132). He was a dun like so many of the Red Line, and also inherited his sire's strong constitution and good temperament, and he proved to be a worthy representative of this line to carry it into the next generation. He remained on the list for twenty years from 1952 to 1972 and had 267 registered progeny. He had a profound influence on the breed during the period when new societies were being formed overseas, and many of his progeny became their foundation stock.

Milleder Archive

Strongbow (90)

Volume VII of the Stud Book

The seventh volume of the Stud Book was published at the end of 1951, covering the period from September 1947 to August 1951, and included 19 stallions and 295 mares. With the exception of five, all the stallions had been bought by the Society as part of the scheme to purchase colt foals which was started in 1934, but after 1947 the numbers of colts bought in had been reduced, and only a few specially selected colts were purchased in later years. There was also a noticeable increase in number of owners living outside Connemara listed in this Volume, which showed how the breed was extending to new breeders who realised the value of owning registered stock. Among those in other parts of Ireland were: Lady Carew, Kildare, Mrs Cochrane, Donegal, Miss Lee Norman, Slane, Col. C. T. Walsh, Kilkenny, Kevin McLoughlin, Donegal.

Jack Bolger won the stallion class at Clifden in 1951 with *Carna Bobby (79)*, and it was the last time that Jack showed the winning stallion, as in October 1951 he moved from Oughterard to Cashel and after 20 years he ceased to be a stallion custodian. During that time he won the stallion class fourteen times with seven different stallions, an achievement which has never been equalled.

He had a record five wins with *Noble Star (17)* in the thirties, he also won twice each with *Innishgoill Laddie (21)*, *Silver Pearl (18)* and *Carna Bobby (79)*, and once each with *Dun Lorenzo (55)*, *Tiger Gill (68)* and *Lavalley Rebel (24)*. Jack handled a great many of the Society's stallions during their first season at stud, and he stood both the T. B sires *Winter* and *Little Heaven* while they were in Connemara, and also had the Irish Draughts *Skibbereen* and *May Boy*. In 1950 he stood four stallions in his yard at Oughterard, but mostly he had two if not three each season.

After his move to Cashel he turned his attention to producing mares for the Show ring, and was equally successful, winning the supreme championship on many occasions, and a steady stream of good ponies passed through his hands.

Jack Bolger with Carna Bobby (79)

80

CHAPTER 6

1952-1959

• Death of Canon Cunningham PP VG • New President Lord Killanin. Two Vice Presidents •
• Visiting Judges • Mare Subsidy Scheme • Clonkeehan Auratum purchased • Death Christy Kerin •
• Volume VIII Stud Book • Draught Rules for Society • Volume VIII Stud Book. • Gelding Register •
• American Connemara Pony Society • Inspections Outside Connemara • TFCs •

Little Heaven (TB) was the last of the approved stallions used to introduce outside blood to stand in Connemara, and he was removed from the list at the end of 1951. In 1952 his son *Carna Dun (89)* was standing at Roundstone with John de Courcey, while the other TB X Connemara sire *Creganna Winter (63)* was placed with Peter Connolly, Bealdangan, and his son *Creg Coneera (82)* was at Inverin with John Hoban.

The Irish Draught blood line was represented by *Farravane Boy (71)* son of *May Boy*, and he stood along side *Carna Dun (89)* at Roundstone. The Blue Line was rather heavily represented with seven stallions from that blood line. *Innishgoill Laddie (21)*, by then aged 18, was moved to Tom Fahy at Kilcolgan, and *Calla Rebel (38)* went to Michael Conroy, Bunowen. *Gil (43)* had been removed from the list, but four of his sons were included, they were *Carna Bobby (79)* and *Cilcairain (78)* who were both in Oughterard, *Tiger Gill (68)* in Cashel, and *Coill Ruadh (80)* at Clifden.

The Red Line had three representatives with *Dun Lorenzo (55)* and his two sons *Dun Orphan (77)* and *MacDara (91)*.

Tully Lad (48), the sole survivor of the Green Line, was not placed during the 1951 or 1952 seasons, but was turned out to grass at Killola. These were the male bloodlines which still remained intact, and the most prolific was the Blue Line.

The Royal Dublin Society again included classes for Connemara ponies at their Spring Show in 1952, and ten pony mares were selected by the Society's inspectors to be exhibited at the Show. This time they were better prepared and favourable reports were received afterwards.

29th Annual Pony Show, Clifden – 13th August 1952

At the 1952 Show a gelding class was included for the first time which attracted good entries. The stallion class was won by *Carna Dun (89)* shown by John de Courcey, and Joseph Walsh, Callowfeenish won the Archbishop's Cup with Lucky Lady (1139) whose dam Film Star (245) won the RDS Silver Medal at Carna in

1941. The Killanin Cup was won by Willie Diamond with Hasty Bits (1405), while Paddy Geoghegan won the Carew Cup with his two year old filly Silver Lining (1444) s. Carna Bobby (79).

Death of Canon Cunningham PP. VF. President of the Society

At a Council meeting held on 7th October 1952 Mr C. J. Kerin announced the sad news that their much loved President Canon Cunningham PP VF had died, and he paid tribute to the assistance and encouragement the late Canon Cunningham had always given to the Society during the long period he had been connected with it. He had been President of the Connemara Pony Breeders' Society for 19 years, and was unfailing in his generous hospitality to the members of the Council on the many occasions when they had been his guests. He had done much to promote the work of the Society, and would be greatly missed.

Lord Killanin Elected President

The Annual General Meeting was held on 31st March 1953 at which a successor to Canon Cunningham was to be appointed, and Lord Killanin was unanimously elected as the new President of the Society. This was a break with tradition in that the three former Presidents had all been priests, and this was the first time a layman had been appointed to the office.

Lord Killanin had been a Vice President of the Society since 1947 and had always shown a great interest in the Connemara pony and the work of the Society. He was Chairman of the Galway Races for sixteen years, a member of the Turf Club, and hunted with the Galway Blazers. He became head of the Olympic Council of Ireland in 1950, and two years later was appointed to the International Olympic Committee. His interests were wide and varied, he was a journalist, an author, and a founder member of An Taisce. He was on the Board of several large companies such

Lord Killanin and Bartley O'Sullivan

as Irish Shell, and was co-author of the Shell Guide to Ireland. The Society was indeed fortunate that a man of his outstanding ability should agree to become its President. Two new Vice-Presidents were appointed and joined Mr C. J. Kerin, they were Very Rev. D. Corcoran PP Clifden, formerly PP of Carna, and Very Rev J. W. Moran PP Rosmuck.

New members of the Council were John Mannion TD. Clifden and E. D. Moran PC. Clifden, John Geoghegan, Carna, Willie O'Malley, Ballinafad, and for the first time six honorary members of the Council were appointed: Tim Cotter, Dublin, Dan Twomey, Dublin, Very Rev Heffernan, Cork, Lt. Col Dan Corry, Dublin, Lady Carew, Celbridge, Col C. H. Walsh Kilkenny.

Lord Killanin assured members of the Council that he would do his best to promote the good work started by the Society, and so ably carried on up to this. The Government policy was to promote the development of our own resources, and he felt the Connemara Pony Breeders' Society was doing its share in such development. Our ponies constituted a valuable asset, and by running one of the most popular small shows in the country, the Society was also helping in the development of the tourist industry.

Death of ECPS Secretary, Miss Spottiswoode

In 1953 the English Connemara Pony Society suffered a sad loss when their founder member Miss Cynthia Spottiswoode was knocked down by a car in Ascot and killed. This was only six years after the forming of the ECPS, and could have been the end of the Society too, but fortunately two very able people took over, John O'Mahony Meade as Chairman and Mrs Louise Barthorp as Secretary, and in their capable hands the ECPS flourished and grew in strength.

30th Annual Pony Show, Clifden – 13th August 1953

The 1953 Annual Show was a special day for Garnet Irwin who won the Killanin Cup with her 3 year old mare Camlin Cilla (1447), and her mare Ciro (551), who was Cilla's dam, won the Archbishop's Cup. In the old mares class Patrick Conneely, Doon, Claddaghduff won the RDS Silver Medal with his mare Doon Lily (1259), and her foal by Carna Dun (89) was placed first in the colt foal class. The Society bought him after the Show and he was registered in 1955 as *Doon Paddy (95)*.

In 1954 another stallion from the Blue Line was added to the list, he was *Inver Rebel (93)*, son of *Lavalley Rebel (24)* and his dam was Inver Bridge (459). He had been bought as a foal at Maam Cross fair, and was bred by Pat (Michael) Mulkerrin, Callowfeenish. He was placed with Joe Little, Bunowen, and replaced *Coill Ruadh (80)* who was rejected for unsoundness in 1953.

Farravane Boy (71) was also taken off the list at the end of the 1953 season, and was subsequently sold to USA where he became No. 1 in the American Connemara Pony Stud Book.

Draught Rules for the Society

The AGM was held in Galway in April 1954 with Lord Killanin in the chair. For the past thirty years the Society had been run by the Council with very simple rules, and there was no real provision for Members of the

Society. Those who wished to support the work of the Society by making a contribution to the Society's funds were most welcome, but this did not entitle the benefactor to any special status. Bartley O'Sullivan had been pressing for some time that the position with regard to "Members" had never been defined, and he proposed that the Rules of the Society should be revised and a suitable constitution for the Society should be drawn up.

It was therefore decided that a sub-committee consisting of Lord Killanin, Sean Keane and Bartley O'Sullivan should be asked to prepare a draft constitution and rules to be submitted to the Council for approval. There were now a number of breeders outside Connemara, both in Ireland and in England, and the question of the registration of ponies outside the Society's district needed to be addressed. It was decided that the rules for registration would also be revised by the sub-committee.

Mrs Barthorp had written to enquire if the Society would permit foals born in England from registered stock imported directly from Ireland to be entered in the Connemara Pony Stud Book. The Council decided that for the meantime the English Connemara Pony Society were to be asked to nominate a suitable judge to inspect their ponies, and to send particulars to the CPBS for approval.

The Society continued to select and sponsor entries from Connemara for the RDS Spring Show, and Sean Keane was in charge of all the arrangements for the ponies travelling from Connemara to the Show. A special "Livestock Train" was provided by CIE, (the railway company) which transported all livestock exhibits travelling to the Show at Ballsbridge and it left Galway at 9am and arrived at a special siding in Ballsbridge opposite the Showgrounds at 2.30pm. Similar Livestock Specials were arranged from other parts of Ireland such as Cork, Limerick, Wexford, Sligo to bring animals to the Spring Show. The trains stopped at all the stations en route, and more animals, cattle, sheep, pigs, or ponies could join the train at each station. The RDS sponsored the travel costs and paid for the journey to the Show, the exhibitor was responsible for the cost of the return trip.

31st Annual Pony Show, Clifden – 12th August 1954

For the first time in 1954, a Visiting Judge was invited to join Christy Kerin and Tim Cotter to judge at the Annual Show at Clifden, and Mrs Nicholson of Kells, Co. Meath, owner of the Arab stallion Naseel, was chosen. The number of entries at the Show had been declining in recent years, and so in order to encourage breeders from the outlying districts in Connemara to bring their ponies to the Show, the Council decided to arrange transport, and lorries were provided from Galway, Kilkerrin, Carna and Recess.

The Stallion Class was the first class of the day, and that year it was decided that the stallion class should be judged outside the Showgrounds on the Fair Green at 11 am. This is where the stables are built today. It could hardly have been considered a safer place for

Lord Killanin presenting cup to Willie Diamond with Five of Diamonds.

showing the stallions than the main showgrounds, as there was no way of controlling the jostling crowds of spectators who lined the road as the stallions were trotted out for the judges, but the judging of the stallion class continued to take place on the Fair Green from 1954 until 1966.

MacDara (91) won the stallion class for Anthony Faherty, Moyard, and the Archbishop's Cup for the best brood mare in the Show, was won by the Christian Brothers, Letterfrack with Pretty Star (998). Willie Diamond won the Killanin Cup with Five of Diamonds (1524), and the Carew Cup went to the winning yearling filly by Carna Dun (89) exhibited by Miss Lee Norman from Slane, with the winning yearling colt also by *Carna*

Clifden Showgrounds in the '50s.

Dun (89), shown by John de Courcey in Reserve. The young stock classes were dominated by *Carna Dun (89)* with his progeny taking the first three places in both the yearling classes, and he was also the sire of the winning two year old filly.

Mare Subsidy Scheme

Earlier that year four members of the Council met with representatives from the Department of Agriculture to discuss a new scheme for retaining selected premium mares to be mated with selected stallions.

The purpose of the scheme was to try to encourage breeders to hold their best young fillies to breed from, and so reduce the number of high class breeding stock being exported out of Connemara.

A small committee was formed to consider the scheme, and it was proposed that six subsidies would be offered in 1955 value £10 each, to selected two year old fillies who were the progeny of registered stock. The selected fillies were to be covered by a stallion approved by the Society, and they could not be sold before reaching the age of six years. The subsidy would also be paid the following year, and inspections for these subsidies and for selection for entries for the Spring Show were held in November 1954.

Society Buys Colt Foal by Arab Stallion, Naseel

In October 1954 the Council decided to buy a dun colt foal bred by Miss Lee Norman, Slane out of her Connemara mare Western Lily (1522) and by Naseel, the Arab stallion owned by Mrs Nicholson, Kells.

Naseel was a quality Arab pony sire, foaled in 1936, he was by Raftan out of Naxina, a light grey and stood 14. 1 hh. Naseel was the most fashionable pony sire in the late 40's and 50's, and Miss Lee Norman, and Miss Berridge, both used him on their Connemara mares. Western lily (1522) was by *Innishgoill Laddie (21)* out of Western Echo (1168) who was by *Paddy (28)*, so she had a solid old Connemara background to blend with the Arab blood.

The foal had been inspected for the Society by Tim Cotter, and he had sent a favourable report in which he stated:

"He is well balanced, full of quality with good bone, good mover, nice head with pony character; he is darker (more golden cream) than Carna Dun but not so dark as MacDara; he has no trace of white or cream in the skin or about the eyes. The only faults I could see are that he is a little short of bone above and below the hocks and that his neck is a little short, but he holds his head very well. I could not fault his colour. I think he is a very good foal. He is well done though not looking his best yesterday as he had been dosed for worms".

Tim Cotter went on to say that it would be difficult to give him the care and feeding he was getting at the present time, and that he could not say if he was worth the high price that was being asked for him. The Council decided to buy him, although his price was £115, the highest they had ever paid for any stallion, and twice what they had paid for *Carna Dun (89)* as a two year old.

Fortunately for the Society they had a most generous offer from Col. Bellingham of Mullingar, Co. Westmeath to keep the colt free of charge until he was ready to be registered, and the Council accepted the offer gladly. He was named *Clonkeehan Auratum*, and was introduced to Connemara very cautiously at first. As a two year old, he was placed with Joe Hoade at Barna for the 1956 season, and was limited to twenty mares selected by the CPBS. An additional fee of £2 with a nomination ticket was charged.

Naseel (Arab)

He moved to Anthony Faherty, Moyard in 1957 and again was limited to twenty mares, but the additional fee was reduced to £1. He was not registered until the Spring of 1958 when he was four years old, and not until after he had spent this two year trial period in Connemara. He was then accepted into the Connemara Pony Stud Book without further restrictions, and registered as number 104. A special class was provided for him at Clifden Show in 1957 to show this quality Arab X Connemara sire to the breeders, and in 1958 he was included in the registered stallion class and was placed 3rd.

He spent one more year with Anthony Faherty at Moyard, and at the 1959 Show he won the stallion class, and his progeny made a big impact, with four sons taking first and second in the yearling colt class, first in the two year old colt class, and first in the colt foal class. In 1960 he was moved to Michael Conroy, Bunowen for three seasons, where he became a most popular sire, with many good mares visiting him, with the result that during that period, 102 progeny were registered by him. He then moved to Moycullen, where he spent his last two seasons in Connemara with Peter Kyne, before being removed from the approved list at the end of the 1964 season.

He spent the remainder of his life outside the district mostly with Tom Whelan at Ardrahan, where mares could still visit him, but the numbers were much fewer than when he was in the heart of Connemara.

Death of Christy Kerin

During the winter of 1954/55 the Council lost one of its most loyal members with the death of Christy Kerin. He was a founder member of the Society, a Vice-President since 1933, and a member of the Inspection committee since 1924. He had a good eye for a horse, and he acted as judge at every Society Show from 1924 to 1954 with only one exception when he was ill. He was a jovial big-hearted man, full of jokes and a great character. He was known as the Mayor of Oranmore and owned a pub in the village. His great interests were horses, racing, hunting and coursing and he kept Thoroughbred sires at Oranmore including the well bred TB. sire Thistleton who was the sire of *Adventure (11)*. He was fully committed to the work of the Society and rarely missed a Council meeting in 30 years. At the time of his death a lament for him was printed in the newspaper.

LAMENT FOR CHRISTOPHER KERIN

He's gone!
Hushed is the lonely village by the sea,
Where dwelt he four score years and five
In peace and harmony.

And in the country round,
Where oft he ranged with horse and hound,
The farmer pauses in his field
To hear that Christy's dead.
He heaves a sigh, and bows his head.

And in the city near,
Where all men knew and loved him,
They'll see his friendly face no more.

The RDS Spring Show in 1955 had an increased entry from Connemara with 19 ponies exhibited by breeders from the West of Ireland. There was an overall entry of 14 in the class for mares of six years or over, and 18 entries in the three, four and five year old class. Three of the first four places in the older mares class went to exhibitors from Connemara.

A surprise arrival at the Show was a dun colt foal by Dun Lorenzo (55) who was born on the first night of the Show to Knollwood (1237), a nine year old mare owned by John McDonagh, Kilkerrin. Mary Kelleher, who is now the Librarian at the RDS Library, is pictured with the new arrival at the Show, offering him a piece of her Frys Chocolate Cream! When the mare and foal were transported back to Connemara after the Show, CIE claimed an extra charge of £13 for the new born foal, which Bartley O'Sullivan disputed as being excessive and unreasonable, and that the unusual circumstances should be taken into account. The foal was none the worse for the journey, whatever it may have cost, and went on to win the colt foal class at Clifden in August that year.

Mary Kelleher

32nd Annual Pony Show at Clifden on 18th August 1955
At the 1955 Show, the President of the English Connemara Pony Society, Mr John O'Mahony Meade was invited to act as the visiting judge with the Society's judges Tim Cotter and T. McD. Kelly. *Carna Bobby (79)* won the stallion class for Festy King, Claddaghduff. Jack Bolger won the Killanin Cup with Cullahara (1601) by Tiger Gill (68), and the Archbishop's Cup for the best brood mare went to Suncloud (1636), owned by Dick Curley, and she was later sold to Mrs Charlotte Read in USA, who was to become the first Secretary of the American Connemara Pony Society in 1957. The RDS Silver Medal for mares over 7 years went to Ballinahinch Grey (1087) owned by Thomas McHugh, Truska.

Draft Memorandum and Articles of Association
A meeting of the Council was held on 11th October 1955 at which the Draft Memorandum and Articles of Association for the proposed company were submitted to the Council by the Secretary, Bartley O'Sullivan, and the following resolution was passed unanimously.

"It is hereby resolved that the Society be formed into a Limited Company not having a share capital, under the title Cumann Lucht Capaillíní Chonamara; that the draft Memorandum and Articles of Association be adopted as the Memorandum and Articles of Association of the Company."

This was the first step to revise the rules of the Society, but it was to take four years before the new Company was finally established. The Draft had to be approved by the Department of Industry and Commerce, and when it was originally sent to the Department written in Irish, no reply was received for a year. In the meantime the Council was unable to make any changes to the rules of the Society, and with more breeders in England and USA as well as other parts of Ireland wanting to register the progeny of registered stock, this delay created many problems for the Secretary, Bartley O'Sullivan.

_____

The exporting of ponies continued both to England and in small numbers to USA, and the stallion *Tooreen Laddie (86)* was bought from the Society by Col. Hume Dudgeon, Dublin, who exported him to USA. A good report was received from the new owner in the States who stated that the stallion had been *"attracting a good deal of favourable attention."*

Volume VIII of the Stud Book

In the introduction to the eighth volume of the Stud Book which was published in the autumn of 1955, it was mentioned that the prices at foal fairs were disappointing, and that home trade had been quieter.

The demand for working horses was declining as mechanisation was gradually creeping into rural Ireland, and to Connemara, and the increased prices for cattle and sheep made pony breeding seem less profitable, with the result that there had been a drop in the number of pony foals being reared.

It was not yet realised that a new and very profitable market was about to open up, and that the Connemara Pony was going to be in great demand overseas and would become an international success in the years to come.

Geldings included on Register

Two more stallions owned by the Society were registered in this Volume, the first was *Camlin Cirrus (94)* by Gil (43), dam Ciro (551) who spent four years on the list from 1955 to 1958, and *Doon Paddy (95)* by Carna Dun (89) dam Doon Lily (1259) who was placed with Paddy Joyce, Oughterard in 1956. In the same year the Council decided to provide a special section in the Stud Book for registered geldings, and they were to be inspected in the same way as the fillies.

33rd Annual Pony Show, Clifden
– 16th August 1956

In 1956 John O'Mahony Meade returned to Clifden to act as visiting judge with Tim Cotter and T. McD Kelly MRCVS at the 33rd Annual Pony Show, and *MacDara (91)* won the stallion class for Anthony Faherty, Moyard. Paddy King, Lehid won the RDS Medal for senior mares with Village Swallow (1061), and Cullahara (1601), a dun five year old mare by Tiger Gill (68), won the

Cushatrough Lass (1650)

89

Archbishop's Cup for Jack Bolger, with Tommy McDonagh taking the Killanin Cup with Cushatrough Lass (1650).

Martin Lee, Dunloughan won the yearling filly class with his Carna Dun (89) filly, who was registered as Flash Girl (1771) and this was the start of her successful showing career. She won her class every year she was shown except as a two year old when she was 2nd. She was one of the mares selected under the new premium mare scheme, and she remained in Connemara to breed six foals, before being sold in 1964 to Tommy McDonagh who sold her to Mrs Westenra from Jersey, Channel Islands for £400, a record price at that time.

Three of her foals were by MacDara (91) and included *Atlantic Storm (139)* who became a Society owned stallion, and three by Clonkeehan Auratum (104) two of which were among the first ponies exported to Germany, Flash Princess (2309) and *Flashy Lad (196)*.

Col. Bellingham lived at Glencara, Mullingar, and he bought a large number of Connemara ponies during the 50's and 60's. He was a regular exhibitor in the Connemara pony classes at the RDS Spring Show and had ten mares registered in his name in Volume IX of the Stud Book. He exported ponies to England and USA and used the prefix Glencara. He also looked after the young colt Clonkeehan Auratum for the Society from a weaned foal to a 2 year old, and took a great interest in the work of the Society. He was invited to act as visiting judge at the 1957 Clifden Show, together with the Society's regular judges, Tim Cotter and T. McD. Kelly MRCVS.

34th Annual Pony Show, Clifden – 18th August 1957

Both the Annual Show at Clifden and the Connemara pony classes at the RDS Spring Show were attracting an increasing number of visitors, and had become the shop windows for the breed. The trade for ponies to the USA had increased dramatically in the space of a few years, and the export of ponies to England also continued. At the 1957 Show at Clifden, ten out of the class of 15 two year old fillies were sold overseas.

The Carew Cup winner for the best one or two year old was a yearling colt shown by Mrs Anne Goodbody and bred by Mrs Kitty Marriott, Moyard. He was by Mac Dara (91) out of her good mare Wireless Wave (477) who won two RDS Silver Medals at Clifden in 1949 and 1951. He was a well made colt, but his coat colour was cream and he had blue eyes, which caused some controversy among breeders. However, at that time there was no ruling against BECs, and he was later registered as the stallion *Marconi (107)* for Stanislaus Lynch, and subsequently exported to Robert Wright, Georgia USA in 1959, where he won many prizes including 1963 Grand Champion and Model Connemara.

His new owner in the States was to become the largest importer of Connemara ponies in the following years, and Stanislaus Lynch who was a well-known horseman, author and equestrian journalist based in Co. Dublin, was commissioned to select suitable ponies for the Rose Hill Herd. He enlisted the help of Michael Clancy from Spiddal, and between them they shipped over sixty ponies to Robert Wright in the late 50's and early 60's.

In those days the journey was long and quite stressful for the ponies, as they were shipped in open crates, lashed to the decks of ocean freighters. The crossing often took more than two weeks, during which time the ponies could scarcely move, and thus unprotected, were subjected to whatever weather the ship found in its path. On arrival at the busy docks in New York, they then faced a long overland journey by lorry to reach their final destination, but their natural hardiness and good temperament ensured that they survived the journey, even if they were described as "looking a bit rough" on arrival.

Among the earliest arrivals in the USA were two stallions, *Tully Nigger (81)* and *Lavalley Pride*, and two mares, Winter Mollie (1323) by Creganna Winter (63) and Victory Gill (1189) by Gil (43), who were bought by Mr George Ohrstrom and his daughter in 1950. The following spring, Whitewood Irish Eve and her brother Whitewood Irish Adam were foaled at

Stanislaus Lynch with ponies from Rose Hill Farm.

the Whitewood Stud in The Plains, Virginia, and were much admired, and soon more Connemara ponies were imported into the USA by other breeders.

American Connemara Pony Society Formed 1957

In 1956 a group of these new breeders in the USA wrote to the Society with their plans to form a Society to promote the Connemara pony in the States, and in 1957 the American Connemara Pony Society came into being with Mrs Charlotte Read, Mass. as its first Secretary, just ten years after the English Connemara Pony Society had been formed.

The new Society decided to have similar rules to the Connemara Pony Breeders' Society, and a copy of the ACPS rules was sent to the Council for approval. The inspection of ponies before registration in the Stud Book had always been central to the policy of the CPBS and the American Connemara Pony Society aimed to follow the same registration procedure.

Creganna Winter (63), the half-bred son of *Winter (TB)*, had been moved out of Connemara after eight seasons, in the winter of 1955, and was sent to James Grealish Roger, Oranmore, where he stood for 1956 and 1957. Sadly in July 1957 he met with an accident, and had to be destroyed, having broken both his hind legs. He left 50 progeny including seven stallion sons, but only one of them, *Creg Coneera (82)* was used in Connemara, and he left few progeny.

Another son *Tarzan (102)* dam Glentrasna Grey (1154) was exported to Robert Wright, Georgia, USA in 1957, and was the first stallion at Rose Hill Farm where he proved to be a brilliant jumper.

Creganna Winter's most outstanding daughter was Winter Roche (1495), dam Dunroche (773) who was owned by Michael Conroy, Bunowen, and she won the Archbishop's Cup three years running in 1957, 1958 and 1959. Her foals included the stallion *Finney Master (306)*, and the mares Dark Winter (2020) and Frosty Winter (2346) and through them this successful female line has carried the Winter blood worldwide in succeeding generations. *Slieve Winter (1377)*, a daughter of Sliabh na mBan (227), was another to leave her mark on the breed through her son *Silver Rocket (523)*.

Tooreen Ross (99) was by *Tooreen Laddie (86)* and his dam Wayfarer (1210) was registered without breeding. He was bred by Michael Walsh, Rosscahill, and registered aged three years in 1957. His sire had been exported to the USA in 1955, and *Tooreen Ross (99)* was bought by the Society in March 1958 from Mark Geoghegan, Oughterard, and placed with James Grealish (Roger), Oranmore for the 1958 season. He then moved to Mikey King at Claddaghduff in 1959 where he remained until the end of 1962.

By 1958 the Council realised that the scheme for subsidising young mares had not been a success, and it was decided to discontinue it. There were problems with the administration of the scheme, and the results had not been satisfactory, as £10 a year was not sufficient incentive for a breeder to hold his young mare if he was offered a high price for her.

The Secretary of the English Connemara Pony Society, Mrs Barthorp wrote on behalf of her Society offering a special prize of £3 to be offered in each class at the RDS Spring Show for the best registered Connemara pony in the class, bred and located in Connemara and exhibited by an owner resident in Connemara. The special prizes were awarded for the first time in 1958, and over the years, Mrs Barthorp became a familiar figure at the ringside, always wearing her emerald green hat, as she waited to present the prizes. It was intended as a mark of encouragement to the owner breeder from Connemara who faced strong competition at the Spring Show from breeders living in Meath, Kildare, or Wicklow and rearing their ponies on better land.

Inspections Outside Connemara – Temporary Foal Certificates

The responsibilities of the Society were now growing, and one of the questions which had to be addressed was the registration of ponies bred outside the Connemara district. The Council decided that when there was an Inspector available, ponies bred in other parts of Ireland could be inspected for an extra fee, and provided that the travelling expenses of the Inspector were paid by the breeder. There were also some ponies being sold for export who were under two years old, which was the minimum age for registration in the Stud Book, and in order to provide these ponies with papers, the regulations for temporary foal certificates were introduced in October 1958.

35th Annual Pony Show, Clifden – 21st August 1958

John O'Mahony Meade, Chepstow once again acted as visiting judge with the two Society judges, Tim Cotter and T. McD Kelly MRCVS. Winter Roche (1495) won the Archbishop's Cup for the second year running for Michael Conroy, with Colman Griffin in Reserve with Windy (782), whose filly foal also won her class. Flash

Girl (1771) was the winner of the Killanin Cup and RDS Medal for young mares, and the stallion class went to *MacDara (91).*

The classes for cattle which had been a feature of the Show for many years were discontinued, although there were still five classes for sheep, but the Country Produce and Home Crafts Classes were as big as ever and well supported, with a total of over 450 exhibits.

The Country Produce classes included poultry, eggs, home made butter, jam, cakes, vegetables, fruit and flowers, while the Home Crafts section catered for hand knitting, crochet, embroidery, hand woven tweed, home made white flannel, leatherwork, rushwork, basket work, spinning, wool-dying from natural dyes, skin curing, and woodwork. These classes were an important element of the Show and were encouraged by the Irish Countrywomen's Association, whose members have continued to act as stewards for this section over the years. At the request of the Very Rev. Chancellor Corcoran P. P. Clifden who was a Vice-President of the Society, the Aeriocht, competitions for Irish Music and Dancing, which had lapsed after the Show moved from Carna, was revived for the 1956 Show, and has continued up to the present day, providing a colourful spectacle for visitors to the Show.

In November 1957, Bartley O'Sullivan had reported to the Council that the problems over the Incorporation of the Society had entailed lengthy correspondence between Mr Gavin, the Society's solicitor and the Department of Industry and Commerce over two years, and it seemed that the fact that the Memorandum and Articles of Association had been draughted in Irish was partly the cause of the delay. It was therefore agreed to submit the Memorandum and Articles of Association in English, but a year later in May 1958, no further progress had been made, and a strongly worded protest at the delay was sent to the Department.

36th Annual Pony Show at Clifden 20th August 1959

Miss Frances Lee Norman, of Clonkeehan, Slane was invited to act as visiting judge at the 1959 Show, and her co-judges were Tim Cotter and T. McD Kelly MRCVS. It was the first year that progeny from *Clonkeehan Auratum (104)* had appeared in any numbers at the Show, and the quality of his stock made a big impression on the youngstock classes. He won the stallion class himself, and his sons were 1st and 2nd in the yearling colts, and 1st in the two year old colts. He also sired the winning yearling filly, and the winner of the colt foal class. Small wonder that when he moved to Michael Conroy the following season he was a very popular sire, and there were 39 progeny registered by him in 1961. However in the senior

Garnet Irwin

Clonkeehan Auratum (104)

classes there was more of a balance, and the prizes were more evenly distributed, with all the sires being represented.

The Killanin Cup went to Village Belle (1855) owned by Paddy King, Lehid and she was to become one of the special mares of the breed whose sons and daughters have continued to carry her good female line with success into the following generations. Glen Nelly (1344), shown by John Mylotte, Carna, was another mare who was successful in the fifties, and she won the RDS Silver Medal for senior mares, and came reserve to Winter Roche (1495) who won the Archbishop's Cup for the third year running for Michael Conroy, Bunowen.

Josie Conroy with Winter Roche receiving cup.

Dun Lorenzo (55) was now aged 18 years and having spent 15 years of the hard life of a stallion travelling the roads in Connemara, it was decided that he should be retired at the end of the 1959 season. He had spent his last four seasons with the Conroys at Bunowen, and Josie Conroy still remembers him as his favourite of all the many stallions who passed through their hands. He was a remarkably tough pony and Josie often tells the story of the day when he was taking *Dun Lorenzo* out on his usual stallion round beside the bicycle, and they met a traveller driving a pony and cart. The traveller's pony was reputed to be one of the best trotting mares in Ireland, but despite trying to overtake Josie and *Dun Lorenzo* for several miles, they couldn't make an inch on them. Having stopped for a chat further along the road, the traveller was full of praise for the old pony and couldn't believe that he was 18 years old and still trotting out as fresh as a much younger pony. He was a very tough breed of pony, and although by today's standards he might not be considered a show winner, yet he had all the stamina and courage which were the real hallmarks of the Connemara pony.

In his 18 years in Connemara, *Dun Lorenzo (55)* had 169 registered progeny, and three of his sons were on the list, *Dun Orphan (77)* from 1949 to 1955, *MacDara (91)* from 1952 to 1972, and *Dun Aengus (120)* from 1962 to 1977.

Not all his progeny were successful in the Show ring, but he had many daughters who were good foundation broodmares, and amongst them were Kingstown Grey (1268), Brown Alice (1419), Lormount (1460), Drimeen Dun (1449), Star of Fahy (1453), Windy Dun (1803), Lor Copper (1947), Glentrasna Brown (1975), Truska Brownie (1997), Dark Winter (2020), Aughris Bright (2131), Early Sunrise (2153) and Wise Sparrow (2270). When he left Connemara, *Dun Lorenzo (55)* was sold in 1960 to Mrs Westaway in Ballina, Co.

Mayo and he spent several years in retirement before he was put down. He left behind him in Connemara a family of sons and daughters who carried on the best attributes of the Red Line, strength, stamina and toughness.

Two other stallions were sold at the end of the 1959 season *Camlin Cirrus (94)* was sold to John O'Mahony Meade, having spent four years with Charles Lynch, Bealadangan, and he left 13 registered progeny including Nansin Ban (1858), and Grey Girl (2021), both dams of future stallions.

Gael Linn (103) was owned by Tommy McDonagh, but was included on the list in 1958 and 1959. He was sold to Stanislaus Lynch after the 1959 Show, and exported to the Hon. O. C. Fisher, House of Representatives, Washington D. C. USA. He left some good progeny including Noreen Grey (2287) who was an outstanding broodmare for the Tulira Stud, also Glen Fanny (2266), dam of *Ballydonagh Bobby (242)* and the Society owned stallion *Ben Lettery (133)* who stood in Connemara from 1963 to 1974.

The Green Line

Among the young stallions who were registered in 1959 were two sons of *Tully Lad (48)* who were both to play their part in carrying on the Green Line into succeeding generations. The first, *Tully Grey (110)*, came 2nd in the two year old colt class that year shown by his owner Thomas Harold, Lanesboro, Co. Longford. He was bred at Moyrus, Carna by Paraic O'Cathain from a *Dun Lorenzo (55)* mare Cait ni Dhuibhir (1428), and spent all his life in Co. Longford with the Harold family, where he was hunted regularly, and competed in show jumping ridden by one of the nine Harold daughters, and won several prizes jumping at Ballsbridge. He was little used as a stallion, but through his son *Dale Haze (794)*, dam Abbeyleix Bluebird (6595), his great-grand son *Moy Hazy Cove (888)* stands in Connemara in 1998 to carry this branch of the Green Line.

The second stallion, *Thunder (113)* was out of a mare by *Lavalley Rebel (24)* called Saint Kathleen (1435), and was bred at Rosmuck by Michael Walsh. He was registered for Jim Lee, Moycullen who sold him to John Brennan, Fort Lorenzo, Galway in 1962. He was a plain pony with a heavy head and was registered as a dark roan, but was more a dark liver chestnut in colour. His most useful son was *Thunderbolt (178)* who was bred from Irene Grey (1899) by

Thomas Harold, Tully Grey (110) and Tommy McDonagh.

95

Farravane Boy (71) and was bought by the Society in 1965, to ensure that the male line from *Mountain Lad (32)* would remain intact.

In 1959 Mrs Charlotte Read, Hon Sec. of American Connemara Pony Society wrote to Bartley O'Sullivan sending a copy of Volume I of their Stud Book, which contained particulars of 21 stallions, 86 mares and 38 foals (temporary foal certificates). The members of Council were very impressed by the excellent way the Stud Book had been produced, and sent their appreciation of the work done by the ACPS for the Connemara pony.

Clifden Fair Green, 1953.

CHAPTER 7

1959-1963

• Adoption of Memorandum and Articles of Association • The New Society. New Studs •
• Death of Bartley O'Sullivan 1960 • Alice Burke Resigns • Sean Keane Acting Secretary •
• Mrs MacDermott Assistant Secretary • Office leaves County Buildings • Volume IX of Stud Book •

The Changeover to the New Society

It was now four years since the Council meeting of 11th October 1955 when the decision was taken to draw up the new Memorandum and Articles of Association, but finally after all the delays, a meeting of the Council was held at the Committee of Agriculture Office, Galway on 22nd December 1959, and the changeover to the new Society took place.

Present were: Lord Killanin in the chair, Messrs. S. Keane, P. O'Scanaill MRCVS. R. Kelly MRCVS. C. Howard, F. McCabe, P. Tiernan, J. Mannion, J. Killeen, E. D. Moran, W. Gavin, solicitor, B. O'Sullivan, Secretary. Apologies were received from T. McD. Kelly MRCVS.

The minutes of the last Council meeting and the Annual General Meeting were read and signed, the audited statement of accounts was adopted, and the solicitor, Mr Gavin, explained the procedure for the changeover of the Society.

In his address, Lord Killanin stated that this was the end of the original Connemara Pony Breeders' Society which was founded at a public meeting at Oughterard on 12th December 1923. He also stated that the only member of that original Society present was the Honorary Secretary, Mr Bartley O'Sullivan. He proposed a sincere vote of thanks to Mr O'Sullivan and to everybody who had worked down the years to bring the Society to the very strong position it now held in the world.

Mr McCabe, seconded the proposal, and also mentioned other outstanding figures in the Society in past years, the late Rev Father C. J. White, the late V. Rev Canon Cunningham, the late Mr Josie Mongan, and others who had helped in forming the Society and fostering its aims. Mr O'Sullivan thanked the members for their kind remarks.

This was the closing of a chapter in the history of the Connemara pony, and the changing from the old Society to the new Cumann Lucht Capaillini Chonamara, marked the end of an era. Many of those men whose vision and determination brought about the formation of the Connemara Pony Breeders' Society were no longer alive, and the only remaining founder members of the Council were: T. McD. Kelly MRCVS, Tim Cotter, Dan Twomey, Michael O'Malley, and Bartley O'Sullivan.

It must have been a poignant moment for Bartley O'Sullivan to have been the only representative of the original Council present at the changeover to the new Cumann.

Cumann Lucht Capaillini Chonamara

The opening meeting of the Cumann Lucht Capaillini Chonamara then followed, and the signatories to the Memorandum and Articles of Association were: Lord Killanin, Sean O'Cathain, Ernest D. Moran, Sean O'Cillin and John Mannion.

The Certificate of Incorporation of the Cumann was produced, and it was ordered that the certificate be framed and hung in the Registered Office of the Society. It was decided that for the time being the Auditor's Office should be the registered office of the Society. An official seal had been ordered for the Society.

The Annual subscription for members was fixed at ten shillings, and all those present were elected members of the new Cumann.

Lord Killanin was elected President, and Rev Father W. Moran PP and T. McD. Kelly MRCVS were elected Vice Presidents.

Three Patrons of the Society were appointed, Most Rev Dr Walsh, Archbishop of Tuam, Most Rev Dr Browne, Bishop of Galway, Very Rev Chancellor Corcoran PP Clifden.

Bartley O'Sullivan was unanimously elected as Secretary, but he regretted that he could not accept his appointment, although he agreed to act as Hon Secretary for a short time until the Cumann could arrange for his replacement. He proposed that his assistant Miss Alice Burke who was already familiar with the work of the Society should be appointed Assistant Secretary. For the past year Miss Burke had written the minutes for Bartley O'Sullivan, and was already doing much of the routine work in the office and in organising the Show. During the thirty five years since the founding of the Connemara Pony Breeders' Society, Bartley O'Sullivan had never missed a Council meeting, and had shouldered the burden of running the affairs of the Society almost single handed. In recent years he had been greatly assisted in the field work and the running of the Show by Sean Keane, but with the growth of the export market, the formation of the first two overseas Societies, and the growing world-wide interest in the Connemara pony, the work load was now considerably greater. He was now seventy years old, and it was understandable that he wished to stand down and hand over the running of the Society's affairs to a younger man.

During the first three months of 1960, two council meetings were held at which the following were elected as ordinary members of the Cumann Lucht Capaillini Chonamara: Eamonn Guy, Main Street, Clifden; Tom Walsh, Market Street, Clifden; T. J. McDonagh, Roundstone; James Lee, Moycullen; Miss Garnet Irwin, Moyard; Graham Tulloch, Moyard; John Daly, Lough Mask House, The Neale; Miss E. B. Berridge, Rathfarnham, Dublin; John Geoghegan, Carna; Michael J. O'Malley, Rosmuck; Mrs E. Petch, Kilbrittain, Co. Cork; Mrs A. B. Flint, Brittas Bay, Co. Wicklow; Sean Ward, Agricultural School, Athenry.

Honorary Members of the Society: Dan Twomey, Dublin; Tim Cotter, Dublin; Lt. Col. Dan Corry, Palmerstown, Co. Dublin; Lady Carew,Celbridge, Co. Kildare; R. J. Curley, Galway; Mr John O'Mahony Meade, President, English C. P. Society; Mrs Barthorp, Hon Sec. English C. P. Society; Mr H. Middendorf, President, American C. P. Society; Mrs Bruce Read, Hon Sec. American C. P. Society; Mrs Y. Cochrane, Northumberland.

Additional Members of the new Council: P. O'Scanaill MRCVS, Clifden; R. Kelly. MRCVS. Galway.; John Geoghegan, Carna; John Daly, Lough Mask House, The Neale.

In the early days of the Cumann Lucht Capaillini Chonamara, many of the breeders were not aware that the new rules now made it possible for them to become members and to subscribe towards the work of the Society, therefore the Council decided to send a circular to all breeders informing them of the conditions of membership of the Society, and the privileges of membership. As the Society was for the most part run by officers of the Department of Agriculture, the small breeder in Connemara did not regard the Society as separate from the Department, and very few became members at that time. There was however a growing interest in the Connemara Pony outside the district, and as more people from other parts of Ireland came to buy ponies, many new studs were established during the sixties, and these new breeders became the early members of the Society.

Miss Lee Norman had already established her Clonkeehan Stud at Slane, in the early fifties, and Miss Berridge had moved to Mervyn, Enniskerry, Co. Wicklow where she started breeding from her good foundation mare Windy Rebel (1473) who was bred by Colman Griffin at Screebe, beside her old home in Connemara.

During the fifties both ladies had used the Arab stallion Naseel on their Connemara mares, and apart from Clonkeehan Auratum (104) several more half-bred progeny were accepted into the Stud Book, notably Mervyn Nasim (2426) who was a lovely quality mare, bred from Windy Rebel (1473). She was the dam of Mervyn Wren (4037) and *Mervyn Pookhaun (528)* who were both to spend their lives at Milford Stud with Tom and Elizabeth Ormsby at Tuam. Two from the Clonkeehan Stud who were registered were Clonkeehan Mayflower (2044) out of Rose of Barna (1337), and Clonkeehan Easter Lily (2163) who was a full sister to *Clonkeehan Auratum (104)*. Later both studs turned to breeding purebred Connemara ponies, and had much success in the Show ring as well as providing the Stud Book with several useful stallions.

Mr and Mrs Donal Brooks came to live at Errislannon in 1957 with their six children and began looking for a pony for the children to ride. They found a brown mare Drimeen Dun (1449), in foal to MacDara (91), and bought her from her breeder, Martin King, Errislannon. Drimeen Dun became the foundation mare for the Errislannon Stud, and in 1958 produced a dun colt foal. Two years later he won his class at the Clifden Show, and was registered as the stallion *Errislannon Coltsfoot (115)*. Drimeen Dun (1449) bred seven foals at Errislannon, and her descendants are still there today. Her most successful daughter, Errislannon Daisy (2533) by Doon Paddy (95) remained at Errislannon, and she produced Errislannon Dana (4769) and Errislannon Diamante (6026) who were both by *Errislannon Sparkler (210)*, the stud's second resident stallion. These mares were sold to breeders in England where they have won many championships. Dana's daughter Spinway Cailin

(6311) bred *Spinway Comet (935)* for Sarah Hodgkins and he is a most successful son of Thunderbolt (178) and represents the Green Line in England. Errislannon Manor later developed into a trekking centre as well as a stud, and became well-known to many generations of young people who learnt to ride there, or had trekking holidays on Errislannon ponies.

In January 1960 a small Connemara pony stud was established in Co. Cork, when the author founded the Coosheen Stud at Kilbrittain. A visit to Connemara resulted in the purchase of a 3 year old stallion *Ceileog (109)* by Clonkeehan Auratum (104), who was bred by Michael Keady, Pollnaclough, Moycullen, from his good mare Pollnaclough Grey (1518). *Ceileog (109)* was bought as a foal by Sean McLoughlin, a school teacher in Moycullen, and he won the 2 year old colt class at Clifden in 1959. Two mares were also purchased, and the three ponies travelled south to become the foundation of the Coosheen Stud. *Ceileog (109)* returned to Clifden twice, in 1961 he came second to his sire in the stallion class, and in 1962 he came back to Clifden once more and won the class.

37th Annual Pony Show, Clifden – 18th August 1960

Col. Dan Corry, was invited to act as visiting judge together with the Society judges Tim Cotter, T. McD. Kelly MRCVS and R. Kelly MRCVS. The winning yearling colt by Dun Lorenzo (55) was bred by P. K. Joyce, Clifden from his mare Rose of Killola (1365) by Winter (TB). He was bought later that year by the Society for £120, and registered as *Dun Aengus (120)*. Michael Conneely, Fahey bred the yearling filly winner, she was by Clonkeehan Auratum (104) from his mare Molly Conneely (562) by Silver Pearl (18), and became the wellknown broodmare Muffy (2157), and reared eleven foals on the hillside on the Sky Road, including the stallion *Murphy Rebel (696)*.

Michael Clancy, Spiddal had been buying ponies since 1955, and through Stanislaus Lynch had exported many to the USA. He had two winners at the 1960 show, Lady May (2018) by MacDara (99) won the 2 year old filly class, and Spiddal Lady (2011) won the Killanin Cup.

Peter Joyce, Ballyconneely won the RDS Medal for senior mares with Lor Sparrow (1264), a mare whose progeny have carried on this famous female line with great success both at home and abroad in succeeding generations. Her filly foal that year by Dun Lorenzo (55) was unplaced in her class, but went on to become an outstanding foundation mare for Jimmy Jones in Carlow who bought her in 1965 to begin his Ashfield Stud, her name was Wise Sparrow (2270). Before leaving Connemara, she bred a daughter by Clonkeehan Auratum (104) who remained with John Joyce in Ballyconneely, she was Wise Cuckoo (2714) and she bred 13 foals including the stallions *Sarsfield (579)* and *Silver Cloud (811)*, and among her many daughters was Maureen's Cuckoo (8799), who became Supreme Champion at Clifden 1989. The Cuckoo progeny are still winning prizes and breeding in Ballyconneely.

Flash Girl (1771) continued her winning ways, and won her class and the RDS Silver Medal for young mares, and then went on to take the Archbishop's Cup for the best brood mare five years old and over. She had a colt foal at foot by MacDara (91) who in time became *Atlantic Storm (139)*.

Death of Bartley O'Sullivan

Sadly this was the last show to be organised by Bartley O'Sullivan, as just one month later, on 14th September 1960, Bartley died in St Bredes Nursing Home in Galway at the age of 71. He was due to retire from his position as Secretary to the County Committee of Agriculture that week, and he still held the post of Hon Secretary of the Connemara Pony Breeders' Society at the time of his death. His contribution to the Society over thirty-seven years was enormous, and the establishment and growth of the Connemara Pony Breeders' Society from its small beginnings in 1923 were largely due to his dedication and hard work over the years. He had been greatly loved and respected by the people of Connemara, and was sadly missed.

He was Joint Secretary with Michael O'Malley from 1924 until his death, although for many years prior to Bartley's death, Michael had ceased to play an active role in the the affairs of the Society. Michael O'Malley should be best remembered as the man whose imagination and and persistence led to the formation of the Society, and were it not for his efforts, the Society might never have been formed. He and Bartley were good friends, and Michael, always the most broad-minded and generous of men, was the first to acknowledge the value of the work done by his Joint Secretary.

Many years later at the celebrations of the 70th anniversary of the Society in 1993 at Oughterard, Michael was quoted by his son Frank, as follows;

Bartley O'Sullivan

"I was Joint Secretary in name only. The work was done by Bartley O'Sullivan. When the history of this Society is being written, I hope that the trojan work that was done by Bartley O'Sullivan in those formative years is recognised by those who come after us. "

Following Bartley O'Sullivan's death, his assistant Miss Alice Burke was appointed as Acting Secretary, with Sean Keane to continue to do the field work. Foaling returns had been introduced earlier that year, and it was suggested that the Agricultural officers in Connemara would help the breeders to fill in the forms and to keep accurate records of the breeding. The deaths also occurred during 1960 of Ernest Moran, Clifden who was a Council member and a signatory to the Memorandum and Articles of Association, and Dick Curley, Galway, a former member of Council who had served on the Inspection Committee from 1955 to 1959 and had given much of his time to the work of the Society. In 1961 the Council decided to move the Annual inspections from early spring to June so that the two year old fillies would be ready for inspection.

Another new breeder in the early sixties was John Huston, the American film director who had come to live at St Clerans, Craughwell, and was a Joint Master of the Galway Blazers. He bought several good mares including Star of Fahy (1453) and Glen Nelly (1344) who he showed successfully for a couple of years, and in 1961 Glen Nelly won her class at both the RDS Spring Show and at Clifden. He later moved into breeding Thoroughbreds, and sold these two mares to Lady Hemphill in 1963, and she used them as foundation mares for her Tulira Stud which she started that year.

At the Spring Show in 1961 there were several new owners exhibiting Connemara ponies for the first time, who were later to become well-known breeders, and among them were Lady de Vesci of Abbeyleix, and Maria Caracciolo, better known now as Lady Maria Levinge, whose Grange Stud was founded the following year.

Colman Griffin, from Screebe was one of the men who travelled to the Spring Show from Connemara, and he was placed with his three year old filly Windy Spring (2053). Her dam Windy (782), now aged 21, was 4th in the class for mares six years or over for her new owner Mrs Naper from Co. Meath, while Windy Rebel (1473), another daughter of Windy (782) took second place in the six year old or over class for Miss Berridge. This was a great tribute to Windy (782), one of the grand old matriarchs of the breed who was dam of the stallion *Rebel Wind (127)*, and among her other good daughters were Windy Dun (1803) and Ard Zephyr (3161).

Ciliarain (78) was withdrawn from the stallion list at the end of the 1960 season having spent 12 years in Connemara, mostly with Bartley Naughton, Costello, and Peter Kyne, Moycullen, but his last year was with Anthony Faherty at Moyard before he was sold to Mrs Duff in Scotland. He had no stallion son registered, but from his 63 progeny he left some useful broodmares including: Ballydonnellan Grey (1593) Ashe Grey (1673), Helpmate (2077), Moycullen Mite (2093), Clifden Molly (2127), Pillagh Beauty (2259), Noreen Ban (2355).

Clonjoy (117), was bought by the Society in 1960 at registration, and placed with James Grealish (Roger) for the 1961 season when he joined the stallion list. He was a blue-grey three year old son of Clonkeehan Auratum

Clonjoy (117)

(104) out of Joyce Grey (933) s. Silver Pearl (18) d. Retreat (320) and was bred by the Christian Brothers at Letterfrack. He was the first of *Clonkeehan Auratum's* sons to be put on the approved list and spent 12 years in Connemara leaving 255 progeny, including 23 registered stallions. Many of his stock were exported as he was in Connemara during the period of expansion when new markets were opening up rapidly.

A second son of *Clonkeehan Auratum (104)* was purchased by the Society in 1961 after he won the two year old colt class for his breeder Michael Lydon, Moyard, and he was registered as *Aura Dun (123)* and he joined the list in 1962, replacing *Clonjoy (117)* at Oranmore for his first season.

38th Annual Pony Show, Clifden – 17th August 1961

Col. Dan Corry was again the visiting judge at the Show in 1961 with Mr T. Cotter, Mr T. McD. Kelly MRCVS and Mr R. Kelly MRCVS and the stallion class was won by *Clonkeehan Auratum (104)*, shown by Michael Conroy. In 2nd place was his son *Ceileog (109)* who had travelled the long journey from Cork by train via Dublin to Galway, and then made the last stage of his journey from Galway to Clifden on one of the CIE lorries which collected the ponies from all over south Connemara to compete at the Show. The stallion was penned in the front of the lorry, the mares and foals loose at the back.

It was another day of triumph for *Clonkeehan Auratum (104)* with his progeny sweeping the board in all the youngstock classes, foals, yearlings and two year olds, and the Carew Cup went to the yearling colt owned by Mrs Anne Goodbody, Moyard with the yearling filly owned by John Joyce, Ballyconneely, in Reserve.

Jack Bolger produced the five year old Cashel Kate (2030) to win her class, as well as the RDS Medal for young mares. It was the first time she had appeared at Clifden, and she really stamped her mark on the Shows in the years to follow. She was bred by John Curran, Kilkerrin, Carna, and her dam was Rebel Kate (736) by Lavalley Rebel (24) out of Droighnean Donn (280) who was also the dam of *Dun Lorenzo (55)*. Her sire is entered in the Stud Book as *Tully Lad (48)* but it is generally accepted that she was by *Carna Dun (89)*.

Jack Bolger with Cashel Kate (2030)

That year Flash Girl (1771) was not eligible to compete in her class, but was able to hold her own in the Championship for the best broodmare, and took the Archbishop's Cup for the second year running.

At two Council meetings held during 1961, four more members joined the Council, they were, Tom Walsh, Clifden, Cornelius Howard, Galway, James Lee, Moycullen, and Miss Garnet Irwin, Ross, Moyard. Also offers of two new trophies for the Annual Connemara Pony Show were received, one was a specially designed bronze plaque depicting a mare and foal presented to the Society in memory of the late Bartley O'Sullivan by his family, to be called the O'Sullivan Perpetual Memorial Plaque and to be awarded to the best Registered Connemara Pony mare with foal at foot by a registered Connemara Pony Stallion. The second trophy was a silver cup presented by Miss Garnet Irwin to be awarded to the foal classes and to be known as the Camlin Cup.

Resignation of Acting Secretary Alice Burke

By the end of 1961 the Acting Hon. Secretary Miss Alice Burke tendered her resignation, which was received with regret by the Council. Miss Burke had assisted Bartley O'Sullivan for many years, and in his tribute to her, Lord Killanin thanked her for all the valuable work she had done for the Society, but most especially for the year since Bartley's death when she had been Acting Hon. Secretary. A new permanent secretary had not yet been appointed, and so a replacement had to be found, and Sean Keane became the acting Hon. Secretary.

Alice Burke

Mrs Phil MacDermott who had worked in the County Committee of Agriculture since 1951, already had a good deal of experience of the work of the Connemara Pony Breeders' Society, and had kindly agreed to help with the work of the Society after Miss Burke's resignation. She was appointed assistant to Sean Keane at the next Council Meeting held in January 1962.

By the end of 1961 the finances of the Society had sunk to the lowest ebb, and there was a credit balance of only £3. 1s. 11d. The situation called for immediate action and a special finance committee was formed to seek extra funding from the Department of Agriculture to put the Society on a sounder footing. With increasing costs, the Society was no longer able to be run efficiently on the slender budget available to date, and there was an urgent need to raise more funds.

Two new council members were elected at the AGM in March 1962, Mr S. O'Donoughue CAO, Galway, and Mr T. J. McDonagh, Roundstone.

Two young stallions had been purchased by the Society and both were put on the list of approved stallions for the 1962 season. They were *Dun Aengus (120)* sire Dun Lorenzo (55) dam Rose of Killola (1365) who was placed with John Walsh, Kylesalia, and *Aura Dun (123)* sire Clonkeehan Auratum (104) dam Early Grey (925) who went to James Grealish (Roger), Oranmore.

Carna Bobby (79), by now aged 15, was removed from the list at the end of the 1961 season and sold to Paddy Lally in Gort for £35. He had served for thirteen years in Connemara and had 88 registered progeny during that time, but his breeding life was far from over, and he remained at stud with Paddy Lally until he died in the winter of 1973. Many of his most famous progeny were sired during this later part of his life, but among the notable ponies sired during his time in Connemara were:

Queen of Diamonds (1934), Atlantic Mist (2175), Atlantic Breeze (2174), Snowdrop (2454), Julie (2246), Bobby's Pride (2331), Anna Maree (2332), Atlantic Surf (2471), Silver Birch of Abbeyleix (2753), and three of his stallion sons, *Paddy's Heaven (137), Island King (122)* and *The Admiral (201)*.

The RDS Spring Show had an increase of entries from outside Connemara, but only seven entries were sponsored by the Society to travel up to Dublin from Connemara. The winner in the class for mares of six years or over was Cashel Kate (2030) owned by Jack Bolger, and the young mares class attracted a large entry of 25 with Willie Diamond winning the class with Flash Judy (2154), a three year old daughter of Flash Girl (1771) by Mac Dara (91).

The Society had approached the RDS with a request to have the Connemara Pony Classes moved from the Spring Show held in May to the RDS Horse Show in August, as it was felt that it would be much easier to present the ponies from Connemara in show condition later in the year. The suggestion was well received by the RDS, but there was a problem about lack of space for stabling at the August Show, and the request had been deferred.

39th Annual Pony Show, Clifden – 16th August 1962

Martin Treacy, Spiddal took over the job formerly held by Sean Keane as chief steward of the Showgrounds, and it was a job he was to continue to do each year until 1974. He became a member of the Society in 1962 and was elected to the Council in 1963.

There was a record entry of 37 in the yearling filly class which was won by Paddy Carr, Dangan, with a filly by Carna Dun (89), while the two year old filly class also had a big entry and was won by Pulleha (2211) by Doon Paddy (95), and she also won the Carew Cup for her owner Miss Faber. The entries in the youngstock classes were of a high standard, and earned favourable comments from the judges. Graham Tulloch won the Killanin Cup with Ocean Melody (2134) by Clonkeehan Auratum (104), who also won the RDS Medal for Young Mares, with Village Belle (1855) in second place for Paddy King, Lehid. Flash Girl (1771) won her class once again, but this year Cashel Kate (2030) beat her for the Archbishop's Cup. The stallion class was won by Mrs Petch with *Ceileog (109)*, with Mikey King taking second place with *Tooreen Ross (99)*.

Ceileog (109)

The judges were Col. Dan Corry, Mr T. Cotter, Mr T. McD. Kelly, Mr R. Kelly.

Office leaves County Buildings 1962

At a Council meeting held in October 1962 Sean Keane told the meeting that he was finding it difficult to cope with the work of the Society in addition to his duties as a full time officer of the Department of Agriculture. He felt that in view of the increasing volume of work, it was no longer possible for the affairs of the Society to be administered by an Hon. Secretary, and it would be necessary to appoint a full time paid secretary.

For many years during Bartley O'Sullivan's time as Hon. Secretary, Council meetings had been held at the County Committee of Agriculture offices, however this custom was now to change, and this was the last Council meeting held at the County buildings. From then on meetings were held in a hotel, and in the absence of a permanent office for the Society, Mrs MacDermott undertook to provide storage space in her flat in Eyre Square for the Society's records.

Volume IX of the Stud Book

Volume IX was published in the Spring of 1963 and covered the period from 1st October 1955 to 1st June 1962. It was a much larger volume than previous ones and contained particulars of 28 stallions, 512 mares and 26 geldings. It was the first time that geldings had been registered, and in contrast to earlier Stud Books when almost all the stallions registered were the property of the Connemara Pony Breeders' Society, in Volume 1X, only five of the 28 entered in the Stud Book were owned by the Society. Among the stallions listed who remained in Ireland in private ownership, there were several who were to have some influence on the breed in the future, they were, *Tully Grey (110)*, *Thunder (113)*, *Camlin Cicada (119)* and *Bridge Boy (124)*.

A number of the stallions had been exported to USA and were entered in the names of their new owners in the States, one had been exported to Portugal, and another, *Island King (122)* was later exported to Australia by John Daly, and he became No. 1 in the Australian Connemara Pony Stud Book.

In the mares register were many of the new owners in both England and USA as well as a good number of new breeders from all over Ireland. The men who were buying ponies for export were among those listed as owners of large numbers of ponies, and included Col. Bellingham, Jack Bolger, Michael Clancy, John Daly, Jim Lee, and Stanislaus Lynch.

The old stallion *Tiger Gill (68)* was removed from the list at the end of the 1962 season, aged 19 and sold to Malahide in Co. Dublin. He had spent 16 years in Connemara and had 100 registered progeny, some of his best included Oorid Belle (1394), Sun Cloud (1636), Nipper of Calla (1407), Copper Coin (1488), Errigal Princess (2295), Coosheen Alanna (2376). He was sold again to Miss Lee Norman in 1964, and spent the rest of his days at Clonkeehan where he had seven more registered progeny including four stallions, three of whom were sold to England. He was a golden dun, and a tremendously tough pony with a wonderful

Tiger Gill (68)

temperament, as well as a great ability to jump, and he passed on these important attributes to succeeding generations.

One of his first foals was Oorid Belle (1394) who was foaled in 1948 and was bred by John Walsh, Oorid, Recess. She was a rather small little grey two year old filly when she was driven down off the hills with a group of ponies to Maam Cross, but when eight strong Connemara men tried to separate her from her companions, she fought like a little tiger, and they had to drive her into the bog to get a halter on her, and finally load her into a trailer. She was driven to Dublin by her new owner Mr Jim Cassidy who had bought her for his daughter Maureen, and the following year she took her young rider hunting and then show jumping. In 1955 she had a remarkable record of winning ten first prizes in a row which meant she had jumped 200 fences without a fault, and in both 1955 and 1956 she won the Pixie Cup awarded by the Show Jumping Association of Ireland for the highest number of wins and placings achieved in a year by a pony not exceeding 13. 2 hands high and ridden by a child under 14 years. Her final triumph in 1956 was to become Champion Pony of the Year at the SJAI Pony Championship at the Indoor Show held at Burton Hall, Stillorgan. The following year she was sold to USA where she continued to demonstrate that she had inherited her sire's remarkable jumping ability, and carried her new young rider to further success.

In the spring of 1963 two new stallions were added to the approved list, *Bridge Boy (124)*, representing the Blue Line, and *Ben Lettery (133)* from the Red Line. *Bridge Boy (124)* sire Tooreen Ross (99), dam Irene (624) was owned and bred by Paddy Geoghegan, and although privately owned, was included on the approved list, and stood at Oughterard. *Ben Lettery (133)*, the two year old son of *Gael Linn (103)* dam Swanee River (1501) was placed with a new stallion custodian, Tommy O'Brien, Canal Stage, Ballinafad for his first season, while *Carna Dun (89)* was moved to Josie Conroy at Bunowen who took over as custodian from his father Michael that year.

CHAPTER 8

1963-1966

• John Killeen new Secretary • Government Grant • Purchased Fair Green • Closed Book 1964 •
• Danish C. P. Society 1964 • Swedish C. P. Society 1965 • Purchase Showgrounds •
• BECs ruling 1966 • Tim Cotter Retires as Judge •

John Killeen Secretary 1963

A Council meeting was held at the Imperial Hotel, Galway on 23rd July 1963 at which John Killeen was appointed permanent Secretary to the Society, and so ended the period of uncertainty which had followed Bartley's death in September 1960.

John Killeen had been a member of the Council since 1951, and was one of the signatories of the Memorandum and Articles of Association of the Cumann Lucht Capaillini Chonamara in December 1959. He had worked with the Department of Agriculture all his life, and in 1920 he was appointed Assistant Overseer in Co. Donegal with a starting salary of £90 per annum. He also received £15 per annum "to provide a bicycle and keep it in perfect mechanical order at all times"!

He married his wife Rose in Donegal in 1927, and they had seven children, four boys and three girls. He moved to Co. Mayo in 1933, before being moved to Galway in 1937, where he became Supervisory Inspector for the Congested Districts which covered a huge area from Donegal to West Cork. He retired from the Department in 1962.

John Killeen

He had an intimate knowledge of agriculture, the farming community, and also the social fabric of the whole Western seaboard. He was a fluent Irish speaker, and his great interests were Gaelic football, particularly Connaught and Mayo football, and the Connemara Pony. He had known and admired Bartley O'Sullivan as a colleague, and he was the ideal choice to succeed him as Secretary of the Connemara Pony Breeders' Society. Mrs Phil Mac Dermott was appointed Clerical Assistant at the same meeting.

John Killeen's wife had died several years earlier after a short illness, and her death left a big vacuum in his life, which was probably one of the reasons he took on the challenging task of Secretary of the Connemara Pony Breeders' Society. When he became Secretary he moved the office of the Connemara Pony Breeders' Society into his own home, which was at Nun's Island in Galway city where he was living at the time with his daughter Mary. In the years to come his address was the cause of much confusion for many overseas pony enthusiasts, and the questions from callers wanting to visit him varied from whether sea or air transport was available to the island, to whether his office was located in a convent!

At the same meeting there was a welcome announcement that the Minister of Agriculture had decided to increase the annual grant to £1000, and it had also been decided to make available to the Society at least £1000 to cover capital costs such as the purchase of stallions, printing of stud books and improvements to the Show grounds. Consideration would also be given to increasing this sum on receipt of satisfactory proposals from the Society as to the steps to be taken to improve and expand the Connemara pony industry.

The Council were most grateful for this much needed help in putting the financial state of the Society on a sounder footing, and decided to invite Mr Smith, the Minister of Agriculture to the Annual Show. In view of the need for increased income and with the improved trade for ponies, it was decided that from June 1964 the registration and transfer fees should be doubled.

By now the Society had bought the Fair Green which was the field next to the main show grounds at Clifden, but there were still difficulties over the purchase of the main show field where the Showing ring was in urgent need of drainage, but nothing could be done until the field was owned by the Society.

40th Annual Pony Show, Clifden – 15th August 1963

The Show was highly successful with a record entry of 276 ponies, and again there was a very good standard in the youngstock classes. The Minister of Agriculture attended the Show and presented the major awards to the winners. John O'Mahony Meade acted as visiting judge together with Col. Dan Corry, Tim Cotter, T. McD. Kelly, and there were also many visitors from overseas, including some pony enthusiasts from Germany.

A new silver cup had been presented for the stallion class by Mr John Alexander from Northumberland, and it was won for the first time by Paddy Geoghegan from Oughterard with his four year old home-bred stallion *Bridge Boy (124)*. The yearling filly class had a record entry of 52 and was won by Paddy Carr with a filly by Carna Dun (89), later registered as Dangan Lass (2486) and the two year old filly class went to Mrs Petch from Cork with Coosheen Alanna (2376) by Tiger Gill (68), who went on to win the Carew Cup for the best yearling or two year old in the Show.

Jack Bolger won the Killanin Cup and young mares RDS Silver Medal with Glen Fanny (2266) by Gael Linn (103), and the Archbishop's Cup, the RDS Silver Medal for Senior Mares and the O'Sullivan Memorial Plaque were all won by Cashel Kate (2030), also shown by Jack Bolger, but now with a new owner.

Mr Trevor Donnelly, a businessman from Delgany, Co. Wicklow, had recently decided to invest in Connemara ponies, and he bought some of the biggest names in the Show ring at that time. Cashel Kate (2030) and Atlantic Mist (2175) were undoubtedly his two top mares, and both were Champions at Clifden on more than one occasion, but he also bought Glen Fanny (2266), Ballinahinch Blue (1752), and Princess (2137).

Cashel Kate (2030) produced three full brothers by Carna Bobby (79) who all became registered stallions and had a big influence on the breed in the years to come. They were *The Admiral (201)*, who stood at Tim Carey's yard in Westmeath, *Ballydonagh Rob (321)* who succeeded his father with Paddy Lally at Gort, and *Sticky (377)* who spent some time as a teaser before he was sold to Holland. Her daughter Ballydonagh Kate (2798) by MacDara (91) was the dam of *Killyreagh Kim (308)* by Carna Bobby (79), and he was given to the Society by his breeder, Col. Creighton and he served on the approved list in Connemara from 1970 to 1986.

Stud Book became "Closed Book" 30th June 1964

At a meeting of the Council held in December 1963 changes in the regulations for registration were discussed, and a resolution was adopted that from 30th June 1964 no pony would be registered whose sire and dam were not entered in the Connemara Pony Stud Book.

This meant that from 1964 onwards the Connemara Pony Stud Book was a "closed book" and no further ponies without particulars of breeding would be accepted for registration. From 1965 foaling returns were also required from breeders and they were to be furnished within one month of the foaling date, giving particulars of sire and dam, date of foaling, sex, colour, and marks of foal. Despite the Stud Book now being closed, the Council felt it was necessary to maintain the rule that all ponies would have to be inspected and passed as suitable for registration after they had reached the minimum registration age of 2 years.

Tooreen Ross (99) had been removed from the approved list at the end of 1963, and spent one more year with Thomas Whelan at Ardrahan, before being sold to Mrs Duff in Cumberland. In his last year at stud in Ireland he was visited by Lady Hemphill's two foundation mares, Glen Nelly (1344) and Star of Fahy (1453). They produced a colt and a filly, and Nelly's son *Tulira Mairtin (214)* became the resident stallion at Tulira, while the filly, Tulira Mavourneen (3026) had a successful show career before retiring to stud. *Mairtin* had all the toughness of his sire and bred hardy active ponies who were great performers, and many went

Lady Hemphill with Tulira Mairtin (214)

on to be good ambassadors for the breed overseas. *Tooreen Ross (99)* was only on the approved list for five years, and left a small family, but among them were some good ponies, including *Bridge Boy (124)* who won the stallion class at Clifden on four occasions.

In 1964 four new young stallions, three of whom had been purchased by the Society, were added to the approved list making a total of thirteen sires standing in Connemara. *Rebel Wind (127)* was a grey four year old son of Inver Rebel (93) out of Colman Griffin's mare Windy (782), and he was placed with John Walsh, Kilkerrin. The second was a dun, *Atlantic Storm (139)* by MacDara (91) and

Rebel Wind (127)

was out of the prizewinning mare Flash Girl (1771) and bred by Martin Lee, Dunloughan, he was placed with a new custodian, Tom Feeney, Carraroe. The third stallion, also a dun, was *Mervyn Storm (140)* who was bred by Miss Berridge, Enniskerry from Windy Rebel (1473) and was by Camlin Cicada (119), a son of Carna Dun (89), and he went to Martin Walsh (Pat), Snabo, Rosmuck. He replaced *Aura Dun (123)* who moved to James Grealish (Roger), Oranmore before being sold to USA at the end of the season.

A three year old son of *Clonkeehan Auratum (104)* bred by John Huston from Star of Fahy (1453) was privately owned and stood with his owner Peter Kyne at Knockranny, Moycullen. He was a dun called *Knockranny Ruby (134)* and his sire stood along side him at Knockranny for one season before *Clonkeehan Auratum (104)* was moved out of Connemara to Thomas Whelan at Ardrahan in 1965.

The list of approved stallions now numbered thirteen, eight of whom were duns, and there was quite a change in the distribution of the blood lines from ten years previously when the list was predominately from the Blue and Red Lines. The influence of the outside bloodlines introduced during the forties and fifties was now much stronger with the *Carna Dun* and *Clonkeehan Auratum* lines making up more than half the list. *Dun Aengus (120)* and *Atlantic Storm (139)* also carried some thoroughbred blood from Winter and Little Heaven on their dams' side.

Blue Line

Bridge Boy (124) ....s. Tooreen Ross (99) ....d. Irene (624)

Rebel Wind (127) ....s. Inver Rebel (93) ....d. Windy (782)

Red Line

Mac Dara (91)...........................s. Dun Lorenzo (55) ....d. Dolan Rose (1132)

Dun Aengus (120) ....s. Dun Lorenzo (55) ....d. Rose of Killola (1365) by Winter

Ben Lettery (133) ....s. Gael Linn (103) ....d. Swanee River (1501)

Atlantic Storm (139) ....s. Mac Dara (91) ....d. Flash Girl (1771) by Carna Dun

Green Line

Purple Line (TB)

Carna Dun (89) ....s. Little Heaven (TB) ....d. Double Dun (803)

Doon Paddy (95) ....s. Carna Dun (89) ....d. Doon Lily (1259)

Mervyn Storm (140) ....s. Camlin Cicada (119) ....d. Windy Rebel (1473)

Orange Line (Arab)

Clonkeehan Auratum (104) .....s. Naseel (Arab) ....d. Western Lily (1522)

Clonjoy (117) ....s. Clonkeehan Auratum (104) ......d. Joyce Grey (933)

Aura Dun (123) ....s. Clonkeehan Auratum (104) ......d. Early Grey (925)

Knockranny Ruby (134) ....s. Clonkeehan Auratum (104) ......d. Star of Fahy (1453)

During the early sixties some ponies were imported into Australia by Mr Fred Wiltshire MRCVS who was an Irish veterinary surgeon living in Australia, and the first was the stallion *Island King (122)*, s. Carna Bobby (79) d. Doon Lass (1311), who in 1963 travelled out by ship in a crate lashed on deck, an even longer and tougher journey than to USA. He was bred at Cashel by Tom Burke, and spent several years with John Daly at Lough Mask House where he ran with a small herd of mares on one of the islands in Lough Mask. *Island King (122)* was the first stallion to carry the Island prefix which John used for the sires who were registered by him. Many of the early ponies exported to Australia were sent out by John Daly to Fred Wiltshire, who then sold them on to new breeders.

John Daly

113

John Daly had been a member of the Council since 1960 and his father Paddy Daly was a Council member in the fifties. The Daly family were always involved in horses, breeding, hunting, show-jumping and racing, and John's uncle Peter kept his own pack of hounds. John started riding on a Connemara pony as a child, and during the mid-fifties and sixties, he became one of the biggest exporters of Connemara ponies, and many ponies carrying his prefix went all over the world. Twelve stallions were given his Island prefix and had noble names, King, Prince, Duke, Earl, Count, Baron, Knight were his earliest ones, and each stallion during his time there was taken out to an island in Lough Mask swimming behind a boat, and left to run with a small group of mares. The mares carried the Easter prefix, although not all would have been bred at Lough Mask, and many more passed through John's hands during the busiest export years.

Island King (122)

Danish Connemara Pony Society Formed in 1964

By 1964, there was a growing interest in Connemara ponies from a number of European countries, and as well as the continued export of ponies to England and USA, a considerable number were also exported to Germany, France, Sweden, Denmark, Belgium and Holland. The prices were also increasing, and this in turn encouraged the breeders, so that more than 400 nominations were taken up in 1964. At the Spring Show that year, Flash Girl (1771) won her class, and was sold later for the highest price ever paid for a Connemara pony at the time.

In August 1964 The Danish Connemara Pony Society was formed with Mrs Gerda Merrild as the first President, and while some of the early imports into Denmark were from England, in 1964 Danish buyers were starting to import direct from Ireland.

The demand for ponies in Germany was particularly strong, with eighteen being exported during the year, and there were plans to start a Connemara Pony Society in Germany.

41st Annual Pony Show, Clifden – 20th August 1964

Mr Jan Harald Koelichen was one of the first to import ponies into Germany, and he brought a large party of pony breeders from Germany to visit the 1964 Annual Show at Clifden. While at the Show he kindly offered to present the Society with a silver cup to be awarded to the Champion Pony of the Show.

A record crowd attended the Show, and for the first time almost all the major awards went to breeders from outside the Connemara district. It was the start of a period when many more pony breeders from other parts of Ireland were establishing studs, and travelling to Clifden to exhibit their ponies, and it caused a certain amount of resentment among the Connemara based breeders who felt it was unfair to expect ponies raised in Connemara to compete on equal terms with ponies raised on the richer lands of Meath or Kildare, Cork or Wexford. Some of the outside breeders were more skilled at turning out their ponies for a show, with the result that a pony who was presented correctly was sometimes able to beat a better pony who was not as well shown. However, it did not take long for the breeders in Connemara to learn how to present their ponies to the highest standards, and the days of bringing a pony to the Show on a piece of old rope with its tail trailing in the mud are now long gone.

Mrs Dan Lanigan O'Keefe was invited as visiting judge and joined the Society judges, Messrs T. Cotter, T. McD. Kelly MRCVS and R. Kelly MRCVS. The stallion class and Alexander Cup was won by a four year old son of MacDara (91), *Lambay Rebel (131)*, owned by Lord Revelstoke, Lambay Island, Rush, Co. Dublin, who with the help of his agent Michael O'Connell, had recently invested in a number of Connemara ponies to start a herd on his island home near to the coast north of Dublin. His prefix of Lambay was to become wellknown worldwide, with many ponies passing through Lambay Island on their way to new homes overseas. *Lambay Rebel (131)* spent three more years on the island before

Lambay Rebel (131) with Michael O'Connell.

being sold to Denmark in 1967 where he became No. 1 in the Danish Stud Book, and laid a solid foundation for the breed in Denmark through his son *Oxenholm Godot*.

The winning two year old filly by MacDara (91), who also won the Carew Cup, was owned and bred by Miss Frances Lee Norman from the Clonkeehan Stud, Slane. Registered as Clonkeehan Tiger Lily (2580), she was a granddaughter of Western Lily (1522), dam of *Clonkeehan Auratum (104)*. Another mare from the same stud, the 16 year old Rose of Barna (1337), won the RDS Medal for senior mares, the Camlin Ciro Cup for her colt foal by Camlin Cicada (119), the Archbishop's Cup for the best broodmare and the O'Sullivan Memorial Plaque for the best Registered Connemara Pony entered at the Show with a foal at foot. The Clonkeehan Stud had also bred the winning yearling colt exhibited by Lord Revelstoke, so it was a day of triumph for Miss Lee Norman and her assistant Miss Susan Traill.

The O'Sullivan Memorial Plaque had been presented by the family of the late Bartley O'Sullivan in his memory, and it was presented to Miss Lee Norman by his granddaughter Caitriona O'Sullivan, whose father Tadhg O'Sullivan was the Irish Ambassador to the United States at the time. It was perhaps a little unfortunate that this trophy, presented in memory of the man who had done so much for the Connemara pony and for the people of Connemara should be won for the first time by a breeder from outside Connemara, but the situation never arose again, as the following year the O'Sullivan Memorial Plaque became a special confined trophy to be awarded to the Best Broodmare with foal at foot bred and located in Connemara, and exhibited by an owner resident in Connemara. A special prize fund was also set up so that extra cash prizes could be awarded to ponies bred, owned and exhibited by a resident of Connemara. This fund was supported for many years by Lord Hemphill, who had become a member of the Council in 1963, and also by Lord Revelstoke and Col. Bellingham.

Susan Traill, Miss Lee Norman and Caitriona O'Sullivan

Later that year, the Irish Export Board Coras Trachtala, sponsored a promotion of Irish goods at Eaton's Department Store in Montreal, and a Connemara mare and foal were shipped out to Canada to feature at the exhibition which was held from 16th to 30th September 1964. The two Connemara ponies were one of the main attractions, and were part of the special events area on the fifth floor of the store. The exhibition was officially opened by the Irish Minister of Industry and Commerce, Mr Jack Lynch, and following the exhibition, the mare and foal became members of the City of Montreal Garden of Wonders!

The stallion list was reduced to eleven in 1965 with *Clonkeehan Auratum (104)* and *Aura Dun (123)* both being removed from the list. However a new three year old stallion, *Errigal Prince (159)* replaced them and he also represented the Orange line being a son of Clonjoy (117). The Society bought him after he had won the two year old colt class at Clifden in 1964 and he was bred by Sean Ward, of the Agricultural School, Athenry. He was placed with Mikey King at Claddaghduff, but only spent two years with him before being sold in 1966, leaving thirty eight progeny. His son *Abbeyleix Ri (290)* was bred by Lady de Vesci out of Queen of Diamonds (1934) and he sired three registered stallions among his ten progeny. *Dun Aengus (120)* was rested in 1965, but returned to the list in 1966 when he stood with Jack Bolger at Cashel for one season.

The RDS Spring Show in 1965 provided three classes for Connemara ponies, which attracted a total entry of fifty-five, and in the class for two and three year olds there was a record entry of thirty-four. In the class for senior mares six years and over, Jack Bolger produced the 20 year old Lucky Lady (1139) by *Gil (43)* to win over Cashel Kate (2030) shown by her new owner Mr Trevor Donnelly, while Michael Clancy won the four or five year old class with Atlantic Breeze (2174), and he also won the 2 or 3 year old class with Atlantic View (2614), a two year old filly by MacDara (91).

Volume X of the Stud Book

During 1965 Volume X was published with particulars of 34 stallions, bringing the total number of registered stallions to 158. There were now 2592 mares on the register with 419 included in this Volume, and a total of 87 geldings had been registered in Volumes 1X and X.

Most of the stallions registered in this Volume were privately owned and only three were owned by the Society. This was a big change from earlier years when the Society had gained complete control of the stallions standing in Connemara, and those sires who were sold to other parts of Ireland were seldom used on registered mares. Now with new studs being developed in Ireland and overseas there was a demand for high class stallions to be used for breeding outside Connemara, and so more breeders were keeping colts up to registration age. Twelve of the stallions registered in Volume X were exported, with four going to Sweden, three to UK, and the others going to Denmark, Holland, Italy, Germany and USA.

42nd Annual Pony Show, Clifden – 19th August 1965

The Clifden Show had the highest ever attendance with a record gate, there were 304 entries in the pony classes, and Miss Berridge joined the Society judges Messrs T. Cotter, T. McD. Kelly, R. Kelly. The growing interest in the Connemara pony in Europe was shown by the many overseas visitors who attended the Show, and there was a keen demand for ponies, with buyers from Germany, France, Belgium and Holland paying good prices.

Jan Harald Koelichen Cup

The new Jan Harald Koelichen Cup for the Supreme Champion of the Show was presented for the first time by Mr Koelichen and the winner was the three year old filly Clonkeehan Tiger Lily (2580), who also won the Killanin Cup, and was bred and exhibited by Miss Frances Lee Norman, Slane. The same owner won the Carew Cup and Reserve Championship of the Show with her yearling colt by Camlin Cicada (119) out of Rose of Barna (1537), so for the second year running the Clonkeehan Stud had scooped most of the major awards.

However, the honour of the Connemara men was upheld by two well-known breeders from Ballyconneely, they were John Joyce, who won the RDS Medal for young mares with Wise Sparrow (2270), and Paddy King, Lehid, who won the senior mare class and RDS Medal with Village Belle (1855) as well as the Archbishop's Cup for the best brood mare, and the O'Sullivan Memorial Plaque for the best mare with foal at foot bred in Connemara and exhibited by a resident in Connemara. Both these mares remained in Ireland, and from them two famous female lines have developed whose progeny continue to breed prize winners in Connemara today.

Wise Sparrow (2270) was sold to James Jones in Carlow later that year and became a most valued foundation mare for the Ashfield Stud, while her filly foal by Carna Dun (89) was subsequently sold to Maria Levinge, she was Dun Sparrow (3025), one of the top brood mares at Grange Stud, who later was Supreme Champion at Clifden in 1972.

John Joyce retained a daughter from Wise Sparrow (2270) to keep this good mare line in Ballyconneely, and Wise Cuckoo (2714) by Clonkeehan Auratum (104) remained with John all her life and bred many outstanding ponies including Maureen's Cuckoo (8799), who was Supreme Champion at Clifden in 1989.

Village Belle (1855) stayed with Paddy King at Lehid until she was 22 years old and by then had bred 17 foals for him, but in 1978, when she had two daughters to follow her at Lehid, she was sold with a colt foal at foot to Mrs Petch and travelled the long journey to Co Cork where she bred two more foals to Coosheen Finn (381), and lived until her thirtieth year. She left a good daughter Coosheen Swallow (7625), who has in her turn become a most successful broodmare.

J. Petch

Village Belle (1855)

The Village ponies are almost legendary today with Belle's daughter Village Star (5146) by Killyreagh Kim (308) providing the two wellknown show winners Village Laura (8097) by Thunderbolt (178) and Village Colleen (8308) by Mervyn Kingsmill (762) for Padraig Hynes, as well as the equally successful Castle Dame (8640) for her owner Henry O'Toole who bred all three ponies. Village Grey (6951) succeeded Village Belle at Lehid with Paddy King, and has been as faithful a breeder as her dam, producing a string of good ponies including the Society owned stallion *Village Boy (927).*

Swedish Connemara Pony Society

The interest in Connemara ponies in Sweden began following an article about Connemara ponies written by Stanislaus Lynch in a Swedish newspaper, and in 1964 two Swedish pony breeders came to Ireland and bought a few ponies. These ponies made such a good impression in Sweden that one buyer bought 26 ponies in 1965, and several more went to individual buyers. Following these imports, a group of nine owners in Sweden got together and in August 1965, another overseas society was founded. The Swedish Connemara Pony Society, named in Swedish "Svenska Connemara Sallskapet" had as its chairman the Countess Andrea Oxenstierna, with Mr Rune Weckner as Vice Chairman, and Mrs Karin Johansson as Secretary.

One of the first mares imported into Sweden by the Countess was Jealous Lady (2301) by Clonkeehan Auratum (104) dam Errisbeg Lass (1425), her breeder was Francis Folan, Roundstone, and she became one of the foundation mares of the Swedish Stud Book with five stallion sons registered in Sweden.

Among the early stallions exported to Sweden were *Roundstone Chief (151)* by Carna Dun (89), *Slieve Dara (146)* by MacDara (91) and *Lambay Inver (162)* by Camlin Cicada (119).

Purchase of Clifden Showgrounds

In September 1965 the protracted negotiations over the purchase of the Showgrounds at Clifden were finally completed, and work was able to start on draining and levelling the field. This work was badly needed to improve the grounds as the Show ring had always been very soft with several boggy patches in it, and now with the aid of the grant from the Department of Agriculture, some essential work could be carried out during the year.

Swedish C.S. Archive

Countess Oxenstierna with Jealous Lady (2301)

Inspections Outside Connemara

The Council was aware of the difficulties arising over the inspection for registration for breeders in Ireland who were outside the Connemara area, and the increasing numbers of ponies being bred in other parts of Ireland was putting a strain on the limited inspection team who now had to cover the whole country. The Society had also become the "parent body" to a growing number of overseas societies, and as each new society was formed it laid down its own rules which were not necessarily the same as those of the Parent Society. This was because the new societies were affiliated to other governing bodies in their own countries and were required to abide by their laws.

In 1964 the English Connemara Pony Society introduced a rule that every pony registered in the ECPS Stud Book would in future be required to have not less than 75% known pure Connemara blood, and as this mitigated against ponies with only one known parent, or by one of the half-bred sires, but who were already registered in the CPBS Stud Book, the rule was not well received by the Council. The feeling was that as the CPBS Stud Book was now closed, all ponies who were already registered in it should be accepted into the stud books of other Connemara pony societies. The Council therefore decided that a meeting should be arranged with the new breed societies to discuss their problems, and if possible set agreed standards for registration.

The 1965 season was the last one in which John Walsh acted as a stallion custodian for the Society. His brother Martin Walsh was the owner of the famous mare, Cuach na Coille (236), and the family had kept a stallion for years before the Society was formed.

John became a custodian for the Society in 1932 when he took *Connemara Boy (9)* and stood him at Kylesalia, Kilkerrin for six seasons. He had *Lavalley Star (25)* for four years, followed by *Gil (43)* 1942 to 1945, and then *Creganna Winter (63)* for two seasons. *Calla Rebel (38)* spent three seasons at Kylesalia, and was followed by *Dun Orphan (77)* from 1951 to 1954. *Carna Dun (89)* 1955 to 1957 was succeeded by his son *Doon Paddy (95)* in 1957/58, and then *Carna Bobby (79)* for three years. *Dun Aengus (120)* spent two seasons there, and the final stallion to stand at Kylesalia was *Rebel Wind (127)* in 1964/65.

John Walsh had been a stallion custodian for thirty-three years and his weekly route was Carna, Moyrus, and Gowla on Mondays; Derryrush, Glentrasna, Maam Cross and Screebe on Wednesdays; and Kilkerrin on Saturdays. It was thanks to the stallion custodians like John that the work of the Society was able to succeed, and they all gave long years of service to the Connemara pony breeders in their district. Now, with modern transport, tarred roads, telephones, it is easy to forget the enormous dedication and time and effort the stallion men gave to the Connemara pony in earlier years. They still play a very important part in the work of the Society, and their contribution should not go unnoticed.

Carna Dun (89) was by now eighteen years old and was sold to Johnny Palmer, Glenlo Abbey in 1966. Although he was now privately owned, he remained on the list and stayed at Glenlo Abbey for another seven years until he was 25 years old, during which time he continued to cover mares and had a further seventy-seven registered progeny, with a number of mares from outside Connemara coming to visit him.

Martin Walsh (Pat) lived at Snabo, Rosmuck in the oldest house in the village, and next door to his cousin Michael Walsh, father of Jackie Walsh. Martin had kept a stallion for the Society since 1953 when he first stood *Creganna*

Garnet Irwin

Carna Dun (89) with Paddy Joyce

120

Winter (63) for one season. In the thirteen years that followed, seven different stallions passed through his hands including *Dun Lorenzo (55)*, *Tully Lad (48)*, *Creg Coneera (82)*, *Inver Rebel (93)*, *Aura Dun (123)*, *Mervyn Storm (140)*. In 1966 he had *Clonjoy (117)*, and it was Martin's last year as a custodian, and he died the following year. He was a colourful character and wore a big moustache, so earning him the nickname "Whiskers". He used to ride the stallions on his regular weekly round, travelling to Camus and Derrynea, Kilkerrin and Carna, Glentrasna and Maam Cross, and he looked so impressive riding on his stallion, he was known as The Prince, and when people heard him arriving in their village, the word would go round . . . "the Prince is coming!" In 1967 *Clonjoy (117)* moved to a new custodian in Snabo, Pat Murphy, and he kept him for three seasons, and travelled the same route as Martin Walsh (Pat) did before him.

Blue-Eyed Cream Ponies

At the AGM held in Galway on 21st March 1966, there was a discussion on the problem of blue-eyed cream ponies, and Dr Peter Cullen said he was particularly interested in the subject, and suggested that in the interests of the breed, steps should be taken to reduce the risk of breeding them by using more dark coloured stallions. Another breeder stated that it was difficult to find a market for the browns and bays as the duns, greys and creams were considered more typical of the breed. Reference was made to the research work done by Dr Parry, a geneticist at Oxford University, on blue-eyed cream ponies, and it was decided that a sub-committee should be formed to do some research on the subject. The members of this committee were: Mr T. McD Kelly MRCVS, Mr R. Kelly MRCVS, Mr P. Scannaill MRCVS, Dr J. Cullen, and Mr Sean Keane.

As a result of the findings of this committee, the Blue-Eyed Cream ponies ceased to be accepted for registration into the Stud Book of the Connemara Pony Breeders' Society, a decision which has been the cause of much controversy between breeders of Connemara ponies, and is a regular point of discussion at the international meetings.

The entries for the RDS Spring Show were continuing to increase, so in 1966 four classes were provided for Connemara ponies and there were sixty entries, although only twelve of these were exhibited by owners from Connemara. Among the prizewinners was Kingstown (2532) bred by John Folan, Errislannon and owned by Joe Gorham and she was 2nd in the four and five year old class. Joe bought Kingstown (2532) at Clifden fair as a yearling, and through her he developed his interest in showing and breeding. She stood 3rd to the Clifden Show champion in 1965, went one better in 1966 when she was placed 2nd to the champion of the Show, and won her class and the RDS Medal in 1967. Joe's first cup winner was her daughter King's Bridge (4374) who won the Archbishop's Cup in 1973. Kingstown was later sold to Mrs Jane Dalrymple, of Boden Park Stud, Co. Meath, but her name is perpetuated by Joe as he now uses it as his prefix.

43rd Annual Pony Show, Clifden – 18th August 1966

Three new studs whose prefixes were to become familiar names in the Show ring during the coming years won their first trophies that year, the American C. P. Society trophy and Carew Cup was won by Lord Hemphill with a yearling filly by Tooreen Ross (99) from the Tulira Stud, while Abbeyleix Molly ((2823) won the two year old filly class and was reserve for the Carew Cup for Lady de Vesci, Abbeyleix, and John Brennan, of Fort Lorenzo, Taylors Hill won the Rose of Barna Cup with Fort Silver (2829). Unusually there was a tie for the Camlin Ciro Cup for the best foal between Michael Conroy's colt and Tommy McDonagh's filly.

The Supreme Championship was won by Jack Bolger with Heather Mixture of Abbeyleix (2709) a lovely three year old dun mare by Clonkeehan Auratum (104) dam Calla Brown (922) who had won her class the previous year for her breeder Francis Burke, Calla, Roundstone.

Heather Mixture of Abbeyleix (2709) with Jack Bolger.

The 1966 show was the last one at which Tim Cotter acted as one of the judges, a duty he had performed for 38 years without a break since 1928 when the Society's Annual Show was held in the grounds of the old workhouse at Clifden for the first time. He was also on the Show committee for the four earlier shows, but was a judge in the Agricultural section rather than in the pony ring. Tim Cotter's co-judges for his last year were T. McD Kelly, Michael O'Connell and Mrs Lanigan O'Keefe.

Michael O'Connell was farm manager for Lord Revelstoke on Lambay Island, and had developed a keen interest in Connemara ponies since 1962, when he started buying foals to rear on the island. It was an ideal place to raise Connemara ponies, with the rough hill grazing providing similar conditions to their native surroundings. With a growing export market, Michael was quick to grasp the opportunity, and many ponies passed through Lambay on their way to new homes overseas. At first he bought ponies and sold them on, but later ponies were bred on the Island, and *Lambay Rebel (131)* was the first of many sires to stand there. He became an active and enthusiastic member of the Society, and judged regularly at Clifden until his untimely death in 1977. A poem written by Lord Revelstoke and printed in the Clifden Show catalogue sums up the feeling of the era.

THE CONNEMARA PONY

Compact, deep-bodied, shortish back,
With sloping withers, there's no lack
Of bone, well-balanced neck and head,
Round hoof'd, upstanding, strong, pure-bred.

Thirteen hands to fourteen one
In cream and grey and black and dun,
Docile, brave with charm and grace
They'll hunt and hack or jump and race.

They love this island very much
We send them North, South, East and West,
The French, the Swedes, the Danes, the Dutch
Come back for more … they are the best.

Lady deVesci, Jack Bolger, Garnet Irwin and Hon. Kate Vesey.

CHAPTER 9

1967-1970

• Volume XI Stud Book • Death of Michael O'Malley •Improvements to Showgrounds •
• Classes RDS Horse Show • New Society Netherlands • Death Two Founder Members •
• French Society Formed • Volume XII Stud Book. • Prefix Rules • International Conference •

By the end of 1966 there were 3000 mares on the register and 201 stallions, and the export trade continued steadily, with a large number of ponies being sold to Sweden, Denmark and Germany. Two ponies were sent to South Africa including the stallion *Clonkeehan Barna Boy (182)* who was Reserve Champion at Clifden in 1965, and several more ponies were sent to Australia, despite the high cost of transport. The following year Volume XI was published, priced 15/, which covered the period from January 1965 to January 1967, and contained particulars of 47 stallions, 418 mares and 66 geldings. This was the largest number of ponies ever registered by the Society in a period of two years, and the Connemara pony had come a long way since that first meeting in Oughterard forty-four years earlier.

Death of Michael O'Malley

During 1967, Michael O'Malley, the man who could be called the "founding father" of the Connemara Pony Breeders' Society, whose vision, determination, and love of the Connemara pony led to the forming of the Society in 1923, died at the age of 83. He became the first Secretary of the Society on the day it was formed in 1923, and had been a Joint Secretary with Bartley O'Sullivan from 1924 until Bartley's death in 1960, although he took a less active role in the administration of the affairs of the Society once it was established. Nevertheless it was largely due to his persistence and dedication to the Connemara pony that steps were taken to save the breed when its future looked threatened. He was a man of action and he put much hard work and enthusiasm into helping to organise the Society's early shows, and maintained his interest in the breed throughout his life. In 1950 he exported the stallion *Tully Nigger (81)* to America, who was one of the first four Connemara ponies to arrive in the States, and led to the forming of the American Connemara Pony Society. Michael O'Malley's contribution towards the revival of the Connemara pony was unique, and without his remarkable sense of purpose, the breed might have gradually faded into oblivion.

In 1965 the Minister of Agriculture had set up a Survey Team to examine all aspects of the Horse Breeding Industry and make recommendations for its development. The report was published in 1966 and commented very favourably on the work of the Connemara Pony Breeders' Society for the promotion and development of the Connemara Pony. It recommended that the Society should be given a grant in-aid to purchase a small farm to keep young colts, and also to provide facilities for breaking and training young ponies for breeders in Connemara and so increase the value of their ponies. This scheme would have been of great benefit to the Society, but sadly it never materialised.

In the meantime the funds for developing the Showgrounds had been exhausted, so the Council decided to appoint a fund-raising committee under the Chairmanship of Lord Hemphill, as more funds were needed to complete stage two of the improvements to the Showgrounds which included plans for providing seating, stabling and toilets.

These were ambitious plans for a Society with very little funds other than the grant of £1000 per annum from the Department of Agriculture, and a grant from the County Committee of Agriculture of £100 a year. The revenue from members subscriptions amounted to only £75, so it was decided to raise the subscription to £2 and also to increase the fees for registration and the entry fees for the Show to try to generate a little more income for the Society.

Connemara Classes move to RDS Horse Show, August 1967

The Royal Dublin Society had been providing in-hand classes for Connemara ponies at the Spring Show in May since 1951, but in 1967 these classes were transferred to the Dublin Horse Show in August. This move had been requested by the Council as it was felt that it would be easier for breeders from Connemara to have their ponies in show condition in August, and also that the Horse Show would provide a better showcase for the ponies with its large gathering of international visitors who were actively interested in horses and ponies.

There were four well filled classes with the biggest entry of 29 ponies in the two year old filly class. It proved to be a good move with great interest being shown in the ponies and several good sales were made.

44th Annual Pony Show, Clifden – 18th August 1967

The Clifden Show was equally successful with an increase in entries and a very high standard of ponies on show. *Bridge Boy (124)* won the stallion class for Paddy Geoghegan, with *Carna Bobby (79)* now aged 21, taking third place for Paddy Lally, Gort. A new class was introduced that year which was confined to Registered

Bridge Boy (124)

Connemara Pony Stallions who were on the Society's list for service in Connemara in 1967, and it was also won by *Bridge Boy (124)*. John Brennan, Fort Lorenzo, won both the yearling classes, and the Carew Cup was won for a second year by Tulira Mavourneen (3036) owned by Lord Hemphill. Lady de Vesci's Abbeyleix Molly (2823) won the Killanin Cup and RDS Silver Medal, and the Championship of the Show and the Archbishop's Cup for the best brood mare went to Cashel Kate (2030) owned by Mr T. R. Donnelly. So once again the major awards went to owners from outside the Connemara district.

Volumes I to VIII of Stud Book Reprinted in 1968

With the growing interest in the breed from overseas and many new breeders in Ireland, the stocks of the early Stud Books had been exhausted, so it was decided to reprint Volumes I to 8 in one book and this was printed in 1968 and cost £3 per copy. Unfortunately the demand for these books was under-estimated, and a further printing had to be made in 1969.

John Curran, Kilkerrin became a new stallion custodian in 1967 and stood *MacDara (91)* for one season. *Doon Paddy (95)* was placed with him in 1968, while *Atlantic Storm (139)* was transferred to Paddy Joyce in Oughterard, and a new four year old stallion, *Toombeola (211)* by Carna Dun (89) dam Silver Belle (1369) who had been bought by the Society, went to Tom Feeney, Carraroe for his first season. *Knockranny Ruby (134)* was sold by Peter Kyne to Sweden and left the list in 1968.

Connemara Pony Society Formed in Holland

Some Dutch visitors had been coming to the Breed Show since 1964, and a few ponies had been imported into Holland each year, but it was not until a party of nineteen breeders visited Ireland in April 1968 and bought two stallions and fifteen mares that the breeders decided to form a Connemara Pony Society in Holland. On 30th March 1968 the new Society was formed, and became the fifth overseas society to represent the growing number of Connemara ponies now being bred outside Ireland.

One of the first ponies to be exported to Holland was the six year old stallion *Glenarde (149)* by MacDara (91), dam Ballinahown Grey (1886) bred by Michael Curran, Ballinahown, and he became No. 1 in the stallion register in the Nederlands

Nederlands C.P. Stamboek

Glenarde (149)

Connemara Pony Stud Book. He was sold by John Brennan, Fort Lorenzo, and was the sire of the winning two year old filly Fort Helen (3287) at Clifden in 1968. He was imported into Holland by Baroness Van Thuyll who also bought the 1966 Clifden Champion, Heather Mixture of Abbeyleix (2709), and she became the first champion mare in Holland. Among other mares who were exported at the same time were: Lor Blue Belle (1712), Errislannon Fuschia (2915), Beauty Queen (2602), Kingstown Swallow (2199) and her two daughters Easter Patricia (3270) and Miss Gortalowry (2982).

The 1968 Dublin Horse Show again attracted good entries in the Connemara classes, and there were 17 entries in a strong class for mares aged six or over, many of them first prizewinners, who came before the judge John O'Mahony Meade, President of the English Connemara Pony Society. It was a battle between Trevor Donnelly's two good mares, and the winner was the 8 year old

Atlantic Mist (2175)

Atlantic Mist (2175) with Cashel Kate (2030) in second place, and two weeks later Atlantic Mist (2175) went on to take the Archbishop's Cup and the Supreme Championship at Clifden.

Further improvements to the Society's showgrounds during the year were limited through lack of funds, but the fund raising had been very successful and £2000 had been collected. The Department of Agriculture had now agreed to give the Society a further grant towards the Showground project by offering £1 for every £1 collected in excess of the £2000 already collected, and another appeal was launched to raise more funds to complete the development project.

45th Annual Pony Show, Clifden – 15th August 1968

There was a record attendance at the Show with many overseas visitors including Jan Harald Koelichen from Germany who presented his cup to the Champion of the Show. The winner of the Stallion Class was Greaney *Rebel (186)*, s. Inver Rebel (93) dam Nansin Ban (1858) owned by Martin McNamara, Flagmount, Co. Clare, and the Killanin Cup was won for the second year by Lady de Vesci with Abbeyleix Molly (2823), and she was also Reserve Champion of the Show. John Brennan produced the winning two year old colt *Marble (254)* who was bred by Martin Mulkerrin, Callowfeenish from his good prizewinning mare Callowfeenish Dolly II (1913). This mare was also the dam of the Supreme Champion of the Show Atlantic Mist (2175), and her full sister Atlantic Surf (2471) was placed 3rd in the five and six year old mare class, shown by Jimmy Jones. The O'Sullivan Memorial Plaque went to Mrs Brooks with Errislannon Heather (2205) by Gael Linn (103).

The class for mares of seven years and over was won by Ashe Grey (1673) by Cilciarain (78), dam Small Change (701) owned by Sean McLoughlin, Moycullen. Sadly Sean died shortly after the Show, but it was fitting that he had a winner at his final show. He was a school teacher in Moycullen, a gentle, kindly man, with a love of the Irish language, and many of his ponies had gaelic names. He was a member of the Council from 1965, and a great supporter of the Connemara pony. His sons Joe and Tom have inherited his love of the ponies and still have ponies today.

Col. Michael Creighton was a new breeder who had started breeding Connemara ponies at his home Killyreagh, near Enniskillen. One of the foundation mares he bought from Trevor Donnelly was Ballydonagh Kate (2798), a daughter of Cashel Kate (2030) by MacDara (91) and she produced a colt foal by Carna Bobby (79). In 1968 Col. Creighton brought the yearling colt to Clifden where he was placed 2nd in his class, and after the Show he most generously donated this colt to the Society. He was named *Killyreagh Kim (308)*, and he spent some time with Graham Tulloch at Shanbolard who kept him until he was ready to join the Society's approved list of stallions in 1970, when he was placed with Josie Conroy. He was to spend 16 years in Connemara and was a popular and successful sire with 242 of his progeny registered in the Connemara Pony Stud Book.

Death of Two Founder Members

At a Council meeting in December 1968, tributes were paid to two men who had died recently who were founder members of the Council, and had both contributed greatly to the work of the Society over many years. Dan Twomey had been a member of the Inspection Committee since it was formed in 1924, when he was Chief Inspector of Livestock for the Department of Agriculture. He served as a member of Council from 1923 to 1952, and became Secretary of the Department of Agriculture, and was made an Honorary member of the Society in 1960. He was a judge at some of the early shows, and maintained an active interest in the work of the Society all his life.

Tim Cotter was a member of the Inspection Committee since it was formed in 1924, and a Society judge for 38 years from 1928 to 1966. He was a founder member of the Council from 1923 to 1959, and was made an Honorary Member of the Society in 1960. He was often sent to inspect stallions which had been offered for sale to the Society, and his meticulous reports in the stallion records bear witness to Tim Cotter's exacting standards. He knew every inch of Connemara which he travelled on his bicycle during his time as an Inspector for the Department of Agriculture, and had a great love of the district, its people and its ponies. Even when he retired to Dublin, he still returned to Connemara twice a year for the Inspections and the Annual Show.

Mervyn Storm (140) by Carna Dun (89) dam Windy Rebel (1473) had been removed from the approved stallion list at the end of the 1968 season having spent five years on the list, two with Martin Walsh (Pat) at Snabo, and three with Tommy O'Brien at Canal Stage. He left 128 registered progeny including the mares Dooneen Grey (3671), Sarena (3994), Grey Hop 2nd (3689), Rusty Glen (4352), and through his son *Clare Charger (310)* two of his granddaughters, Trabane Castle (5959) and Miss Charger (6400) feature in the pedigrees of some of today's stallions. *Mervyn Storm (140)* spent the rest of his life as a teaser at a stud in Dunboyne, Co. Meath, but left some valuable old bloodlines in his stock in Connemara.

Four new stallions joined the approved list in 1969, two owned by the Society, and two owned privately. *Thunderbolt (178)* was a six year old son of *Thunder (113)* and had been bred by John Brennan out of his mare Irene Grey (1899) by Farravane Boy (71). He came onto the list representing the Green Line which was a welcome increase to the gene pool, as there had been no stallion from that line on the list for more than a decade. However he only remained on the list for three seasons, one with Mikey King at Claddaghduff, and two with Stephen Curran at Kilkerrin, before being replaced on the list by his son *Thundercloud (459)* in 1973.

The second Society-owned stallion was *Ardilaun (261)*, a three year old son of *Carna Bobby (79)* bred by Joe McNamara, Craughwell from his mare Ganty Jane (2300) by Tully Lad

J. Petch

Thunderbolt (178) with Mikey King.

(48), so he also carried the Green Line on his dam's side. The other two stallions were the four year old *Kimble (227)* by Dun Aengus (120) dam Inver Colleen (2202), owned by Willie Diamond, Tully, and already a prizewinner at Clifden, and *Paddy's Boy (183)* a three year old son of *Paddy's Heaven (137)*, whose dam Swangate (2649) was also by Tully Lad (48) and he was owned by Paddy Geoghegan, Oughterard.

In March 1969, the death was announced of Sean O'Donoughue, CAO. Co. Galway Committee of Agriculture. He had been a member of Council since 1962, and had administered the nomination scheme on behalf of the Society from the County Buildings. Following his death, this valuable assistance was not continued by his successor, and from 1970 onwards the nomination scheme was administered by the Secretary of the Society. This amounted to a lot of extra work for Mr Killeen and his assistant Phil MacDermott, but no funds were available to increase their small wages.

A new member of the Council that year was Graham Tulloch, who was to give many years valuable service to the Society and was a highly respected and knowledgeable horseman. He had returned from abroad in the mid-fifties to take over the family farm Shanbolard at Moyard, and built up a herd of Connemara ponies using the prefix Ocean, which came from his foundation mare Ocean Melody (2134). She was an attractive dun mare by Clonkeehan Auratum (104) and won the Killanin Cup in 1962 and the RDS Silver Medal for young mares in 1964. He had a naturally good eye for stock, and was soon made a member of the Inspection Committee, and he also acted as a Society judge for many years.

New Stables Built at Showgrounds

The work on the Showgrounds was finally able to go ahead in 1969 thanks to a generous grant of £2000 from Bord Failte, and an additional grant of £2000 from the Department of Agriculture as well as over £2700 donated by individuals in response to the fundraising appeal, and 24 new stallion boxes were built at the Showgrounds in time for the Show as well as some precast concrete seating erected around the ringside for spectators.

The stables were made available for breeders who had travelled some distance to the Show to keep their ponies in overnight, but had to be vacated on show day, when they were to be used to stable the stallions entered for the Show. Stabling in Clifden at show time has always been a problem, and with more ponies coming to the Show from outside Connemara every year, the new stables were a great improvement on what was available previously. Ponies have been known to be stabled in the garage at the Bank, the bottle store behind a pub, and even in the cells in the old town jail! Joe Gorham was appointed caretaker of the Showgrounds in 1970, and it has been his job each year to sort out the stabling arrangements during the Show, a difficult task, but he always does his best to look after everyone.

46th Annual Show, Clifden – 21st August 1969

The Show was an even bigger success than the previous year, with a record attendance and 347 entries in the pony classes. There were large numbers of foreign buyers paying big prices for ponies, and among the many visitors were representatives from all the new overseas societies with large parties of breeders from Sweden and Germany. The Show had also become a major tourist attraction in the area, so Clifden was crammed with visitors on Show day. In a newspaper article a journalist describing the Show asked "How high can a Connemara Pony jump? … in price!"

Bridge Boy (124) won both the stallion classes, and as always gave an impressive display. He was a great showman and like his great-great-grandsire *Rebel (7)* he enjoyed standing on his hind legs and showing off to the crowd. Abbeyleix Molly (2823) won her class for the fourth year running for Lady de Vesci, this

Abbeyleix Molly (2823) with Lady deVesci.

131

time it was the Archbishop's Cup and RDS Silver Medal, and she was also reserve Champion for the second time. Abbeyleix Molly was bred in Clifden by Senator John Mannion out of his mare Clifden Molly (2127), and when sold to Lady de Vesci as a yearling, she went to live in the Midlands, but she really seemed to enjoy coming back to her native Connemara every year, as she always sparkled in the Show ring at Clifden.

The Killanin Cup was won by Ballydonagh Deirdre (3423), a four year old daughter of Cashel Kate (2030) by Carna Bobby (79), bred by Trevor Donnelly, and she went on to win the Jan Harald Koelichen Cup and became Supreme Champion of the Show.

During the year a beautiful book about the Connemara pony was published in German under the title "Connemara, Pferdeland am Meer". It was written by the internationally known author of books about horses, Ursula Bruns, and beautifully illustrated with black and white photographs taken by a gifted young photographer Dirk Schwager. The author and photographer had spent many hours together studying the ponies in their natural surroundings, and the result was a fascinating and informed study of the Connemara Pony. The book was later translated into English by Anthony Dent and published under the name "Connemara, Seaboard of the Horses. "

Following the success of the 1969 Annual Show, a Council meeting was held, and it was decided that the time had come to hold an International Conference of Connemara Pony Societies in order to exchange information and discuss mutual problems. It was hoped that regulations for the registration of all Connemara ponies could become standardised, and it was important that all the newly formed societies should meet with the Connemara Pony Breeders' Society to discuss how best this could be achieved.

It was to be a two day Conference, and the dates chosen were Friday 21st and Saturday 22nd August 1970, which would be the two days following the 47th Annual Show at Clifden. A number of committees were formed, and the Organising Committee was chaired by the President of the Society, Lord Killanin. There were also three sub-committees: Technical chaired by Sean Keane; Finance chaired by Lord Hemphill; Social and Reception chaired by Mrs Maeve Kelly.

Each established Connemara Pony Society was to be invited to send items for the agenda and to nominate two delegates to attend the conference. Observers were also to be invited from countries where societies were likely to formed in the near future, and places were to be offered to members of the Connemara Pony Breeders' Society.

New French Connemara Pony Society

Some breeders in France had been importing Connemara ponies since 1963, and once they started to be recognised in France, their numbers grew rapidly, and in 1969 the new French Society was formed. It was called the Association Francaise du Poney Connemara and M. Chagnaud was its first President. He imported his first mare in 1965, and two years later he bought the stallion *Island Earl (177)* s. Carna Dun (89) from John Daly, and this sire became the foundation sire for the breed in France. He gained a reputation as a sire of jumpers, and eight of his ten registered sons were used at the National Haras (studs) throughout France. In the early seventies the Connemara pony took off in France, and it became the fastest growing overseas society, with fourteen stallions and ninety-five mares in the Connemara section of the Stud Book by 1973.

Volume XII of the Connemara Pony Stud Book was due to be published in 1969, but because of a serious fire at the printers' works, the publication date was delayed until February 1970. This volume covered the period between January 1967 and January 1969 and it reflected the growing demand for Connemara ponies with an even bigger number of ponies being registered than in the previous two year period. It contained a total of 676 registrations consisting of the particulars of 80 stallions, 502 mares and 94 geldings. This was the last volume of the Stud Book to be published without an index of the ponies, and in future all Stud Books from Volume XIII onwards included an index of ponies and their stud numbers.

A member of the Society, Miss Susan Traill, who helped Miss Lee Norman with the ponies at Clonkeehan Stud, kindly offered to compile an index of the first 12 volumes of the Stud Books, and undertook to do this on a voluntary basis. It was quite a formidable task, with a total of 4047 ponies to be indexed (without the aid of a computer), and it was an invaluable piece of work, which is still extremely useful when trying to trace a pony in the early years of the register.

Rules for Prefixes – Increase Membership from 100 to 200

At the AGM held on 11th March 1970 tributes were paid to the late Col. Bellingham who had died during the year. He had been a great benefactor of the Society and had given his support to the Society in many different ways. His ponies carrying the Glencara prefix had been exported to America and many other countries, and he had acted as a judge in England on several occasions.

The question of prefixes had been raised on several occasions in the past, and it was finally included in the regulations for registration following this meeting. Prior to 1970 many breeders and dealers were using a prefix on all ponies who were owned by them at registration age, and this was causing some confusion with buyers from overseas. From 1970 onwards, a breeder was entitled to register a prefix with the Society for life, and it could not be used by another person. The breeder with a registered stud prefix could use the prefix for all ponies bred by the stud, and the prefix would be added to the name of the pony at the time of registration, but it could no longer be used for a pony who had not been bred by the stud. It was also ruled that a prefix could not be used as a suffix.

There was now a waiting list for membership of the Society, which under the Articles of Association had been restricted to 100 members, and so an application was made to have the rules amended so that the number of members could be increased to 200. This amendment was passed at an EGM held following the AGM on 27th March 1971, and twenty-four people who had been on the waiting list were made members of the Society. More breeders in Connemara were now keen to join the Society, although the majority of the members were still from outside Connemara.

In 1970 Mrs Brooks of Errislannon Manor offered to provide weekly training sessions at the Show grounds for ponies and riders, and this was started on 10th April that year. She also held training courses at Errislannon to encourage the education of ponies and riders, and as a result of this training, a highly successful innovation at the 1970 Annual Pony Show was an historical pageant held during the lunch break, which was designed and produced by Mrs Brooks, and enacted by the pupils from her riding centre.

47th Annual Pony Show, Clifden – 20th August 1970

With the International Conference being held the following day, a large number of foreign delegates were expected to attend the Show, so there was a big increase in entries, and 499 ponies were catalogued. The classes for youngstock were huge, and in particular the yearling filly class which had a total of 88 entries.

Kimble (227) with Willie Diamond

John Brennan, Fort Lorenzo had three home-bred entries in the class, and took the 1st 2nd and 4th prizes with Tommy McDonagh just managing to squeeze into third place and deny John a clean sweep! The winner was Fort Viola (4267) by Carna Bobby (79), dam Fort Pansy (3041), 2nd was Fort Holly (4266) by Clonkeehan Auratum (104) dam Irene Grey (1899) and 4th was Celebration Cream (4270) by Marble (254), dam Moycullen Mite (2093). It was a quite unique achievement, and one that has never been repeated.

A strong class of twenty-seven stallions filled the ring, with *Bridge Boy (124)*, already a winner on three previous occasions, being challenged by the five year old dun *Kimble (227)* owned by Willie Diamond. On the day it was *Kimble (227)* who won the class, and in second place was his son *The Fugitive (368)*, the winning two year old colt, who was bred by Pakie Coyne, Renvyle and owned by Charlie Lydon MRCVS, Westport, and *Bridge Boy (124)* was placed third.

The Camlin Ciro Cup for the best foal went to a filly foal by Bridge Boy (124) and her dam was the 20 year old Cregg Lassie (1737) owned by Jim Walsh, Cregg, Oughterard. Joe Carr, Dangan, won the yearling colt class with a son of *Rebel Wind (127)*, who was registered a year later for Paddy Carr as *Dangan Dun (415)*, and his dam Breath of Spring (3137) took the five to six year old class for Michael Conroy, Bunowen.

Errislannon Daisy (2533) won the O'Sullivan Memorial Plaque, for Mrs Brooks, and Trevor Donnelly's Atlantic Mist (2175), who had no foal at foot, won her class and became the Supreme Champion of the Show for the second time, with the stallion *Kimble (227)* the Reserve Champion.

The Show was an outstanding success, with the large group of visitors being shown the cream of the youngstock of Connemara, and in the class for mares of seven years or over with foal at foot, forty-eight wonderful mares and foals provided a feast of all that is best in the Connemara pony. The class was won by Trevor Donnelly's Cashel Kate (2030) with Finola of Leam (3036) in second place for Jack Bolger. However, as well as these super mares, each year there are many mares in the broodmare classes who are not placed in the Show, but who are the real backbone of the breed, and also part of its history, and their progeny have made the the Connemara pony famous in many different countries throughout the world.

First International Conference for Connemara Pony Societies

The following day the First International Conference for Connemara Pony Societies was opened by the Minister of Agriculture Mr James Gibbons at University College Galway, and there were delegates from all the overseas Connemara Pony Societies, Great Britain, United States of America, Sweden, Denmark, Holland and France, as well as from the Connemara Pony Breeders' Society. There were also representatives from countries where Connemara Pony Societies had not yet been established, Germany, Belgium and Italy, and a total of 200 delegates attended the conference.

In his opening address the President of the Connemara Pony Breeders' Society Lord Killanin welcomed all the delegates, and said that since the foundation of the Society in 1923 when the ponies were limited to Connemara and when their main purpose was as a working pony, to the present day when the ponies had become a major export, conditions had changed considerably. It was felt that the time had come to call a conference so that the Connemara pony breeders of the world could meet, and that the many points of mutual interest, and possibly of difference, could be freely discussed.

The first session of the Conference was then opened by Mr Sean Keane with an illustrated talk on the Connemara Pony in which he gave a brief history of the city of Galway, and of Connemara and the Connemara pony. This was followed by a lecture on Equine Diseases and Control given by Dr. B. Farrelly, MRCVS. and the afternoon session had two more talks, one by Dr. L. B. Moore MRCVS. on Equine Nutrition, and the second by Miss Susan Traill on Schooling the Connemara Pony. This session was then finished by the Showing of a film on the Connemara Pony.

The second day was taken up with a series of ten minute talks given by a delegate from each society, followed by discussions about the points raised. Several of the societies stated that blue-eyed cream ponies were not accepted into their stud books, and there were problems with ponies growing over height and not being eligible for registration. Some of the societies also required two generations of pure Connemara blood in the pedigree of a pony being registered in their stud book, and this caused some difficulties for ponies bred in Ireland from the half-bred sires or from some of the foundation stock who had been registered without known breeding. These were the main points of difference raised, and there were some useful exchanges of views, and the overall feeling of the Conference was one of optimism and goodwill between the societies. It was proposed that a Round Table Conference should be held in Clifden the following year on the morning after the Show, to continue discussions between the societies.

Parade of Stallions at Tulira Castle

At the end of the Conference, the delegates were invited to visit Tulira Castle where a Parade of stallions took place, with a commentary given by Miss Berridge. It was a lovely setting for a unique occasion, and the stallions paraded in order of seniority with the twenty-four year old *Carna Bobby (79)* leading the parade, followed by *Carna Dun (89)* aged twenty two, *MacDara (91)* aged twenty-one, *Clonkeehan Auratum (104)* aged sixteen, and *Thunder (113)* aged thirteen. These five stallions represented the five stallion lines still intact, the Blue, Red and Green lines tracing back to the original foundation sires, and the Purple and Orange lines representing the Thoroughbred and Arab blood of the two half-bred sires. The young stallions presented included *Cregmore Dun (223)*, s. Tooreen Ross (99), d. Smokey (1198), *Marble (254)*, s. Rebel Wind (127), d. Callowfeenish Dolly II (1913) *Ballydonagh Rob (321)* s. Carna Bobby (79) d. Cashel Kate (2030) and *Jolly Roger (397)* s. MacDara (91) d. Callowfeenish Dolly II (1913).

Milleder Archive

Carna Bobby (79)

The parade was followed by a riding and dressage display given by members of the local Pony Club, and a jumping demonstration was given by Miss G. Kerins riding Waltzing Matilda (2625), s. Carna Dun (89) owned by Mr Jim Norton. Afterwards a reception was given in the Castle by Lord and Lady Hemphill, and the evening ended with a Medieval Banquet at Dunguaire Castle, Kinvara.

The Conference had been a great success, largely due to tremendous amount of effort and hard work which was put into it by the organising committee and the three sub-committees. John Killeen and Mrs Phil MacDermott especially put in a lot of extra work in running the Show and the Conference, and because of their efforts, the three days ran very smoothly. The Society also received

J. Walshe

Waltzing Matilda (2625)

major sponsorship from the Department of Agriculture, Bord Failte, Coras Tractala, and Callaghans of Dame Street, Dublin.

J. Walshe

Clonkeehan Auratum (104) at Tulira Castle.

Shortly after the Conference, John Killeen suffered the sad loss of his daughter Mary, who had lived with him at Nun's Island since the death of his wife some years earlier. It was a very traumatic time for him, and later he left Nun's Island, and moved in with his son Sean, his daughter-in-law Mary and their four children at Ard na Mara in Salthill, so Salthill became the Society's new office from 1st September 1972. Phil MacDermott also lived in Salthill, and as the work in the Society increased, she was on hand to give more assistance when needed. John Killeen was never a nine-to-five man, and during his years as Secretary he always provided an office in his home and was used to people calling at all times including weekends and public holidays. Even in his later years he never complained or objected if a call came day or night. Indeed with the interest in ponies extending to United States and Australia, this sometimes meant a phone call in the early hours of the morning from some overseas caller, but everyone was treated with the utmost courtesy.

Carna Dun (89) with Paddy Carr at Tulira Castle, 1970.

CHAPTER 10

1971 - 1975

• *Documentary film* • *Australian Society Formed* • *EGM to Increase Council* • *Volume XIII Stud Book* •
• *German Breeders Group Formed* • *Death of Patron Dr Walsh* • *Killanin Resigns* •
• *Sean Keane New President* • *Farewell to Old Stallions* • *Ponies to Paris Show* •
• *Volume XIV Stud Book* • *Ist Clifden Gymkhana* • *Ist Chronicle* • *Ponies to Aras an Uachtarain* •
• *Bord na gCapall replaces Dept of Agriculture, increases grant* • *Four new Council Members* •

A film entitled "Connemara and its Ponies" was made by David Shaw Smith in 1970 and was shown on RTE during 1971. It was a beautifully made film, which followed the seasons in Connemara, and showed a foal being born, the Annual Inspections, the Clifden Show, and the pony's place in the life of a family in Connemara. The commentary was written by Lord Killanin, and there were some beautiful shots of Connemara and the ponies in their natural surroundings. The film was widely shown on television, and in cinemas and on airlines worldwide, and gave the Connemara pony some good publicity.

In 1971 there were twelve approved stallions in Connemara, with *Clonjoy (117)* not placed for that season, and *Paddy's Boy ((183)* was taken off the list. *Killyreagh Kim (308)* had joined the list in 1970, but sadly his breeder Col. Creighton who had donated him to the Society died that year, and so he never saw any of his progeny.

The export trade had slowed down in 1970, but in 1971 there was a better demand and ponies were sent to Sweden, Denmark, Holland France and Germany during the year. The export of ponies to USA had been seriously curtailed by the lack of direct shipping from Ireland to America, and if ponies were transported through English ports, the new regulations in the UK with regard to the transport of horses involved lengthy delays at the ports which added considerably to the shipping costs. The Society asked the Horse Board and the Department of Agriculture to see if anything could be done, as it was a major problem in the export trade to the United States.

Connemara Pony Breeders' Society of Australasia Formed

Fred Wiltshire MRCVS had been importing Connemara ponies into Australia since 1963, and the breed had gained in popularity and grown in numbers, with the first Australian-bred foal born in 1967.

Four years later, on St Patricks Day 1971, the Connemara Pony Breeders' Society of Australasia was formed, and became the seventh new society to represent the Connemara pony overseas. The founding members of the

Society included Colin and Margaret Kelly, Frank Tynon and Harold Baldwin. Fred Wiltshire became the first President of the Society, and was both its inspiration and driving force.

His first imported stallion *Island King (122)*, (no. 1 in the Australian Stud Book) stood at Connemara Park, near Lancefield, Victoria, and was certainly the foundation sire for the breed in Australia, with fifteen sons registered by him, all but two carrying the Connemara Park prefix. The first registered mare who went out in 1965 was Ardan (2465), s. Inver Rebel (93), d. Leam Lassie (1838), bred by Coleman Sullivan, Leam, and she proved to be an outstanding broodmare, with six registered stallion sons, and twenty-three foals during her long life. She was only 12. 3 h. h. and just three years old when she left Ireland, but she was remarkably tough and imperturbable, and lived to the age of thirty. She travelled out with a filly foal at foot, Easter Mask (2940) by Island Prince (136) and produced a full brother in Australia, who became the stallion *Connemara Park Kenneth*. Two more mares went out the following year, Noreen Ban (2355) by Cilciarain (78) with Easter Peak (3239) at foot, and Renvyle Rebel (2728) by Tooreen Ross (99), and these were the first foundation mares for the breed in Australia.

It was a sad blow for the new Society when Fred Wiltshire's untimely death two years later, following a tractor accident on his farm, deprived the Connemara world in Australia of its most ardent supporter, and it took some time to recover from his loss. Fortunately there were others to pick up the reins, and the Connemara Pony Breeders' Society of Australasia grew and prospered.

48th Annual Show, Clifden – 19th August 1971

The Show had almost as many entries as the previous year, and this year the Supreme Championship of the Show went to *Kimble (227)* who gave a fine show in the stallion class. Lady Carew was the visiting judge, and the Carew Cup for two year old fillies was won by Abbeyleix Holly (4225) shown by her breeder Lady de Vesci, who had also won the same cup with Holly's dam Abbeyleix Molly (2823) in 1966. Abbeyleix Holly (4225) was also the Reserve Champion of the Show.

Hill Country (2504) won the RDS Silver Medal for the best broodmare aged seven or over with foal at foot, and her owner Jimmy Jones also won the Archbishop's Cup with Atlantic Surf (2471). The winning yearling filly s. Rebel Wind (127) d. Dancing Spanner (1750) was owned and bred by Tommy

J. Walshe

Abbeyleix Holly (4225) and Ashfield Loyal Sparrow (4424).

140

McDonagh, and was to become one of the most successful ponies he ever owned, her name was Roundstone River (4746).

The first Round Table Meeting was held the day after Clifden Show 1971, at the Great Southern Hotel, Galway, and delegates from the overseas societies met with members of the Council and the technical sub-committee which had been formed for the International Conference the year before. It was a successful meeting, and M. Chagnaud, President of the Association Francaise du Poney Connemara submitted a copy of the rules the French Society proposed to adopt.

During 1972 the Society lost another benefactor with the death of the Most Rev. Dr Walsh, the former Archbishop of Tuam, who had been a Patron of the Society since 1940. He was the first person to present a perpetual trophy to the Society for the Annual Show, and his beautiful silver cup which became known as the Archbishop's Cup was first awarded in 1944, and was won by Cuach na Coille (236).

New Inspection Committee

The Council decided it was time to review the Inspection Committee which had been reduced to four following the deaths of some of its longstanding members. With increasing numbers of ponies being bred outside the Connemara district, it was felt necessary to enlarge the Committee, and appoint Inspectors to cover all four provinces of the country. The new Inspection Committee included the following: T. McD Kelly MRCVS. R. Kelly MRCVS. P. O'Scannaill MRCVS. Col. D. Corry, S. Keane, M. O'Connell, D. Kenny, T. Duggan, Miss Berridge, Mrs Petch, Mrs Lanigan O'Keefe, Miss Lee Norman, Major Davison.

Connemara Pony Breeders' Society – 1972

Patron
Very Rev Chancellor Corcoran, Clifden.

President
Lord Killanin, St Annin's Spiddal.

Vice Presidents
T. McD. Kelly MRCVS, Raheen Park, Athenry.
Very Rev Canon Moran PP Oranmore.

Secretary   **Hon Secretary**
John Killeen, Ard na Mara, Salthill.   Sean Keane, Newcastle, Galway

Lord Killanin, St. Annin's, Spiddal, Galway.

T. McD. Kelly MRCVS. Raheen Park, Athenry.

John Mannion, Hulk Street, Clifden.

R. Kelly MRCVS, Penrose, Dalysfort Road, Galway.

John Daly, Lough Mask House, The Neale, Co. Mayo.

Miss Garnet Irwin, Ross, Moyard.

T. J. McDonagh, Roundstone, Connemara.

Lord Hemphill, Tulira Castle, Ardrahan.

Graham Tulloch, Shanbolard, Moyard.

Miss E. Berridge, Mervyn, Enniskerry, Co. Wicklow.

Very Rev Canon Moran PP, Oranmore, Galway.

Sean Keane, Newcastle, Galway.

P. O'Scannaill,MRCVS, Clifden.

John Geoghegan TD, Carna, Connemara.

Tom Walsh, Market Street, Clifden.

Jim. Lee, Moycullen.

Martin Treacy, Spiddal.

Michael Clancy, Spiddal.

Lt. Col. Dan Corry, Palmerstown, Co. Dublin.

The Council was limited to twenty members by the Memorandum and Articles of Association and membership of the Society was open to people resident in Eire. This meant that breeders in Northern Ireland could only become honorary members of the Society, and as a result some Northern breeders suggested they might form an Association to promote the Connemara Pony in the North.

The Council was not in favour of this idea, and so it was decided to:

(a) Amend the Memorandum and Articles of Association so that residents in Northern Ireland could become ordinary members of the Society.

(b) Increase the membership of the Council from twenty to twenty-four. This increase would enable the Society to have a representative from each province on the Council.

These amendments were passed at an EGM held on 28th March 1972.

Volume XIII of the Stud Book

A new volume of the Stud Book was published in March 1972 and was priced at £1. 50. The overall number of ponies registered in the two year period from January 1969 to January 1971 showed a big increase on the previous volume with a total of 961 ponies including 150 stallions 687 mares and 124 geldings. This was the first volume of the Stud Book to include an index of the ponies with their registered numbers as well as indexes of the owners of stallions, mares and geldings. It contained a much greater amount of information, and although the volume was of a similar size, the print was much smaller than in earlier volumes.

Thunderbolt (178) had only spent three seasons on the list when he left Connemara at the end of the 1971 season, and was sold as a teaser to Alan Lillingston at Mount Coote Stud, Kilmallock, Co. Limerick in the spring of 1972. He left a small group of progeny including a son *Thundercloud (459)* who replaced him as a Society stallion in 1973. *Thunderbolt (178)* had some good daughters including, Hillside Star (4774), Ceres (4775), Loobeen Meg (4809), Rossinver Dolly (5225), Martin's Pride (6013), Ashfield Gipsy (5504). Unfortunately his son did not prove as successful a sire, and was not popular with the breeders, leaving only thirteen progeny.

Doon Paddy (95) retired from the stallion list at the end of 1971 having spent 15 years in Connemara, and lived out his last years with Joe McNamara in Craughwell until 1977. He left 222 progeny, and a son, *Lough Easkey (166)* dam Rambling Colleen (1563) succeeded him on the stallion list for one season in 1972, but had few registered progeny. No other son from either *Carna Dun (89)* or *Doon Paddy (95)* was bought at this time by the Society, but two sons of *Doon Paddy (95)*, *Glyntown Paddy (259)* and *Silver Rocket (523)* both privately owned, were later to provide sons to continue the Purple Line. It was not until 1985 that a grandson of

Doon Paddy (95)

Doon Paddy (95) was bought by the Society, and he was *Seafield Silver Rogue (823)* by Silver Rocket (523).

Doon Paddy (95) left some good daughters including Betsy Bay (2075), Errislannon Daisy (2533), Blue Moon (2542), Rinso (2731), Merry Dolly (4340), Winnie the Pooh (4349), Ganty Gina (7187), and many more who made their name overseas.

Clonjoy (117) was not placed in Connemara in 1971 but returned to the list in 1972 and stood with Tommy O'Brien at Canal Stage for his last season in Connemara.

The new members of the inspection committee were invited to attend the Annual Inspections in Connemara which took place 15th to 17th May 1972, and a visitor from Germany, Mrs E. von St. Paul was also welcomed as an observer on the inspection tour. Mrs von St Paul was the delegate who spoke for Germany at the International Conference in 1970 and was one of the first people in Germany to develop an interest in the Connemara pony. Special inspections for registration were also carried out by the Society's inspectors in other parts of the country during the year, and these were largely individual inspections rather than at centres, because the breeders were widely scattered throughout the country. In all, 34 stallions, 432 mares and 74 geldings were registered during the year.

German Breeders Group Formed 1972

During 1972 Mrs E. von Paul and some friends joined together to form a group of breeders and friends of the Connemara pony in Germany, and this was the foundation of the Connemara Pony Interessengemeinshaft which grew into today's thriving Connemara Pony Society in Germany.

Connemara ponies had been imported into Germany since the mid-fifties, at first mostly geldings for riding, but in 1962 Mr Jan Harald Koelichen, who had a business in Sligo and a house in Bantry, Co. Cork, imported some good mares for breeding including Sheelagh Shrue (2405), Breedog (2050), Autumn Retreat (2192), and Abbeyleix Heather (2406), and in 1965 he presented the Connemara Pony Breeders' Society with the beautiful Championship Cup for Clifden Show. Sadly Mrs E. von St Paul died in 1973, only a year after forming the group, but the Connemara Pony has flourished in Germany, and there are many enthusiastic breeders. Among them is Mr Hillnhutter, who has given many outstanding driving displays with his stallion *Golden Dan (342)* s. Ben Lettery (133) d. Ballydonnellan Grey (1593), leading a team of four grey Connemara ponies driven one behind the other.

Bachmann

Golden Dan (342) with Herr Hillnhutter.

49th Annual Pony Show, Clifden – 17th August 1972

The latest improvement to the Showgrounds was the provision of a judges hut in the centre of the Showing ring which looked very smart. It was also the first year that T. McD. Kelly did not act as one of the judges, although he was still actively involved in the centre of the ring where he acted as a referee judge, a position which he continued to hold up to the year he died. He was by this stage the last remaining founder member of the original Council which was formed in 1923, and had been a Society judge and a member of the Inspection Committee for forty-eight years. It was a tremendous record of service and commitment to the Connemara pony.

The visiting judges for the Show in 1972 were two judges from Holland, Mr. W. Goedhart, and Mr D. Modderman, and they acted with two judges from the Society's panel, Mrs Lanigan O'Keefe, and Mr Michael O'Connell. The Stallion class was won by *Carrabaun Boy (353)*, by MacDuff (209) owned by John Luskin, Cong Co. Mayo, the Carew Cup was won by Tommy McDonagh with Roundstone River (4746), who also won the Confined Championship and was Reserve Champion of the Show. Lady de Vesci's Abbeyleix Molly (2823) won

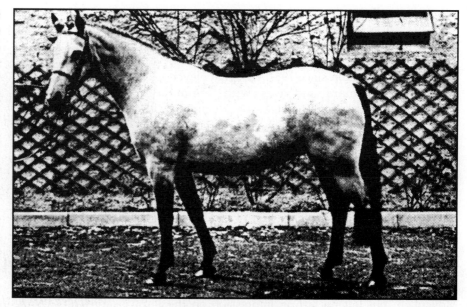

Dun Sparrow (3025)

the RDS Silver Medal in the senior mare class, and her daughter Abbeyleix Holly (4225) won the Killanin Cup for best three year old mare.

The Archbishop's Cup was changed to the four year old mare class that year and went to John Brennan's Fort Cora (4107), and the Supreme Champion of the Show was Dun Sparrow (3025), bred by John Joyce, Ballyconneely, and owned by Maria Carraciolo (Lady Maria Levinge), Rathfarnham, Co. Dublin.

A Round Table Meeting was held in Clifden the day after the Show, and representatives from the overseas societies met with members of the parent society. This became an annual meeting when breeders from different countries could come together to discuss problems and share views with other breeders.

The end of the 1972 season saw the retirement of one of the Society's longest serving stallions, *Mac Dara (91)*, who had spent twenty years on the approved list in Connemara, and was now aged twenty three. He spent his last four years in Connemara with Peter Kyne at Knockranny, Moycullen, but he also spent three years with him in the early sixties, so there was a special bond between them, and he was Peter's favourite pony. Together they took part in the parade of stallions at Tulira Castle for the International Conference in 1970, and ten years earlier they won the stallion class at Clifden Show. Peter Kyne served as a member of the Council from 1965 to 1970, and stood a Society stallion from 1953 to 1972. During those years he stood *Carna Bobby (79), Cilcairain (78), MacDara (91), Clonkeehan Auratum (104), Knockranny Ruby (134)*, and finally *MacDara (91)* again. Peter became very ill shortly after the old pony retired, and sadly he died some weeks later. *MacDara* spent his final years in Carlow with Jimmy Jones, and his last son *Ormond Oliver (653)* was foaled there in 1975.

Another stallion who retired that year was *Clonjoy (117)* who was aged fourteen and had been a Society stallion since 1961. He spent eleven years in Connemara and was with Tommy O'Brien, Canal Stage for his last season. He moved to Frank Quinn at Ardrahan where he spent his retirement years. He left two hundred and fifty-five registered progeny including twenty-three stallion sons. Many of his progeny went overseas, and among his best-known sons were *Errigal Prince (159), Island Duke (208), Tulira Rambler (281), Clare Lad (312), Rosmuck Master (340), Robber Boy (604),* and *Cnoc Dabuide (606).*

MacDara (91) with Peter Kyne at Tulira.

His five year old son *Rosmuck Master (340)* replaced him on the list in 1973 and spent three seasons with Patrick Mulkerrins, Knockerasser, Moycullen, but left no lasting impression on the breed.

Clonjoy's list of daughters is extensive and includes, Evening Joy (2754), Lambay Lassie (3254), Callowfeenish Beauty (3605), Little Cashel Hill (3983), Walnut Brown (4082), Wireless Wave (3641), Callowfeenish Doll (3642), Bay Lady (3971) Corn Flake (4028), Windy Joy (4298), Gaelic Heather (4335), Home Lover (4735), Story of Slieve na mBan (5136), and there were others who left Connemara as young ponies and left no progeny in Ireland, but made their name overseas.

Lord Killanin Resigns

At meeting of the Council on 28th November 1972, a letter was received from Lord Killanin in which he explained that he had been elected President of the International Olympic Committee, and it was necessary for him to give up many of the voluntary and honorary positions which he held. He therefore tendered his resignation as President of the Connemara Pony Breeders'Society, and suggested that Sean Keane should become Acting President until the next AGM, when a new President could be elected.

Lord Killanin had served twenty years as President of the Society, and during that time he had seen it grow from a Society run on simple lines by a small group of dedicated people, to a Society which had become the Parent Body to a large group of Connemara Pony Societies now established throughout the world. The Connemara pony had found a new role as a riding pony of world renown, and with an increasing export trade, it had become an international success.

Despite many other commitments, Lord Killanin had devoted much time and energy to the affairs of the Society, and with his guidance, the Society was made into a Limited Company in 1959. He was also Chairman of the first International Conference for Connemara Pony Societies in 1970, and its success was largely due to his organisation and leadership. The Society was fortunate to have had as President a man of such wide experience to steer it through the years of expansion and growth with a steady hand.

Sean Keane agreed to become Acting President until the next AGM, and the members of the Council joined him in congratulating Lord Killanin on his new appointment as President of the International Olympic Committee, which was a great honour for him and for his country, and they wished him every success in his challenging new office.

Sean Keane Elected President

The AGM was held on 23rd March 1973, and at the Council meeting which preceded it, Sean Keane was elected President of the Society, and Lord Killanin formally handed over office to him. When Lord Killanin took office in 1952, he was the first layman to become President, his three predecessors were all priests, and this was the first time an officer from the Department of Agriculture was elected President of the Society.

Sean Keane became a member of Council in 1943, and had always taken an active part in the running of the Society. He worked with Bartley O'Sullivan for eighteen years, and through his work in Connemara he had developed a great knowledge of the ponies and their breeders. During those years he saw the start of the export trade to England and the USA in the forties and fifties, and in fact one of the mares sent to the States was named Keane's Selection. He had been chief steward of the the Annual Show for many years, and was Acting Secretary during the period between Bartley O'Sullivan's death and John Killeen being appointed as Secretary of the Society. It was clear that Sean Keane would be an active President, and fully involved in the running of the Society.

At this meeting a new Council member was also appointed, John Brennan, Fort Lorenzo, Taylors Hill, Galway. He had been a successful breeder since the early sixties, and bought his first pony at Maam Cross in 1962. It was at his suggestion that two riding classes were included in the

Connacht Tribune

Sean Keane, Lord Killanin and John Killeen.

147

schedule for the 1973 Clifden Show after a lapse of many years, and a silver cup was presented by Mr and Mrs Donal Brooks as a perpetual trophy for the riding classes, to be known as the Errislannon Cup.

A dinner was held following the AGM at which Lord Killanin was thanked for his long years of dedication to the work of the Society. He became a Vice President in 1947, and had succeeded Canon Cunningham as President of the Connemara Pony Breeders' Society in March 1953. In recognition of his twenty six years in office, he was presented with a Charles II lidded Galway Tankard (c. 1680) made of solid silver. A silver pendant was also presented to Lady Killanin.

During the seventies many of the old stallions who had served in Connemara for the past two decades were coming to the end of their days, and the Society found that it was difficult to replace them, as many of the good young colts were being bought for high prices by breeders from overseas. There was a further problem in the breeding herd in that many of the good broodmares were also growing old, and their owners needed to keep a good daughter as a replacement, but during those vital years in the late seventies, some valuable lines were lost because the best of the stock had been exported, and in some cases it was too late to breed a follower.

1971 *Thunderbolt (178)* sold. *Doon Paddy (95)* retired.
1972 *Mac Dara (91)* retired. *Clonjoy (117)* retired.
1973 *Carna Bobby (79)* and *Carna Dun (89)* died. *Kimble (227)* sold.
1974 *Ardilaun (261)* sold.
1975 *MacDara (91)* died. *Ben Lettery (133)* sold. *Bridge Boy (124)* sold.
1976 *Clonkeehan Auratum (104)* died.
1977 *Atlantic Storm (139)* retired. *Dun Aengus (120)* died.
1978 *Rebel Wind (127)* died. *Doon Paddy (95)* died.
1979 *Clonjoy (117)* died.

Three young stallions joined the list in 1973:
Thundercloud (459) s. Thunderbolt (178) d. Claddagh Queen (3681)
Roundstone Oscar (337) s. Rebel Wind (127) d. Dancing Spanner (1750)
Rosmuck Master (340) s. Clonjoy (117) d. White Lor (1863).

Sadly none of them were worthy successors for their respective sires, and they left very few progeny in Connemara.

In May 1973 a Connemara Pony show was held by Miss Berridge at her home, Mervyn, Enniskerry, Co. Wicklow to encourage breeders of Connemara ponies in the Leinster region, and it was also an inspection centre and two members of the inspection committee acted as judges.

The Irish Horse Board, Bord na gCapall, arranged to send two Connemara ponies to the Horse Show at the Salon du Cheval in Paris at the end of May, and they were part of an exhibition of Irish horses at the Show and provided great publicity for the breed. The export trade to France was growing rapidly, and this was an opportunity to show the Connemara pony to the French public. Sean Keane, who was a member of the Horse Board, went with the ponies to Paris, and afterwards they were sold in France.

50th Annual Pony Show, Clifden – 16th August 1973

Despite rather wet weather there was a good attendance, and the entries were well up to average. The riding classes were well supported, with 48 entries between the two classes. They took place during the lunch interval and the winner of both classes and first winner of the Errislannon Cup was *Marble (254)*, the seven year old grey stallion owned by John Brennan, Fort Lorenzo, and ridden by his son Johnny. *Marble* showed perfect manners under saddle, and then came out to display all his vigour and presence in the open stallion class which he won from *Coosheen Finn (381)*. He also won the Confined Championship, but had to be content with Reserve in the Supreme Championship of the Show.

Roundstone River (4746) continued her supremacy in the three year old class and won the Killanin Cup as well as

Connacht Tribune

Marble (254)

being reserve to *Marble (254)* in the Confined Championship. The Archbishop's Cup went to Joe Gorham's King's Bridge (4374), and Jimmy Jones, Carlow won the RDS Medal and the senior broodmare class with Lambay Starry Eyes (3248). The winner of the two year old filly class and the Carew Cup, was Boden Park Maythorn (5195) s. Mervyn Grey Monkey (347) d. Clonkeehan Whitethorn (2796) bred Mrs Jane Dalrymple, Ashbourne, Co. Meath, and owned by Graham Tulloch, Shanbolard, and she went on to win the Jan Harald Koelichen Cup and was made the Supreme Champion of the Show. She combined some of the best early breeding from Camlin, Mervyn and Clonkeehan Studs, and was a great-grand daughter of two former champion broodmares at Clifden, Rose of Barna (1337) and Cashel Kate (2030).

The Minister of Agriculture, Mr Mark Clinton, who attended the Show, was greatly impressed by the display of ponies, and presented the Jan Harald Koelichen Cup to the Champion of the Show.

1973 saw a greater number of ponies exported than in any previous year, and with the substantial increase in prices, many of the best prizewinning youngstock were being sold abroad. It was hard for a small breeder to refuse a big price for his pony, but good ponies were being sold in large numbers, and some fears were beginning to be expressed that too many valuable youngstock were leaving the native herd before they reached breeding age. There were however many more ponies being registered each year, and the market was welcomed by breeders who needed buyers for the ponies they produced.

In November 1973, one of the best known stallions of his era was laid to rest at the age of twenty-five. *Carna Dun (89)* was foaled in 1948 and was one of *Little Heaven's* first crop of foals. He was bred in Carna by John Mylotte, and made his first appearance at Clifden Show in 1950, as a big, strong, lively two year old colt where he won his class, and went on to win the Carew Cup for youngstock champion. He was bought by the Society after the Show, and joined the approved list of stallions in 1951, spending his first season with Brendan Burke, Patches, Claddaghduff. He moved to Roundstone the following season, and John de Courcey produced him to win the Stallion Class at Clifden in 1952. During his years on the list from 1951 to 1973 he had a total of 292 registered progeny, and although many of his sons went overseas, two sons were owned by the Society, and joined their sire on the list. They were *Doon Paddy (95)*, who served in Connemara from 1956 to 1971, and *Toombeola (211)* who spent just two seasons on the list 1968/69, before being sold. Three other sons who remained in Ireland and made their contribution to the breed were *Camlin Cicada (119)*, *Little Joe (165)* and *Kilgreaney Lad (216)*, while another son, *Finney Master (306)* spent four seasons in Moycullen with Johnny Lee and left 55 progeny, before going to France and later to Sweden.

Carna Dun (89) will be best remembered for his daughters, and among them there were three who won the Supreme Championship at Clifden, Cashel Kate (2030), Dun Sparrow (3025) and Belle of the Ball (3122).

He also sired a number of other top prizewinners at Clifden, many of whom became great broodmares, and they included: Cushatrough Lass (1650), Flash Girl (1771), Callowfeenish Pride (1912), Callowfeenish Dolly II (1913), Breedog (2050), Coosheen Petronella (2203), Ardnasillagh Honey (2373), Arctic Moon (2377), Errisbeg Rose (2895), Abbeyleix Molly (2823), Lambay Starry Eyes (3248), Roundmount (3353), Ocean Bambi (4372) and many more.

Many of the *Carna Dun (89)* stock inherited the tremendous jumping ability which came from his sire *Little Heaven*, and although some of his progeny may have lacked pony characteristics, they were tough and were also great performers in the hunting field or in the Show jumping arena.

The same winter another old veteran, *Carna Bobby (79)* died at Gort with Paddy Lally at the age of twenty seven. Born in 1946, he was bred by Pat Mulkerrin (Tom), Callowfeenish, Carna, his sire was *Gil (43)* and his dam the well-known mare Carna Dolly (442) whose sire was *Buckna (TB)*. He was bought with a group of colt foals at Maam Cross Fair by Tim Cotter and Bartley O'Sullivan, and was produced by Jack Bolger to win the stallion class at Clifden as a three year old in 1949. He won it again every other year until 1959, when he was second to *Clonkeehan Auratum (104)*. He was on the Society's list from 1949 to 1961, when he was sold to Paddy Lally in Gort, and he remained with him for the rest of his life. He had a total of 305 registered progeny, and two thirds of those were foaled after he left Connemara. While he was on the approved list, he spent six years in the Oughterard and Moycullen districts, before moving to Festy King at Claddaghduff for four seasons, and his last three years in Connemara were spent with John Walsh at Kilkerrin.

His list of 47 stallion sons is impressive, and among them were *Island King (122)*, *The Admiral (201)*, *Ballydonagh Bobby (242)*, *Ardilaun (261)*, *Ballydonagh Rob (321)*, *Leam Bobby Finn (297)*, *Lambay Bobby (299)*, *Killyreagh Kim (308)*, *Sticky (377)*, *Coosheen Finn (381)*, *Bloomfield Bobby (362)*, *Ashfield Bobby Sparrow (444)*, *Ashfield Sparrow (583)*, *Grange Bobbing Sparrow (623)*, *Tantallon Bobby (626)*.

When *Carna Bobby (79)* moved to Paddy Lally in Gort, the new studs were being established outside Connemara, and a stream of visiting mares came from Ballydonagh, Abbeyleix, Ashfield, Grange, and Leam Studs. The resulting list of progeny is full of outstanding ponies who graced the Showrings and jumping arenas during the 60's, 70's, and 80's, and brought further acclaim for the breed.

He was the sire of the Supreme Champion at Clifden on nine occasions, Atlantic Mist (2175), in 1968, 1970, Ballydonagh Deirdre (3423), in 1969, Rambling Home (3383), in 1975, Inish Aluinn (5329),in 1976, Gloves Misty (6535),in 1982, 1986, 1988, *Killyreagh Kim (308)*, in 1984.

Also among his progeny were two of the top Grade A show jumpers of their day, the mare Currycahill Katie (4411), and the legendary stallion, *Ashfield Bobby Sparrow (444)*, who won the Junior European Show Jumping Derby at Soder in Germany when jumping on the Irish team in 1980.

Then a host of lovely mares, many of them dams of future stallions, Queen of Diamonds (1934), Julie (2246), Anna Maree (2332), Atlantic Surf (2471), Silver Lace (2723), Ganty Mint (3979), Ashfield Loyal Sparrow (4424), Abbeyleix Holly (4225), Fort Viola (4267), Ganty Jane II (4828), Ashfield Silver Cloud (5894), Abbeyleix Fiona (6257), and so many more.

Carna Bobby (79) put a stamp of quality on his progeny, they were predominantly grey, and many of them had lovely heads and free movement. He was one of the great sires of his era, and his son *Killyreagh Kim (308)* carried on his line in Connemara, while another son *Ballydonagh Rob (321)* succeeded him at Gort with Paddy Lally. One of his visiting mares was Finola of Leam (3036) who was brought over from Wales by her owners John and Phyllis Meade, as they hoped to breed a stallion from *Carna Bobby (79)*. It was a bold plan and one which deserved to succeed, and it did. She stayed at Gort for three seasons, where she produced three sons, and two became the well-known stallions *Leam Bobby Finn (297)* and *Coosheen Finn (381)*. *Leam Bobby Finn (297)* returned to Wales, and was the first Connemara stallion to win over all other native breeds at the Ponies of Britain Show in 1973, and he and his progeny have been outstanding ambassadors for the breed in England. *Coosheen Finn (381)* was bought as a foal by the Author, and spent all his life at Coosheen Stud in Co. Cork, where he bred many prizewinning ponies, and sired the Supreme Champion at Clifden in 1979, 1980 and 1983.

Volume XIV of the Stud Book

Volume XIV of the Stud Book was published early in 1974 priced at £2. 00 per copy, and again there was an increase in the number of ponies registered in the two years it covered, 1971 and 1972. The number of stallions registered had dropped to 86, but 850 mares and 144 geldings brought the overall total to 1080, the first time that over 1000 ponies had been registered in a two year period.

The stallion list in 1974 was reduced to ten following the death of *Carna Dun (89)* during the winter, and *Kimble (227)* also left the list and was sold to Sweden. *Kimble (227)* left a comparatively modest list of 43 registered progeny, but among them were two sons who have really contributed to the breed, His first foal, *The Fugitive (368)*, dam Loobeen Lily (2919), foaled in 1968 and bred by Pakie Coyne, Renvyle, has been a successful sire for Clair Studdert in Co. Meath, and *Abbeyleix Owen (496)* who was bought by the Society, replaced his sire on the approved list in 1975, and has remained in Connemara on the Society's list for twenty three years.

J. Petch

The Fugitive (361)

Following the success of the riding classes at the 1973 Clifden Show, the Council decided to run a Gymkhana in Clifden on 13th June 1974. Its aim was to encourage the owners and breeders of Connemara ponies to train them and school them, and to promote an interest in riding and jumping in the Connemara district. The use of the pony had changed dramatically since the foundation of the Society. In the early days most of the ponies were used for work and were trained for harness and saddle, but with the coming of the motor car and the tractor, the pony's traditional role had disappeared, and many of the mares were now used purely for breeding. Mrs Brooks of Errislannon had started training classes for local children and their ponies three years earlier, and she and a band of enthusiastic helpers organised the gymkhana games which were enjoyed by children and spectators alike. There were also five jumping classes, two for horses and three for ponies, and the day was a great success.

First Connemara Chronicle

In the Spring 1974 the first edition of the Connemara Chronicle was published by the English Connemara Pony Society and edited by Pat Lyne whose dedication and enthusiasm for the Connemara pony ensured the success of this new venture. It was a timely production, with so many new societies being formed worldwide, the Chronicle was to become a link between all the Connemara pony societies, and Pat Lyne remained its editor until 1985.

The first edition was sold for 50p, and was welcomed by breeders from around the world, with letters of congratulations being sent to the Editor from John Killeen, Connemara Pony Breeders' Society, Mrs M. Kelly, from Australia, Mrs Merrild from Denmark, and Mr Oomen from Holland.

Connemara Ponies at Aras an Uachtarain

The Minister of Agriculture, Mr Mark Clinton was most impressed with what he saw when he visited the Show at Clifden in 1973, and he suggested that it would help to promote the breed if some Connemara ponies were kept in the grounds of Aras an Uachtarain, Phoenix Park, Dublin, the residence of the President of Ireland. He thought this would provide a good opportunity for guests of the President to see Connemara ponies, and admire Ireland's native breed. Following this suggestion, six Connemara mares, some with foals at foot, were selected and brought to Phoenix Park in the summer of 1974. The mares were Ganty Heather (4873), Fort Flora (5531), Fort Hazel (5533), Moy Maeve (5567), Knockdoe Walnut (5736) and Funny Girl (5691).

Independent Newspapers

President Childers meets the Connemara ponies.

On 15th October 1974 the President gave a reception at Aras an Uachtarain for the Minister of Agriculture, the breeders of the six mares and members of the Connemara Pony Breeders' Society. It was a relaxed and pleasant occasion, and President and Mrs Childers received the party from Connemara and showed great interest in the ponies. Only a month later the news of President Childers sudden death from a heart attack came as a great shock to the nation, and it was of particular sadness for the group from Connemara who had met him so recently. He had only been a short time in office, and had been a very popular President.

51st Annual Pony Show, Clifden – 15th August 1974

The Show again had a large entry with 428 in the pony section, and the judges were Miss Lal Berridge, Mr Donal Kenny, Miss Judy Preston, and Mr Michael O'Connell. The winning stallion *MacDuff (209)* by Dun Aengus (120) dam Callowfeenish Pride (1912) was shown by John Luskin, Cong and later sold to France, and in the two year old colt class the winner, *Gold Fort (551)*, a son of *Marble (254)*, was shown by Graham Tulloch for his delighted new owner, M. Lyon from France, and later he became Reserve Champion of the Show.

The Killanin Cup went to Boden Park Maythorn (5195), also shown by Graham Tulloch, but this time the Supreme Champion of the Show was Roundstone River (4746) bred and owned by Tommy McDonagh and she also won the Archbishop's Cup, and the Confined Championship for ponies owned and bred by a resident of

Connemara. It was a proud day for Tommy McDonagh, as this mare had won her class at Clifden each year since she was a yearling and had also won the Confined Championship and been Reserve Champion in 1972.

She won her class at the RDS Horse Show earlier in the month, and a picture of Tommy McDonagh leading Roundstone River (4746) in the parade of prizewinners featured on the front cover of the Horse and Hound magazine. After the Show, Roundstone River (4746) was also sold to France, to Hubert Laurent, as a foundation mare for his Melody Stud. She has bred many good foals for him, and in 1997, her daughter Dance River Melody, by his stallion Idenoir, was Supreme Champion at the National Breed Show at Poitiers, France.

Roundstone River (4746) with Tommy McDonagh.

During the following winter of 74/75, one of the best of the old type Connemara pony stallions died at the age of twenty five. He was *MacDara (91)*, son of *Dun Lorenzo (55)* and was bred in Roundstone by John McCahill from Dolan Rose (1132) who was by Lavalley Star (25). He was born in 1949 and bought by the Society for £25 after he had won the yearling colt class at Clifden in 1950. He more than repaid the investment, with two hundred and sixty-seven registered progeny, and many of his sons and daughters went abroad to become foundation stock for the new societies overseas. He was registered as a two year old and joined the approved stallion list in 1952, spending his first five years with Anthony Faherty, Moyard.

He spent twenty-one seasons in Connemara, and his time was divided mostly between Bunowen and Moycullen, with one season in Kilkerrin in 1967. He retired to Jimmy Jones in Carlow in 1972 and spent two years there before he died.

MacDara, meaning Son of the Oak, was the name of the patron saint of the fishermen of Carna and Cilcairain, and every year on the 16th July, the Feast day of MacDara, the fishermen take pilgrims out to the Saint's island where traditional prayers are said. *MacDara (91)* was the real old stamp of dun pony with all the strength and stamina of the Red Line, tracing back to *Connemara Boy (9)*, and he came from the best of native stock with no outside blood. He was a dark dun with a thick black mane and tail, an attractive pony head and large kindly eyes. Many of his progeny were dun or bay, they were tough hardy ponies, and had wonderful temperaments. He won the stallion class four times in 1954, 1956, 1958, and 1960, and was second on two other occasions.

He was succeeded by his son *Atlantic Storm (139)* who joined the list in 1964, and his last son *Ormond Oliver (653)* who was foaled in 1975, and became a Society-owned stallion in 1977.

He had thirty-three registered stallions sons, among them were *Gael Linn (103)* and *Marconi (107)*, who both went to USA. *Lambay Rebel (131)* went to Denmark, *Slieve Dara (146)* to Sweden, *Glenarde (149)* to Holland, *Bantry Oak (168)* to Germany, *MacNamara (175)*, *Thos. of Oakleigh (176)* and *Atlantic Sentinel (239)* to England, *Murrisk (217)* to France. *Atlantic Hero (339)*, *Errislannon Coltsfoot (115)*, *Atlantic Storm (139)* and *Ormond Oliver (653)* remained in Ireland, and the last two were both owned by the Society.

He also left the breed some good broodmares, many were never shown, but they have proved themselves through their progeny. They include Ripple (1708), Dairina (1726),Loobeen Lily (2919), Castletown Lady (2009), Flash Judy (2154), Kingstown Swallow (2199), Queen of the Hills (2449), Rock of Cashel (2464), Clonkeehan Tiger Lily (2580), Breath of Spring (3137), Ballydonagh Kate (2798), Winning Trump (3965), Glencastle Valley (4102), Wise Little Pet (4366), Ashfield Blue Molly (6761).

The Half-Bred Register

The Stud Book had now been closed since 1964 and there were some members of the Council who were concerned that the gene pool was too small and there was a risk of in-breeding.

Miss Garnet Irwin had bought a small thoroughbred sire called *Speck*, Sire: Romany Air, dam: Goudhurst. He was a 15 hands bay, and was foaled in 1961. He stood at Mrs MacCartan's Clooncormack Stud, Hollymount, Co. Mayo, and in 1973 Miss Irwin offered to allow 12 nominated mares from the Connemara area to visit her stallion at a fee of £6 plus nomination.

The purpose of this new venture was to introduce new blood into the breed, and it was hoped that a half-bred register would be opened to record the progeny of this cross. Dr Austin Mescal and Mr Donal Kenny of the

J. Petch

Speck (TB) with Jimmy Canavan.

155

Department of Agriculture were appointed to study the whole question of introducing outside blood gradually in order to avoid in-breeding.

The following year at the Round Table Meeting held the day after the Show in 1974, Dr Austin Mescal and Mr Donal Kenny gave a short talk on the half-bred register which it was proposed should be set up in order to introduce some outside blood in a controlled and cautious manner. It was to be a long term programme, with the female progeny of nominated mares mated to the stallion *Speck* or other selected stallions of outside blood being eligible for the half-bred register after inspection at two years of age. These fillies would then be mated to selected Connemara stallions, and their female progeny would be crossed back to Connemara stallions again until 87. 5% pure Connemara blood had been achieved, and then they would be accepted into the main Stud Book.

The next year a second Thoroughbred stallion was inspected and approved for the service of a limited number of nominated Connemara mares and in 1975 he joined *Speck* on the list of outside sires whose female progeny would be eligible for the supplementary register.

He was a small Thoroughbred bay horse, foaled 1967, called *Tellipy*, sire: Le Levanstell, dam: Pretty Nippy, and he stood at stud with Martin McNamara, at Lakeview House, Flagmount, Co. Clare.

These two sires were available for the service of a limited number of nominated mares from the Connemara area by special arrangement with the Connemara Pony Breeders' Society, and they remained on the list until 1985. *Speck* moved to Jimmy Canavan's Stud at Moycullen in 1979 and stayed with him until he died in 1986.

The programme would perhaps have been more suitable for a breeding station than for a group of individual breeders in Connemara, and although some mares visited *Speck* and *Tellipy*, and the resulting first cross fillies were inspected, the full breeding programme was never followed through.

The Council had now received authority to increase its membership from 20 to 24 members, and at a Council meeting held on 3rd December 1974 it was decided to elect one new member of Council from each of the four provinces of Ireland. The following members were appointed.

Ulster: Mrs Patricia MacKean, 51, Loughanmore Road, Antrim.
Leinster: Mr Michael O'Connell, Lambay Island, Rush, Co. Dublin.
Connaught: Mr Donal Kenny, 6. Beech Grove, Oranmore, Galway.
Munster: Mrs Elizabeth Petch, Seaview, Kilbrittain, Co. Cork.

In February 1975 Bord na gCapall brought a group of Irish horses and ponies to Germany to exhibit them at the Essen Equitana Horse Show. Every recognised breed of horse and pony was exhibited at the Show, and included in the Irish group was John Brennan's stallion *Marble* (254) representing the Connemara Pony. He was shown both in hand and under saddle, and behaved impeccably. There was a very large attendance of international visitors at the Show, and the Irish exhibit attracted much attention, which helped the promotion of the breed.

Bord na gCapall had also been appointed by the Minister of Agriculture to take over all functions relating to the breeding, production, and improvement of non-thoroughbred horses, and the first step taken by the Bord in February 1975 was to increase the grant-in-aid to the Connemara Pony Breeders' Society to £2,500 which was greatly appreciated by the Council.

Two more stallions were removed from the list at the end of the 1974 season, *Ardilaun (261)* and *Ben Lettery (133)* and were sold out of Connemara. *Ardilaun (261)* by Carna Bobby (79) was bred by Joe McNamara, Craughwell, out of his mare Ganty Jane (2300) who was by Tully Lad (48). He was foaled in 1966 and spent the year he was registered with B. J. Bermingham at Kinvara before being put on the approved list for the 1969 season. He spent six years in Connemara three with Tommy O'Brien at Canal Stage, and three in Carraroe with Tom Feeney, and had one hundred and twelve registered progeny. One of his sons, *Silver Finn (451)* dam Finola Of Leam (3036) spent a few years at Killyreagh Stud with Mrs Creighton, but *Ardilaun (261)*, unlike his sire, *Carna Bobby (79)* left little impression on the breed.

Ben Lettery (133) by Gael Linn (103) dam Swanee River (1501) was bred by Anthony Conroy, Lettery, Ballinafad, and was bought by the Society for £100. He joined the list as a two year old in 1963, and spent his first three seasons with Tommy O'Brien, Canal Stage. He then moved to John Mulkerrins at Moycullen for three years, followed by three years with Tom Feeney at Carraroe, and his final three years in Connemara were spent at Kilkerrin with Stephen Curran. He represented the Red Line through his grandsire *MacDara (91)*, and had all the rugged strength of that good old breeding. He had 242 registered progeny, and his most outstanding son, *Golden Dan ((342)* went to the Hillnhutter family in Germany where he founded a dynasty of his own. Many of his daughters made good broodmares, and among them were Glenlo Spring (3042), Lambay Winnie (3251), Juliet (3623), Bright Cherry (4277), Callowfeenish Colleen (5133), Hippy Mistress (5156), Snowdrop's Surprise (5674), Summer Gladness (6361), Callowfeenish Katie (6639), and Party Gay Girl (6730).

Ben Lettery (133) was sold to Lambay Island in 1975, and although he left no stallion son to follow him on the list in Connemara, many of his daughters remained to pass on his best attributes.

In the Spring of 1975 the annual inspections were held in Connemara during May, and for the second year there was a slight drop in the number of ponies registered. This may have been partly due to the number of ponies being exported before reaching registration age, but it was the start of a disquieting trend which was to continue over the following years.

Abbeyleix Owen (496) by Kimble (227) dam Queen of Diamonds (1934) was bred by Lady de Vesci at Abbeyleix, he was bought by the Society and joined the approved stallion list in Connemara as a four year old in 1975. He was a much stronger and plainer pony than his sire, and his good bone, strength and substance were valuable qualities which were needed to blend with the some of the lighter mares. He was placed with Josie Conroy for his first three seasons, and his first crop of foals produced some good fillies who were to become wellknown names in the future, they included Silver Sparrow (6898), Errisbeg Dolly (69400, Grey Rock Star (6947) and Village Grey (6951). He was to have a long and fruitful life in Connemara and served for twenty three years on the Society's stallion list.

A second young stallion who joined the list that spring was *Tulira Snowball (561)*, a three year old grey bred at Tulira, he was by Tulira Mairtin (214) out of a good mare from the Windy line, Julie (2246). He only remained in Connemara for two seasons and left four registered progeny.

The gymkhana was held for the second year at the Showgrounds in Clifden on 1st June 1975 and once again it proved very successful with five jumping classes and the usual gymkhana games. It had very good entries in all classes, but it was a little disappointing for the organising committee that it not well supported by the general public.

52nd Annual Pony Show, Clifden – 21st August 1975

By now Clifden Show had become an established international event with breeders from all over the world visiting the Show on a regular basis. Representatives from all the overseas societies were at the Show, which added a cosmopolitan air, with many different languages being spoken at the ringside. The Round Table Meeting held each year on the day after the Show had helped to bring the members of all the societies together, and Clifden had now become the place where breeders of Connemara ponies from all over the world met annually. There were 409 entries which included 67 entries in the riding classes, and the Show committee decided it was necessary to divide the main ring in two for some of the classes to keep the Show running up to time. This was not a very popular move, but with increased entries and more classes, it was unavoidable.

The stallion class was won by *Mervyn Pookhaun (528)*, a four year old grey by The Admiral (201) dam Mervyn Nasim (2426). He was bred by Miss Berridge, Enniskerry, and owned by Mrs Liz Ormsby, Cloghans Hill Tuam. *Killyreagh Kim (308)* stood second and also won the Confined stallion class. There was a strong class of two year old fillies with some lovely ponies among the fifty-three entries. It was won by Ballinaboy Breeze (6030) by Ballydonagh Rob (321) dam Evening Joy (2754), owned and bred by Col. Tony Morris, Ballinaboy, with Michael Lee, Moycullen coming a close second with his dun filly Inishnee Dun Damsel (6101) by Killyreagh Kim (308). The four year old class was won by another daughter of Killyreagh Kim (308), Village Star (5146), whose owner Paddy King, Lehid got a loud cheer from the ringside when he was presented with the Archbishop's Cup.

Ballinaboy Breeze (6030),
Lady Carew, Col. A. Morris and Sean Keane.

The Supreme Champion of the Show was Rambling Home (3383) by Carna Bobby (79) owned by Padraig Hynes, and winner of the senior mares class and RDS Medal. It was a memorable day for Padraig Hynes as this was his first big success in the Show ring, and although since then he has won many more Championships, and has produced a string of prizewinning ponies, Rambling Home (3383) always remained a very special pony for him. He bought her as a foal at Maam Cross, and still treasures her first rosette, a third prize at Ballinrobe Show.

The Confined Championship went to the two year old filly Ballinaboy Breeze (6030), who was also Reserve Champion of the Show. It was a good year for local breeders, with many of the top awards staying in Connemara, and it was also a successful show for *Carna Bobby (79)* whose progeny dominated the prizewinners. The judges were Mrs Dan Lanigan O'Keefe, Mr Graham Tulloch, Mrs E. Petch and Mr C. Lydon MRCVS.

Ruth Rogers

Rambling Home (3383) with Padraig Hynes and Sean Keane.

In October 1975 a group of forty horses were flown from Shannon to Australia on a DC8 Jet. This was the first time such a large number of horses were flown in one plane on a long-haul flight, and included in the group were six Connemara ponies bought at Clifden after the Show. They all arrived in good condition, and it must have been a much less stressful form of transport than in a crate lashed to the deck of a ship, the only drawback being the very high cost.

Another well known stallion served his last season on the approved list in 1975 and was sold to Denmark in January 1976. *Bridge Boy (124)* was foaled in 1959 and was bred and owned by Paddy Geoghegan in Oughterard. He was by Tooreen Ross (99) out of Mark Geoghegan's good mare Irene (624) by Innishgoill Laddie (21) and carried some of the toughest blood lines from this branch of the Blue Line. He was always privately owned but was included on the approved list from 1963 to 1975 and stood with the Geoghegans in Oughterard. He first appeared at Clifden as a four year old in 1963 and won the stallion class, beating *MacDara*

(91) and *Carna Dun (89)*. He showed tremendous presence in the ring and was the delight of cameramen as he enjoyed showing off to the crowd. He also won the open stallion class in 1965, 1967 and 1969, and the Confined Class in 1969, and again in 1974 when he was reserve in the Confined Championship.

His time in Connemara spanned the years when the export trade was at its height, and many of his 279 progeny went overseas. *Tulira Colman (215)* was one of his sons who spent a brief time in England before going to Mrs M Kelly in Australia where he was a successful performance sire, and his partbreds when crossed with Thoroughbred mares were outstanding. Another son *Ardnasillagh O'Flaherty (730)* made his name in Denmark where he became a successful dressage pony, and was later sold to Finland.

Two grandsons of *Bridge Boy (124)* who remained in Ireland to carry on his line were *Clonkeehan Captain Cook (423)* son of Marco Polo of Clonkeehan (236), who spent all his life with Mrs MacKean in Co. Antrim and bred many useful ponies, and *Ard Conneely (898)* by Ard Bridge Time (277), who won the Supreme Championship at Clifden in 1992 for his breeder Mrs Heather Wright, and spent several years at stud in Ireland before being sold overseas.

One of his many daughters who left Ireland was Brigitte (7242), dam Betsy Bay (2075). She was bought by Bent Nielsen in Denmark, and he bred her lovely daughter Oxenholm Bardot (7251) who was the outstanding mare of her day at three International Festivals in 1977, 1979 and 1981. Many others were successful mares overseas, among them were Blioscan (2961), Lune Star (3194), Strandhill Colleen (3645), Boogie Woogie (4547), Canrower Jacqueline (4302), Ardnasillagh Amethyst (5332), and some of those who remained in Ireland included Mrs Mulligan (3024), Coosheen Tansy (3328), Lucky Smokey (3735), Windy Mountain (3910), and Canrower Rebecca (6625).

Ruth Rogers

Lucky Smokey (3735) owned by Murty McGrath.

CHAPTER 11

1976-1980

Early in 1976, two men who had already given many years to the Connemara pony were elected as members of the Council, they were Willie Diamond, Tully and Jack Bolger, Cashel. Both men had a deep knowledge of the ponies and their breeding, and had been involved with the ponies all their lives. They represented the long established breeders in Connemara, and they both had a good eye for a pony, and many winners had passed through their hands.

Another name was added to the Council later that year when John Luskin, Cong was elected in October 1976. He had already produced two stallions to win the stallion class in Clifden, *Carrabaun Boy (353)* in 1972, and his sire *MacDuff (209)* in 1974, and had further success in 1977 when he produced *Milford Hurricane (568)* to win his class, and then take the Supreme Championship of the Show.

Two new young stallions joined the list in 1976, *Sarsfield (579)* and *Ardnasillagh Magnus (547)*, replacing *Rosmuck Master (340)* and *Bridge Boy (124)*. *Sarsfield (579)* was a three year old grey dun by Killyreagh Kim (308) and was bred at Ballyconneely by John Joyce out of his good *Clonkeehan Auratum (104)* mare Wise Cuckoo (2714). He was bought by the Society and remained on the list for five seasons.

Ardnasillagh Magnus (547) was a four year old dun by MacDara (91) dam Blondie (3120), and he replaced *Bridge Boy (124)* at Oughterard with Paddy Geoghegan and was owned privately.

J. Petch

Sarsfield (579)

Volume XV of the Stud Book

A new volume of the Stud Book was published in 1976 and covered the period from January 1973 to October 1975. It contained the particulars of 1420 ponies including 95 stallions, 1150 mares and 185 geldings.

Since the first inspections in 1924 a total of 617 stallions, 6200 mares and 701 geldings had been registered, and there was a noticeable increase in the number of geldings coming forward for registration.

The annual inspections took place in May as usual, and there was another slight drop in the numbers compared to the previous year. It was to prove a difficult year for pony breeders throughout Europe as there was a severe drought during the summer, which caused an acute shortage of grazing and hay in England and in Europe. This meant a drop in sales of ponies during the year, and some of the ponies who were bought by breeders from overseas, had to be kept in Ireland, where the drought was not so severe, until supplies of feeding stuffs improved in Europe.

For a third year a gymkhana was held in Clifden at the Showgrounds, and it was again most successful with good entries in most classes. There were special classes confined to children and ponies from the Clifden Union which were very popular, and with the encouragement of training classes provided by Mrs Brooks at Errislannon, there was a growing interest in riding among the children in the district.

Death of T. McD. Kelly MRCVS

In June 1976 the Society lost one of its longstanding Vice Presidents with the death of T. McD. Kelly MRCVS, or Tommy Kelly as he was known to his friends. Aged 87, he was the last surviving founder member of the Society and had served on the Council for fifty-three years. He had acted as a member of the inspection committee since 1924, and was one of the judges at the first Show in Roundstone in 1924.

Since then he had acted as a judge or referee judge at almost every show up to the year before he died. He was a well respected horseman, and a keen racing man, his small neat frame was ideal for a jockey and he rode in many races in his younger days. He also enjoyed hunting and show jumping, and was recognised as one of the top horse vets in the country in his day, often travelling to Limerick to vet a horse for Lord Daresbury. His commitment to the Connemara Pony Breeders' Society was remarkable, and he maintained his interest in the ponies and the work of the Society throughout his long life. He could remember right back to the early beginnings of the Society, and when asked a few years before he died if the ponies had improved over the years, his reply came back, "*Of course, they're much better now, there were some terrible 'yokes' when we started!*" His familiar figure in his tweed suit with the brown felt hat pulled well down over his

T. McD. Kelly MRCVS

eyes would no longer be seen in the centre of the ring, and his presence was missed at Clifden later that summer.

53rd Annual Pony Show, Clifden – 19th August 1976

At the Clifden Show in 1976, *Killyreagh Kim (308)* won the Open and Confined stallion classes for Paddy Folan, Camus, who had him looking really well, and in second place was John Luskin's *Cnoc Dabhuide (606)* shown by his new owner Bent Nielsen from Denmark. Another son of Carna Bobby (79), *Grange Bobbing Sparrow (623)* won the two year old colt class for Maria Carraciolo, and the Archbishop' Cup for the best four year old mare was won by Boden Park Rosethorn (5728) sire Clonkeehan Nimbus (229) owned by Miss C. Featherstonhaugh from Kildare.

In the five and six year old class, the winner was Inish Aluinn (5329) s. Carna Bobby (79) dam Inish Carra (3601), bred by C. T. Lydon MRCVS and owned by Mr Hank Verschuur from Holland. This mare went on to win the Supreme Championship of the Show, much to the delight of her new owner who was there to lead her in the ring, and he was well supported by a large group of breeders from Holland who were visiting the Show. The Society-owned stallion *Killyreagh Kim (308)* was the Reserve Champion.

COPA Meeting

Ireland had become a member of the European Community in January 1973, and COPA was a group of farming organisations within the EEC which acted as an advisory body to the EEC Commissioners. COPA held a meeting in London in September 1976 to meet representatives of the pony breed societies to discuss the problem of common standards for registering ponies of the same breed within the EEC. As a result of this meeting the English Connemara Pony Society decided to send two of their Council members to Ireland to discuss the matter with their Parent Body.

Connacht Tribune

Killyreagh Kim (308) with Paddy Folan.

A meeting was held in October in Galway between representatives from Bord na gCapall, the Department of Agriculture, the Council of the CPBS, and Mr and Mrs O'Mahony Meade and Miss Pat Lyne who were representing the ECPS. After a full discussion, the two societies agreed, in principle, common standards for acceptance into the respective stud books.

The main difference between the regulations of the two societies was that the ECPS did not inspect fillies prior to registration, but Mr Meade proposed to recommend to the members of the ECPS that all Connemara ponies should be inspected for registration in the ECPS Stud Book after they reach a minimum registration age of 2 years.

This was the first step along the road to harmonisation of the rules between societies which has been ongoing for many years, and with an increasing number of societies being formed worldwide, it has been difficult at times to find a united way forward.

Clonkeehan Auratum (104) sire Naseel (Arab), dam Western Lily (1522), bred by Miss Lee Norman, Slane, was the founder of the Orange Line and he brought the infusion of Arab blood which the Society introduced in 1956. He had spent the years after he retired from the Society's list in 1964 with Thomas Whelan at Ardrahan, and it was there in October 1976 that he was put down at the age of twenty-two.

Clonkeehan Auratum (104) was introduced gradually, being limited to 20 mares for his first season, and he spent a relatively short time on the approved list, but his progeny made a huge impact in Connemara in the early sixties, where he became a very popular sire, and his stock dominated the Show ring with their extra quality and lovely heads. The export trade was growing, and many of his attractive offspring were sold to overseas buyers from Sweden, Denmark, Holland, Germany or France.

Heather Mixture of Abbeyleix (2709) who won the Supreme Championship in 1966 was typical of the best of his stock, and showed all the quality and presence of her sire. He was particularly successful when mated to the heavier type of pure Connemara mare, but less so when crossed with the daughters of Carna Dun (89), when some of the progeny showed too much influence of outside blood and lost their native pony characteristics. He had a total of 205 registered progeny including nineteen stallions, and two of his sons won the stallion class at Clifden, *Ceileog (109)* in 1962 and *Ballydoogan Clondagoff (157)* in 1966, both were owned privately. His sons *Clonjoy (117)* and *Aura Dun (123)* were owned by the Society, and *Clonjoy (117)* was his best son and left some good progeny in Connemara. In his last year at Ardrahan he sired another son *Ashfield Alex (771)* bred by Jimmy Jones, Carlow out of his good mare Lambay Starry Eyes (3248), and he was bought by the Society and stood in Connemara for seven seasons, but he did not have the same impact on the breed as his sire.

Among his many successful daughters were, Muffy (2157), Solitude (2132), Ocean Melody (2134), Keehaune Belle (2310), Frosty Winter (2346), Jealous Lady (2301), Flash Princess (2309), Kingstown (2532), Ballinahinch Beauty (2545), Nimble Fingers (2522), Oranmore Stardust (2583), Lehid Star (2913), Heather Mixture of Abbeyleix (2709), Wise Cuckoo (2714), Turf Fire (2720), Village Dun (2759), Fort Silver (2829), Fort Irene (4105), Fort Cora (4107), Fort Holly (4266), Tulira Lily (6592).

Clonkeehan Auratum (104) gave his progeny quality and a little more spirit, but some lacked the bone and substance of the old Connemara pony, and were not kept for breeding. However many of these lighter ponies made attractive riding ponies and there was a ready demand for this type of pony in Europe. The best of his daughters who remained in Connemara proved to be consistently good broodmares and were able to live the same tough life as the purebred ponies.

Michael O'Connell had started his interest in Connemara ponies in 1962 when he first bought foals to rear on Lambay Island. Since then he became increasingly involved with the affairs of the Society and was made a member of the Council in 1974. He was also a member of the inspection committee and travelled to England, France and Denmark as an inspector and judge. He was a great ambassador for the Connemara pony and for his country, and he willingly shared his knowledge of the breed with many new breeders who visited Lambay. He developed a big export trade to Europe, and one hundred and sixty-five ponies were registered under the Lambay prefix, although not all of these were bred on the island, and probably as many more spent some time on the Island before being sold on to a new home overseas.

Michael first judged at Clifden in 1966, the same year in which Tim Cotter judged for the last time, and he became a regular judge at Clifden in the following years, and in 1976 he judged at both RDS Horse Show and at Clifden. He was a most enthusiastic worker for the Society and his untimely death early in 1977 at the age of fifty-four was a great loss to his family, as well as to the Council and to his many friends in the Connemara pony world. Sadly the Lambay herd was dispersed after Michael's death, and visitors were no longer able to experience the magic of a trip to the island.

Michael O'Connell at the RDS Horse Show.

The Annual inspections in 1977 saw another drop in the number of ponies presented for registration, with the total for the year being 349 in comparison with 447 in 1976 and 472 in 1975. It was a disturbing trend, but there was also a recession in the export trade, and with prices improving for cattle and sheep, the breeder in Connemara was tending to reduce the number of ponies in favour of cattle or sheep which gave a better return. The pony was no longer an essential part of working the farm, and the tradition of always having a pony about the place had largely died out, and so the number of ponies being bred in Connemara was falling each year.

Two young stallions were removed from the list at the end of the 1976 season, *Thundercloud (459)* and *Tulira Snowball (561)*, and sadly neither left any impression on the breed. The stallion list for 1977 included two new young stallions who were purchased by the Society, the first was *Skryne Bright Cloud (622)* by Clonkeehan Nimbus (229) dam Aughris Bright (2131), bred by Mrs Waring Willis, Tara, Co. Meath, he was a three year old dark grey, and was placed with Paddy Folan, Camus. The second new stallion was *Ormond Oliver (653)* a dun two year old by MacDara (91). He was his last son, foaled in Kilkenny, and was bred by William Brennan from his mare Ashfield Judy (5505). There were ten stallions on the list in Connemara in 1977, but for the three oldest sires it was to be their last season, and in June of that year *Dun Aengus (120)* who was nineteen years of age, died when running out in a field with his mares.

Dun Aengus (120) was born in Clifden in 1958 and he was the second son of *Dun Lorenzo (55)* to stand in Connemara on the Society's list of approved stallions. He was very different to Dun Lorenzo's other son *MacDara (91)*, he had a smaller lighter frame and was a light dun. His dam Rose of Killola (1365), who was chestnut, was a daughter of the T. B. sire Winter, and her dam Ivy Lass (815) was by Innishgoill Laddie (21) out of a T.B. racing mare, known in Connemara as Irish Lady. *Dun Aengus (120)* combined both sides of the old pony breeding in Connemara, on one side the tough hardy working pony stock from the Red Line through his sire *Dun Lorenzo (55)*, and on the other side, his dam Rose of Killola (1365) came from a line of great racing mares, and she and her dam and grand-dam won many races in Connemara. She may have had more thoroughbred than Connemara blood, but she was an exceptional mare, and lived until she was thirty-four years of age as a much loved family pet.

J. Petch

Dun Aengus (120) with Mikey King.

Dun Aengus (120) was bought by the Society in 1960 from his breeder P. K. Joyce, the well known butcher from Clifden, and was placed with John Walsh, Kilkerrin for his first season in 1962. He spent the next fifteen years in Connemara, moving between Claddaghduff, Cashel, Moycullen, Bunowen and Oughterard. In 1977 he went to Paddy Folan at Camus, when he was nineteen years of age, and he died during the summer.

He left two hundred and nine registered progeny, and among his sons were *Kimble (227)* Supreme Champion at Clifden in 1971, who was then sold to Sweden, *MacDuff (209)*, the winning stallion at Clifden 1974 was sold to France, *Atlantic Currach (294)* who went to Holland, *Moycullen Dan (226)* to Belgium and *Camlin Comet (378)* to Scotland.

Calla Boy (694) and *Maam Hill (728)* remained in Ireland and *Maam Hill (728)* was on the Society's list from 1980 to 1986. His daughters included Gentle Breeze (2684), Alnabrone Rebel (2691), Starlight Venture (3149), Kilcloghan Lady (3163), Hillswood Helena (3268), Riverside (6931), Knockabout Lady (6933), and one of his outstanding geldings was Pat Aengus (G809) who won many prizes under saddle.

Dun Aengus (120) left his mark on the breed through his grandson *Abbeyleix Owen (496)*, son of Kimble (227), who joined the Society's list in 1975, and it was through him that the Red Line was passed to future generations.

MacDuff (209) with John Luskin.

First International Connemara Pony Show, Denmark

The Danish Connemara Pony Society, under the leadership of their new President, Mr Bent Nielsen, staged an International Connemara Pony Show at Roskilde in Denmark on 30th and 31st July 1977, and invited all Connemara pony breeders in Europe to bring their ponies to the Show. Mrs Dan Lanigan O'Keefe was invited as the senior judge from Ireland, and she was joined by Mrs Anna Aaby Wodschow from Denmark, and Mr Friedlander from Sweden.

Only one intrepid breeder from Ireland braved the long journey to Denmark with her ponies, and she was the indomitable Mrs Margo Dean from Kells, Co. Meath. She had an incredibly difficult journey, but arrived in time to represent the breed's native country at this first International Show. A group of English breeders led by Mrs Cecilie Williams took eight ponies to the Show, Mr Hillnhutter and some of the German breeders also brought ponies, and there were forty ponies from Sweden. There were about 200 Connemara ponies at the Show, and the classes were dominated by Mr Nielsen's Oxenholm Stud who had thirty-nine ponies entered.

The Supreme Championship of the Show was won by *Marble (254)* who had been imported by Mr Nielsen in September 1976, and he was an outstanding Champion, having lost none of his grace and presence since he left Ireland. The Reserve Champion was the lovely five year old Danish bred mare Oxenholm Bardot (7251) sire Rosenharley Mac Milo (233) dam Brigitte (7242), and she carried some of the best old blood lines in Connemara, tracing back to two famous old mares Retreat (320), and Cregg Lassie (1737). Good weather, combined with wonderful organisation by the Danish Society, made the Show a great success, and breeders came from twelve different countries to visit the first International Connemara Pony Show.

54th Annual Pony Show, Clifden – 18th August 1977

Many of the overseas visitors who had been at the International Show in Denmark travelled on to Ireland to attend the Clifden Show. The stallion class had twenty-eight entries and was won by a five year old dark grey *Milford Hurricane (568)*, owned by John Luskin, Cong, and bred by Mr and Mrs Tom Ormsby at Cloghan's Hill, Tuam. His sire, *Mervyn Bowsprit (338)*, was bred by Miss Berridge and was a grandson of *Calla Rebel (38)* through *Strongbow (90)*. In second place was the Society's new stallion *Skryne Bright Cloud (622)* shown by Paddy Folan, Camus, and he had joined the approved list that season. He was a dark grey three year old son of *Clonkeehan Nimbus (229)* was a great-grandson of *Carna Dun (89)* through *Camlin Cicada (119)*, and he represented the Purple Line.

The two year old colt class went to *Grange Finn Sparrow (659)* by Coosheen Finn (381) owned by Joe Day, Wexford, and Coosheen Samba (6678), won the 2 year old filly class and Carew Cup for Mrs Petch. The Confined Championship winner was Joe Gorham's Belle of the Ball (3122) who won the senior mares class, and Mrs Brooks won the Archbishop's Cup with Errislannon Diamante (6026) and was reserve in the Confined Championship.

The Supreme Champion of the Show went to John Luskin's stallion *Milford Hurricane (568)*, and Reserve Champion was the winner of the Killanin Cup, Lady de Vesci's attractive three year old filly, Abbeyleix Fiona (6257) by Carna Bobby (79) dam Finola of Leam (3036). It was a most successful show held in beautiful weather and there was a record attendance which was important for the Society as the gate receipts at the Show contribute a large part of the Society's funds.

―――――――

By the Spring of 1978, Connemara had lost all three of the last remaining older

J. Walshe

Abbeyleix Fiona (6257)

168

stallions from the 1977 list. *Dun Aengus (120)* had died during the summer of 1977. *Atlantic Storm (139)* had been retired from the list at the end of the season aged seventeen and had moved to Jimmy Jones in Co. Carlow. *Rebel Wind (127)* spent the winter of 1977/78 in Wexford with Lady Maria Levinge, and was due to return to Connemara for the 1978 season when he became ill very suddenly and died. It was later diagnosed that he had died from cumulative ragwort poisoning, and his death was a big loss to the Society.

Rebel Wind (127) was foaled in 1960 and was by Inver Rebel (93) out of Colman Griffin's good mare Windy (782). He was bought by the Society in 1963 from his owner Mrs Naper, Oldcastle, Co. Meath and cost £175. He spent his first two seasons with the veteran stallion custodian John Walsh, Kylesalia, who had kept a stallion for the Society since 1932, and these two years with *Rebel Wind (127)* were John's last as a custodian. *Rebel Wind (127)* was a small tough little stallion, he measured 13 hands and was the real old stamp of pony, carrying no outside blood in his pedigree. He was a prolific sire and in the fourteen years he travelled the roads in Connemara, he had a total of 334 registered progeny, which was a record number by a stallion owned by the Society.

J. Petch

Rebel Wind (127).

He had many daughters who became good broodmares and among them were Garafin (3350), Homeward Bound (3354), Sparrow Hill (3661), Gipsy Moth (3675), Trixie (3998), Lehid Wild Wind (4003), Roundstone River (4746), Bunowen Saga (4764), Breath of Wind (5188), Grey Belinda (5983), Cregg View Colleen (6031) and many more. His most outstanding son was undoubtedly *Marble (254)*, and several other good sons went overseas including, *Atlantic Rebel (295)* who spent some time in England before going to Australia, and *Ocean Wind (323)*, who went to Holland. *Roundstone Oscar (337)*, was on the approved list for five seasons 1973/77 before being sold to Canada, and his son *Ballinaboy Barry (655)* was owned by the Society for two seasons, but neither were successful sires.

Another son of *Rebel Wind (127)* was *Dangan Dun (415)* bred by Josie Conroy from his good mare Breath of Spring (3137), and he spent his life with Paddy Carr at Dangan. He provided the link into the next generation to carry on this line in Connemara, as his son *Atlantic Cliff (663)* was the sire of *Mervyn Kingsmill (762)* who joined the approved list in 1983.

One of *Rebel Wind's* last sons to be registered was *Murphy Rebel (696)*, he was foaled in 1976 and was a son of Muffy (2157), the well-known little mare by Clonkeehan Auratum (104) who lived all her life on the Sky Road with her breeder, Michael Conneely and was a great broodmare. *Murphy Rebel (696)* was owned by

Stephen Heanue, Clifden, and he was included on the approved list in 1982 at the age of six, although he remained in private ownership. He left Connemara in 1990 when he was sold to Philip McMahon, Belturbet, Co. Cavan, and some of the best of his progeny made their name after he had left the district, including three who became Supreme Champions at Clifden in the 1990s.

Rebel Wind (127) died at the beginning of May just as he was about to return to Connemara for the covering season, and the Council was most grateful to Graham Tulloch who kindly made the generous gift to the Society of his stallion *Ocean Minstrel (420)* to replace his sire on the list in Connemara for the 1978 season.

There were several other new stallions added to the list for that season, two were owned by the Society and two privately. The Green Line had another representative in *Ardnasillagh Casey (654)*, a three year old son of *Thundercloud (459)*, but he was only on the list for one season and left few progeny. The second was *Ballinaboy Barry (655)* who spent two years in Connemara but was not a successful sire. Willie Diamond, Tully owned a three year old son of *Killyreagh Kim (308)* called *Davy D. (671)*, and he joined the list that season, and finally *Greaney Rebel (186)*, by Inver Rebel (93) dam Nansin Ban (1858) who had won the stallion class in 1968, and was now aged fifteen, was also included, and stood with his owner Henry Whyte, at Salthill, Galway.

Death of Sean Keane

The AGM which was held on 21st March 1978 at Salthill was well attended, and it was announced that the Council proposed to produce a colour brochure on the Connemara Pony and a sub-committee had been formed to work on the project. A number of other topics were discussed at the meeting which was chaired by the President of the Society Mr Sean Keane, and it came as a great shock to the members when just over a month later they learned of his death on 30th April at the age of sixty-eight.

Sean Keane had been elected to succeed Lord Killanin in March 1973, and had served for five years as President of the Society. He had been a most active President, and had done much to promote the Connemara Pony both at home and overseas. He was first elected a member of the Council in 1943 and over the following thirty-five years had devoted a great deal of his time and energy to the affairs of the Society. As an inspector for the breed he travelled all over Ireland to do special inspections for registering ponies, and also carried out inspections in England and in Europe.

Sean Keane

He was a member of the Commission of Enquiry on the Horse Breeding Industry, which was set up in 1965, and on the recommendations of the Commission the Irish Horse Board, Bord na gCapall was established, and Sean Keane became a member of the Board. He was also a member of the Breeding Committee which advised the Board on horse and pony breeding. During his years on the Council he saw the Society grow and prosper, and his knowledge of the ponies and the breeders in Connemara would be greatly missed.

Presentation to John Killeen by RDS

During the Spring Show in May a special award was made to Mr John Killeen by the Royal Dublin Society, and he was presented with a silver ash tray which was given in recognition of his record of having attended the Spring Show every year for sixty years without a break. It came as a complete surprise to him, and he was delighted at the gesture, and very proud to have been selected to receive the award.

Martin Treacy Elected President

A Council Meeting was held on 16th June 1978 at which Canon Moran, Vice President, took the chair, and Mr Martin Treacy was elected as the new President to succeed Sean Keane. Martin Treacy was born in 1914 at Derreen, Abbeyknockmoy, near Tuam, and having studied agriculture at the Albert College, Glasnevin, he joined the Department of Agriculture in 1932. He moved to Spiddal where he met his wife, and they lived at Ballydonnellan and had a large family of five boys and two girls. He was a great cyclist, and in the early years he covered most of Connemara on his "High Nellie" bicycle, which was supplied to field officers by the Department of Agriculture. He had succeeded Sean Keane as Area Inspector for Western Connemara in 1961, and he also followed him as Chief Steward of the Showgrounds at Clifden, a job which he did for many years. He was a brilliant Irish speaker, with a great knowledge of the language, and he was a valued member of a committee of language experts who worked on the Irish-English dictionary. They held frequent meetings to translate new words, interpret

Martin Treacy

colloquial expressions, and update the dictionary. He was not a pony man, but knew the people of Connemara through his work in the district, and having been a member of the Council since 1963, he took an active interest in the affairs of the Society.

Michael O'Connell Memorial Trophy at RDS Horse Show

The RDS Horse Show continued to provide four classes for Connemara ponies, and in 1978 the judges were Miss Pam Forman from England and Mr Graham Tulloch from Moyard, Co. Galway. For the first time a Championship Class was included and the 1st and 2nd prizewinners from each class were eligible to compete. A silver cup had been presented in memory of the late Michael O'Connell as a perpetual challenge trophy and the first winner was Tulira Mavourneen (3026) owned by Lord Hemphill, Tulira. The reserve was the two year old filly Ballinaboy Mermaid (6952) owned and bred by Col. Tony Morris, Ballinaboy, Clifden

55th Annual Pony Show, Clifden – 17th August 1978

Once again the weather was ideal, and there was a very large attendance at the Show. The stallion class and RDS Medal was won by *Coosheen Finn (381)*, s. Carna Bobby (79), owned by Mrs Petch, and in second place was *Ormond Oliver (653)* shown by Tommy O'Brien who also won the Confined Stallion Class. Col. Tony

Morris won the Carew Cup with his two year old filly Ballinaboy Mermaid (6952) by Ocean Minstrel (420), and Jimmy Jones won both the Killanin and Archbishop's Cups with Ashfield Blue Molly (6761) by MacDara (91) and Ashfield Lor Sparrow (6254) by Carna Bobby (79). Joe Gorham's Belle of the Ball (3122) by Carna Dun (89) won the Senior mare class and RDS Medal, and took the Confined Championship for the second year, but this year she went one better and became Supreme Champion of the Show.

A special class was included in the Show for the first time for fillies or mares entered in the half-bred register, the progeny of *Speck* or *Tellipy* out of a registered Connemara mare. There were only three entries which was perhaps an indication that the half-bred register had not met with much support from breeders. The class was scheduled again in 1979 and 1980, but with only two or three entries each year the class was dropped, and the scheme never really made any significant progress.

J. Petch

Coosheen Finn (381)

The Round Table Meeting was held the day after the Show, and many of the breeders from different societies were able to meet to discuss various matters of interest. The Swedish Connemara Pony Society had decided to hold an International Show in Sweden in early August 1979 and the venue chosen was Vetlanda, in a beautiful area of southern Sweden. All friends of the Connemara pony from all over the world were invited to attend the Show. After the meeting Mr Nielsen from Denmark showed a film taken at the first International Show at Roskilde in 1977 which was greatly enjoyed.

During the early part of the winter the Council was to lose three more members, and with the death of John Mannion, who had been a member of the Council since 1951, the Society lost an old friend. He was one of the signatories to the Memorandum and Articles of Association at the Council meeting held on 22nd December 1959 when the new Cumann was formed, and he had served as a member of the Council for twenty-seven years. He had been nominated by the Clifden Town Improvements Committee, and had done a great deal of work for the Society over the years, especially in matters relating to Clifden. He had a life long interest in pony racing, and often acted as judge or starter at the Clifden Races. One of his best known ponies was Clifden Molly (2127), dam of Abbeyleix Molly (2823), who was such a successful mare for Lady de Vesci, and some of Clifden Molly's progeny still remain in Clifden. During his life he served as a County Councillor, a Member of Dail Eireann and a Member of the Senate.

Death of Martin Treacy

The Society suffered another sad loss when the newly elected President, Martin Treacy died suddenly on 22nd November 1978 while attending a meeting in Dublin. He had only been President of the Society for five months and his death was a great shock to his family and members of the Council. He was sixty-four years of age and had been due to retire from his job with the Department.

In early December the Society bade farewell to another good friend when Jack Bolger passed away. He was one of the greatest pony men of his day and had a fund of knowledge about the ponies and their breeding. The first stallion he stood for the Society was Noble Star (17) in 1932, and he produced him to win the stallion class for four years running until the rules were changed! He had a good eye for a pony, and was a great showman and could produce his ponies looking really well. Many good ones passed through his hands including the Supreme Champions Cashel Kate (2030) and Heather Mixture of Abbeyleix (2709), but his greatest contribution to the Society was his handling of the stallions during the early years. His son Bobby has inherited his love of the Connemara pony, and has made sure that the Bolger tradition carries on with four Supreme Champions at Clifden in the 1990s.

Two vacancies on the Council were filled at a meeting in early November when Lady de Vesci, Abbeyleix, and Joe Gorham, Clifden were elected, and following Martin Treacy's death another meeting was held on 15th December 1978 at which three more members were elected to the Council. They were: John M. Mannion TD, Clifden, who replaced his father on the Council; Dermot Power, B. Agr. Sc. Galway, and Owen Crehan, Galway, who both worked in Connemara for the Department of Agriculture. Owen Crehan was also appointed Joint Treasurer of the Society.

Basotho Pony Project

During 1978 a programme to improve the Basotho pony in the state of Lesotho in southern Africa was established which was sponsored by the Irish government as part of Ireland's development aid programme to the Third World. Donal Kenny had been assigned to Lesotho by the Department of Agriculture in 1976, to evaluate and research the project, and following his report, the Basotho Pony Project was born. Donal Kenny became its director and in 1978, a team from the Department of Agriculture led by J. O'B. Gregan MRCVS went to Lesotho to start the Lesotho National Stud at Thaba Tseka.

As part of the project, two Registered Connemara Pony Stallions were bought by the Irish Government and presented to Lesotho, and they were to be mated with selected Basotho pony mares at the stud at Thaba Tseka, in

Connacht Tribune

The two stallions for Lesotho.

an experimental breeding programme. The two stallions were the six year old *Milford Hurricane (568)* sire Mervyn Bowsprit (338) dam Mervyn Silver Grey (4449) who was the 1977 Supreme Champion at Clifden owned by John Luskin, and *Crockaun Connemara (674)* sire The Fugitive (368) dam Silver Lace (2723), a three year old owned by Willie Fahy, Corrandulla. The stallions left Ireland in December 1978 and travelled out to Lesotho in the care of Pat Lenihan, Assistant Manager of the project. After 30 days quarantine in Capetown, they travelled across the Great Karoo Desert to their new home in the mountains of Lesotho, where they settled in quickly, and were covering mares within two weeks of their arrival at the stud.

Ireland's involvement in this project was sought by the Lesotho Government because the Basotho pony breed was in serious decline, and the success which had been achieved in Ireland with the development of the Connemara pony indicated that it might be possible to conserve the Basotho pony in a similar way. It was an inspired idea and the project has been a very successful one, and several grooms from the Lesotho stud, including Gilbert the head groom, have visited Ireland and joined the annual inspection tour in Connemara.

Donal Kenny Elected President

A Council meeting was held on 8th February 1979 at which Mr Donal Kenny was elected as President of the Connemara Pony Breeders'Society. He became the seventh person to hold the office, and was the third official from the Department of Agriculture. He had been an Inspector of Livestock for many years and had been based in Galway, but was moved to Dublin in 1977. He was somewhat reluctant to take on the job of President because he no longer lived in Galway, and only accepted on the understanding that he would fill the gap until someone else could be found. In accepting the office he said that he took a deep interest in the Connemara pony which was a great national asset, and he paid tribute to the founders of the Society and he hoped to try to continue to foster and develop the breed.

Ridden Connemara Pony of the Year Award Scheme

In 1979 the Council introduced a new Ridden Award Scheme, and its aim was to highlight the achievements of registered Connemara ponies in the performance field, and so promote the Connemara as a versatile riding pony. The scheme was run on a points system and was open to all registered ponies taking part in a variety of different competitions, show jumping, eventing, working hunter, ridden show classes, driving, and the pony gaining the most points throughout the year won the special award. John Brennan offered to provide a trophy for the winner, and Graham Tulloch gave a prize for the breeder of the winning pony.

The winter of 1978/79 was one of the hardest and longest in living memory, and the rain continued through the Spring and Summer making it very difficult and costly to save hay and grain crops. The market for Connemara ponies was depressed, and this meant that the decline in the numbers of breeding ponies in Connemara continued, and the situation was one of serious concern to the Connemara Pony Breeders' Society. During the boom years when the export trade had been very bouyant, many of the best youngstock were sold overseas for big prices, but now the demand from Europe for breeding stock had slowed down as the overseas societies had established studs in their own countries, and the need to return to Connemara to buy more stock had lessened. However, the Connemara pony has always been essentially a product of its own environment, and many of its best attributes are nurtured by a natural upbringing in its native land of bog and mountain, and therefore the Society needed to take steps urgently to provide an incentive scheme to encourage the traditional breeders in Connemara to continue to keep a mare for breeding. These men had produced the Connemara pony for generations, and were the backbone of the pony industry.

Two new stallions owned by the Society were added to the list for the 1979 season. The first was *Slyne Head (710)*, a dark grey two year old by Tulira Snowball (561) who was placed with Michael King, Claddaghduff, but he only remained on the list for one season. The second was *Ashfield Alex (711)* by Clonkeehan Auratum (104) dam Lambay Starry Eyes (3248), a bay two year old, and he stood with Joe Nee, Oughterard. The Thoroughbred stallion Speck belonging to Miss Garnet Irwin who had been standing at Mrs MacCartan's stud in Hollymount Co. Mayo, moved to Jimmy Canavan at Moycullen, and remained there until his death in 1986. The half-bred register made very little progress as a breeding programme, but Speck became a well-known sire of show jumpers, and was visited by mares from all over Ireland.

The 1979 annual inspection tour was held at 26 centres in Connemara during May, and a total of 266 ponies were registered during the year which included registrations from other parts of the country.

J. Petch

Ashfield Alex (711) with Joe Nee.

Volume XVI of the Stud Book

In 1979 the sixteenth volume of the Stud Book was published and contained the particulars of 1089 ponies which were registered over a three year period, and included 94 stallions, 900 mares and 85 geldings. Since the first registrations began in April 1924, 711 stallions and 7100 mares had been inspected and passed for registration in the Connemara Pony Stud Book. The Society had come a long way since its early beginnings and took pride in the registration system which had been established in which every pony in the Stud Book had been inspected prior to registration.

Judges Day 24th April 1979

Many more shows throughout the country were now including classes for Connemara ponies, and in some cases the judges at these shows had no knowledge of the breed. The Council appointed a sub-committee to prepare a set of guide-lines for judges and also to make a list of judges considered suitable for judging Connemara pony classes. Those whose names were put on the list were invited to attend a judges day which was held on 24th April 1979 at Rockmount Riding Centre and two veterinary surgeons, Mr Pat Daly MRCVS and Mr R. Kelly MRCVS, together with two experienced judges, Mrs Dan Lanigan O'Keefe and Mr John Daly gave a demonstration and talk about judging Connemara ponies.

In June 1979 a group of 120 members of the International Federation of Agricultural Journalists from 20 different countries were attending a Congress in Dublin. During their visit they toured Connemara and the Connemara Pony Breeders' Society organised a judging competition at Oughterard Showgrounds for the visiting group. Ten prizewinning Connemara pony mares were assembled and prejudged by three of the Society's judges: Mrs Dan Lanigan O'Keefe, Mr R. Kelly MRCVS and Mr Pat Daly MRCVS.

The ponies were then paraded for the visiting journalists, and the judges described what to look for when judging a Connemara pony. The winner of the competition was a member of the Japanese delegation who was presented with an inscribed silver trophy. The competition was most interesting and was greatly enjoyed by the visitors who took numerous photographs for publication in their various magazines, which was valuable publicity for the breed in many different countries.

The RDS Horse Show invited Mr John O'Mahony Meade to judge with Mr R. Kelly MRCVS and although the classes were smaller than in previous years, the standard was good. The class for mares of six years or over was won by the 13 year old Lambay Starry Eyes (3248) s. Carna Dun (89) owned by Jimmy Jones, Carlow, and she went on to win the Championship and the Michael O'Connell Trophy with Abbeyleix Bluebird (6594) in Reserve. *Coosheen Finn (381)* achieved a hat trick in the young mare classes with three of his daughters winning their class. They were Lady de Vesci's four year old Abbeyleix Bluebird (6594), and three year old Abbeyleix Folly (7045), and Mrs Petch's two year old Coosheen Nutmeg (7183).

56th Annual Pony Show, Clifden – 16th August 1979

Heavy clouds hung over Clifden on Show day, and the rain poured down from early morning. The sun did come out in the afternoon, but the mud in the ring made it very hard for the ponies and handlers.

The show had received generous sponsorship from Waterford Glass, and *Abbeyleix Finn (675)* owned by Herbert Glynn, Castlebar, Co. Mayo won the magnificent Waterford Glass Trophy which was presented to the winner of the stallion class. He was a four year old by Abbeyleix Ri (290), bred by Lady de Vesci out of Finola of Leam (3036), and later he was sold to Holland. In second place was *Tantallon Bobby (626)* by Carna Bobby

(79) owned by Michael Clancy, Spiddal, while *Greaney Rebel (186)* won the confined class for Henry Whyte, Salthill.

The Lady Carew Cup for the best two year old filly was won by Coosheen Nutmeg (7183), the Killanin Cup went to Lady de Vesci's Abbeyleix Folly (7045) and the Archbishop's Cup was won by Coosheen Samba (6678), and again all three mares were by *Coosheen Finn (381)*. Jimmy Jones won first and second in the five or six year old mare class with Ashfield Silver Cloud (5894), and Ashfield Lor Sparrow (6254) both by Carna Bobby (79), and Mrs Breege Curran, Moycullen won the Confined Championship with Queen of the Hills (2449) by MacDara (91) dam Ashe Grey (1673) and her colt foal by Killyreagh Kim (308) also won his class. Joe McLoughlin, Moycullen showed the yearling filly winner who stood reserve to her dam Queen of the Hills (2449) for the Confined

J. Petch

Coosheen Nutmeg (7183)

Championship, she was by Rory Ruadh (517) and was also a grand daughter of Ashe Grey (1673), who won at Clifden in 1968 for Joe's father Sean McLoughlin.

The Supreme Champion of the Show and the Jan Harald Koelichen Cup went to the two year old filly, Coosheen Nutmeg (7183), bred and exhibited by Mrs Petch, and the Reserve Champion was the stallion *Abbeyleix Finn (675)*. These two ponies were both related to the remarkable old mare Finola of Leam (3036) who was dam of *Abbeyleix Finn (675)* and also the dam of *Coosheen Finn (381)*, sire of Coosheen Nutmeg (7183).

Finola of Leam (3036) was owned in her later years by Lady de Vesci, and died at Abbeyleix in October that year aged twenty-one, and her legacy to the breed through her progeny was to stamp her as one of the outstanding broodmares of her time. Her sire *Lavalley Rebel (24)* by Rebel (7), was foaled in 1935, he was one of the early Society-owned stallions and was sold to Mr and Mrs Meade, in Wales in 1949. Her dam Waterfield Grey (1270), had no known breeding, and was sold to the Meades by Jack Bolger, and they renamed her Teresa of Leam after Jack's wife Teresa.

Finola of Leam (3036) was foaled at Leam Stud in 1958, and bred three foals in Wales for the Meades, before coming to Ireland to visit *Carna Bobby (79)*. Having bred three colts, the Meades chose *Leam Bobby Finn (297)*, foaled in 1967, to take back to Wales and were persuaded to sell Finola of Leam (3036) to their old friend Jack Bolger. He sold the 1968 colt foal to Mrs Petch, in Co. Cork and he became *Coosheen Finn (381)*, and in 1972 Finola of Leam (3036) was sold to Lady de Vesci with a filly foal at foot by *Atlantic Storm (139)*. She was named Fionnuala (5508) and in time became the dam of Abbeyleix Flora (7539), *Abbeyleix Fionn (810)* and *Boden Park*

Finnard (899). Two more of Finola of Leam's progeny went to Australia, one was Abbeyleix Fiona (6257) by Carna Bobby (79), who won the Killanin Cup and was Reserve Champion at Clifden in 1977, and the other was Abbeyleix Finbar by *Ballydonagh Rob (321)* who became a stallion at Glenormiston Stud in Queensland for Barton and Sue Clarke.

During 1979 the Council had a series of discussions with Bord na gCapall, the Irish Horse Board, which was the Government agency with responsibility for the non-thoroughbred horse industry in Ireland. Among the topics under discussion were the funding of the Society, purchase of stallions, registrations, and the proposed introduction a passport to replace the

Finola of Leam (3036) with Lady deVesci.

existing registration certificate, which would be a much more comprehensive document, and would include sketch markings of the animal. Further discussions were to be held with Bord na gCapall to ensure that the Connemara Pony Breeders' Society would remain in control of the Connemara Pony Stud Book, the inspections for registration, and the issuing of the passports.

Stallion Committee

The Council decided to appoint a Stallion Committee to look into the selection and the location of the Society's stallions, and the following were its members. Mr R. Kelly MRCVS, Mr Graham Tulloch, Mr John Brennan, Mr John Daly, Mr Dermot Power, Mr John Luskin, Mr Donal Kenny.

In October 1979 they inspected all the Society owned stallions in Connemara, and decided to remove *Ballinaboy Barry (655)* and *Slyne Head (710)*. The Green Line was again without a representative on the Society's list as the young stallion *Ardnasillagh Casey (654)* had died at the start of the 1979 season. His grand sire *Thunderbolt (178)* had been sold to Mr Alan Lillingston in Co. Limerick, and had spent the last eight seasons as a teaser at Mount Coote Stud. He was by now sixteen years old, but the committee decided to try to bring him back to Connemara in order to retain this valuable blood line. They wrote to Mr Lillingston, who kindly agreed to exchange *Thunderbolt (178)* for *Ocean Minstrel (420)*, and *Thunderbolt (178)* returned to Connemara in 1980, and went to his former custodian Mikey King at Claddaghduff, where he stood for the next three seasons.

Death of John Killeen

The Connemara Pony Breeders' Society suffered a great loss with the sudden death of John Killeen on 27th October 1979, and Connemara pony breeders from all over the world shared in the sadness of his family and many friends at the loss of this very special man who had given so much of himself to the service of others. Following his retirement, after a distinguished career with the Department of Agriculture, John Killeen was appointed Secretary of the Connemara Pony Breeders' Society in 1963, and he gave sixteen years of dedicated service to the Society. While he was Secretary he served four Presidents, Lord Killanin, Seane Keane, Martin Treacy, and Donal Kenny. He was respected and loved by his many friends at home and abroad, and his integrity, charm and unfailing courtesy made him a wonderful ambassador for the Connemara Pony Breeders' Society.

J. Petch

John Killeen

John Killeen's days with the Society were before the mobile phone and lap-top, his method was a note on the envelope taken while at the Show or inspection or at Maam Cross Fair. This note would then be meticulously acted upon when he returned to the office. John Killeen died at the age of 82, at six o'clock in the evening on the Saturday of the Maam Cross Fair bank holiday weekend. He was sitting at the desk in his office signing a Society certificate. He had given over 60 years to the development of agriculture and the Connemara Pony Breeders' Society. He had enjoyed life to the full in his own quiet way, and he is remembered with respect and great affection by all who knew him.

At the Dublin International Horse Show at the Royal Dublin Society on Sunday 18th November a moving tribute was paid to the late John Killeen by Captain Tommy Ryan on behalf of the Show Committee. The Chairman of the Show, Mr John Bland made a presentation to representatives of Mr Killeen's family, Mr Michael Killeen and Mrs Kathleen Terry.

Earlier at the same show the prizes were awarded for The Ridden Connemara of the Year 1979, and the first pony to win the Award was an 8 year old mare Park Cherry (5422) by Marble (254) owned by Michael Lenihan, Kilmacthomas, Co. Waterford, and ridden by his son Paul. In second place was Mrs Mary McCann's 9 year old stallion *Ashfield Bobby Sparrow (444)* by Carna Bobby (79), and third was Currycahill Katie (4411)a 10 year old mare also by Carna Bobby (79). The Award Scheme had been very successful in its first year of operation, and was providing valuable publicity for the breed.

J. Walshe

Kimble showing high spirits.

CHAPTER 12

1980-1984

Appointment of New Secretary

Mrs Phil MacDermott had been assistant secretary to John Killeen for sixteen years and had also done work for the Society during Bartley O'Sullivan's term of office when she was employed in the County Committee of Agriculture Office in Galway. She had been assistant to Sean Keane when he was Acting Secretary in the years between Bartley O'Sullivan's death and John Killeen's appointment as Secretary. Since the death of John Killeen in October 1979, she had been asked to take over as Acting Secretary, and at a meeting held on 28th March 1980, the Council unanimously agreed to appoint Mrs Phil MacDermott as Secretary of the Society. She was very well qualified for the job as she already had a thorough knowledge of the work of the Society and for many years had been responsible for the Show catalogue, and did the job of Show Secretary involving much of the organisation of the Show. She had also prepared the last eight volumes of the Stud Book for publication, and handled much of the routine paper work in the office. Phil MacDermott was married with two children, and the family lived in Salthill. She agreed to move the office into her home and the new address for the Connemara Pony Breeders' Society was: 73, Dalysfort Road, Salthill, Galway.

The Society was fortunate that such an able successor to John Killeen was there to pick up the reins, and with Phil MacDermott as Secretary, the continuity was maintained and the changeover was smooth and easy.

Bord na gCapall Increase Grant

Following a final discussion between representatives of the Council and Bord na gCapall, the grant in-aid to the Society was increased from £2500 to £7500 in 1980, and this enabled the Society to continue and develop its work for the Connemara Pony. It was also agreed that the identity and autonomy of the Connemara Pony Breeders' Society would be maintained.

In line with the new type of registration for all ponies in Ireland which Bord na gCapall had started in 1979, the Council decided that the Society would begin to replace the registration certificate with a passport system in 1980. Although it was planned that passports would be issued to all Connemara ponies registered in the following year, in fact it was several more years before the passport system was established.

Colt Inspection Centre at Maam Cross

Several new regulations were introduced in connection with the new type of registration, and at the Annual Inspections in the Connemara area held on 13th to 15th May 1980, sketch markings were taken for the first time. Sketch markings were also included on all foaling returns, and all colts to be registered in the Connemara area were brought together to one centre for inspection at Maam Cross on 13th May 1980.

A total of 250 ponies were registered during the year, 12 stallions, 199 mares and 39 geldings which was only sixteen less than in the previous year.

A memorial fund was set up in memory of the late Mr Sean Keane and Mr John Killeen, and members were asked to subscribe to a fund which would provide a suitable memorial to two men who had given so many years to the work of the Society. Mr Owen Crehan the Hon Treasurer, was to administer the fund.

The 7th Annual Gymkhana was held at the Showgrounds at Clifden on 1st June, it was a beautiful sunny day, and was greatly enjoyed by everyone taking part. Unfortunately the Connemara pony classes at the RDS Horse Show in August were not so lucky, and the rain fell relentlessly all day. The judges were Miss Pat Lyne from England and Mr Michael Clancy, Spiddal, and it was difficult for judges and exhibitors alike as the Show ring was hock deep in mud and very slippery. The Champion and winner of the Michael O'Connell Trophy was Mrs Phyllida Collier's twelve year old Crancrower Goblin Girl (4036) by Checkpoint Charlie (167) with Mrs Petch's three year old Coosheen Nutmeg (7183) in Reserve.

57th Annual Pony Show, Clifden – 21st August 1980

At the Clifden Show the beautiful Waterford Glass Trophy for the winning stallion went to Mrs Ormsby's *Mervyn Pookhaun (528)* who had previously won the class in 1975. Two of his sons won the yearling and two year old colt classes at the Show, and his full sister Mervyn Wren (4037) was second in the senior mares class which made it a good day for the Milford Stud.

The winner of the Carew Cup, who had also won her class in Dublin, was Ballymadun Kate (7434) by Clonkeehan Nimbus (229) dam Cashel Kate (2030) owned by Mr M. J. Murphy, Clontarf, Dublin, a lovely quality dun filly, and in second place was another dun, Graham Tulloch's Ocean Amber (7408) by Loobeen Larry (670) who was to remain at Shanbolard, replacing her dam Ocean Melody (2134) who had died aged twenty.

J. Petch

Mervyn Pookhaun (528)

The winner of the Killanin Cup was Coosheen Nutmeg (7183) by Coosheen Finn (381) owned and bred by Mrs Petch and the Archbishop's Cup went to Noel Mannion's Grey Rock Star (6947) by Abbeyleix Owen (496) dam Breath of Wind (5188) bred by Josie Conroy, Bunowen, and these two mares had the final battle for the Championship. The Confined Championship went to Grey Rock Star (6947), and she was also Reserve Champion of the Show, but the Supreme Championship and the Jan Harald Koelichen Cup was awarded for the second year running to Coosheen Nutmeg (7183). It is a record which still stands, for although several ponies have won the Supreme Championship on more than one occasion since the Jan Harald Koelichen Cup was first presented in 1965, Atlantic Mist (2175) in 1968 and 1970, Gloves Misty (6535) in 1982, 1986 and 1988, and Coral Misty (8642) in 1995 and 1997, no other pony has been Supreme Champion at Clifden in two consecutive years.

1980 was the second year for the Ridden Connemara Pony of the Year Award Scheme, and it had been a successful year for Connemara ponies who had competed in a variety of events. The presentation of the 1980 Connemara Pony Breeders' Society Award took place at the Dublin Indoor International Show at the Royal Dublin Society on Sunday 16th November and the winner was the 10 year old stallion *Ashfield Bobby Sparrow (444)* by Carna Bobby (79), dam Wise Sparrow (2270), owned by Mrs Mary McCann, Hartwell Stud, Kill Co. Kildare and ridden by Edward Doyle. *Ashfield Bobby Sparrow* was selected to jump for the Irish Pony Team at Soder in Germany and La Hulpe in Belgium, and won two International competitions, including the Grand Prix in Belgium, the biggest event in the European

M. Ansell

Ashfield Bobby Sparrow (444)

Championships. He also won the Irish 148 cms Pony Derby at Millstreet and was reserve hunter pony champion there. The breeder's prize went to Jimmy Jones, Carlow, who bred the winning pony.

Stallion Custodian Awards

The stallion committee introduced an Award Scheme for the stallion custodians in 1980, and cash prizes were awarded for the three best kept stallions owned by the Society standing in Connemara.

The 1980 Award was won by Josie Conroy with *Skryne Bright Cloud (622)*. In second place was Tommy O'Brien with *Ormond Oliver (653)*, and third prize went to Joe Nee with *Ashfield Alex (711)*.

The Society also purchased a new stallion in 1980, he was *Maam Hill (728)*, a three year old dun, sire Dun Aengus (120) dam Bay Lady (3971), bred by Martin Mulkerrin, Callowfeenish. He was put on the approved list for Connemara in 1981 and was placed with Tommy O'Brien for his first season. *Sarsfield (579)* was removed from the list at the end of the 1980 season and moved to Milford Stud with Tom and Liz Ormsby for 1981.

The Society's list now consisted of nine stallions, seven owned by the Society, and two in private ownership.

Blue Line

Killyreagh Kim (308) ....s. Carna Bobby (79) ....d. Ballydonagh Kate (2798).
Greaney Rebel (186) ....s. Inver Rebel (93) ....d. Nansin Ban (1858). (p)
Davy D. (671) ....s. Killyreagh Kim (308) ....d. Diamond's Fancy (4023). (p)

Red Line

Abbeyleix Owen (496) ....s. Kimble (227) ....d. Queen of Diamonds (1934).
Ormond Oliver (653) ....s. MacDara (91) ....d. Ashfield Judy (5505).
Maam Hill (728) ....s. Dun Aengus (120) ....d. Bay Lady (3971)

Green Line

Thunderbolt (178) ....s. Thunder (113) ....d. Irene Grey (1899).

Purple Line (T. B)

Skryne Bright Cloud (622)..........................s. Clonkeehan Nimbus (229) ....d. Aughris Bright (2131)

Orange Line (Arab)

Ashfield Alex (711) ....s. Clonkeehan Auratum (104) ....d. Lambay Starry Eyes (3248)

The Annual Inspections were held in Connemara in May and again the centre for the colt inspection in Connemara was at Maam Cross. Inspections were also held at a number of centres throughout the country during April and a total of 215 ponies were registered during the year compared to 250 in 1980 and 266 in 1979.

The 8th Annual Gymkhana which was due to be held at Clifden on 31st May had to be cancelled because of appalling weather conditions. Heavy rain during the previous week caused serious flooding in the Showgrounds and it was not possible to transfer to another date. The holding of a gymkhana under SJAI rules was dropped in future years as the Council felt that a gymkhana for local children would be more suitable, and this proved to be a popular decision.

The Danish Connemara Pony Society hosted their second International Connemara Festival at Roskilde on 24th to 26th July 1981. There were 250 entries with visitors bringing ponies from Sweden, Germany, France, Holland, England and Ireland to compete with a strong entry from Denmark.

The weather was very unkind, and unrelenting rain over the two days made conditions appalling in the ring. However the warmth of the Danish hospitality and the enthusiasm and cheerfulness of everyone taking part overcame the weather, and the festival was an enjoyable time for the Connemara pony breeders who gathered at Roskilde from many different countries.

J. Petch

Cossack Rider with five Connemara Mares.

Marble (254), the pony who had dominated the past two International festivals was not at this one, and it was sad that "The White Gentleman" as he was affectionately known in Denmark, had died earlier in the spring aged fifteen. The Supreme Champion of the Show was the mare Oxenholm Bardot (7251), and the Reserve was *Rory Ruadh (517)*, both owned by the Oxenholm Stud.

A Connemara Gala was performed each day and included a wonderful driving display representing different breeds, Cossack riders standing on the backs of two ponies and driving three more in front, disco jumping, and a vaulting display by a team of young girls from Germany on a delightful 21 year old grey mare called Dolly. She was registered as Autumn Retreat (2192) s. Carna Dun (89) d. May Retreat (1569), and was one of the first ponies imported into Germany by Jan Harald Koelichen in 1965.

There was an increase in entries at both the RDS Horse Show and at the Annual Pony Show at Clifden and both shows were blessed with fine weather. The Champion Connemara pony at Dublin Horse Show was Noel

Mannion's consistent winner Grey Rock Star (6947) by Abbeyleix Owen (496),d. Breath of Wind (5188) bred by Josie Conroy, and in Reserve was Garryhack Lady (5477) s. Sticky (377) owned by Joe Day, Ballycogley, Co. Wexford who won a large class for senior mares which had twenty-two entries.

Talk on the Basotho Project

On the evening prior to the Annual Pony Show at Clifden a meeting was held for members and delegates from the overseas societies to meet members of the parent society. There were representatives from five different countries, and during the evening a most interesting illustrated talk was given by Mr J. O'B. Gregan MRCVS on the Basotho Pony Project. He showed slides of the two Connemara pony stallions on the project, and Crocaun Connemara (674) had proved that he had an exceptional talent for jumping, and was the star performer at the National Stud at Thaba Tseka.

The project was making good progress, and in the 1980/81 season 30 foals were born, while 48 mares were in foal for the 1981/82 season. All foals born at the stud would be carefully selected with the best fillies being retained for breeding. Selected colts would be retained on the stud until three years old, and then sold to farmers who had shown an interest in the project, and there was keen rivalry between the local farmers to select their own stallion. The stud had already become a show piece, and many VIPs, national and international who visited the area, had been to see the Basotho Pony Project, and were very impressed and full of complimentary remarks on Ireland's involvement in it.

58th Annual Pony Show, Clifden – 20th August 1981

Clifden Show was blessed with fine weather in 1981 and the sunshine brought out a record crowd at the Show. Mrs Phyllis O'Mahony Meade was the visiting judge with Mrs Lanigan O'Keefe, Mr R. Kelly MRCVS and Mr Pat Daly MRCVS, and there were 320 ponies entered in the Show.

The winner of the open stallion class was *Fort Doolin (719)* a four year old bay by Rory Ruadh (517), bred by John Brennan out of Fort Lady (2648) by Thunder (113), owned by Padraig Curran, Moycullen, and shown by his son Gearoid. Another four year old stood in second place, he was *Bobby Brown (731)*, by Abbeyleix Ri (290) dam Brown Bird (4991) and was bred in Co. Laois by James Ryan.

The Confined Stallion class was won by *Thunderbolt (178)* who had returned to Connemara that season, and although he was eighteen years old,

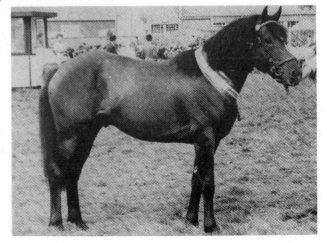

Fort Doolin (719)

186

he really sparkled on the day, and stood proudly at the head of the class for his old friend Mikey King. *Greaney Rebel (186)* by Inver Rebel (93) who was also aged eighteen, owned by Henry Whyte was in second place, and these two stallions carried their years lightly and showed the strength and substance which some of the younger stallions lacked.

Joe Gorham won the Carew Cup with Ocean Gipsy (7609) s. Loobeen Larry (670), dam Gypsy Moth (3675), and Lady de Vesci took the Killanin Cup with Abbeyleix Golly (7424) who was the third daughter of Abbeyleix Molly (2823) to win it, and as Molly also won it twice herself, it was quite a family record.

The RDS Medal for five and six year old mares went to the Dublin Champion, Noel Mannion's Grey Rock Star (6947),

Irish Farmers' Journal

Grey Rock Star (6947), Champion RDS, 1981.

and she went on to be Reserve Champion for the second year, while the Supreme Champion of the Show was the winning stallion, Padraig Curran's *Fort Doolin (719)*.

This young stallion's sire *Rory Ruadh (517)* was never shown in Ireland, but was sold to Bent Nielsen in Denmark, and was Reserve Champion of the Show at the Danish International Festival in July. *Fort Doolin (719)* was later sold to France but he left one son in Ireland, *Abbey Fort (824)* dam Abbeyleix Flora (7539).

Connemara Ponies Display at European Championships, Millstreet

The European Pony Show Jumping and Dressage Championships came to Ireland for the first time in 1981, and were held at Noel Duggan's Green Glens Centre at Millstreet, Co. Cork on 20th to 23rd August. It was a big International Event with ponies from all over Europe competing in the Championships, and the Connemara Pony Breeders' Society was invited by the organisers to put on a display of Connemara ponies on the Saturday evening.

The exhibition was held in the indoor arena in front of a large audience, and it began with a group of mares shown in hand, including many prizewinning and champion mares of the breed, and then four stallions were paraded, and a series of ridden displays followed. Among the highlights of the evening were the individual displays of dressage given by three of the international competitors, all of whom were riding purebred Connemara pony stallions. The first representing Sweden, was Susanne Gielen riding *Varnsbergs Neptunus*, who was bred in Sweden by Countess Oxenstierna, sire Lambay Inver (162), dam Jealous Lady (2301), and the second stallion was **Fireman**, an 11 year old from France ridden by Robert Lamblot. The third display was given by the Danish rider Lotte Andersen riding her Danish-bred 8 year old stallion **Cecil**, and the next day they won the individual title in the European Dressage Championship and brought much credit to the Connemara pony. The grand finale of the evening was an exhibition of jumping by the two top show jumping Connemara ponies, **Ashfield Bobby Sparrow (444)** and Currycahill Katie (4411). They and their young riders Mark Leddy and Zandra Flynn gave a thrilling display of four bar jumping, with the jumps reaching a final height of 5'2".

Connemara Pony on Stamp

On Friday 23rd October 1981 the Irish Post Office issued the fourth set of stamps in its series depicting the Fauna and Flora of Ireland. This issue featured famous Irish horses, and the stamps were in four denominations and five separate designs.

The horses depicted on the stamps were the Thoroughbreds Arkle and Ballymoss representing the steeplechaser and the flat racer, the Show Jumper Boomerang, the Irish Draught Stallion King of Diamonds, and the Connemara Pony stallion **Coosheen Finn**. The paintings for the stamps were done by Wendy Walsh who was the artist for all the Flora and Fauna series.

Coosheen Finn was selected by the Irish Post Office to represent the Connemara pony because he was the winning stallion at Clifden in 1978, the leading sire in 1979 when his progeny won the two, three and four year old classes at Dublin and again at Clifden, and he was also the sire of the Supreme Champion of the Show at Clifden in 1979 and 1980. He was chosen for the 36p stamp, which was the airmail stamp to USA and Australia, because so many people from the West of Ireland had emigrated to those countries, and it was thought that they would appreciate receiving a letter from home with a Connemara pony on the stamp.

The Awards for the winners of the 1981 Ridden Connemara Pony of the Year were presented at the Dublin Indoor International Horse Show at the RDS on 14th November. The winner was Tantallon Gaye Roberta (6155) owned by Mrs Juliet Perrin, Newbridge, Co. Kildare, with Mrs Anne Gormley's Currycahill Katie (4411) again taking second place, and in third place was Pat Aengus (G809), a six year old gelding from Co. Galway ridden by Gerald Dillon. Three of the ponies in the top four places in the Award Scheme were selected to represent

Ireland on the working hunter team which competed at Peterborough in England in September, they were Tantallon Gaye Roberta (6155), (1st) Pat Aengus (G809), (3rd) and Master Aengus (G512), (4th). Both the geldings were sons of *Dun Aengus (120)*.

Two Council Members Resign

At a meeting in early December, the Council received a letter from Miss Garnet Irwin to say she was resigning from Council, she had been a member of Council since 1961 and was a great supporter of the Society. She had been a breeder of Connemara ponies for many years and her Camlin ponies were known worldwide. She had a great knowledge of the ponies, and in her early days she was a keen jockey, and was the only girl riding against the men in the pony races in Connemara. Her foundation broodmare Ciro, was bred from the 20 year old mare, Swallow II (473), who was

Garnet Irwin on Camlin

Garnet's first racing mare. Ciro (551) by Silver Pearl (18) was foaled in 1938, she was Swallow's only foal, and was the best mare Garnet ever had. She won 10 first prizes at Clifden between 1949 and 1962 and also won her class at the RDS the first year the Connemara classes were held at the Spring Show in 1951. She was a great jumper, and she and Garnet frequently competed against horses in novice jumping competitions and once they cleared a five foot wall at Castlebar show. Ciro's only daughter Camlin Cilla (1447) won the Killanin Cup in 1953 and was the dam of *Camlin Cicada (119)* and Camlin Capella (2350) both by Carna Dun (89). The Council accepted Miss Irwin's resignation with regret, and Padraig Hynes, Canal Stage, Ballinafad was elected as a new member of Council to take her place. Garnet Irwin no longer lives in her old home Ross, Moyard, but lives nearby at Camlin, and still takes a keen interest in the ponies and the people who breed them.

Another longstanding member of the Council who resigned in March 1982 was Lord Hemphill, who was first elected to the Council in 1964. He had been a very generous supporter of the Society and for many years had given a cash prize to the Clifden Show for special prizes for ponies bred owned and exhibited by residents in Connemara. He was a most able chairman of the finance committee for the International Conference in 1970, and he and Lady Hemphill had also been hosts to the conference delegates at their home Tulira Castle after the parade of stallions. Connemara ponies had been bred at Tulira since 1963, and the Tulira ponies had earned a worldwide reputation as hardy active performance ponies who excelled as eventers and working hunter ponies. Lord Hemphill's place on the Council was taken by Mr Charles Lydon MRCVS, Westport, Co. Mayo.

The Society owned stallion *Skryne Bright Cloud (622)* left the stallion list at the end of the 1981 season having been in Connemara for five seasons. He spent two years with Paddy Folan at Camus and three with Josie Conroy at Bunowen, and then he was sold to Sam Morrison in Portadown, Co. Armagh. He was a representative of the Purple Line in the fourth generation and carried both the *Carna Dun (89)* and *Winter TB* blood on his sire's side, and the Red and Blue Lines on his dam's side. He lacked some pony characteristics, and was more a strong small horse than a pony, which came through the TB blood in his male line, but he also passed on the outstanding jumping ability which carries down through this line. He had six registered sons, and *Robin Hood (806)* d. Village Grey (6951) and *Silver Cloud (811)* d. Wise Cuckoo

J. Petch

Skryne Bright Cloud (622) with Josie Conroy.

(2714) are two who have continued this branch of the Purple Line into the fifth generation. He had sixty-eight registered daughters, among them were: Blue Jean (7568), Airfield (7784), First Love (7690), April Cuckoo (7714), Harvest Home (7901), Glen Lady (8094), Grey Rock Lucky Star II (7859), June Cuckoo (8083), Inishnee Daisy (8077) and Bunowen Pier (8081), and three of these were prizewinners at Clifden in 1982.

Two new names were added to the stallion list in 1982, the first was *Murphy Rebel (696)* s. Rebel Wind (127) d. Muffy (2157) who was a six year old grey owned by Stephen Heanue, Bridge Street, Clifden. The second was *Fort Boffin (759)* a four year old cream dun by Rory Ruadh (517) dam Fort Lady (2648) who was lent to the Society by his breeder John Brennan and stood with Joe Nee, Oughterard. He was a full brother to *Fort Doolin (719)*, the 1981 Clifden Champion, but was quite a different type of pony, and showed more native pony characteristics.

The Annual inspections were held in Connemara from 18th to 20th May and once again the number of ponies registered was less than the previous year with 178 ponies in 1982 compared to 215 in 1981.

Society's Funds Critical

The Society suffered a further setback when the grant in-aid from Bord na gCapall which had been reduced by £1000 to £6500 in 1981 was reduced drastically in 1982 to £3000. The Society had always been funded to a large extent by grant in-aid from the Department of Agriculture, and since 1972 this grant had been administered by Bord na gCapall.

On 27th May 1982 at a meeting between members of Bord na gCapall and the Council, the Chairman of the Bord Mr Peter Needham told the Council that the Bord would give a grant of £3000 towards the breeding schemes, but no financial assistance would be available for the administration costs of the Society. It was suggested that some of the administration work could be done at the Bord's offices at Tallaght, Co. Dublin, but this was not acceptable to the Council, and there was a strong feeling among the members of the Council that if the administration of the Society's affairs was transferred to Dublin, it would destroy the Connemara Pony Breeders' Society. Mr Donal Kenny stated that the best way the Bord could help the Society would be to give adequate financial aid to allow the Society to continue its work in Connemara, and also help towards the promotion and sale of Connemara ponies. However the Bord was adamant, and the grant for 1982 remained at £3000 which was a severe blow to the Society. Fortunately Waterford Glass continued their generous and valued sponsorship for the Annual Pony Show, and the membership fees and registration fees were raised to increase the income of the Society, but the financial state of the Society was critical.

On Sunday 6th June a local gymkhana was held in the Showgrounds in Clifden and over seventy children took part in an exciting programme of pony classes and gymkhana games. The day was organised by Mrs Brooks, who over many years has put a huge amount of effort into encouraging the local children in Connemara to enjoy their ponies, and the day was greatly enjoyed by both the competitors and spectators.

A new show for Connemara ponies made its debut in 1982 when Ballinalee Show was held on 13th June, in the village of Ballinalee, Co. Longford. It was organised by Miss Clair Studdert and Mr Harry Farrelly and received great support from breeders, with 161 Connemara ponies taking part. It was the first time a show confined solely to registered Connemara ponies had been held outside Connemara, and with an increasing number of breeders in the Midlands, the Show was welcomed enthusiastically, and was an outstanding success. It is now a popular annual event and has gone from strength to strength over the years. The Champion of the Show was Mrs Jane Dalrymple's Clonkeehan Whitethorn (2796) and the Reserve Champion was the winning stallion *Grange Bobbing Sparrow (623)* shown by his breeder Lady Maria Levinge.

The World Show Jumping Championships were staged at the Royal Dublin Society Showgrounds at Ballsbridge from 8th to 13th June 1982, and ten Connemara Ponies were given the honour of leading the parade of all the nations as they left the arena following the opening ceremony. This welcoming ceremony was a spectacular display representing many

Reggie Scanlon at the World Championships.

different organisations involved in equestrian sport in Ireland. Mr Reggie Scanlon drove his pair of dun Connemara geldings in the driving display, and Connemara ponies also took part in a pageant of Irish Horse Breeding organised by Bord na Capall at the Championships. The ten ponies in the parade were led by *Ashfield Bobby Sparrow (444)*, and included some of the leading ridden Connemara ponies.

The Round Table Meeting was usually held the day after the Clifden Show, but in 1982 it was decided to replace it with an informal meeting which was held the evening before the Show at the Clifden House Hotel. Breeders from many of the overseas societies including England, France, Germany, Holland and Australia who were visiting the Show were able to renew friendships and exchange information with Irish breeders and it provided a very enjoyable opportunity to get together before the Show. The evening was so successful, it became a regular feature of the arrangements for Clifden Show in future years.

59th Annual Pony Show, Clifden – 19th August 1982

There were good entries for the Show which was held the following day with 294 ponies entered in sixteen classes including two riding classes. The judges were Miss Susan Lanigan O'Keefe, Mr P. J. Foy, and Mr C. T. Lydon MRCVS.

First and second in the Open Stallion class went to two sons of Carna Bobby (79) and the winner was the 16 year old *Ballydonagh Bobby (242)* shown by Joe Day, Wexford, with Michael Clancy's *Tantallon Bobby (626)* in second place, and the winning three year old colt *Milford Hard Times (758)* s. Mervyn Pookhaun (758) took third place for Michael Flynn, Castlebar. *Abbeyleix Owen (496)*, won the Confined stallion class for Bartley O'Malley, with *Murphy Rebel (696)* second.

Mrs Brooks with Errislannon Ayesha (4767), Confined Champion.

192

Noel Mannion, Murvey had two winners, the first was his yearling filly by Skryne Bright Cloud (622) dam Lucky Star (3367), and his six year old Grey Rock Star (6947) won the 5 and 6 year old class for the second time, this time with a foal at foot by Skryne Bright Cloud (622) who was 3rd in her class. The two year old filly class and the Carew Cup was won by Airfield (7784) owned by Thomas Mullen, Moyard, and second in this class was John Joyce's April Cuckoo (7714), both these fillies were also by Skryne Bright Cloud (622), who was removed from the list that season, but had left some promising fillies in Connemara.

The three year old class was a close contest, and the eventual winner of the Killanin Cup was Mrs Petch's Coosheen Swallow (7625), with Castle Lady ((7605) second for Henry O'Toole. It was something of a family affair as Coosheen Swallow's

Mary Tarry

Eddie Madden with Gloves Misty (6535), Supreme Champion.

dam Village Belle (1855) was the granddam of Castle Lady, and Village Belle won the Killanin Cup in 1959.

The class for mares of seven or over was the biggest of the day with forty-four mares filling the ring. The winner, who had also won this class in 1981 was Eddie Madden's lovely grey mare Gloves Misty (6535), with the Dublin Champion Garryhack Lady (5477) second for Joe Day. The third prize winner in this strong class was Errislannon Ayesha (4767) owned and bred by Mrs Brooks, Errislannon, and this mare won the Confined Championship and took the O'Sullivan Memorial Plaque and the Clonkeehan Cup. Gloves Misty (5477) went on to become Supreme Champion of the Show, and Joe Day's stallion *Ballydonagh Bobby (242)* was Reserve

The winner of the riding class at Clifden was the 15 old gelding Tulira Rocket (343) s. Tulira Paddy (188) dam Noreen Grey (2287) owned and bred by Lady Hemphill, and ridden by Noel Murphy from Athenry. Rocket had spent some years in England where he had been Champion in ridden Mountain and Moorland classes

Tulira Rocket (343) with Noel Murphy.

three times. He then returned to his breeder at Tulira, and having competed successfully throughout the season, he became the winner of the 1982 Ridden Connemara Pony of the Year Award, and the presentation of the Award was made at the Dublin Indoor International Show at the Royal Dublin Society in November.

The 1982 Society's Stallion Awards for the three best kept stallions owned by the Society went to: 1st Bartley O'Malley with *Abbeyleix Owen (496)*, 2nd Tommy O'Brien with *Maam Hill (728)* and 3rd Josie Conroy with *Ashfield Alex (711)*.

Donal Kenny, President of the Society, had a number of meetings with Bord na gCapall during 1982, and had requested that the grant in-aid for the Society would be increased in 1983, as lack of funds was severely curtailing the work of the Society. At a meeting held in March 1983, Donal Kenny told the Council that the finances of the Society were in a critical state, and there was only £329.25 in the current account. The Society had very limited means of generating income, the principal sources being the proceeds of the Annual Show, registration and transfer fees and members subscriptions. Therefore the Society depended to a great degree on state aid and sponsorship in order to carry on its work.

It was important to appreciate that the work of the Society since its inception was very much a service to the people of Connemara, and was not profit orientated. A sub-committee was formed to seek ways to improve the finances of the Society, and in order to generate some extra income all the fees were increased for 1983.

New Society Logo

It was announced at the AGM that the Council had decided to hold a competition to find a suitable design for a logo for the Society to be used on passports and all documents and stationery, and designs should be submitted by 1st June 1983. Mrs Marion Swift Clarke kindly offered a cash prize for the designer of the winning logo, and eleven designs were entered in the competition. The entries were judged by the Council, and the winning logo was designed by Mr Tom Farrell, Clara, Co. Offaly who was a graphic artist working at the Kilkenny Design Workshop.

The new logo was launched at the 60th Annual Pony Show at Clifden, it appeared on the cover of the Show catalogue, and it was also used on special T shirts and sweat shirts to commemorate the 60th anniversary which were sold to raise funds for the Society. After the Show Lady de Vesci presented a cheque for £900 to the Society which was the result of her efforts in the organising and selling of the shirts.

A new young stallion was added to the approved list in 1983, he was *Mervyn Kingsmill (762)* a three year old grey bred by Miss Lal Berridge Enniskerry, Co. Wicklow from her prizewinning mare Mervyn Blue Charm

(4605). His sire *Atlantic Cliff (663)* was little known in Ireland, but was bred by Michael Clancy and was by Dangan Dun (415), his dam Hillswood Helena (3268) by Dun Aengus (120) won her class at RDS Horse Show in 1973. *Atlantic Cliff (663)* was sold to John Daly, and he leased him to Miss Berridge for two seasons to run with her mares, before selling him to Holland. His only foals in Ireland were four colt foals born at Enniskerry, three of them were gelded, but the fourth one foaled in 1980, was kept as a colt, and he was *Mervyn Kingsmill (762)*. *Abbeyleix Cypress (241)* s. Doon Paddy (95) dam Silver Birch of Abbeyleix (2753) also spent two years with Miss Berridge, and Kingsmill's dam Mervyn Blue Charm (4605) was one of his five foals. Later as a gelding, Abbeyleix Cypress went on to be an outstanding show jumper, owned by Eugenia Murray and was European Showjumping Champion in France, as well as being a Champion working hunter pony and a good all-round performance pony.

Mervyn Kingsmill (762) had a mixture of some of the best bloodlines in his pedigree, and his arrival in Connemara caused much interest and speculation. He was sent to Mikey King for his first season and was to spend five seasons at Claddaghduff. He replaced *Thunderbolt (178)*, now aged twenty, who was moved to Festy Mulkerrin for his last season in Connemara. The Society had purchased a colt foal by *Thunderbolt (178)* out of Peter Molloy's mare Dooneen Grey (3671), and it was hoped that he might be the one to follow his sire and retain his valuable bloodline in Connemara. The two privately owned stallions *Greaney Rebel (186)* and *Davy D (671)* were removed from the stallion list for the 1983 season, and *Killyreagh Kim (308)* moved to Tommy O'Brien, while *Maam Hill (728)* joined *Abbeyleix Owen (496)* with the O'Malley brothers at Carraroe.

The annual inspection tour was held at 26 centres in Connemara from 17th to 19th May, and other inspections were held throughout Ireland at various centres and at some shows. The overall total of ponies registered during the year was 223 which was a slight increase on the previous year, but not enough to mark any change in the declining numbers of ponies being bred in Connemara, and there were only 209 nominations awarded to registered mares in the Connemara area.

The RDS Spring Show included a class for ridden Connemara ponies for the first time in 1983, and it was well supported, although unfortunately the day was very wet. However, despite the difficult conditions, the judge Mr Tony Cox did an excellent job, and the winner of the class was Eugenia Murray's Mervyn Blue Tac (7179) by *Sticky (377)* dam Mervyn Blue Charm (4605), a half sister to *Mervyn Kingsmill (762)*, she has since been a consistent winner for Judy Cazabon.

Ballinalee Show was held for a second year and with extra classes and more sponsorship it was another successful day. Shows were also held at Roundstone, Spiddal, and Oughterard, and other shows providing classes for Connemara ponies were Westport, Galway, Athenry, Ballinasloe and Hollymount.

The European Hunter Pony Championships took place at the Royal Dublin Society Showgrounds at Ballsbridge on 28th and 29th May. Teams came from Germany, England, Scotland and Wales to compete, and three Connemara ponies travelled from Germany on their Hunter Pony Team. It was good to see Connemara ponies returning to Ireland representing another country at the Championships, and the breed was well represented for Ireland by Tantallon Gaye Roberta (6155) who was on the winning Leinster Team.

Tantallon Gaye Roberta (6155) was a consistently good performance pony and later in the year won the Award for the Ridden Connemara Pony of the Year for the second time. She previously won the Award in 1981, and another former winner, Park Cherry (5422) who won the 1979 Award, was in 2nd place.

Following the success of the ridden class at the Spring Show, The RDS agreed to include a ridden class for Connemara ponies at the Horse Show as well as the four in-hand classes already in the schedule.

There was a good response for the new class with 31 entries coming before the judge, Mr John Moore, and the winner was Pat Aengus (G809) owned by Mr Sean Hardiman, Galway. Unfortunately the led classes were not so well filled, and only three were entered in the four to five year old class. All three came from

Tantallon Gaye Roberta (6155), Champion Working Hunter Pony.

Connemara and it was disappointing that they had travelled to Dublin only to find no opposition there. The strongest class of the day was for mares of six or over, and it was won by Eddie Madden's Gloves Misty (6535) with Coosheen Samba (6678) in second place for Mrs Petch, and these two ponies were made the Champion and Reserve Champion of the Show.

60th Anniversary

1983 was the 60th Anniversary of the founding of the Connemara Pony Breeders' Society, and the former President of the Society, Lord Killanin was invited to be the special guest of honour at the 60th Annual Show to celebrate the occasion. On the evening before the Show, many visitors from the overseas societies and members of the Connemara Pony Breeders' Society gathered together for an informal evening at the Clifden House Hotel.

Lord Killanin was invited to speak to the large gathering of breeders present, and he expressed his optimism for the continued success of the Society. He also stressed the importance of international co-operation to ensure that the Connemara Pony which is now renowned throughout the world continues to maintain its high profile in the equine world.

60th Annual Pony Show, Clifden – 18th August 1983

The 60th Annual Show took place the following day, and many officials from the overseas Connemara Pony Societies came to visit the Show, including the President of the French Society, M. Jean Pierre Boisseau, accompanied by M. Rene Louis Chagnaud, a former President. Mr Herbert Imping President of the German Society with Mr Kurt Hillnhutter, Mrs Inger Schroder Secretary of the Danish Society and Mr Eric Bus. Mr and

Mrs John Williams, longstanding supporters of the Show, representing the English Connemara Pony Society. Mr Tadhg O'Sullivan, Irish Ambassador in Washington, also attended the Show and was there to present the O'Sullivan Memorial Plaque, given in memory of his father, the late Bartley O'Sullivan, the former secretary of the Society. There were 290 entries at the Show, and the judges were Mr R. Kelly MRCVS and Mr Pat Daly MRCVS with Mr J. Brennan referee.

The winning two year old filly and winner of the Carew Cup was Lady de Vesci's Abbeyleix Delphinium (7908) s. Coosheen Finn (381) d. Callowfeenish Dolly II (1813), and the three year old colt winner was a full brother, *Abbeyleix Dolphin (777)*, also bred by Lady de Vesci, and shown by his new owner Padraig Curran, Moycullen.

Mikey King had a good day with the Society's new stallion, *Mervyn Kingsmill (762)* who was second in the Two and Three Year Old Colt class, he then won the

Liz Harries

Abbeyleix Dolphin (777) with Padraig Curran.

Confined Stallion class and was third in the Open Stallion class. The winner of the Open stallion class and the Waterford Crystal Trophy was *Ballydonagh Cassanova (370)*, owned by Mr Joe Murphy, this 15 year old stallion had tremendous presence in the ring and was a real showman. Bred by Mr Trevor Donnelly, he was by Checkpoint Charlie (167) and his dam was the former Supreme Champion, Atlantic Mist (2175). The three year old mare class provided another win for Lady de Vesci when she won the Killanin Cup with April Cuckoo (7714), who had also won her class in Dublin, and the Archbishop's Cup went to Joe Gorham's Ocean Gipsy (7609).

The largest class of the day was for mares of seven or over which had forty-one entries with many former prizewinners filling the ring. The first three mares were very close and there was very little between them, the winner was Silver Sparrow (6898) owned by Michael Clancy, a seven year old grey mare by Abbeyleix Owen (496) dam Sparrow Hill (3661), who was bred by Peter Joyce, Ballyconneely, and whose full brother was the

*Lord Killanin with Joe Murphy
and Ballydonagh Cassanova (370).*

stallion *Cuchulainn (789)*. In second place was Coosheen Samba (6678), and Gloves Misty (6535), the Dublin Champion and 1982 Champion at Clifden, was placed third this time. Silver Sparrow (6895) won the Confined Championship, with the four year old winner Ocean Gipsy (7609) in Reserve, and the Supreme Champion of the Show and the Jan Harald Koelichen Cup went to the two year old filly, Lady de Vesci's Abbeyleix Delphinium (7908) with Silver Sparrow (6898) the Reserve Champion.

Callowfeenish Dolly II (1913), was bought by Lady de Vesci in 1978, and Abbeyleix Delphinium (7908) and *Abbeyleix Dolphin (777)* were the last two foals from this fine Carna Dun mare. She was bred by Martin Mulkerrin at Callowfeenish, and her dam

Lady deVesci with Supreme Champion Abbeyleix Delphinium (7908)

Callowfeenish Dolly (437) was aged twenty when she was foaled in 1956. She was one of the most outstanding mares of her day, and future generations of her progeny still grace the Showrings of today.

Less than two weeks after the Show, members of the Society were shocked to learn of the untimely death of Mr Joe Murphy who had shown his winning stallion with such pride at Clifden. He lived in Dublin but had a farm in Co. Mayo and had a fatal accident when his car ran into some loose horses on the road in the dark when driving home. He was a keen breeder and a strong supporter of the Society, and his death was a great loss to his wife and family and to his many friends in the Society. His daughter Emer became a member of the Council ten years later.

First All Ireland Ridden Connemara Pony Championship

This new Championship was held at Oughterard Show on 28th August 1983, and qualifiers were held at 12 different shows throughout the country. The competition was for registered Connemara ponies 148cms and under ridden by children between the ages of 10-16 on 1st Jan 1983. The Championship attracted the top ridden ponies from all over Ireland, and it was very successful thanks to the hard work of Jimmy Canavan and Frank Joyce, two members of the Oughterard Show Committee, who organised the competition and gave a lot of time to promoting the new Championship at shows all over Ireland throughout the summer.

The first winner of the Championship was Diamond's Cracker (6168), s. Roundstone Oscar (337) d. Silver Tassie (4151), a seven year old dun mare bred by Willie Diamond, Tully, and owned by Mrs Ian Fox,

Summerhill, Co. Meath, and she received the Cannon Ball Trophy, which was presented to the Show by Gerry O'Neill, Lisdoonvarna.

The Championship was an important step forward in promoting the Connemara pony as a performance pony in Ireland, and the All Ireland Championship at Oughterard has now become an annual event, and is an established date in the calendar for the ridden Connemara pony.

Tulira and Abbeyleix Studs Dispersed

Just twenty years after it was established, the famous Tulira Connemara Pony Stud was dispersed at a sale held at Tulira Castle on 8th September 1983. Having sold the estate to an American lady Mrs Breeden, Lord and Lady Hemphill had moved to Raford House, Kiltulla, and although some old favorites went with them to Raford, most of the herd was sold, and it was a sad day when fifty-six ponies were put up for auction at Tulira. The Stud was founded on two good mares bought from John Houston in 1963, Glen Nelly (1344) who was the dam of *Tulira Mairtin (214)* and Star of Fahy (1453). The first pony to achieve success in the performance field for the Hemphills was the outstanding gelding Patsy Fagan (G59), s. Tooreen Ross (99) d. Smokey (1198), bred by Murty McGrath, Cregmore, and ridden by one of the Hemphill children, he was the individual winner of the Irish Pony Club Championship on three occasions as well as winning many International Events.

The aim of the stud was to breed a hardy active pony with good strong limbs which would make a tough performance pony, and some suitable mares from the best old pure bloodlines in Connemara were bought to run with *Tulira Mairtin (214)*. The most successful of these foundation mares was undoubtedly Noreen Grey (2287) s. Gael Linn (103), d. Rebel Noreen (1413) who was bred by John Joyce (Peter), at Derrada East, Recess and she bred thirteen foals, among them the top class performance ponies *Tulira Rocket (343)*, Tulira Maria (4433) and *Tulira Nimble Dick (476)*. Over the years Tulira ponies were exported to nine different countries and were renowned for their strength and boldness across country. At the sale Mrs Breeden bought some of the best mares to continue

Noreen Grey (2287)

breeding at Tulira and all the ponies found new homes in Ireland. Five years later, in 1988 the Tulira Stud was re-established at Raford House.

Only two months after Clifden Show Lady de Vesci suffered a sad loss with the death of her husband in October 1983, and within a few months she left Abbeyleix and moved to England so that her son Tom could take over the estate. The herd of ponies at Abbeyleix, which had been built up with such care over twenty-one years, was dispersed, and the mares were all sold to breeders who were trusted friends. Since 1962, many lovely ponies had passed through Abbeyleix on their way to new homes overseas and were registered with the Abbeyleix prefix, although they were not all bred at Abbeyleix. However over the years a small herd of good broodmares was established, and in later years all ponies carrying the Abbeyleix name were bred there. The most successful and the favourite of her foundation mares was Abbeyleix Molly (2823), who won every class at Clifden during her showing career. Two other outstanding mares who spent their last years with Lady de Vesci were Finola of Leam (3036) and Callowfeenish Dolly II (1913), and both bred well into their old age.

There was never a resident stallion at Abbeyleix, but several good stallions were bred there, including the well-known Society owned stallion, *Abbeyleix Owen (496)*, as well as *Abbeyleix Cypress (241)*, *Abbeyleix Ri (290)*, *Abbeyleix Finn (675)*, *Abbeyleix Fionn (810)*, and *Abbeyleix Dolphin (777)*. Lady de Vesci enjoyed showing her ponies and had many successes at Dublin, Galway and Clifden, the ponies brought her great joy, and so it was with great sadness that she decided to sell them and leave Abbeyleix. Her champion Abbeyleix Delphinium (7908) was sold to England, but all the other mares went to new homes in Ireland.

In early October a Seminar was held in Clifden which was attended by pony breeders from all over Connemara. It was organised by the Connemara Pony Breeders' Society, and consisted of lectures and practical demonstrations on all aspects of pony production, nutrition, general husbandry, training, showring presentation and marketing. It was a day long seminar and was well attended, and there was a high percentage of young people present which was encouraging. The day was organised by Mr Dermot Power and Mr Pat Mulrooney of ACOT, and part of the demonstration was filmed by a French TV unit.

The annual foal fair was held as usual at Maam Cross on 31st October 1983, and a competition was held for the best foal of the fair. A cup had been presented for the competition by Mr Michael Keogh, Maam Cross and it was won by Mr Paddy Hoade from Headford.

Social at Maam Cross

Another new innovation in 1983 was the Social at Peacocke's, Maam Cross which was held on 19th November 1983 and about 200 pony breeders and friends gathered at Maam Cross for a very enjoyable social evening.

During the evening the Stallion Awards for the three best kept stallions for the year were presented by the sponsors, the Bank of Ireland, Galway. Tommy O'Brien and Josie Conroy shared first prize for the stallions *Killyreagh Kim (308)* and *Ashfield Alex (711)* and Mikey King was in third place with *Mervyn Kingsmill (762)*.

The upkeep of the stallions owned by the Society had been sponsored by Udaras na Gaeltachta, Furbo, Co. Galway, and their representatives were also at the social to present a cheque for £500 to Donal Kenny. In a year when the grant in-aid from Bord na gCapall had been greatly reduced, the assistance from these locally based sponsors was very encouraging for the Society, and also during the year the Clifden District and Community Council had made a collection in the Clifden area, and had raised over £1000 for the Society's funds.

Two stallions left the list at the end of the 1983 season, and one of them was *Thunderbolt (178)*, He was twenty years old and had been brought back to Connemara for three seasons, two of which he spent with Mikey King in Claddaghduff, and his last season was with Festy Mulkerrin at Callowfeenish. During those three years some good mares visited him, and from his two years at Claddaghduff he had two really good daughters who have been consistently successful in the Showring, Village Laura (8097) and Dooneen Star (7871). In his last year at Callowfeenish he had five more fillies and they were Hazel Dun (8289), Callowfeenish Wave (8329), Kilkerrin Surf (8330), Homeward Bound 2nd (8279) and Shee Gaoth (8499), and they have all remained to breed in Ireland, with the exception of Callowfeenish Wave (8329) who was sold to France. The Society had already bought the colt who was a full brother to Dooneen Star (7871), and it was hoped that he would carry on the Green Line where the previous sons of *Thunderbolt (178)* had failed. Sadly he did not fulfill his early promise, and although the Society registered him as *Thunderstorm (796)* and he spent one season on the stallion list, he was not a success in Connemara and was sold to the Ennistown Stud in Co. Meath.

Milleder Archive

Spinway Comet (935)

Thunderbolt (178) was bought by a syndicate of five breeders in England, and he spent the remaining eleven years of his life at Cocum Stud with Mrs Cecilie Williams. He rewarded the syndicate by breeding 30 foals during his time in England, including the ECPS Champion stallion *Spinway Comet (935)*. He sired his last foal aged twenty nine, and finally was put down at the age of thirty-two.

The second stallion to leave the list in 1983 was *Fort Boffin (758)* who had spent two years at Oughterard with Joe Nee, but only five mares were registered by him, and as there seemed to be so few breeding mares in the area, no Society-owned stallion was placed in Oughterard in the following years.

A new stallion joined the approved list in 1984, he was *Loobeen Larry (670)* a nine year old dark bay, and he was leased from his owner Graham Tulloch, Shanbolard, Moyard. By Killyreagh Kim (308) dam Loobeen Meg (4809), he was bred by Mrs Rosemary Tierney, Lettergesh West, Renvyle, and his dam was by Thunderbolt (178). He was a big stallion, and was needed at Carraroe where the mares tended to be smaller, and was placed with Bartley O'Malley who also had *Maam Hill (728)* in his care, and *Abbeyleix Owen (496)* moved to Festy Mulkerrin in Callowfeenish. *Sarsfield (579)* had been removed from the approved list in 1980, and he was now located with Sean Conneely, Cregduff, Spiddal.

At a special ceremony held in Dublin in February 1984, John Brennan was honoured by the Equestrian Federation of Ireland in recognition of his contribution to equestrian sport. He had been a successful breeder of Connemara ponies since the early sixties, and a member of the Council of the Connemara Pony Breeders' Society since 1973. He had also been Chairman of the Galway Riding Club, District Commissioner of Galway Pony Club, was a member of the executive committee of the S. J. A. I. and Chairman of the Galway County Show. He was presented with the F. E. I. Badge of Honour by President Hillery, who thanked him for his sound leadership and voluntary effort, and his huge contribution to equestrian sport in the West of Ireland.

President Hillery with John Brennan.

In the Spring of 1984 the Council lost one of its longstanding members with the death of Mr Jim Lee, Moycullen, who had been involved with Connemara ponies both as a dealer and later as a breeder since the early fifties. He was elected to the Council in 1961, and his yard at Moycullen was the traditional centre for the annual inspections for many years. His family-run pub in the main street in Moycullen was a place where people gathered at the end of the first day of the inspection tour, and he and his wife Pauline were generous and kindly hosts to the many overseas buyers who came to see Jim's ponies.

He would buy forty or more foals at weaning time each year, and during the years when the export trade was at its height, he ran the foals on for two or three years, and he had large groups of mares running together for buyers to see, but it was not always easy to select the one they wanted from a herd flashing past at the gallop! Jim Lee first showed a mare at the RDS Spring Show in 1957, and his first winner there was in 1961 when he won with Grey Girl (2021), but there are no records of the number of ponies which passed through his hands, and many of them were sold to overseas buyers as well as to Michael O'Connell on Lambay Island. His sons Michael and Johnny inherited his interest in the ponies and continued to breed ponies after Jim's death, using the Moy prefix, and one of his favourite mares who was never sold was Windy Cove (2870) by Tooreen Ross (91). She had her last foal when she was twenty-four years of age, and he became the stallion *Moy Hazy Cove (888)* by Hazy Dawn (849), and is now owned by the Society. At a Council meeting held on 14th May 1984, Mr Johnny Lee was appointed a member of the Council to fill the vacancy due to his father's death.

At the AGM held on 6th March 1984 the President, Donal Kenny told the members that the Council had been informed by Bord na gCapall that the grant in-aid for the Society was to be £2000 in 1984, which was £1000 less than the grant given in 1983, and this was going to leave the Society seriously short of funds. The Council proposed that a monthly draw would be held in order to generate up to £6000 extra income which was needed for the running of the Society and members were invited to suggest other ways of raising funds so that the Society could continue to do its work for the Connemara pony. The Society was fortunate to still have the substantial sponsorship for the Annual Show which was given most generously by Waterford Glass each year as well as valuable crystal trophies.

In April 1984 the Society lost one of its longstanding members with the death of Miss Frances Lee Norman of Clonkeehan Stud, Slane. She had established her Connemara Pony Stud in the early fifties, and bred *Clonkeehan Auratum (104)* from her mare Western Lily (1522). She won most of the major awards at Clifden for two years running in 1964 and 1965, with the result that the following year the Council decided that special prizes should be offered for ponies bred, owned and exhibited by residents in Connemara. Miss Lee Norman showed her support for the Council's decision by presenting the Clonkeehan Trophy to the Society in 1966, and it is still awarded each year to the winner of the Confined Championship.

Her homebred stallion *Clonkeehan Nimbus (229)* s. Camlin Cicada (119) d. Dark Winter (2020) sired many good performance ponies, and was the sire of *Skryne Bright Cloud (622)* and through him the Purple Line was carried into the fourth generation.

Miss Lee Norman was a respected judge for the Society, and was invited to judge at Clifden in 1959, one of the first ladies to receive that honour. She was made a Society inspector in 1972 and acted as an inspector for the North of Ireland, she also visited Denmark on several occasions to judge at the Danish inspections. In later years when she became crippled with arthritis, she founded the Irish Driving Society, which owed much of its success to her enthusiasm and forthright personality, and in 1981 she was honoured by the Equestrian Federation of Ireland for her contribution to driving in Ireland. Her name will long be remembered as the breeder of *Clonkeehan Auratum (104)*, who had such a big influence on the breed in the early sixties, and whose attractive progeny were sold to many buyers from all over Europe.

The Annual Registration inspections were held in Connemara from 15th to 17th May 1984 at 23 centres, and during April inspections were also held at other centres throughout Ireland. In all 210 ponies were registered for the year, but the number of live foals born in 1983 in Connemara was only 120 which was the cause of much concern to the Council. The stallion committee had proposed that the nomination fees should be increased for 1984, but because the Society was so lacking in funds, the Council felt it was not possible to make any changes in the fees for 1984. Many of the old districts in Connemara which had been famous for their ponies in the past now had no breeding stock left, and on the inspection tour it was sad to find no ponies waiting at some of the centres where in earlier times there would have been 20 or more fillies.

Once again the entries for the led classes at RDS Horse Show were a little disappointing with the three year old mare class only attracting three entries. Mr R. Kelly MRCVS and Mr M. Clancy were the judges, and the

Championship was won by Mr Jimmy Jones with Ashfield Silver Cloud (5894) with Mrs Breege Curran's Abbeyleix Flora (7539) in Reserve.

Unveiling of Memorial to Sean Keane and John Killeen

On the eve of the Annual Pony Show at Clifden a special ceremony took place at the Showgrounds when a new ticket office and a granite wall plaque in memory of Mr Sean Keane and Mr John Killeen were officially unveiled. Dr Michael Killeen, son of the late Mr John Killeen performed the unveiling ceremony which was attended by members of the Keane and Killeen families and members of the Society. Mr Sean Keane had been an active member of the Council for over thirty years and had served as President of the Society from 1972 to 1978. Mr John Killeen was Secretary of the Society from 1963 to 1979 and during his term of office had done much to promote the Connemara pony worldwide, and the memorial was to honour two men

Donal Kenny, President, Mrs Phil MacDermott, Secretary and Owen Crehan, Treasurer at the unveiling ceremony.

who had both given many years of committed service to the work of the Connemara Pony Breeders' Society. The unveiling took place on a beautiful warm sunny evening, and the simple ceremony was followed by the annual informal meeting of overseas guests, breeders and friends at the Clifden House Hotel, when the guest speaker was Dr Austin Mescal, Chief Inspector of the Department of Agriculture.

61st Annual Pony Show, Clifden – 16th August 1984

The Show was held in brilliant sunshine, and there was a very good attendance which was a welcome boost for the Society's funds. There were 316 entries with 40 entries in the ridden classes, and good support for the gelding class which was reintroduced after a lapse of many years. The judges were Mr Jimmy Jones from Carlow and Miss Ginette Mason from England with Mr R. Kelly MRCVS as referee.

The young stock classes were well filled, with the two or three year old colt class going to Sean Dunne's two year old *Abbeyleix Fionn (810)* by Ashfield Sparrow (583) dam Fionnuala (5508), while the winner of the Carew Cup for the best two year old filly was Village Laura (8097), by Thunderbolt (178) dam Village Star (5146) owned by Padraig Hynes. Both these ponies were going to make their mark in the years to come, and came from two of the best female lines. Michael Clancy's three year old mare Atlantic Peace (7903) by Tantallon Bobby (626) won the Killanin Cup and her dam Errisbeg Rose (2895) was another famous mare, and the

Archbishop's Cup was won by Finisglen Belle (7700) s. Killyreagh Kim (308) for Sean Keane, Moycullen.

The Confined Stallion Class was won by the seventeen year old *Killyreagh Kim (308)* who was produced looking really well by Tommy O'Brien and shown by Tommy's daughter Ann, and he went on to win the Open Class standing above another son of Carna Bobby (79), Michael Clancy's *Tantallon Bobby (626)* who had been in second place for three years running. The five and six year old mares class was won by Hidi Rambler (7301) whose sire Dunmore King (668) was by *Killyreagh Kim (308)*, and second to her was the Dublin winner Abbeyleix Flora (7539), while the senior mares class had fifty entries and was a close contest between Gloves Misty (6535) and Silver Sparrow (6896) with Gloves Misty (6535) emerging the winner. The Confined Championship was won by Michael Clancy's three year old Atlantic Peace (7903), and the Supreme Championship of the Show was awarded to *Killyreagh Kim (308)* who really showed himself well and was a credit to the O'Brien family. It was a successful Show, and the beautiful warm weather helped to make it a relaxing and enjoyable day for the many visitors who were at the Show.

J. Petch

Killyreagh Kim (308), Supreme Champion.

205

Colts on the loose at Maam Cross.

CHAPTER 13

1984-1987

• Launch of New Book • Two New Overseas Societies • Volume XVII Stud Book • Headage Grants •
• Passports • Society Stallions Bloodtyped • Marketing Group • Financial Crisis •

A new book about the Connemara pony, "Shrouded in Mist" written by Pat Lyne was published in 1984, and was launched at an evening party at O'Gorman's bookshop in Galway just before the Clifden Show. It was the first time an in depth study of the Connemara pony from the earliest times up to 1963 had been made, and in the course of her research for the book over a period of seven years, Pat Lyne had met many people and made many friends in Connemara. She first visited Connemara in 1964, and bought her first Connemara pony, Arctic Moon (2377), by Carna Dun (89) from her breeder Mark Geoghegan, Oughterard. Through this chance purchase she became interested in the breed, and later established her own Chiltern Connemara Pony Stud in Herefordshire. In 1970 she was elected to the Council of the English Connemara Pony Society, and in the same year she returned to Connemara as a delegate at the International Conference, and visited the Clifden Show. This visit prompted her to learn more about the breed, and in time she found that she had lost her heart to Connemara, its people and its ponies.

In 1973 she joined the English Connemara Pony Society's panel of judges, and since then has become a well known judge for the breed, and she was the first editor of the Connemara Chronicle which she started in 1974 as a journal produced by the English Connemara Pony Society. As editor of the Connemara Chronicle she realised that an increasing number of people were becoming interested in the Connemara pony, and there was a need for more information about the origins and the development of the breed. Her aim in writing "Shrouded in Mist" was to fulfil that need, and her book has now become a valuable source of information, and is used by breeders of Connemara ponies all over the world as a book of reference.

J. Petch

Pat Lyne with Colman Griffin.

The second All Ireland Ridden Connemara Pony Championship was held at Oughterard Show on 26th August and the twelve qualifiers from shows held throughout the country came to Oughterard to compete for the top award. The winner was a seven year old grey gelding Lambay Master Ash (G904) by Moy Village Master (603) dam Fort Ash (4640) who was bred on Lambay Island by Lord Revelstoke and owned by Gail Miller, Athy, Co. Kildare.

Later in the year the results of the 1984 Performance Award Scheme were announced and the Ridden Connemara Pony of the Year for the third time, was Mrs Juliet Perrin's Tantallon Gaye Roberta (6155). It was the last year the Performance Award Scheme was held, because the entries had not increased over the years, and there was not sufficient support for the scheme.

Volume XVII of the Stud Book

A new volume of the Stud Book was published in 1984 covering four years of registrations, and it contained particulars of 1103 ponies, consisting of 84 stallions, 480 mares and 179 geldings. During this period the sale of ponies to overseas buyers had decreased, but a new market was developing in Ireland, and with more people taking up riding as a leisure activity, an increasing number of riding centres, Pony Clubs, and trekking centres were being established, and this created a better home trade for Connemara ponies. However the decline in the numbers of breeding stock in Connemara was still the cause of much concern, because although there were more ponies being bred outside Connemara, the small breeder in Connemara was still the backbone of the breed, and it was vital to maintain the breeding stock in Connemara at its present level.

On 2nd October 1984 a group of EEC Officials of the Special Agricultural Committee visited Connemara and were invited by the Connemara Pony Breeders' Society to a demonstration of Connemara ponies which was staged at the Society's Showgrounds at Clifden. The ponies were shown in-hand as well as being ridden and jumped, and the demonstration was very well received by the visitors. The Special Agricultural Committee deals with the Headage Grant Scheme, and members of the Council were able to meet the officials at the demonstration and request that Connemara ponies be included in the Headage Grants Scheme, which they hoped would provide an added incentive for the small breeder in Connemara to continue to keep a breeding mare.

The Annual Social was held at Peacocke's at Maam Cross on 17th November and about 200 breeders and friends had a very enjoyable evening. During the evening the awards were presented for the best kept stallions, and 1st prize went to Tommy O'Brien with the 1984 Supreme Champion at Clifden, *Killyreagh Kim (308)*, and Mikey King was in 2nd place with *Mervyn Kingsmill (762)*.

Two New Overseas Societies

Two new overseas societies were formed in 1984, one in Finland and the other in New Zealand, and they were welcomed into the ever increasing group of overseas societies breeding Connemara ponies all around the world. There were already a number of Connemara ponies in both countries before the Societies were formed, in Finland their ponies were mostly imported from neighbouring Sweden and Denmark, while the small group of breeders scattered widely through New Zealand relied on Australia for most of their early stock.

Three New Council Members were elected at a meeting of the Council on 4th March 1985, they were Mr Jimmy Jones, Carlow, who had been a prominent breeder since the early sixties, Mr Pat Mulrooney from ACOT, who had been involved in the running of the seminars and demonstrations for the Connemara Pony for several years, and Mr Sam Morrison, who had been a breeder for many years based in Portadown and represented the North of Ireland on the Council in place of Mrs Pat MacKean, who had resigned.

The Annual Inspections in 1985 were held at 23 centres in Connemara in May and there were also three inspection tours to other parts of the country, including trips to the North and South, but the number ponies registered was again lower than the previous year with just 180 being accepted into the Stud Book, and there were only 225 nominations awarded to registered mares in Connemara which was a significant decrease compared to earlier years.

The financial state of the Society was much improved in 1985 with grant in-aid from Bord na gCapall increased to £5000, and as a result the Society was able to purchase a two year old colt, and he was registered as *Seafield Silver Rogue (823)*, and joined the approved list in 1986. Bred by John Tarpey, Rahoon, Galway, sire Silver Rocket (523) dam April Anita (7553), he was a grandson of *Doon Paddy (95)*, and so became a new representative for the Purple Line.

The summer of 1985 was one of the wettest for many years, and very little hay was saved in Connemara, and so with winter keep being in such short supply, there was poor trade for the foals at the autumn foal fairs.

62nd Annual Pony Show, Clifden – 15th August 1985

The bad weather also affected the Show which was held on a wet and dreary day with the result that the attendance by the general public was badly affected, and the gate receipts were down considerably. A party of twelve breeders from the American Connemara Pony Society visited the Show and there were also breeders from Holland, Sweden, Germany and France. The guest Speaker at the pre-show reception was the Minister of Agriculture, Mr Austin Deasy, and he brought the welcome news that after many years of campaigning by members of the Council, the Connemara pony was to be included in the Headage Grant Scheme, and payments would begin in 1986. It was hoped that this grant would provide an incentive to the breeders in Connemara to keep their breeding mares.

J. Petch

Mervyn Kingsmill (762)

There were 322 entries for the Show, and the judges Mr John Luskin and Miss Pat Lyne had well filled classes, despite the bad weather. Both the Confined and the Open Stallion classes were won by the Society's five year old *Mervyn Kingsmill (762)* for Mikey King, Claddaghduff, with the 1984 Champion *Killyreagh Kim (308)* in second place. In the Open Stallion Class there was an interesting group of three half-brothers all bred from Lady Maria Levinge's mare Dun Sparrow (3025) standing in 5th, 6th and 7th place, they were *Grange Bobbing Sparrow (623)* s. Carna Bobby (79), *Grange Finn Sparrow (659)* s. Coosheen Finn (381), and *Grange Sand Sparrow (589)* s. Clonkeehan Bowman (315), a unique breeding and showing achievement.

The two and three year old colt class was won by Sean Dunne, Portarlington, with his three year old colt *Abbeyleix Fionn (810)*, and the Society owned colt *Seafield Silver Rogue (823)* was in second place. The winning three year old filly was Village Laura (8097), owned by Padraig Hynes, who also won her class the previous year, and was to do so many times again in her successful showing career, and the Archbishop's Cup for the best four year old went to Michael Clancy's Atlantic Peace (7903) who was also a winner in 1984 and the Reserve Champion at RDS Horse Show.

The largest class of the day was the class for mares of seven years or over with an entry of fifty-five, and the ring was filled with some of the top mares of the breed. Both the Supreme Champion of the Show and the reserve were from this class with Silver Sparrow (6898) s. Abbeyleix Owen (496) winning the Championship for Michael Clancy, Spiddal, and in Reserve was Joe Gorham's Silver Fort (7281) s. Rory Ruadh (517) d. Fort Hazel (5533).

The Champion Silver Sparrow (6898) was later sold to France where she joined the 1974 Clifden Champion, Roundstone River (4746) at Hubert Laurent's Melody Stud.

J. Petch

Michael Clancy with Silver Sparrow (6898)

The Reserve Champion Silver Fort (7281) had the distinction of having been foaled at Aras an Uachtarain, in the Phoenix Park, Dublin, as her dam was one of the mares presented to the late President Childers, and when the mares subsequently returned to Connemara to become the resident herd at the Connemara National Park at Letterfrack, she was bought by Joe Gorham.

A Connemara Pony Breeders' Society Newsletter was produced during 1985, compiled by Miss Siobhan Brooks,

Silver Fort (7281) and foal.

and two issues were sent out to members during the year. It was welcomed by members and contained details of show dates and results, and other items of news for breeders. Minutes of the Council meetings were no longer circulated to members, and the newsletter provided a valuable link between the Council and the members of the Society.

Champion at Olympia

The Finals of the Ridden Mountain and Moorland Championships, held each year at the Christmas Show at Olympia in London, had become the most hotly contested Championship, with qualifiers from all the native pony breeds competing for the coveted top award, and a very high standard of presentation and performance was required from all the finalists.

In 1985 the pony who was made the Supreme Champion was an eleven year old Irish-bred Connemara gelding, Phineas Finn (G. 760), s. Coosheen Finn (381) d. Turret Tina (4980), bred by Lady Colthurst, Blarney Castle, Co. Cork, owned by Mrs P. Clarkson, Saffron Walden and ridden by her daughter Sophie. Connemara ponies, bred in England had won the Supreme Award on four previous occasions, but this was the first time that a pony bred in Ireland had become the Champion.

How proud Michael O'Malley would have been to have known that his epic journey from Connemara to London seventy-three years earlier to show his ponies in the Grand Hall in Olympia was worthwhile, his faith in his beloved native pony was justified, and that the Connemara pony was now acclaimed as the best all-round native riding pony not only at Olympia but worldwide.

The Society-owned stallion *Ashfield Alex (711)* was removed from the approved list at the end of the 1985 season having served in Connemara for seven seasons, but with only 65 registered progeny and just one registered son, he left little impression on the breed. He spent his first four years in Oughterard with Joe Nee, and his next three with Josie Conroy at Bunowen, and after leaving Connemara he spent several seasons in Donegal with Clive Evans before being sold to England. He was the last son of *Clonkeehan Auratum (104)*, but did not make the same impact as his sire, and no son of his was kept by the Society.

Two new stallions joined the list in 1986, the first was the three year old colt *Seafield Silver Rogue (823)* who was purchased by the Society and placed with Josie Conroy at Bunowen. *Seafield Silver Rogue (823)*, sire Silver Rocket (523) was a grandson of Doon Paddy (95), and was the first representative of the Purple Line on the list since 1981. His dam April Anita (7553) was a prizewinning mare by Abbeyleix Owen (496), and her mare line traced back to Sliabh na mBan (227), winner of an RDS Silver Medal at Carna in 1936.

J. Petch

Seafield Silver Rogue (823)
with Josie Conroy

211

The second stallion was the four year old *Thunderstorm (796)* s. Thunderbolt (178) d. Dooneen Grey (3671), who was bought by the Society to carry on the Green Line, and stood for one season with Mikey King, but he did not prove a successful sire and had no registered progeny from his one year on the list. He moved to Co. Meath at the end of the season, and so sadly another attempt to keep the Green line intact came to nothing.

Loobeen Larry (670) remained on the list, but left Carraroe where he had spent two seasons with Bartley O'Malley, and returned to his owner Graham Tulloch at Shanbolard.

Headage Scheme – Passports Introduced

Two new schemes were introduced in 1986 which had been in the pipeline for several years, and for the first time passports were issued by the Connemara Pony Breeders' Society to all Connemara ponies registered in the Stud Book during 1986. Headage payments were paid in respect of Connemara ponies owned by farmers who lived in severely disadvantaged areas, which included Connemara, and registered Connemara pony mares who qualified for the scheme received £32 per head. The headage payments were welcomed by the Society and it was hoped they would encourage breeders in Connemara to retain their good breeding mares.

Society Stallions Blood-Typed

The Council decided that in future all the stallions owned by the Society should be blood-typed, and blood-typing of Connemara ponies for the verification of breeding would be carried out when it was deemed necessary. This was the first step towards full blood-typing for all Connemara ponies which became established in 1991.

These new schemes entailed a lot of extra administration work for the Secretary, as the passports were issued by the Society, and all the paper work for the headage scheme was also processed through the office. With the Society's lack of funds, it was not possible to provide an assistant secretary, and so the increased workload fell to Mrs Phil MacDermott, who since Mr Killeen's death had been solely responsible for the day to day running of the affairs of the Society, as well as the compiling of the Stud Books and the organisation of the Annual Show. All this was accomplished cheerfully and efficiently, without the aid of a computer, but in the years to come the extra volume of work became an increasing burden, and was too much for one person to handle.

The Annual Inspections were held in Connemara during May and were followed by tours to other parts of the country in late May and early June, and a one-day trip to the North of Ireland in October, with a total of eight days to cover all the centres. The members of the inspection team have always offered their services free, and through the years their commitment has been a very valuable contribution towards the work of the Society.

The number of ponies registered throughout the year was 188, including 13 stallions, 141 mares and 34 geldings, and under the Nomination Scheme, 224 nominations were awarded to registered mares in the Connemara area.

Connemara Pony Exporters and Marketing Group

On 9th March 1986 a public meeting was held at Peacocke's, Maam Cross, at which a new group was formed called the Connemara Pony Exporters and Marketing Group. The chairman of the meeting was Mr Pat Mulrooney, and the purpose of the group was to provide training facilities in Connemara so that ponies could be trained and schooled professionally to a high standard, and to market these trained ponies both at home and abroad. Mrs Ann Jocelyn, Cashel was the founder of the group, and having seen the growing demand for trained ponies, she had built an outdoor training centre at her home in Cashel. It was planned to set up a pilot scheme for training ponies at her centre, and the group would maintain close links with the Connemara Pony Breeders' Society. During 1986 there was a good demand on the home market for the potential riding pony of 148 cms, and also a number of ponies were exported to England, France, Germany, Sweden, Belgium, Austria, Italy and Spain.

The two classes for ridden Connemara ponies were again held at the RDS Spring Show and the RDS Horse Show, and there was a rather unique double, with Mrs Janet McLoughlin Minch winning the 4 and 5 year old class at both shows with Tulira Searchlight (G1018), while the 6 year old and over class was won at both shows by Purple Hills (6372). This mare owned by Mrs Pam More O'Farrell went on to win the All Ireland Ridden Championship at Oughterard in August for the second year running.

One of the best known men in Connemara who had been involved with Connemara ponies all his long life, died in June 1986 at the great age of ninety-five years. He was Mark Geoghegan from Oughterard who was one of the early stallion custodians, and the first stallion he kept for the Society was *Black Paddy (8)* in 1926, followed by *Rebel (7)* in 1927 who he showed that year at Carna to win the stallion class and the RDS Silver Medal. *Adventure (11)* was the next Society-owned stallion to stand with Mark Geoghegan in 1929, 1930 and 1931, and in 1953 he had *Farravane Boy (71)* for his last season on the approved list. Mark Geoghegan was a fearless horseman, and from the time he was a small boy he could sit up on an untrained pony and tame it in a few hours. He was also a great man to drive a gig, and he was one of three men who rode the famous *Cannon Ball* in the Oughterard races. The ponies were his life, and he drove them, worked them, rode them, raced them, and cared for them in his own special way.

Silver Gray (143), foaled in 1926, was registered in Volume II of the Stud Book, and was the first mare registered in Mark Geoghegan's name. She was the dam of his good mare Irene (624) by Innishgoill Laddie (21), and Irene (624) was the dam of the stallion *Bridge Boy (124)*. Speculation (295) was another of his early mares and was a daughter of Adventure (11), foaled in 1930, in later years his son Paddy had *Bridge Boy (124)* who was included on the approved list from 1963 to 1975.

A new show was added to the Connemara calendar in 1986 with Ballyconneely holding its own show on 20th July for the first time. The enthusiastic show committee was headed by Siobhan Brooks as President, with Josie

Conroy as Chairman, and the Show was well supported with 180 ponies entered, as well as good entries in the craft and country produce section. One of the nice features of this show is a class for veteran mares aged 20 years or over, which was introduced in its second year, and the Show has now become a popular annual event.

63rd Annual Pony Show, Clifden – 21st August 1986

Again the weather was mixed with heavy showers in the morning, but a better gate that the previous year. The judges were Lady Maria Levinge and Padraig Hynes and there were 280 entries in the pony classes. The winner of the Open Stallion Class was James de Courcey's seven year old Grade A show jumping stallion *Cuchulainn (789)*, sire Abbeyleix Owen (496) dam Sparrow Hill (3661), who was a full brother to the 1985 Supreme Champion, Silver Sparrow (6898). Later he was made Confined Champion with the winner of the five or six year old mare class, Michael Clancy's Atlantic Peace (7903) in Reserve. *Mervyn Kingsmill (762)* was placed second in the Open Class, and won the Confined Stallion Class for Mikey King. The Archbishop's Cup was won by a

James de Courcey with Cuchulainn (789)
receiving the Waterford Glass Trophy from Alf Nicholson.

daughter of Abbeyleix Owen (496), Owen's Lady (8066) owned by Jackie Walsh, Snabo, Rosmuck, and in the class for mares of seven years old or over the winner was Eddie Madden's Gloves Misty (8535), who went on to become Supreme Champion of the Show for the second time. The Reserve Champion was the three year old Killanin Cup winner Whiterock Princess (8144), owned and bred by Pat Taaffe, Drogheda, Co. Louth, by a little-known stallion *Traigh Bhuidhe (411)*, who was a son of MacDara (91), out of Ashfield Judy (5505) and a full-brother to *Ormond Oliver (653)*. The ridden classes had good entries and were judged by John Moore, who also did his usual job as a well-informed and excellent commentator at the Show.

At the end of the 1986 season Paddy Folan, Camus moved to Rosmuck, and ceased to be a stallion custodian for the Society. When living at Knockadave, Camus, he first took a Society-owned stallion in 1970, and *Clonjoy (117)* spent one year with him, and he was followed by *Rebel Wind (124)* in 1971 to 1973, who was a favourite sire. He was also fond of *Killyreagh Kim (308)* who he kept for the next three seasons, 1974 to 1976, and produced him to win the Open and Confined Stallion Classes and become the Reserve Champion of the Show at Clifden in 1976.

In 1977 he had two stallions, the old *Dun Aengus (120)* who died that summer, and the three year old *Skryne Bright Cloud (622)*, who also spent 1978 at Camus along with *Ardnasillagh Casey (654)*. In 1979 and 1980 *Sarsfield (579)* was placed with him, and the last stallion *Ormond Oliver (653)* remained with him from 1981 to 1986. Paddy travelled the stallions on a regular route three days a week, Camus and Derrynea on Mondays, Kilkerrin and Carna on Wednesdays, Glentrasna and Maam Cross on Saturdays until 1980, but from 1981 onwards he only travelled the stallion by arrangement. Paddy Folan had a great love for the ponies, and his stallions were always well looked after and kindly handled, it was a sad day for the Society when he decided to give up keeping a stallion.

Killyreagh Kim (308) spent his last four years in Connemara with Tommy O'Brien, and was retired at the end of the 1986 season, aged nineteen, and moved to Jimmy Jones in Carlow. He served for seventeen years in Connemara, and although in later years he was not such a prolific sire, during his time on the approved list he had 238 registered progeny. Among his twenty-two registered stallion sons, three were on the Society's list, *Sarsfield (579)*, *Loobeen Larry (670)*, and *Davy D (671)*, and several more made their names overseas, notably *Kings Ransom (584)* who went to England and then to France.

J. Petch

Tommy O'Brien with Killyreagh Kim (308)

Many of his long list of daughters were sold overseas, and among his most successful were Village Star (5146), Ballinaboy Bracken (5648), Dolan Lucky Star (5686), Inishnee Dun Damsel (6101), Lehid Lovely Princess (6427), Purple Hills (6372), Lor Ruadh 2nd (6387), Lehid Linda (6443), Village Miranda (6271) Spinway Cailin (6311), La Eanair (6600) Windy Sunshine (7218), Kingstown Molly (7604), Finisglen Belle (7700), Sliabh na mBan Peggy (7851) and Gillian (8071).

J. Petch

Jimmy Jones with Atlantic Storm (139) in Carlow.

Atlantic Storm (139) having spent nine years in semi-retirement with Jimmy Jones in Carlow, was put down in the autumn of 1986 at the age of twenty-six. He covered a few mares right up to his last season, and two foals were born to him in 1987. One of his daughters, foaled in 1965, was Boden Park Hailstones (8445), dam Frosty Morning (5680) bred by Mrs Jane Dalrymple, and she became a successful pony in the Show ring, and won the Killanin Cup at Clifden in 1988.

Bord na gCapall Grant Ceased in 1987

The Council was informed in early 1987 by the Chief Executive of Bord na gCapall, that due to the uncertain future of the Board, the Connemara Pony Breeders' Society would no longer receive a grant in-aid from the State, which in 1986 had been £5000. This was a grave blow, as since the Society was founded in 1923, it had received an annual grant from the State which had been a valuable contribution towards the work of the Society, and was its main source of funding.

At a Council meeting held on 19th February 1987, Donal Kenny outlined the cutbacks which were necessary until other funding could be found for the Society. The administration costs were to be reduced to a minimum, and the Nomination Scheme would have to be discontinued unless it received grant in-aid from the Co. Committee of Agriculture. The subsidy for providing a blacksmith in the Connemara area would cease, and the publishing of a newsletter would be discontinued. Fees for passports and registration certificates were to be increased, and the stallion list to be reviewed and a small number of stallions retained by the Society. In order to make the Society self financing, it would be necessary to get increased sponsorship for the Showgrounds, the Show catalogue, and for individual classes at the Annual Show.

Proposed Review of Memorandum and Articles of Association

He also proposed that it was time to reorganise the Society's rules, and that although the current constitution of the Connemara Pony Breeders' Society had served the Society well in the past, the closed nature of the Council deprived the ordinary member of any active participation in the running of the Society. Under the definitions of the Memorandum and Articles of Association drawn up in 1959, the Council had the power to elect its own members without recourse to the ordinary members of the Society, but for some time the membership of the Society had been increasing steadily, and the members were now urging that the rules of the Society should be made more democratic. In response to this, the Council decided that a review committee should be set up to study ways of restructuring the Society's rules in regard to the election of Council members, and to review the Memorandum and Articles of Association.

The Council decided that because of the cutback in the grant from the Co. Committee of Agriculture for the nomination scheme, a sum of £5 would be paid to each stallion owner for each live foal born in 1987 produced by a nominated mare of 1986, instead of payment of nomination fees for mares covered in 1987. This was to lead to the gradual phasing out of the Nomination Scheme which had been in operation since the founding of the Society, and the payments on live foals ceased after the 1989 season.

At the Council meeting held prior to the AGM on 26th March 1987, Mr Eamonn Hannan, St. Endas, Moycullen was elected as a member of the Council. He had been a member of the Society since 1983.

New Stallions on List

A new young stallion owned by the Society joined the approved list of stallions standing in Connemara for 1987, he was *Canal Cormac (848)*, a two year old colt by Thunderbolt (178), dam Rambling Home (3383), bred by Padraig Hynes. He was *Thunderbolt's* last son born in Ireland, and so he represented the Green Line, and he was placed with a new stallion custodian Dudley Nee, Camas, who had taken over that district from Paddy Folan. *Fort Dara (718)*, a ten year old bay by Rory Ruadh (517), was leased to the Society for the season and placed with Bartley O'Malley at Carraroe, and James de Courcey's *Cuchulainn (789)*, the Champion Stallion at Clifden in 1986, was also included on the list.

John Brennan, Pat Mulrooney, Roderic Kelly, Mrs Phil MacDermott, Donal Kenny and Dermot Power.

CHAPTER 14

1987-1990

• Review of Articles of Association • Deaths of two Council Members • New Inspection Committee •
• New Members on Council • Decline of Ponies in Connemara • International Rules • EGM •
• Donal Kenny Retires •

The newly appointed Review Committee held its first meeting on 19th May 1987 to study the Memorandum and Articles of Association, and to consider ways of restructuring the rules of the Society. The members of the sub committee were: Mr D. Kenny, Mr J. Jones, Mr D. Power, Mrs E. Petch, Mr P. Hynes, and Mr E. Hannan, and they were conscious that care would be needed to ensure that any changes being proposed would be in the long term interests of the Society. The committee was asked to make a report to the Council by the end of the year.

On 28th May 1987 a deputation from the horse industry including representatives of the Connemara Pony Breeders' Society met the Minister of Agriculture to discuss the future of the Irish Horse Register following the disbanding of Bord na gCapall. The representatives of the Connemara Pony Breeders' Society stressed that the Society wished to maintain its independence, and intended to continue publishing its own Stud Book, but some financial aid was requested.

In response to an appeal for fund raising at the AGM several members arranged functions on behalf of the Society during the summer, and Mrs Phyllida Collier and Miss Maureen Goodbody organised a very successful evening at the Kilruddery Estate, Bray, Co. Wicklow at which £1200 was raised. Mrs Bay Goodwin also held a coffee morning and donated the proceeds to Society funds.

The Annual Gymkhana had a change of venue in 1987 when it moved to Errislannon Manor where a new sand arena had been provided. Mrs Brooks kindly offered to hold the gymkhana there in order to provide greater safety for the children who would no longer have to ride their ponies from Errislannon to Clifden on the roads.

The new Connemara Pony Export and Marketing Group held their first show for performance ponies at the Cashel Training Centre on 26th July, when thirty-two ponies took part, and the Show was recorded on video which was available for sale. The group had been successful in marketing a number of Connemara ponies both at home and overseas. Another new show in Connemara was held on the same day, when Claddaghduff held its first show with an entry of 120 ponies. It was a successful show and has now become a regular feature on the Connemara show calendar.

For the second year the entries in the in-hand classes for Connemara Ponies at the RDS Dublin Horse Show were disappointing with only 23 entries in the four classes, although the quality of the entries was of a high standard. The Champion of the Show was the five year old Village Laura (8097), owned by Padraig Hynes.

With the Society's funds at such a low ebb, staging the Annual Pony Show would have been difficult without the considerable help of the Clifden Pony Show Festival Committee who organised a collection in the town of Clifden. With the proceeds they kindly sponsored the pre-show reception in Clifden on the eve of the Show, and also contributed £800 towards the cost of printing the catalogue, as well as paying for some necessary repairs to the Showgrounds prior to the Show.

64th Annual Pony Show, Clifden – 20th August 1987

The Show in 1987 will be long remembered as the wettest show in the history of the Society. Torrential rain fell all through the previous night, and continued relentlessly through the morning of the Show. The Show was postponed for an hour, but when it was decided to go ahead, the Owenglin river was already beginning to overflow its banks and flooding the Show ring. The waters continued to rise, until the railings on the lower side of the ring were submerged and the water had reached the judges hut in the centre of the ring. However the Show went on despite the weather, and by noon the rain ceased and the river subsided rapidly so that by the afternoon the whole ring could be used again.

Eithne MacDermott

Showgrounds – Morning and Afternoon.

The judges were Mr P. J. Foy and Mrs Petch, with Mr R. Kelly MRCVS the referee judge, and in the morning the youngstock classes were judged in a small upper portion of the ring which was not under water. These classes were dominated by *Mervyn Kingsmill (762)*, with his daughters filling the first three places in both the yearling and three year old classes. The yearling winner was Henry O'Toole's filly out of Village Star (5146),

220

and a full sister to this filly, Village Colleen (8308), won the three year old class and the Killanin Cup for Padraig Hynes. Another Kingsmill daughter, Jennifer Rose (8528), won the two year old class and the Carew Cup for Peter Molloy, Claddaghduff and *Mervyn Kingsmill (762)* won the Confined Stallion class for Mikey King for the third year in a row.

The Open Stallion class was won by Joe Day from Co. Wexford with his 21 year old *Ballydonagh Bobby (242)*, and his daughter Ashfield Grey Sparrow (8155) took the Archbishop's Cup for Jimmy Jones.

The Supreme Champion of the Show went to Padraig Hynes' Village Laura (8097), and her dam, Village Star (5146), owned by Henry O'Toole had a special day, having produced three winning daughters at the Show, including the Supreme Champion.

Despite the appalling weather in the morning, flooding on all the roads approaching Clifden, and a bus strike, all combining to prevent a good attendance at the Show, when the sun came out after lunch, a large and enthusiastic crowd gathered in the afternoon and enjoyed a memorable day.

Alexander Evans (19) and William (14), sons of Mr and Mrs Clive Evans, Bruckless House, Bruckless, Co. Donegal, showed great enterprise when they rode their Connemara ponies Sweet Wall Wanda (8389) and Bruckless Gaffalla (G. 1204) from Donegal to Clifden to take part in the Show. They travelled through Donegal, Sligo, Mayo and into Clifden via Leenane, and rode a lap of honour around the Show ring on Show Day. On their journey from Donegal they made a collection on behalf of the Riding for Disabled Association, and were helped along the route by members of the Association.

At the Oughterard Show held at the end of August, the winner of the All Ireland Ridden Connemara Pony Championship was Tulira Searchlight (G. 1018) owned by Mrs Janet McLoughlin Minch, Tara, Co. Meath, who was also a winner at the RDS Spring Show.

Dr Percy Weissman of Cloonisle, Cashel and of Canada, was a man who had taken a very practical interest in the Society's breeding programme, and had been a great benefactor for the Society for several years. He was particularly interested in Connemara ponies and in maintaining the breed in its native habitat of Connemara. To encourage this, he provided a very valuable sponsorship towards the upkeep of the stallions owned by the Society standing in Connemara. This generous support helped the Connemara Pony Breeders' Society to carry out a vital part of its breeding programme, and with Dr Weissman's death in October 1987, the Society lost a generous and loyal friend.

At the end of the 1987 season *Maam Hill (728)* was removed from the list, having spent six years in Connemara, two with Tommy O'Brien and four with Bartley O'Malley. He was a son of *Dun Aengus (120)*, and was also a light dun, although he was a larger and stronger pony than his sire. He was not widely used in Connemara, and only left fifty registered progeny, with just one registered son, *Loughlum Sadat (812)*. One of Maam Hill's daughters, Misty Glen (8075), is dam of the stallion *Bushmills Coral Blue (977)* who was awarded the highest marks in the 1995 Stallion Performance Test.

J. Petch

Maam Hill (728)

J. Petch

Ormond Oliver (653)

Another stallion owned by the Society left Connemara after the end of the 1987 season, he was the twelve year old *Ormond Oliver (653)* who was the last son of *MacDara (91)* to serve in Connemara. He moved to Jimmy Jones in Co. Carlow who has always favoured the *MacDara* line, and both *MacDara (91)* and his son *Atlantic Storm (139)* spent their final years with him at Ashfield Stud. *Ormond Oliver (653)* had been on the list for ten seasons, spending four years with Tommy O'Brien, six with Paddy Folan, and his last year with Festy Mulkerrin, but he was not as popular a sire as his father, and only left eighty registered progeny during his time in Connemara, including two stallions, *Ballinaboy Charlie (749)* and *Newbridge Oliver (905)*. Among his daughters were, Derrylea Peggy (7729), Persil (7878), Loughconeera Snowdrop (8277), Dawn Mist (8311) and Derryvoniff Harp (8617).

Festy Mulkerrin, Callowfeenish, decided not keep a stallion for the Society in the 1988 season as there were very few breeding mares left in the district. This was a sad reminder of the steady decline in the number of breeding mares in Connemara, but particularly in the Carna district, which had once been famous for its mares, and some of the best ponies were bred there. The primary function of the Connemara Pony Breeders' Society being the conservation and development of the breeding population in Connemara, the current situation, with breeding stock being sold out of the district, and an annual drop in the number of foals born in Connemara, was of grave concern to the Society. A new financial package for the breeding of Irish Draughts had recently been announced by the Department of Agriculture, and the Society hoped to secure a similar incentive scheme for the Connemara Pony.

Death of two Council Members

It was with great sadness that members of the Connemara Pony Breeders' Society heard the news in November 1987, of the untimely death of John Brennan, Fort Lorenzo, Taylors Hill, after a short illness. John Brennan, was a native of Castleblaney, Co. Monahan, and moved to Galway in the fifties, where he became a prominent building contractor, and he also had a great interest in the equestrian world. His many commitments included being a member of the Executive Committee of the Show Jumping Association of Ireland, he was also an active member of the Galway Race Committee, and the Chairman of the Galway County Show. John's interest in the Connemara pony began in the early sixties, and he became a keen breeder and judge, and established his stud at Fort Lorenzo. He produced many prizewinners in the sixties and seventies, and his ponies, who carried the Fort prefix, were exported all over the world. One of his most famous ponies was the stallion *Marble (254)* who he bought at Maam Cross Fair as a foal, and another was Fort Cora (4107) by Clonkeehan Auratum (104) who won many prizes in her day, and is still living with the Brennan family aged thirty. He was elected a member of the Council in 1973 and also served as a member of the stallion committee, and his work for the Society over many years will be remembered with gratitude. His integrity and commitment made him a respected member of the Council, and his sound advice based on his wide experience was always tempered by solid common sense. With John's death, the Society lost a most valued member and friend.

In January 1988, the Society lost another true friend, with the death of Miss Lal Berridge, who was one of the longest standing members of the Society. She was born in London in 1910, but having lived much of her early life at Ballinahinch and Screebe, she had a deep love of Connemara and its ponies. She was the first woman to be elected to the Council in 1950, and served as a member of the Council for 27 years. She was also a Society inspector, and a respected judge at Clifden on many occasions. At the International Conference in 1970, she spoke on the development of the Connemara pony through the work of the Connemara Pony Breeders' Society.

She moved to Wicklow in 1959, and her work in promoting the Connemara pony included running her own Connemara Pony Show for several years at Enniskerry. Here at Mervyn, she started breeding from two Connemara mares, and her small stud produced many successful ponies including the stallions *Mervyn Pookhaun (528)* and *Mervyn Kingsmill (762)*, and both these stallions won the coveted stallion trophy at Clifden. The success of *Mervyn Kingsmill* and his progeny at the Clifden Show in 1987 must have given her great pleasure, and was a fitting tribute to a dedicated breeder whose life-long interest was the Connemara pony.

J. Petch

Miss Lal Berridge

There were eight stallions on the approved list for stallions standing in Connemara in 1988, four belonging to the Society, and four owned privately. *Mervyn Kingsmill (762)* moved to Josie Conroy, Bunowen, and *Seafield Silver Rogue (823)* went to Bartley O'Malley at Carraroe, replacing *Maam Hill (728)* and *Fort Dara (718)* who had both left the list. *Abbeyleix Owen (496)* remained with Tommy O'Brien, and *Canal Cormac (848)* was with Dudley Nee, Camas.

One newcomer was *Granard Storm* (737) a ten year old dark dun son of Atlantic Storm (139), dam Martins's Pride (6013) by Thunderbolt (178), and his granddam was Callowfeenish Pride (1912). He was lent to the Society by Jimmy Jones, Carlow and placed with Mikey King, Claddaghduff. The other three stallions on the list, *Loobeen Larry* (670) Graham Tulloch, *Cuchulainn* (789) James de Courcey, and *Murphy Rebel* (696) Stephen Heanue, were privately owned and they stood with their owners.

New Inspection Committee

At a Council meeting held prior to the AGM on 29th March 1988 it was decided that the stallion committee and the inspection committee would be amalgamated, and the following members were appointed.

Mr D. Power (chairman), Mr D. Kenny, Mr R. Kelly. MRCVS,
Mr G. Tulloch, Mr P. Scanaill MRCVS, Mrs E. Petch,
Mr J. Luskin, Mr J. Jones, Mr J. Lee, Mr J. Gorham.

Two members who had served on the Council for many years, decided to make way for new members, and sent letters of resignation to the meeting.

Michael Clancy, Spiddal was elected to the Council in 1968 and had given twenty years of service to the Society. He had been involved with ponies since the fifties, and many good ponies carrying his Atlantic prefix were exported all over the world. He was a Society judge, and his keen eye for a pony contributed to his many successes. Atlantic Storm, Atlantic Mist, Atlantic Breeze, Atlantic Surf, Atlantic Currach, Atlantic Peace and Silver Sparrow were some of the outstanding ponies produced by him, and although his interests have now turned more towards thoroughbreds and racing, he still keeps some good Connemara mares for breeding, and his ponies continue to compete successfully at shows.

J. Petch

Michael Clancy with his mare
Atlantic Peace (7903)

Sam Morrison, Portadown served as the Northern Ireland representative on the Council, and he gave valuable help to members of the inspection team when they visited the North. He has been breeding ponies for many years, and ponies carrying his well known Holiday prefix have gone all over the world. He still continues to be a regular exhibitor at the Annual Show. The Chairman paid tribute to both members, who had made a valuable contribution to the work of the Society over the years.

There were now four vacancies on the Council to be filled, and the following were elected as new members: Mr Johnny Brennan, Lady Maria Levinge, Mr Padraig Curran, Mrs Nicola Musgrave.

At the AGM, Mr Donal Kenny announced that a Directive on Zootechnical Regulations regarding the Harmonisation of the rules for Equine Stud Books had been proposed by the EEC Commission. Some sections of this directive would have serious consequences for the Connemara Pony Breeders' Society. In particular the role of the Connemara Pony Breeders' Society as the Parent Society for the Breed in the matter of defining standards for registration in the Irish Stud Book would be in question. The President suggested that the Society should take the lead in this area, and proposed that a meeting with representatives of the overseas Connemara pony societies should be held in Clifden on the eve of the Connemara Pony Show 1988.

The Annual Inspections were held in Connemara in May, and during the year the inspection team travelled to other centres all over Ireland. In all 16 stallions, 164 mares and 53 geldings were passed, a total of 233 ponies, and the slight increase in numbers from previous years might have been encouraging, had it not been for the more disturbing fact that the number of ponies registered by breeders in the Connemara area was only 35% of the total.

The entries in the in hand classes at the RDS Dublin Horse Show were again disappointing with only twenty-two entries in the four classes, and unfortunately the high cost of entry and stabling at the Show was the reason given by breeders for not taking their ponies to Dublin. The Championship in the Connemara pony classes was won for the second year by Padraig Hynes with Village Laura (8097), with Jimmy Jones, Carlow, taking Reserve with Ashfield Saile (8013).

J. Petch

Jimmy Jones with Ashfield Saile (8013)

International Rules Meeting for Overseas Societies

A meeting of the Overseas Societies was held in Clifden on 17th August 1988, the day before the Annual Show, and delegates from England, France, Denmark, Holland, Sweden, Germany, Finland and the Parent Society together with representatives of the Department of Agriculture, met to discuss how best to implement the directive from the EEC on harmonising the rules and regulations which govern each individual society worldwide. The meeting was chaired by Donal Kenny, and it was agreed that the proposed legislation to harmonise the rules would affect many of the Connemara pony societies, and although there were many points on which all societies could agree, the major differences centred around the requirement for inspection prior to registration, and the standards required for entry into the Stud Book. The Connemara Pony Breeders' Society was given a mandate at the meeting to draft proposals for a set of International Rules for all societies which would be discussed at the next meeting of the overseas societies to be held in Clifden on the day before the 1989 Show.

A sub-committee was set up to work on the draft rules, and consisted of the representatives of the Connemara Pony Breeders' Society who had attended the meeting, Mr D. Kenny, Mr D. Power, Mr. J. Jones, Mrs E. Petch.

The Pre-Show reception was held at the Celtic Hotel, Clifden on the eve of the Show, and once again it was sponsored by the Clifden Committee who had collected generous contributions from over sixty business establishments in Clifden to sponsor the evening. Representatives of the overseas Societies who had attended the meeting joined breeders and exhibitors from all over Ireland for an enjoyable evening. The guest speaker was the Minister of Agriculture Mr Michael O'Kennedy TD, and in his speech he acknowledged that the Connemara Pony held an important place in the Irish horse and pony breeding industry, and he assured the breeders that this was fully appreciated by the Irish Government.

65th Annual Pony Show, Clifden – 18th August 1988

Clifden Show took place the following day, and the day dawned fine and sunny, which was a welcome relief after the appalling weather of the previous year. A large and enthusiastic crowd gathered to see 300 ponies being judged by Miss Susan Lanigan O'Keefe and Mr Padraig Curran, and for the first time a dog show was also included which was organised by Mrs D. Geddes and proved a great success.

The confined stallion class was won by the 17 year old *Abbeyleix Owen (496)* shown by Tommy O'Brien who had produced him in top form, and he also stood second in the Open class which was won by 6 year old *Abbeyleix Fionn (810)*. The winning two year old colt was *Garryhinch Prince (861)*, a son of Abbeyleix Fionn (810) owned by Joe Gorham, and the Carew Cup winner was Coosheen Kittiwake ((8683) by Glyntown Paddy (259), owned by Mrs Petch, with Bobby Bolger's Coral Misty (8642) in second place. The three year old winner of the Killanin Cup was Boden Park Hailstones ((8445) s. Atlantic Storm (139) owned by Mrs Jane Dalrymple, and Lady Maria Levinge's four year old Callowfeenish Wave (8329) by Thunderbolt (178) won the Archbishop's Cup.

Padraig Hynes won the five and six year old class with Village Laura (8097) and went on to take the Confined Championship, but in the class for senior mares, the winner was Eddie Madden's lovely 14 year old mare Gloves Misty (6535), who then won the Jan Harald Koelichen Cup and became the Supreme Champion of the Show for the third time in her showing career. This was a record achievement, for not only was she a champion in the Showring, Gloves

J. Petch

Gloves Misty (6535)

226

Misty was also a successful broodmare, having produced seven foals in seven years including the winning yearling colt at the Show, as well as working on the farm for the Madden family.

At the end of the 1988 season two of the Society owned stallions, *Maam Hill (728)* and *Canal Cormac (848)*, were sold, and left Connemara, while *Granard Storm (737)*, who had spent one season with Mikey King at Claddaghduff, moved to Mr Clive Evans in Donegal, and *Ashfield Alex (711)* returned to Connemara to stand with Graham Tulloch at Moyard.

Granard Storm (737) was the last stallion which Mikey King held at Claddaghduff for the Society, and he retired after having been a stallion custodian for thirty years. He took over from his father Festy who stood *Innishgoill Laddie (21)* for his last season in Connemara in 1954, and *Carna Bobby (79)* for four years from 1955 to 1958, and Mikey's first sire in 1959 was *Tooreen Ross (99)* who he held for four seasons. He travelled his regular weekly route, leading his stallion from his bicycle to Letterfrack and Tully on Wednesdays, Recess, Cashel and Roundstone on Fridays (staying overnight in Roundstone), Clifden and Ballyconneely on Saturdays and Fair days. He continued this route until the end of the 1973 season, when he stopped the Friday route, but for the next ten years he still travelled the Wednesday and Saturday routes until 1983, when he travelled the stallion by arrangement.

During his time as a custodian Mikey handled thirteen different stallions, they were, *Tooreen Ross (99), Inver Rebel (93), Dun Aengus (120), Errigal Prince (159), Thunderbolt (178), Doon Paddy (95), Lough Easkey (166), Atlantic Storm (139), Sarsfield (579) Slyne Head (710), Mervyn Kingsmill (762), Thunderstorm (796), and Granard Storm (737)*.

He always kept his stallions looking very well, and won the Confined stallion class on six occasions, once each with *Lough Easkey (166)* and *Thunderbolt (178)*, and four times with *Mervyn Kingsmill (762)*, who also won the Open Stallion class in 1985 which must have been a proud day for Mikey.

One of the longest living mares in Connemara died peacefully in her own field at Lehid during the winter of 1988/89. She was Lehid Rose (1417), foaled in 1949, and had she lived another few months she would have reached the remarkable age of forty years. She lived out all the year, with just a little extra feeding in the winter, and was still carting hay for her owners the Conneelys at Lehid at the age of thirty-seven. She was bred by Val Gorham, Truska, Ballyconneely, sire Clough Droighnean (67), and her dam Little Nell (988), by Silver Pearl (18) was one of the outstanding mares of her era. Her sire was from the same dam as *Dun Lorenzo (55)*, and so Lehid Rose came from a tough line of ponies. One of her daughters, Lehid Love (2912) by Carna Dun (89) won a cup at the Clifden Races in

Lehid Rose (1417)

227

the sixties with Michael Conneely riding, another daughter by Clonkeehan Auratum (104) was Old Rose (3142) who took fourth place in the class for veteran mares at Ballyconneely Show in 1989 aged 27 years. Descendants from Lehid Rose (1417) are still breeding at Lehid today, and many more of her progeny went overseas.

At the end of 1988 the Department of Agriculture announced in a press release that the headage scheme was to be increased to £70 per head, and would be payable in respect of eligible registered mares in all disadvantaged areas in which cattle headage grants were paid.

Another new young stallion, owned and bred by Jimmy Jones, joined the approved list for stallions standing in Connemara for 1989. He was *Ashfield Festy (859)* a three year old son of Granard Storm (737), dam Atlantic Surf (2471), and he was placed with Tommy O'Brien, Canal Stage. *Abbeyleix Owen (496)* moved to Dudley Nee at Camus, *Mervyn Kingsmill (762)* remained with Josie Conroy, and *Seafield Silver Rogue (823)* stayed at Carraroe with Bartley O'Malley.

It was a great loss for Connemara when James de Courcey's good Grade A jumping stallion *Cuchulainn (789)* died at the young age of ten years. He was Champion Stallion at Clifden in 1986, and had been on the list of approved stallions for two seasons. He only left 26 registered progeny, but from his five registered stallions, two sons, *Coral Star (890)* and *Slisneoir (925)*, have remained in Connemara, and a third son *Rocky (914)*, bred by Joe Gorham from his mare Silver Fort (7281), who was an impressive winner of the Junior and Supreme Championships at Clifden in 1991, was sold to the USA.

One of his daughters is a full sister to *Rocky (914)*, Kingstown Silver (9033), and others are Castlestrange Sparrow (9092), Dooneen Moonlight (9283), Tassie's Cailin (9282).

Review Committee Report

The Review Committee made their report to the Council at a meeting in February 1989 when the proposed changes to the Memorandum and Articles of Association were discussed at length. The principal recommendations were that four members of the Council should retire each year on rotation, ordinary members of the Society would have power to elect members to the Council, and a minimum of 13 members of the Council should reside in Connemara.

Some of the Council members representing the Connemara area expressed serious reservations about the review, and many feared that the proposed amendments would diminish the role of the Connemara district as the cradle of the breed, and that the Council would lose many of its members who were based in Connemara. It was the feeling of the meeting that in view of the number of changes which had occurred recently in the membership of the Council, the proposed amendments should be postponed for at least a year.

There were two vacancies on the Council which were filled at this meeting by Mr John Enda Feeney, Spiddal, and Mrs Joan Hawkins, Dangan, Galway.

The AGM was held on 31st March 1989, and the members of the Society were very critical of the Council's decision to postpone action on the report of the review committee for one year, and were very dissatisfied that members still had no say in the running of the Society. The matter was raised again at the next Council meeting held in May 1989, and the Council then agreed to put the proposed amendments to the Memorandum and Articles of Association to an Extraordinary General Meeting in January 1990.

Following a mild Winter and Spring, the ponies all looked very well on the Annual Inspection tour which took place in Connemara on 16th/18th May, but there was another drop in the number of ponies registered in Connemara, and there were no ponies at several of the centres. At Ballyconneely, where in the past there would often be twenty or more, there were only four, two 2 year olds fillies, a gelding, and one three year old filly shown by her breeder John Joyce. She was given the name Maureen's Cuckoo (8799), and was by Mervyn Kingsmill (762) out of John Joyce's good mare Wise Cuckoo (2714), who sadly died that year shortly after foaling aged 26 years.

Despite the small number of fillies forward for inspection, two of the fillies seen during the 1989 inspection tour in Connemara were to become future champions at Clifden. During the year the inspection team made several trips to other parts of Ireland, and in all 19 stallions, 172 mares and 39 geldings were passed, making a total of 230 ponies registered in 1989.

Volume XVIII of the Stud Book was unable to be published in 1988, due to the Society's serious lack of funds, but in June 1989, a Connemara Pony Festival was held in Innishannon Co. Cork to raise funds towards the cost of printing the new Stud Book. It was organised by breeders in the Munster area, and centred around a 21st birthday celebration for the well-known Connemara stallion Coosheen Finn (381), and 200 people came to see him parade with a group of his progeny. Members from seven branches of the Pony Club took part in various gymkhana games during the day, and a sum of over £2500 was raised for the Stud Book fund.

Entries for the Dublin Horse Show were marginally up on previous years, with a high standard of quality. All four classes were won by breeders from Connemara, with ponies who were to dominate the Show ring in the years to come, three of them becoming Champions at Clifden. The two year old class went to Mrs Josie Joyce's Cailin Ciuin (8785), and Bobby Bolger won the three year old class with Coral Misty (8642). Padraig Hynes won with his five year old Village Colleen (8308), and then having won her class, Village Laura (8097) took the Championship for the third year running, which was quite an achievement.

In July 1989 the Danish Connemara Pony Society celebrated its 25th Anniversary with a Jubilee Show held over

Equestrian Photographic Services

Village Laura (8097) RDS Champion 1987, '88 and '89.

two weekends, and the President of the Connemara Pony Breeders' Society Mr Donal Kenny was invited to judge the Shows together with Mr Dermot Power.

Overseas Societies Meeting

On 23rd August 1989 the second meeting of the overseas societies was held at Clifden on the eve of the Annual Show. Two more overseas societies were formed during the year in Austria and in Belgium. Representatives from England, Germany, France and Finland met members of the International Committee of the Connemara Pony Breeders' Society, and good progress was made in agreeing the draft document of International Rules which would be acceptable under EEC legislation and acceptable to all Connemara Pony

Equestrian Photographic Services

Village Colleen (8308) with Padraig Hynes.

Societies. Much work still needed to be done to achieve full harmonisation and to enable draft rules to be submitted to all Societies including the Connemara Pony Breeders' Society, but there was general agreement on the broader issues.

Later the same evening the pre-Show reception was held at the Clifden Bay Hotel, and once again the evening was sponsored by the Clifden Committee. The Minister of Agriculture, Mr Michael O'Kennedy TD. made a lively and interesting speech, and the many overseas visitors to the Show as well as the representatives of the Overseas Societies had an opportunity to meet members, breeders and friends, making it a very enjoyable evening.

66th Annual Pony Show, Clifden – 24th August 1989

There were a large number of overseas visitors at the Show including breeders from England, France, Holland, Germany, Sweden, Finland, USA, Australia and New Zealand. Once again the weather was unkind, and rain marred some of the enjoyment in the afternoon, but it was an excellent Show with an entry of 328 ponies, which was the highest for a number of years. The Dog Show was again a very successful added attraction to the Show, and the

Abbeyleix Fionn (810) with Sean Dunne.

Aeriocht with its competitions for Irish music and dancing was very popular with the visitors to the Show.

The Connemara Pony Breeders' Society was honoured to have a most distinguished guest, the President of Ireland, Dr Patrick Hillery visiting the Show, and he presented a Waterford crystal bowl to the winner of the Confined Stallion Class, Josie Conroy with *Mervyn Kingsmill (762)*. In the Open Stallion Class Sean Dunne's

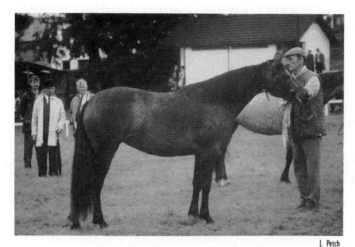

J. Petch

J. Petch

John Joyce with Maureen's Cuckoo (8799)
Supreme Champion.

Carole Seigne with Templebready Starling (8829)
Reserve Champion

Abbeyleix Fionn (810) won the Waterford Crystal Stallion Trophy for the second year running, and his sons stood first and second in the 2 to 3 year old colt class. This year the Show was dominated by the younger mares, and John Joyce's outstanding three year old filly, Maureen's Cuckoo (8799) won her class and the Killanin Cup and went on to win the Confined Championship, the Jan Harald Koelichen Cup and the Supreme Champion of the Show. Reserve Champion was the two year old winner, Templebready Starling (8829) owned and bred by Mrs Carole Seigne, Crosshaven, Co. Cork, and Peter Molloy's winning four year old Jennifer Rose (8528) was Reserve in the Confined Championship. The judges were Mr Paddy Carr and Mr Michael Casey, with Mr R. Kelly MRCVS as referee.

The winner of the riding class was Leoni (8378) owned and ridden by Lucy McEvilly, and they went on to become the winners of the All Ireland Ridden Connemara Pony Championship at Oughterard two weeks later.

Extraordinary General Meeting

The year 1990, the start of a new decade, also saw the beginning of big changes in the Society, and on 18th January 1990 an Extraordinary General Meeting of the Connemara Pony Breeders' Society was held at the Sacre Coeur Hotel, Galway. The purpose of the meeting was to amend the Memorandum and Articles of Association, which had been in place since December 1959, when rules for the new Cumann Lucht Capaillini Chonamara had been formalised under the guidance of the President of the Society, Lord Killanin.

In the thirty years since then, the Society had grown and changed considerably from the small group of dedicated people involved in the preservation of the breed and the interests of the small breeder in Connemara. The Society had now become an organisation with much more diverse responsibilities, and as well as looking after the small breeder in Connemara, it served a large number of owners and breeders throughout the whole of Ireland, and was also the Parent Society to a group of twelve overseas societies, with representatives of the Society heading the International Rules Committee. The Council acknowledged that it was necessary to update the rules and make them more democratic, but at the same time it was important to maintain continuity in the work of the Society.

The main changes which were proposed were:

1. Membership of the Society to be increased to 1,000.
2. Membership of the Council to represent all of Ireland, but with not less than 13 members of Council to be resident in the Society's district of Connemara.
3. Four members of Council to retire on rotation every year, and be eligible for re-election.
4. An ordinary member to be eligible for election to the Council if he/she is nominated by four members of the Society.

From the panel of candidates submitted to the AGM, two to be elected to the Council by the members at the AGM, and two to be appointed by the Council at the next Council meeting following the AGM.

There were 19 formal resolutions proposing the amendments which were put to the fifty-three members present, and they were individually voted on and all were passed. Some of the members felt that the changes were too limited, but it was a step towards a more democratic structure of the rules of the Society, and as the new rules would come into effect at the AGM in March 1990, it was suggested at the meeting that they should be given a trial period.

Donal Kenny Retires from Office as President

At a Council meeting held on the same day as the EGM, the President, Donal Kenny told the Council that he had now completed eleven years in office, and that he would not be seeking re-election at the next Council meeting. Donal Kenny had been elected as President of the Connemara Pony Breeders' Society in 1979 following the sudden death of Martin Treacy, and his years in office had not been easy, particularly because of the fluctuating state of the Society's finances, and the growing concern over the decline in the breeding stock in Connemara. The death of John Killeen in the same year that he took office was a serious loss for the Society, but Donal Kenny was fortunate that Phil MacDermott was able to provide an office in her home, and take over the running of the Society's affairs so smoothly. A new inspection team had been set up which enabled inspections for registration to be carried out throughout the whole country more efficiently, and Passports were introduced in 1986, the same year that headage payments were first granted to Connemara ponies. In 1988 he set up the International Rules Committee to

Donal Kenny

harmonise the rules of all Connemara pony societies, and this task would have important longterm implications for the Society, and his final major undertaking while in office was the review of the Constitution of the Society leading to the amendments to the rules for the election of members of the Council.

CHAPTER 15

1990 -1993

• Election of New President • Two Council Members Elected at AGM • Secretary Resigns •
• Society Office Moves to Clifden • New Secretary • Volumes XVIII and XIX Stud Book. •
Stallion Inspections to Centres. • Blood-typing all Foals • Grants for Breeders • Connemara Pony •
• Quadrille • Display in Paris • Stallion Performance Test. • 70th Anniversary •

On Friday 23rd March 1990, at the Council meeting held prior to the AGM, two candidates were nominated for the office of President, Mr Eamonn Hannan and Mr Dermot Power. All twenty-four Council members were present, and following a vote, Mr Eamonn Hannan was elected to become the eighth President of the Connemara Pony Breeders' Society.

Eamonn Hannan had been a member of the Society since 1983, and had been elected to the Council in 1987. He was a member of the Review Committee who had proposed the amendments to the rules of the Society, and had been appointed as the representative for the Society on the Horse Breeding Advisory Committee established in December 1989. He was Chief Executive of the Western Health Board, and he brought his considerable administration skills to his new office as the President of the Connemara Pony Breeders' Society.

The Two Vice-Presidents appointed were Mr Dermot Power, Galway, and Mr T. J. McDonagh, Roundstone, and they joined Canon W. Moran, Oranmore who held that office for life.

Four Senior Council Members Retire

It was decided at the meeting that the method of retirement from the Council under the new rules would be by seniority, and the four longest serving members of the Council who retired that day were: Mr P. O'Scanaill MRCVS, Mr. D. Kelly MRCVS, Mr G. Tulloch, Mrs E. Petch.

All four were senior members of the Inspection Committee:
* Mr P. O'Scanaill MRCVS had served as a member of Council since 1947,
* Mr R. Kelly MRCVS had been a Council member since 1949,
* Mr Graham Tulloch was elected to the Council in 1969,
* Mrs E. Petch had been a member of the Council since 1974.

Outgoing Council 1990

Back Row: *Jimmy Jones, John Luskin, Willie Diamond, Johnny Lee, Owen Crehan, Johnny Brennan, John M. Mannion, Pat Mulrooney.*
Middle Row: *Padraig Hynes, Dermot Power, Mrs Joan Hawkins, Padraig Curran, Lady Maria Levinge, Graham Tulloch, Mrs Nicola Musgrave, Joe Gorham, Peadar O'Scannaill, John Enda Feeney.*
Front Row: *Tommy McDonagh, Mrs Phil MacDermott, Rev Canon Moran, Donal Kenny, Eamonn Hannan, Mrs Elizabeth Petch, Roderic Kelly.*

AGM Friday 23rd March 1990

The AGM was held following the Council meeting, chaired by the new President, Eamonn Hannan, and there were 70 members present.

It was announced that blood-typing of all registered Connemara Pony Stallions would be introduced in 1990. Prior to this only stallions owned by the Society had been blood-typed, but with many more privately-owned stallions standing throughout Ireland, this was a necessary step towards full blood-typing for the breed.

The Council also proposed to introduce computerisation to the office, and had received a generous offer of a computer from Digital, and a cash contribution towards the cost of the programme from Mr and Mrs Hugh Musgrave.

Two Council Members Elected at AGM

There were seven nominated candidates for the election by the members for two places on the Council, and the four retiring Council members were also entitled to stand for re-election. The two new Council members who were elected were, Mr J. J. Gorham, Claremorris, son of Joe Gorham, Clifden. and Miss Eugenia Murray, a solicitor from Dublin. Two of the retiring Council members were elected to the Council at the next Council Meeting, Mr Graham Tulloch, and Mr P. O'Scannaill MRCVS, but when Graham Tulloch did not wish to be re-elected, Ms Siobhan Brooks Naughton was elected in his place.

Senior Council Member Retires

Mr Roderic Kelly MRCVS was one of the most senior Council members who retired from the Council under the new ruling, and he left the Council having given forty-one years of service to the Connemara Pony Breeders' Society. He was a nephew of the founder member T. McD. Kelly MRCVS, and first joined the Council in 1949, joining the Inspection Committee the following year, and for forty years he travelled with the inspectors on the annual inspection tour in Connemara without charge to the Society.

He judged in Dublin and Clifden on many occasions, and in 1976 he took over from his uncle as Referee Judge at Clifden where his cheerful presence in the centre of the ring will be remembered by many. His wife Maeve also contributed to the work of the Society for many years when she helped in the ticket office on Show day, and she also chaired the Social Committee for the International Conference in 1970.

Secretary Resigns

On 24th April 1990 Mrs Phil MacDermott gave notice of resignation from her position as Secretary of the Society which she had held since John Killeen's death in 1979. She had given many long years of service to the Society, and had also acted as Assistant Secretary to both Sean Keane and John Killeen. During her thirty years with the Society she had worked on producing ten Volumes of the Stud Book, and in recent years she had coped cheerfully with an increasing workload in the Society's office as well as running the Annual Show. Volume XVIII of the Stud Book, the tenth book Phil MacDermott had compiled for the Society, was ready to go to print as she left office, and would be a lasting testimony to the valuable contribution she made to the Society over many years. During her years in the Society office from the early sixties she had seen the huge expansion in the role of the Society, with increasing exports leading to the formation of many new overseas societies, and her vast knowledge of the ponies and their breeders both in Ireland and worldwide would be greatly missed.

Mrs Phil MacDermott

The new President, Eamonn Hannan, took on the work of re-organisation straight away, and a number of sub-committees were formed to deal with the various aspects of the Society's work. There were several new committees dealing with office computerisation, equestrian matters, public relations and education, a new Stud Book committee, and with new faces in the Council, there were fresh ideas and a feeling of optimism for the future of the Society.

The list of Approved Stallions standing in Connemara in 1990 was reduced to six, with one new addition, the three year old *Smokey Duncan (871)*, leased to the Society by his owner Graham Tulloch, and standing with Josie Conroy at Bunowen. He was bred by Murty McGrath, Cregmore, and was by Westside Frank (817) dam Smokey Jane Grey (7477). His sire, who went to Germany, was by Bobby Brown (731), who was sold to USA, and this line traces back through seven generations to *Clonkeehan Auratum (104)*, while his dam was grand-daughter of the famous mare Smokey (1198) by Gil (43) who was the foundation mare of Murty McGrath's great line of ponies.

The Annual Inspections were held at 20 centres in Connemara during May and inspections were also held in other parts of the country and a total of 296 ponies were registered including 27 stallions, 80 geldings, and 189 mares, but again there was a decline in the number of ponies presented in Connemara.

Connemara Pony Quadrille

A new innovation in 1990 was the Connemara Pony Quadrille and the idea was started by a group of enthusiastic young riders in Galway who got together after the Clifden Show and decided to make a musical ride. The twelve children, all riding registered Connemara ponies, started training in December 1989 with Mrs Anita Cahill in David Moore's indoor arena, and they also received some help from Miss Iris Kellett. After months of hard work, and enthusiastic backing from parents and sponsors, they performed the musical ride at Galway County Show, then at Salthill,

Connemara Pony Quadrille at the RDS Horse Show.

and finally in the main arena at the Royal Dublin Society Horse Show, where their performance was a triumph.

The riders, who wore green jackets with a shawl of saffron tweed draped from one shoulder, were all mounted on grey ponies, and they were a credit to all those who had helped them to bring the Connemara Pony Quadrille to the Royal Dublin Society Horse Show.

Death of Graham Tulloch

The news of the sudden death of Graham Tulloch in July came as a shock to his many friends in the Society, and left a great sense of loss and sadness throughout the whole of Connemara and beyond. A kind and gentle man, Graham Tulloch was a true friend of the Connemara Pony Breeders' Society and as a member of the

Council, he could always be depended on for his sound advise and practical help. He was also a valued member of the Inspection committee, and was a knowledgeable and well-respected judge. He built up his herd of high-class Connemara ponies which carried the Ocean prefix from his first prizewinning mare Ocean Melody (2134), and stood his stallion *Loobeen Larry (670)* at Shanbolard.

He was always generous with his time and help to others, and often drove his neighbours ponies to shows in his lorry. He also held stallions for the Society at Shanbolard when they needed special care or a winter on good land, and he lent his own stallions to the Society whenever there was a need. In 1990 he leased his latest young stallion *Smokey Duncan (871)* to the Society, and after his death, this stallion was generously donated to the Society by his executors.

His ponies including his stallion *Loobeen Larry (670)* passed to his niece Mrs Nicola Musgrave, who carries on the Tulloch family's strong ties with the Connemara Pony at Cleggan Farm where she

Milleder Archive

Graham Tulloch with Loobeen Larry

has established a small breeding herd, and her ponies carry the Annilaun prefix. Nicola was elected to the Council in 1988, and since then has given generously of her time to the work of the Society as an Inspector and as a Judge both at home and overseas. She has encouraged the promotion of the Connemara gelding for many years, and sponsors the gelding class at the Clifden Show in memory of her mother, the late Mrs Anne Goodbody.

Mr Owen Crehan who had served as Hon Treasurer for many years resigned from the Council at the end of July, and he was succeeded as Hon. Treasurer by John M. Mannion. Owen Crehan had been a member of the Council since 1978, and as well as his duties as Treasurer, he had also acted as General Steward of the Showgrounds for fifteen years. His place on the Council was filled by Mrs Jane Dalrymple, Ashbourne, Co. Meath.

New Secretary Appointed – Society's Office Moves to Clifden

Miss Marian Turley B.Sc. H.Dip. Eq.Sc. from Galway was appointed as the new Secretary to replace Mrs MacDermott whose resignation was due take effect in July, and the Society's Office was moved from Galway to Clifden in July 1990 into the Gate Lodge at the gates of the Hospital. Marian started as Secretary to the Connemara Pony Breeders' Society on 1st August 1990, and had little time to become familiar with her new job before the Annual Clifden Pony Show on 16th August. However she coped very well, and the Council was grateful to Johnny Lee who undertook the task of dealing with the Show entries and producing the Show catalogue during the changeover.

The International Connemara Pony Society Meeting 1990

A meeting of the International Connemara Pony Societies was held on 15th August at the Abbeyglen Hotel and eleven countries were represented, with delegates from England, USA, Denmark, Sweden, Holland, France, Germany, Australia, New Zealand, Switzerland and Italy. The meeting was chaired by Donal Kenny and good progress was made with the drafting of the proposed International Rules. A new and fuller description of the Connemara Pony was introduced, which was approved by Council, and was used in Volume XVIII of the Stud Book. A dinner was held after the meeting for the delegates which was attended by the Minister of Agriculture Mr Michael O'Kennedy, and afterwards he was the guest speaker at the Annual Pre-Show Reception, which was hosted by the Clifden Community Council.

67th Annual Pony Show, Clifden – 16th August 1990

The Annual Show was held the following day, and for the first time for several years the sun shone all day and there was a large attendance. The big number of delegates from the overseas societies made it a very international occasion, and the entries showed an increase, with 361 in the pony classes.

The Judges were Mr Pat Daly MRCVS, Miss Eugenia Murray and Mr J. Jones. The winner of the three year old colt class was *Smokey Duncan (871)*, beautifully produced by Josie Conroy, and he went on to win the Open Stallion Class with the 19 year old *Abbeyleix Owen (496)* standing in 2nd place. This was a great achievement for the Society stallions as the Confined Stallion Class had been dropped and the strong Open Class included several former winners.

The Killanin Cup for the best three year old filly class was won by the RDS winner Cailin Ciuin (8785) owned by Mrs Josie Joyce, while the Archbishop's Cup went to Bobby Bolger's Coral Misty (8642). Three of *Mervyn Kingsmill's* progeny headed the 5/6 year old mares with Peter Molloy's Jennifer Rose (8528) the winner, while Michael

J. Petch

Josie Conroy with Smokey Duncan (871)

Clancy's Atlantic Peace (7903) won the 7/9 year old class and Kingstown Molly (7604) owned by Malachy Gorham took first place in a big class of senior mares. It was encouraging that all the first prizewinners with one exception were owned and exhibited by residents in Connemara, and all but one have remained in Connemara as breeding mares.

Both the Confined and Supreme Championships were dominated by the two winning three year olds, and on the day the filly Cailin Ciuin (8785) was made the Reserve Champion, and the Jan Harald Koelichen Cup

238

for the Supreme Champion of the Show went to the stallion *Smokey Duncan (871)*. It was a proud moment for Josie Conroy, but one tinged with sadness too, knowing that his old friend Graham Tulloch was not there to share his moment of triumph.

During the afternoon presentations were made in the Showring to the retiring President Mr Donal Kenny, and to Mrs Phil MacDermott, the former Secretary, in recognition of their many years of service to the Society.

This was followed by a parade of the veteran stallion *Little Joe (165)*, who at the age of 27, looked very fit and well and was shown by his owner Sean Stagg. He was the last surviving son of *Carna Dun (89)*, and was bred at Cregg, Oughterard by Jim Walsh from his good mare Cregg Lassie (1737). He had spent his life since he was a foal with the Stagg family at Hollymount, Co. Mayo, and was a regular winner at the pony races as well as being a Grade A Show Jumper. He got a great reception from the crowd, and many would remember Sean riding him at Clifden Races. He lived on for a further five years and died peacefully at home aged thirty-two.

Ruth Rogers

Smokey (1198)
g.g. grand dam of Smokey Duncan (871)

Connemara National Park Ponies

The herd of Connemara ponies now living at the Connemara National Park at Letterfrack was established in 1980 when four of the original mares who were presented to President Childers in 1973 returned to their native Connemara to become the foundation of the herd at the National Park. 83,000 visitors come from all over the world each year to see the Park, and have an opportunity to admire our native breed in their natural surroundings.

In October 1990 the Park was visited by Queen Beatrix of the Netherlands, and having seen the herd of Connemara ponies including the three filly foals born in the Park that year, she gave her permission that they would be named after the last three Dutch Queens, Wilhelmina, Julianna and Beatrix.

Volume XVIII of the Stud Book

A new Stud Book was published in January 1991, and contained details of ponies registered from 1984 to 1988, with a total of 1,046 ponies including 71 stallions, 780 mares and 195 geldings. This book had been compiled by Mrs Phil MacDermott before she left office, but due to lack of funds it had not been published at the appropriate date. This meant that that a further volume needed to be published to bring the records up to date, and this was achieved in October 1991. Volume XVIII contained the new description of the Connemara Pony which had been adopted at the International meeting in 1990.

POINTS OF THE CONNEMARA PONY

Height: The height of a breeding Connemara pony is 133cms to 148cms

Colours: Grey, black, brown, dun, with occasional roan and chestnut, palomino and dark-eyed cream.

Type: Compact, well-balanced riding type with good depth and substance and good heart room, standing on short legs, covering a lot of ground.

DESCRIPTION OF THE CONNEMARA PONY

Head: Well-balanced head of medium length with good width between large kindly eyes. Pony ears, well-defined cheekbone, jaw relatively deep but not coarse.

Front: Head well-set onto neck. Crest should not be over-developed. Neck not set on too low. Good length of rein. Well-defined withers, good sloping shoulders.

Body: Body should be deep, with strong back, some length permissible, but should be well-ribbed up and with strong loins.

Limbs: Good length and strength in forearm, well-defined knees and short cannons, with flat bone measuring 18cms to 21cms. Elbows should be free. Pasterns of medium length, feet well shaped, of medium size, hard and level.

Hind Quarters: Strong and muscular with some length, well-developed second thigh (Gaskin) and strong low-set hocks.

Movement: Movement free easy and true, without undue knee-action, but active and covering the ground.

CHARACTERISTICS

Good temperament, hardiness, staying power, intelligence, soundness, surefootedness, jumping ability, suitable for a child or adult.

The Society owned stallion *Mervyn Kingsmill (762)* was removed from the list at the end of the 1990 season, and was sold to England in the Spring of 1991. Kingsmill had been on the approved stallion list for eight years, spending five years with Mikey King, two with Josie Conroy and his last season with Dudley Nee. During his years in Connemara he had 121 registered progeny, including 14 sons registered as stallions, and 79 daughters. He won the Confined Stallion Class five times, and was consistently in the first three in the Open Class, winning it in 1985.

His attractive progeny were frequent prizewinners in the eighties, and his lovely daughter Maureen's Cuckoo (8799) was Supreme Champion of the Show in 1989. Other successful daughters include, Shining Flame (8298), Village Colleen (8308), Heather Cuckoo (8509), Hillside Star (8525) Jennifer Rose (8528), Dooneen Castle (8648), Castle Dame (8640), Moy Dawn (8934), April Dolly (9538).

His son *Village Boy (927)* was bought by the Society and joined the approved list in 1992, and *Streamstown Larry (930), Matchmakers Lad (937), Murvey Mario (943), Ard ri Cunga (946)* and *Windy's Boy (993)* are among his fourteen registered sons.

Colt Inspection Centres – Blood-typing

The Inspection Committee decided that from 1991 the colt inspections would take place at Riding Centres and at the Clifden Showgrounds, and blood-typing was to be introduced for all foals born in 1991 and their dams.

New Incentive Schemes

In January 1991 the Minister of Agriculture announced a new grant-aided incentive scheme for the Connemara pony, which it was hoped would encourage breeders to keep their young mares.

It consisted of two parts:

(1) For foals born in 1991/1992/1993, who would qualify, on registration, for a grant of £150.

(2) A young brood mare scheme in which a Connemara mare aged 4,5,or 6 years would receive a grant of £500, (or £400 in non-disadvantaged areas) on registration of her first foal in the years 1991, 1992 and 1993.

Other incentive schemes were also announced with grant-aid available for stabling fencing etc, and the purchase of stallions with certain conditions. This package was announced at the AGM in March, and although it was generally welcomed, some fears were expressed that it would lead to a large increase in the number of foals being bred, and there might not be a market for them.

In February 1991 Mr Donal Kenny, former President of the Society resigned from the Council, and also as Chairman of the International Rules Committee. He had been Chairman of the International Rules Committee since it was formed in 1988, and had put a great deal of time and effort into the drafting of the rules. His able and courteous chairmanship of the International meetings would be missed by all those who had worked with him on the harmonisation of the rules during the previous three years.

Johnny Lee died suddenly and unexpectedly in March 1991, and the news of his death came as a great shock to his family and many friends in Connemara. He had been involved in ponies all his life, and was a keen breeder and exhibitor for many years. He had a great knowledge of the breed, and ponies carrying the Moy prefix were exported all over the world by the Lee family. Johnny Lee succeeded his late father Jim as a member of Council in 1984, and was made a member of the Inspection Committee in 1988. He was an active member of the Council, and had made a considerable contribution to the work of the Society over the years. His home-bred stallion *Moy Hazy Cove (888)* sire Hazy Dawn (849), dam Windy Cove (2870), was the third generation of a line of stallions he had bred, descending from *Tully Grey (110)*, and following Johnny's death, Moy Hazy Cove *(888)* was included on the Society's list, and became the new representative of the Green Line but this time through *Tully Grey (110)* instead of *Thunder (113)*.

There were just five stallions on the approved list for 1991, *Abbeyleix Owen (496)*, *Ashfield Festy (859)*, *Seafield Silver Rogue (823)*, *Smokey Duncan (871)* and *Moy Hazy Cove (888)*, and for the first time there was no representative of the Blue Line since *Murphy Rebel (696)* had been sold.

Moy Hazy Cove (888)

AGM 24th March 1991

During the year many new members had joined the Society, and over 130 members attended the AGM on 24th March. Four Council members retired at the meeting, and the two members elected at the AGM by the members were Mrs Jane Dalrymple and Mr Joe Gorham. At a subsequent Council meeting in April, Mr Michael Lee was appointed to take his brother's place on the Council, and Ms Siobhan Brooks-Naughton, Willie Diamond, John Luskin, James Canavan and Joseph O'Neill were appointed to fill the remaining vacancies.

The Annual Inspections were held in Connemara in May 1991, but the tour was reduced from three days to two, and the colts were inspected at Clifden Showgrounds instead of at Maam Cross. For the first time all the markings were taken by a veterinary surgeon who travelled with the inspection team, and this step together with the blood-typing of all ponies was aimed at tightening up the Society's registration procedure.

Book Launch

On the evening of 15th May 1991 following the second day of the inspection tour in Connemara, the Society hosted a launching party for a new book by Miss Pat Lyne at the Alcock and Brown Hotel. It was an enjoyable evening with more than 100 members and breeders present.

The new Book "Out of the Mist", written as a sequel to Pat Lyne's successful first book on the Connemara pony "Shrouded in Mist", studies of the development of Connemara ponies in the fifteen other countries to which they had been exported. In this book Pat Lyne traces the links between the ponies' roots in Connemara and the new lands to which they travelled, and follows the progress of the ponies in the many different countries and climates where the breed is now established. "Out of the Mist," as well as being a delightful study of Connemara ponies and their many new owners worldwide, has also become a valued book of reference.

The Connemara Pony Quadrille

The Connemara Pony Quadrille continued to give performances at a number of shows during 1991 and were well received wherever they went. The group had further training courses during the winter with Miss Iris Kellett, and they gave a very polished display at Galway County Show, Kildalton Agricultural College, National Show Jumping Championships, Salthill, RDS Horse Show, and finally at the Annual Connemara Pony Show at Clifden. The breed gained excellent publicity through these performances, and great credit was due to the riders and their parents, their trainers and sponsors, and Eugenia Murray who made the arrangements on behalf of the Connemara Pony Breeders' Society.

Connemara Pony Display in Paris

The Connemara Pony received further publicity later in the year when a group of six ponies and their riders, aged from eight to eighteen, were invited to give a display at the Salon du Cheval in Paris in December 1991. The ponies were shown in-hand, show jumping and ridden side-saddle, and the display really caught the imagination of the packed audiences in Paris, particularly the side-saddle demonstration. Comdt. Ronnie MacMahon acted as Chef d'Equipe, and the trip was organised by Eugenia Murray, while Lady Maria Levinge and Mrs Phyllida Collier were responsible for preparing and running the Society's Stand. The trip to Paris was a memorable one for all those who took part, and was also a unique opportunity to promote the Connemara Pony.

International Rules Meeting

An International Meeting was held in Clifden on the eve of the Annual Show, and delegates from England, France, Germany, Holland, Italy, Finland, Austria, Sweden, New Zealand, United States, Australia met the representatives from the Parent Society. The final draft of the International Rules which had been worked on since 1988, was ratified at this meeting, and the rules were subsequently approved at a Council meeting and circulated to all the overseas societies.

68th Annual Pony Show, Clifden – 15th August 1991

The Clifden Show had a record entry of 425 ponies, and for the second year the weather was kind and there was a large attendance. The judges were Miss Eileen Parkhill MRCVS, Mr Jimmy Canavan, and Mr Michael Higgins, who had a very long day in the ring with so many ponies entered.

A Junior Championship, for the best one, two or three year old pony in the Show was introduced for the first time, and the Lee Memorial Trophy was won convincingly by the winning 2 year old colt, *Rocky (914)* by Cuchulainn (789) dam Silver Fort (7281). He was owned and bred by Joe Gorham, who also bred the champion colt foal from the same mare, but his sire was *Moy Hazy Cove (888)*. The Stallion class had twenty eight entries and was won by Tulira *Finn MacCool (715)* by Tulira Mairtin (214), shown looking really well by his owner Murty McGrath.

In an interval following the stallion class, the Connemara Pony Quadrille gave a delightful performance, which was much

Jo Jo Gorham with Rocky (914)

243

appreciated by the big attendance. The mares classes were all strongly contested, with John McLoughlin's Milford Wren (8067) winning the seven to nine year old class, and the senior mares class which was biggest class of the day with forty entries was won by Finisglen Belle (7700) for Sean Keane of Moycullen.

However, the Championship was dominated by the stallions, and the Supreme Championship of the Show went to the two year old colt *Rocky (914)* who was outstanding on the day, and the Reserve Champion was the winning stallion *Tulira Finn MacCool (715)*.

Tulira Finn MacCool (715)

Volume XIX of the Stud Book
Another volume of the Stud Book was published in October 1991 which was the second volume to be published in one year. This new volume brought the registrations up to date and covered the period from 1989 to 1991 with a total of 857 ponies registered including 59 stallions, 598 mares and 200 geldings. The publishing of this volume would not have been possible without the financial support of the Department of Agriculture, Udaras na Gaeltachta and funds raised by members of the Society. A noticeable feature of Volume XIX was that many more of the stallions listed were registered for new owners in Ireland, and the breeding of Connemara ponies had now extended throughout the whole of Ireland from North to South.

Clifden Mart Sale
For the first time in 1991 a catalogue sale of Connemara ponies was held at Clifden Mart on the October Bank Holiday Monday, the same weekend that the traditional Maam Cross Foal Fair has been held for generations. The new move to selling by auction was viewed cautiously at first, but since then the number of Sales has increased, and the Sales at the Clifden Mart have now become an accepted part of the Connemara year with a Sale held the day following Clifden Show, a Spring Sale and the October Sale has now become a three day Sale. The Fair at Maam Cross survives, and long may this traditional old fair continue, although now with the huge increase in traffic, it has become a more hazardous way to sell foals than in days long ago.

First Stallion Performance Testing Scheme
Performance testing for Connemara pony stallions was introduced for the first time in January 1992 when a group of eight stallions were selected by the inspection team to undergo twelve weeks training at a centre where they would be assessed on their conformation,temperament, soundness, ease of riding and athletic ability. The trainer chosen for this scheme was Mr Philip Scott, a well-known producer of high quality show horses, and the eight selected stallions spent twelve weeks at his yard at Ballina. During the programme they were assessed at intervals by Mr Jack Doyle and Comdt. Ronnie MacMahon, and at the end of the course there

was a performance day when the stallions were all ridden and jumped before an interested audience of owners and breeders. The scheme was made possible by the financial assistance from the Department of Agriculture and EC funding, and it proved so successful, that it was planned to hold another course later in the year.

Two Council Members retired at the AGM in March 1992, they were Lady Maria Levinge and Mr Johnny Brennan, who had both joined the Council in 1988. Lady Maria Levinge started breeding Connemara ponies in the early sixties and her Grange ponies have been exported all over the world. She is well-known as a judge both at home and overseas, and has always given her time unstintingly to the work of the Society.

Lady Maria Levinge

Johnny Brennan succeeded his late father, John Brennan as a member of Council, and since 1979 he had acted as a ring steward at the Clifden Show.

Mr Pat Mulrooney and Mrs Phyllida Collier were elected to the Council by the members at the AGM and Mr Henry Whyte Jnr. and Mr Jimmy Jones were appointed at the next Council meeting. Membership of the Society was increasing steadily, and forty new members joined the Society in March 1992.

Two new stallions were included on the stallion list for Connemara in 1992. *Village Boy (927)*, a 3 year old son of Mervyn Kingsmill (762), dam Village Grey (6951) bred by Paddy King was placed with Joe Gorham, Clifden, and *Matchmaker's Lad (937)*, a 2 year old grey also by Mervyn Kingsmill (762) dam Foreglass Matchmaker (6897), bred by Mark Conroy, Ballyconneely, who was bought as a foal by the Society, joined *Ashfield Festy (859)* to stand with Tommy O'Brien. The 21 year old *Abbeyleix Owen (496)* remained with Jimmy Canavan at Moycullen, *Seafield Silver Rogue (826)* with Bartley O'Malley *Smokey Duncan (871)* with Josie Conroy and *Moy Hazy Cove (888)* with Dudley Nee, Camus.

Stallion Parade at Kill

A group of breeders in Leinster, led by Miss Maureen Goodbody, Mrs Phyllida Collier and Mrs Jane Dalrymple, organised a successful Stallion Parade at Kill on 12th April 1992, when 23 stallions took part in an exhibition of Connemara Pony Stallions, and it was interesting to see their progeny groups who were shown with their sires. There was a large attendance of breeders, and a commentary was given on each pony in the parade. The stallions were very well presented and were a credit to their owners, and the parade was led by two sons and three grandsons of *Carna Bobby (79)*. Three stallions owned by the Society took part in the exhibition, with **Abbeyleix Owen (496)** representing the Red Line, *Smokey Duncan (871)* the Orange Line and *Village Boy (928)* the Blue Line.

The Connemara Pony Breeders' Society had a stand at the Spring Show for the first time in 1992 which was set up by Mrs Joan Hawkins, and manned by a number of members of the Society, and it attracted a lot of favourable comment. Because of its success, the Council decided to take a stand at the RDS Horse Show, which was again manned by members of the Society, and the stand has become a regular feature at the RDS Show.

The Annual Inspections were carried out during April and May and there was an extensive tour from North to South. Colts were inspected at Kill, Claregalway and Clifden and there was also an appeal day for colts held in July. A total of 29 colts were passed with 246 fillies and 72 geldings.

During 1992 four well-known ponies, all of them Clifden Champions, came to the end of their days. The oldest of them was 27 year old Dun Sparrow (3025) by Carna Dun (89) who was Champion at Clifden in 1972, and a much loved foundation mare for Maria Levinge. Padraig Hynes had his first big success with Rambling Home (3383) by Carna Bobby (79),when she was Champion in 1975, but sadly she had to be put down aged 26, and later in the year Eddie Madden's three times Clifden Champion, Gloves Misty (6535) died aged eighteen. Finally, the Society-owned, 1984 Clifden Champion, *Killyreagh Kim (308)*, who had contributed so much to the breed, was put down at the age of twenty-five.

Breeders Group

Donegal breeders were the first to bring Connemara ponies to Clifden Show from outside the district when in 1948 Kevin McLoughlin, Portnoo brought his 3 year old colt for registration and showed two mares, and Mrs Yseult Cochrane, Stranorlar won the Killanin Cup and RDS Medal with her mare Solus na Bhflaitheas (1090). Since those early days there have been many other breeders in Donegal, among them the late John McCaffery, Dr George Luke, and Kieran Guinness. By 1992 there were some thirty breeders in the County, and they became the first to form their own marketing group, known as Connemara Pony Breeders (Donegal), which has the support of the Connemara Pony Breeders' Society, and has its own sales list. Clive Evans, Bruckless, acts as co-ordinator for the group, and although its principal aim is to market stock, the group also serves as a focus of interest for breeding in the area.

The group had 22 fillies for registration in 1992, and at the end of the season, the Society's stallion *Seafield Silver Rogue (823)* was bought by a Donegal breeder, Mr Joe McGlinchey, Stranorlar. Joe set about training Silver Rogue to harness, who took to his new task well, and is shown all decked out for a wedding!

Seafield Silver Rogue (823) with Joe McGlinchey.

The RDS Horse show included a stallion class for the first time which was won by Sean Dunne's *Abbeyleix Fionn (810),* and he was reserve to the Champion, Bobby Bolger's Coral Misty (8642) who was the winner of the senior mare's class.

69th Annual Pony Show, Clifden – 20th August 1992

Although the morning was wet, the weather improved by the afternoon, and a very large crowd gathered to watch the stallions being judged. There were 402 entries in the pony classes, and despite the large entry, the judges Mrs Judy MacMahon and Mr Sean Stagg managed to complete the judging by 6. 30pm.

The Junior Champion was the winner of the 2 and 3 year old colt class, *Little Rascal (931)* by Seafield Silver Rogue (823) dam Trabane Castle (5959), a three year old grey shown by Thomas Keaney, he was smaller than many in his class, but a real pony type. The Stallion class was won by the five year old *Ard Conneely (898),* a grandson of Bridge Boy (124) who was bred and exhibited by Heather Wright and her mother Mrs Margo Dean. His sire Ard Bridge Time (277) and his dam Ard Khana (6262), were

Ard Conneely (898) Supreme Champion

both bred by the owners, and *Ard Conneely* was beautifully produced by Heather and gave a lovely show. Through his dam *Ard Conneely (898)* traces back to Lor Ruadh (1715) bred by Thomas Keaney, Murvey, who kept the same line of breeding since Silver Spray (328).

The five and six year old mares class was strongly contested, and the winner was Peter Molloy's Dooneen Castle (8648), with Josie Joyce's Cailin Ciuin (8785) second. Padraig Hynes won the 7/9 year old class with Sliabh na mBan Cailin (8500), by Abbeyleix Owen (496) and she went on to win the Confined Championship, with Dooneen Castle in Reserve. The Supreme Champion of the Show was the stallion *Ard Conneely (898)* with Sliabh na mBan Cailin (8500) the Reserve Champion. Both ponies were most beautifully presented and were outstanding on the day. During the afternoon the Society's 21 year old stallion *Abbeyleix Owen (496)* was paraded by Jimmy Canavan, looking extremely well, he was placed third in the stallion class, and also had two cup winners and the Confined Champion among his progeny at the Show.

Sliabh na mBan Cailin (8500) Reserve

247

Two stallions left the stallion list for Connemara after the 1992 season, and the first was *Seafield Silver Rogue (823)* was sold to Mr Joe McGlinchey in Donegal, and the second was *Ashfield Festy (859)*, who had been leased to the Society for four seasons, and was taken back by his owner Jimmy Jones.

For almost thirty years Jimmy Jones has been one of the most dedicated members of the Society, and has worked tirelessly for the Council as an inspector, a judge and a loyal supporter of the Connemara pony. His great knowledge of the pedigrees of the ponies is the result of many years of studying the breed, and his contribution to the work of the Society has been exceptional. His Ashfield Stud has produced many good ponies who have made their way to many countries overseas, and *Ashfield Sparrow (583)* and *Ormond Oliver (653)* still run with their mares on the hill above Carlow. Several of the Society's stallions have spent their retirement in Carlow, and Jimmy has also leased some of his own stallions to the Society. When *Ashfield Festy* left Connemara, he embarked on a new career as a successful show jumper, and he is also siring good performance ponies.

The Second Stallion Performance Testing Programme

The second test commenced on 28th November 1992, and a further ten stallions, aged between three and six years, were selected to take part in the twelve week training programme which again was held at Philip Scott's yard at Ballina. The course was completed on 21st February 1993, and the stallions were assessed during the course and at the end of the twelve weeks by Mr Jack Doyle and Comdt. Ronnie MacMahon. All the stallions were beautifully turned out for the final day when they were ridden and jumped, and the stallion who gained the most marks from this group was Mrs Mary Rabbitt's *Monaghanstown Fred (922)*, who Philip Scott described as a good balanced ride, and a potential all-rounder.

In January 1993, the Connemara Pony received some very good publicity in a four page article about the breed which appeared in Cara, the in-flight magazine for Aer Lingus. The article was written by Anna Mundow who attended the 1992 Clifden Show, and she was assisted in her research for the article by Mrs Bay Goodwin who collected material from other breeders. Some lovely photographs were included in the article which were taken at the Show, and there was also a photo of a Connemara pony on the cover of the magazine.

The Connemara Pony Breeders' Society lost another good and valued friend in early February with the sudden death of John Moore, and he would be sadly missed, especially at Clifden Show where for many years his familiar voice was known to thousands through his job as the Show Commentator. He was also a judge for the breed, and on several occasions managed to step down from his commentary box during the lunch interval to judge the riding classes at Clifden. He had many interests, and had the distinction of being Chairman of the SJAI in the year the Irish Team won the Aga Khan Trophy outright. He was also President of the Irish Rugby Union in its Triple Crown year, and shortly before his death, he was proud to see his son David celebrate 21 years with the Rockmount Riding Centre.

AGM 21st March 1993

More than 140 members attended the AGM held on 21st March 1993, and there was a lively debate when it was announced that the Council proposed to raise the age of colts being presented for inspection from 2 years to 3 years in 1994. While the majority of members present were in favour of the change, there were some who felt the decision should not have been taken without the views of the members being heard. The two members who were elected to the Council at the AGM were the out-going Council members Mrs Nicola Musgrave and Mr John Enda Feeney. At a subsequent meeting of the Council, Mrs Joan Hawkins and Miss Emer Murphy, Dublin, were appointed to the remaining places.

Inspections in 1993

During April and May, 104 colts were presented for registration at the colt inspections which were held three centres, Kill, Claregalway and Clifden. Many of the colts presented did not reach the high standard required by the inspection committee, and only seven colts were accepted for registration. The number of ponies presented in the South Connemara area was noticeably down when the inspection tour of Connemara was held in May, and 290 ponies were registered throughout Ireland, 7 colts, 205 fillies and 78 geldings. All the two year olds presented for inspection in 1993 had been blood-typed as foals when the scheme was introduced in 1991, and with such a good response by the breeders, it was hoped that in one or two more years a fully blood-typed breeding herd of Connemara ponies would be established. The Connemara Pony Breeders' Society was the first to introduce blood-typing for all pure-bred stock prior to registration, and the scheme was the most comprehensive in the country outside the Thoroughbred sector.

The O'Malley brothers Bartley and Thomas have been great supporters of the Society over the years, and since 1979 they have held a stallion for the Society. The first stallion was *Abbeyleix Owen (496)* who spent four seasons in Carraroe. *Maam Hill (728)* joined them in 1983, and *Loobeen Larry (670)* spent two years there followed by *Seafield Silver Rogue (823)* from 1988 to 1992.

In 1993 the Society's 3 year old stallion *Moy Johnny's Pride (938)* by The Kid (877) dam Castle Park (7838) was placed with Bartley O'Malley and has remained with him. The other four Society stallions on the list in 1993 were *Abbeyleix Owen (496)*, *Smokey Duncan (871)*, *Moy Hazy Cove (888)* and *Village Boy (927)*, and these five stallions have remained on the list of stallions standing in Connemara for the Society.

J. Petch

Bartley O'Malley with Moy Johnny's Pride (938)

70th Annual Pony Show, Clifden – 19th August 1993

The Clifden Show was the highlight of the year in which the Society celebrated the 70th Anniversary of its foundation, with 370 entries in the pony section. There was a large number of overseas visitors including a party of fifty French breeders, and the judges were Countess Merveldt and Mr Michael Casey. The yearling filly class was won by an attractive daughter of Callowfeenish Mairtin (846) d. Village Colleen (8308), owned and bred by Padraig Hynes, and she became the Junior Champion, with Val Noone's winning two year old filly, Crusheen Connie (9660), s. Corbally Con (613) d. Nansin Bhan 2nd (7822) the Reserve. A strong three year old class was won by Noel Sweeney, Bunowen with Irishtown Beauty (9447), and the Archbishop's Cup went to Thomas Mullen, Moyard with his four year old Over the Hill (9286).

The foals were judged during the lunch break by Mrs Phyllida Collier and Mr Sean Feeney, and the winning filly was bred by Joe Gorham out of his winning 5/6 year old mare, Kingstown Silver (9033), while John McLoughlin's Milford Wren (8062), who was the winner of the senior mares class, also produced the winning colt foal. Henry O'Toole won the 7/9 year old class with Castle Dame (8640), and the winner of the Stallion Class was Bobby Bolger's *Coral Prince (934)*, a four year old son of Murphy Rebel (696), d. Snowdrop's Surprise (5674) who showed great presence in the ring, and moved very well. The Championships were not judged until late in the evening, and by then the rain was pouring down which rather marred the end of the Show. Bobby Bolger's stallion *Coral Prince (934)* won the Confined Championship and went on to become the Supreme Champion of the Show, with Padraig Hynes' yearling filly and Junior Champion taking the Reserve.

The ridden classes were judged by Lady Maria Levinge and the Champion Ridden Pony was Bunowen Mist (9452), owned by Oliver Roche, Co. Wicklow.

Milleder Archive

Bobby Bolger with Coral Prince (934) Supreme Champion

International Societies Meeting

The Meeting of the International Societies took place the day after the Clifden Show on Friday 20th August and thirteen countries were represented. In the morning there was a display and commentary on a number of Connemara ponies in the Showgrounds, when the ponies were assessed by some of the Irish judges. The delegates then adjourned to the Abbeyglen Castle Hotel where the reports from each Society were presented.

70th Anniversary of the Connemara Pony Breeders' Society – 12th December 1993

The Connemara Pony breeders' Society celebrated its 70th Birthday with a large gathering of members and friends who came to a special meeting in the Corrib Hotel at Oughterard, just seventy years after the first inaugural meeting, to mark the occasion and to honour the men who founded the Connemara Pony Breeders' Society on 12th December 1923.

Among the two hundred people present were two former Presidents of the Society, Lord Killanin and Mr Donal Kenny, and the first Joint-Secretaries of the Society, were represented by their sons Mr Frank O'Malley and Mr Tadhg O'Sullivan, who both spoke about their fathers' work for the Society. Mr Michael D. Higgins TD. Minister for Arts, Culture and the Gaeltacht, made an amusing speech, and was one of fifteen speakers on the platform. Lord Killanin spoke of his memories of the earlier days of the Society, and Bobby Bolger spoke on behalf of the breeders. Bobby's great-uncle William Roe was a member of the First Council, and his father Jack Bolger first stood a stallion for the Society in 1932.

Josie Conroy kept everyone amused as he recalled the day when as a small boy aged six he saw his father riding up the lane to their house on the first stallion to stand at Bunowen, he was *Adventure (11)* and the year was 1937. A Society stallion had been held by the Conroys every year since then, first with his father Michael, and then with Josie since he took over in 1963.

There were many other speakers, all representing organisations who have given support to the Connemara Pony Breeders' Society over the years, and in their speeches they paid tribute to the men whose vision and determination had founded the Society in 1923, and congratulated the Connemara Pony Breeders' Society for what had been achieved over seventy years.

It was a delightful occasion and a unique gathering of the many people who this remarkable pony has linked together in friendship, and the celebrations were made even more special by the delicious birthday cake made by Mrs Stephanie Brooks and shared by everyone at the birthday tea provided by the Lady members of the Council.

A special brooch was also made to mark the 70th Anniversary, which bore the Society Logo on a green enamel ground.

Michael Connaughton

The Birthday Cake.

251

Speakers at 70th Anniversary Celebrations
Seated: Sean O'Neachtain, Lord Killanin, Michael D. Higgins TD, Eamonn Hannan, Donal Kenny, Roderic Kelly MRCVS.
Standing: Bobby Bolger, Frank O'Malley, Patsy Geraghty, Dr Austin Mescall, Henry Tierney, Dermot Power, Elizabeth Petch, Ado Kenny, Tadhg O'Sullivan.

CHAPTER 16

1994-1998

• 3rd Stallion Performance Test • Computerisation • Death T. J. McDonagh • Pony Club Award •
• New Vice President • 4th Stallion Performance Test • Volume XX of the Stud Book • New Brochure •
• Quality Broodmare Scheme • 5th Stallion Test • Death of Canon Moran • 6th Stallion Test •
• Judges Training • President Retires • New President Elected • 75 Years •

Another group of ten stallions aged between four and six years were selected to take part in the ten week training programme from 16th October 1993 to 8th January 1994, and again the programme was held at Philip Scott's yard. The stallion who gained the most marks in the third programme was *Templebready Fear Bui (880)*, owned by Dan O'Brien, Dripsey, and bred by Mrs Carole Seigne in Co. Cork. The three stallion performance tests had been made possible by the financial support received from the EC fund, and twenty-eight stallions had now benefited from this worthwhile training scheme.

AGM 13th March 1994

There were several changes in the Council in 1994, with Mr J. J. Gorham being appointed as Treasurer to replace Mr John M. Mannion, and Mrs Jane Dalrymple retired and did not seek re-election. Mr Bobby Bolger was elected to the Council for the first time at the AGM and Mr Joe Gorham was re-elected. At a Council meeting following the AGM both Mr P. O'Scannail MRCVS and Miss Eugenia Murray were re-elected.

Annual Inspections

The grants for foals introduced in 1991 as an incentive scheme for breeders, ceased in December 1993, and as a result of the scheme, there had been a significant increase in the number of foals born in each successive year, from 498 foals in 1991 to 901 in 1994. One of the main purposes of the scheme was to try to increase the number of mares being kept and bred in Connemara, and while there had been a slight rise in the number of foals born in Connemara, the majority of the breeding mares were in fact outside the district. This was the first year that colts had to be a minimum of three years of age before being presented for registration, and in all 10 colts were passed. 288 fillies and 117 geldings were also registered making a total of 415 ponies which was a big increase compared with 290 ponies passed in 1993. The Inspection tour in Connemara was held on 10th and 11th May and several visitors from England, USA and France came to see the inspection team at work.

During May, Pat Lyne travelled on a extensive tour of Ireland to launch "Reflections Through the Mist," her third book about Connemara ponies. This latest volume was written as a sequel to her two earlier books, and in it Pat shares her memories of her thirty year association with Connemara, its people and its ponies. It reviews the thirty years from 1963, and contains colourful portraits of many of those who have contributed to the remarkable progress of the Connemara pony. The new book, which completed the Trilogy, was well received by the many breeders and friends who met Pat along her journey, and her reflections have given much pleasure to breeders from all over the world who share her love of the Connemara pony.

Computerisation

The computerisation of the office began in May 1994, and the systems analysis, which was carried out by two graduates from University College Galway, was completed in October 1994. Then the big task of inputting all the office records since 1923 began, and continued into 1995, when the next volume of the Stud Book was compiled with the aid of the new computer. It was a sign of the improved financial state of the Society, compared to sixty years earlier when the Council did not have sufficient funds to supply the Secretary Bartley O'Sullivan with a typewriter, and suggested that he might look out for a secondhand one!

The Annual Pre-Show Reception was held on the eve of the Show in the Clifden Bay Hotel, and as usual it was sponsored by the Clifden Community. Owners and breeders were joined by many overseas visitors who were in Clifden for the Show and for the annual meeting of the International Pony Societies which took place the day after the Show. During the evening a presentation was made to Dr Austin Mescal to mark his retirement as Chief Inspector of the Department of Agriculture. For many years Dr Mescal had been closely associated with the Connemara Pony Breeders' Society, and had given the Society much support over the years.

71st Annual Pony Show, Clifden – 18th August 1994

Show day dawned grey and wet, and the youngstock classes were judged in the rain in very slippery conditions. The judges were Mr Jimmy Jones and Mr P. J. Foy with Mr Bob Blackburn the visiting judge, and there were 400 entries. Peter Molloy's quality dun colt s. Streamstown Larry (930) d. Dooneen Star (7871) won the yearling colt class and went on to be the Youngstock Champion, with the winning 3 year old filly Castle Countess (9785) shown by Padraig Hynes in Reserve. In the afternoon the sun came out, and a large crowd

Peter Molloy with Youngstock Champion. Bob Blackburn

254

including many overseas visitors gathered to watch the judging of the stallion class. Every year the stallion class provides the high spot of the Show, and when twenty-three stallions filled the ring the crowd was buzzing with excitement. *Smokey Duncan (871)* was full of high spirits, and was well shown by Josie Conroy to win the class for the second time, with Bobby Bolger's *Coral Star (890)* s. Cuchulainn (789) in 2nd place.

The 5-6 year old mare class went to a very typical mare Queen Gillian (9494) s. Murphy Rebel (696) d. Gillian (8071) also shown by Bobby Bolger, while the consistent winner Cailin Ciuin (8785) owned by Mrs Josie Joyce, won the 7-9 year old mares class. John Joyce won the senior mares class with Heather Cuckoo (8509), and her foal by *Smokey Duncan (871)* was the Champion foal. The Confined Championship and the Clonkeehan Cup went to Queen Gillian (9494) with the stallion *Smokey Duncan (871)* in Reserve, and Queen Gillian (9494) then went on to take the Supreme Championship of the Show, with Cailin Ciuin (8785) the Reserve Champion.

It was a special day for Bobby Bolger, winning the Championship for the second time in two years, as he won it the previous year with his stallion *Coral Prince (934)*, and the cup was presented to him by his father's old friend John O'Mahony Meade who was visiting the Show.

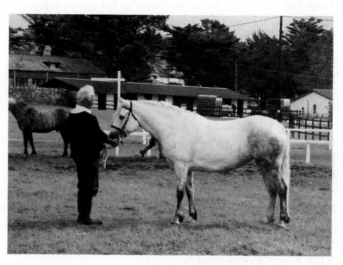

J. Petch

Queen Gillian (9494) Supreme Champion.

Death of T.J. McDonagh

Tommy McDonagh's death on 26th October brought great sadness to his many friends in Connemara, and to the many pony breeders from all over the world who had known him over the years. Tommy was born in 1913 at Derrylea, and was the second of ten children. His father and grand-father both had a great interest in the ponies, and his father Michael was one of the pony men listed in Michael O'Malley's booklet. Tommy inherited this love for the ponies and always ran about twenty on the mountains. When he married his wife Mary, he moved to the island of Inishnee, where she came from, but in 1955 they moved to Roundstone, and his butcher's shop was familiar to everyone who had an interest in the Connemara pony. He held a Society stallion at Derrylea from 1937 to 1943, and in 1940-41 he held the two stallions *Noble Star (17)* and *Clough Con (37)* who he used to travel together leading them from his bicycle.

Tommy MacDonagh

255

Tommy enjoyed showing his ponies and one of his proudest moments was winning the Supreme Championship at Clifden in 1974 with Roundstone River (4746). Many other well-known ponies passed through his hands over the years and found their way to new homes overseas, and he had a deep knowledge of the breed which he was glad to share with others. He became a member of the Council in 1962, and held the office of Vice-President of the Society from 1990 until his death. His last journey from the church to Gurteen cemetery was in a horse-drawn hearse driven by Paddy Geoghegan, with two grey Connemara ponies leading the cortege. Tommy will long be remembered with great affection by all who knew him.

Pony Club Award

In October 1994, Mrs Stephanie Brooks, Errislannon, the District Commissioner of the Connemara Branch of the Pony Club was nominated for the Lady Sylvia Carew Award which is given to those people who have done unstinting voluntary work for the Pony Club over many years. Since the early sixties she had encouraged the children in Connemara to ride and enjoy their ponies, and during that time she taught many of the children in the Clifden area to ride, including several of today's prominent breeders. In 1978 she formed the Connemara Branch of the Pony Club, and she provided her own ponies for rallies for children who did not have their own. The Award was given to ten people in 1994, and Mrs Brooks fully deserved to be among them and to be recognised for her remarkable work for the children in Connemara. Many more riding centres have since been established in Connemara, and another branch of the Pony Club has been formed at Oughterard, proudly called the Cannon Ball Pony Club, but Mrs Brooks was the person who showed the way.

New Vice-President

There were further changes on the Council in 1995, and following the death of Tommy McDonagh, Mr Peadar O'Scannaill MRCVS was elected as a Vice-President of the Society. He had been a member of the Council since 1947, and was the longest serving member of the Inspection Committee. Mrs Phyllida Collier and Mrs Nicola Musgrave both resigned from the Council, and Mr John Luskin, Mr Jimmy Canavan, Mr Michael Lee and Mr John M. Mannion were re-elected. Three new members also joined the Council for the first time, Mrs Mairin Browne, from Co. Cork, Mr Wilson Boyd, Co. Tyrone, and Mr Miceal Higgins, Athenry.

The 1995 Inspections took place during April and May and the tour in Connemara was on 9th and 10th May. There were 22 colts, 323 fillies, 131 geldings registered in the Stud Book as well as 15 entered into the Sports section of the register, and this gave a total of 491 which was the largest number of ponies registered in one year. 964 foals were blood-typed during the year which was another record, but the market had not increased sufficiently to absorb the number of foals now being produced, and this in turn was to lead to lower prices.

72nd Annual Pony Show, Clifden – 17th August 1995

The 1995 Annual Show was the biggest for many years, and was held in brilliant sunshine which brought a very large crowd to enjoy the Show. The judges were Lady Hemphill, Mr John Luskin and Mrs Anne Rolinson, and with an entry of 450 ponies, they had a long hot day in the ring. The two year olds dominated the Junior

Championship which went to the winning two year old colt by Slisneoir (925) dam Gold Label (8863), owned by Patrick Conneely, Ballyconneely, with John Riordan, Donabate, Co. Dublin taking the Reserve with Lishmar Fiona (10124) s. Murphy Rebel (696) d. Moy Dawn (8934). The winner of the Killanin Cup was the three year old Coosheen Breeze (9991) s. Coosheen Finn (381) d. Scarteen Mistral (83535) owned by Ciaran Curran, Moycullen.

Garryhinch Finn (924) s. Abbeyleix Fionn (810) d. Kilbracken Queen (7221) won the stallion class for Seamus O'Neill, Co. Offaly, and was a full brother to two other Clifden prizewinning colts, *Garryhinch Prince (861)* and *Garryhinch Millrace (883)* bred by Sean Dunne. The winner of the 7/9 year old mare class was Coral Misty (8642), who

Killanin Cup Winner, Coosheen Breeze (9991).

went on to become Supreme Champion of the Show. Bred by Pat Mullen, Roundstone, s. Murphy's Rebel (696) d. Gurteen Misty (8085), her grand-dam was the former three times champion Gloves Misty (6535), and she was shown by her owner Bobby Bolger. This win was a unique achievement for Bobby Bolger, who had taken the Jan Harald Koelichen Cup for the third time in a row with three different ponies, and it was also a hat trick for *Murphy Rebel (696)* who was the sire of all three ponies. The winning two year old colt and Junior Champion was the Reserve Champion of the Show. The Champion Ridden Pony was Canrower Liath (G1524) owned by Deirdre Geoghegan, Oughterard. On Show night the

Coral Misty (8642) Supreme Champion

first "Annual Showdown" was held at the Abbeyglen Hotel when there was an official presentation of the Championship trophies. Music was provided by two bands, and more than three hundred people enjoyed the evening.

Twelve countries were represented at the International meeting which was held the day following the Show at the Abbeyglen Hotel, and a delegate from each country reported on their affairs for the year and the activities relating to the International committee.

Fourth Stallion Performance Test

A fourth group of ten stallions completed their Performance Test in 1995, this group was trained by Padraig Foy at his Equestrian Centre at Drummindoo, Westport, and they had their passing out parade on Sunday 10th December 1995. The stallion who came out of the assessment with the highest points was *Bushmills Coral Blue (977)* owned by Mr Hugh Cochrane, Ballymoney, Co. Antrim. He was a four year old grey stallion by Coral Star (890) dam Misty Glen (8075), and his breeder was Mr Thomas Keaney, Cashel.

Volume XX of the Stud Book

Volume XX of the Stud Book was published in December 1995 and contained particulars of 1654 ponies registered during the four year period from 1992 to 1995, and included 75 stallions, 1136 mares and 443 geldings. Blood-typing for foals had been introduced in 1991, and all registered stallions were already blood-typed, so that all the ponies registered in this volume born from 1991 onwards were blood-typed before inspection.

To conform with the new International Rules, several new sections were included in this Stud Book. For the first time there was an International Section which contained seven entries, one stallion and six mares which were transferred on arrival in Ireland from approved Societies overseas. There were eight entries in the Sports Section for ponies over 148cms at the time of inspection, but whose progeny would be eligible for entry into the main Stud Book if within height at the date of inspection. The final new category was the Sports Register which contained particulars of ponies not deemed suitable for breeding but who were entitled to identity documentation under EC rules for all equines.

AGM 10th March 1996

There were 140 members present at the AGM, and two of the members of Council who retired did not seek re-election, Mr Pat Mulrooney and Mrs Siobhan Brooks-Naughton. Mr Willie Diamond and Mr Michael Higgins were elected to the Council at the meeting, and the remaining places were filled at the next Council meeting by Messrs Joe O'Neill, Frank Joyce, and Padraig Hynes. The Annual subscription for members had remained unchanged since 1986, and it was agreed at the AGM that the subscriptions should be increased from £10 to £15 with effect from January 1997. The draw for a raffle took place during the AGM, and the first prize was a gelding which had been donated to the Society by Mr Seamus O'Neill, Co. Offaly, and the winner was Mrs Kerry King, Ballyconneely.

New Brochure

For several years Siobhan Brooks-Naughton had been the Editor of the Newsletter for the Society, which she had offered to compile and produce on a voluntary basis, and it served as a welcome link between the Council and the members of the Society. She now handed over the newsletter to Ms Emer Murphy who was made the new PRO for the Society. Emer Murphy had also been working on a new colour brochure for the Society which was brought out in April 1996, and was printed in Irish, English French and German. The Society received considerable financial support from the Irish Horse Board for this publication.

Annual Inspections

There was a noticeable increase in the number of registrations since the incentive schemes for breeders were introduced in 1989-1991, which had been aimed at retaining young breeding mares in Ireland, particularly in Connemara. Undoubtedly the scheme had succeeded in increasing the number of breeding stock, but not all the foals produced were of a sufficiently good standard, and now it was necessary for the Society to try to impress on breeders to be more selective, and to breed only from good quality stock, in order to maintain the best attributes of the breed.

The Annual Inspections were held during April and May, and a group of over sixty overseas delegates joined the inspection tour in Connemara, with visitors from USA, Canada and Europe following the route for the two days. A total of 478 ponies were registered throughout Ireland compared with 491 in 1994, and included 9 stallions, 339 mares, and 116 geldings. 5 ponies were entered in the Sports Section, and 9 ponies in the Sports Register.

A meeting of the International Committee for Connemara Pony Societies was held on Friday 17th May to review and amend the International rules, and this was finalised at the second International meeting on Wednesday 14th August 1996.

In July the Chief Veterinary Officers of the European Communities held a Conference in Galway, and while they were in Connemara they were invited to visit the Showgrounds at Clifden where the Society staged a display of Connemara ponies. Stallions, broodmares, youngstock and ridden ponies took part in the display, and a quadrille was performed by members of the Connemara Pony Club, trained by Mrs Brooks, and her daughter Siobhan Brooks-Naughton. The visitors were most impressed with the quality of the breeding stock on display, and also with the age of some of the ponies in the quadrille, with one still performing aged twenty-eight.

73rd Annual Pony Show, Clifden – 15th August 1996

The Show was fortunate this year and the weather remained fine all day which brought out a large crowd, there were 374 entries catalogued although not all were forward on the day. The judges were Mr Joe Gorham and Mr Padraig Hynes, and in the youngstock section the Junior Champion was the winning two year old colt s. Abbeyleix Owen (496) d. Castle Dame (8640) owned and bred by Henry O'Toole, Clifden, with Liam Walsh's yearling filly by Village Boy (927) in Reserve. Winner of the two year old filly class was John Folan, Errislannon with

J. Petch

Village Boy (927)

259

Moorland Trixie (10758) by Westside Mirah (892) d. Easter Trixie (8005), bred by Mrs Brigid Snow, Errislannon.

The stallion class was won by *Village Boy (927)* s. Mervyn Kingsmill (762) d. Village Grey (6951) shown by Tommy O'Brien, and he went on to win the Confined Championship, and was Reserve Champion of the Show. The Supreme Champion of the Show was Cailin Ciuin (8785), Mrs Josie Joyce's golden dun mare s. Abbeyleix Owen (496) d. Wireless Wave (3641), who had already been the Champion at Dublin, and her breeder was Martin Walsh, Carna.

The foal classes were judged during the lunch break, and Ms Tuula Pyoria from Finland was the visiting judge with Mr Jimmy Jones and Mrs Elizabeth Ormsby.

Equestrian Photographic Services

Cailin Ciuin (8785) Supreme Champion.

The Champion foal was a filly by Village King (941) d. Ginger (8481) owned by Sean Conneely, Oughterard, and the Champion Ridden Pony was Killyreagh Mistral (G1359) ridden by Sarah Cahill, Kilmaine, Co. Mayo.

On Show night the Annual Showdown party was held at Foyles Hotel, and the official presentation of the Championship trophies was made to the winning owners.

The winner of the 1996 All Ireland Ridden Connemara Pony Championship at Oughterard for the second year running was the ten year old gelding Doninga Bobby (G1322), s. Ormond Bobby (795) dam Tulira Therese (7811), ridden by 14 year old Jean Santry from Cork. They had a spectacular season, winning 23 championships in the Show ring, and ended the year winning three awards from the Irish Pony Society including the Aran Bobby Cup for the best purebred Connemara pony in the IPS working hunter section.

Quality Broodmare Scheme

The Department of Agriculture had already put in place a Quality Broodmare Scheme for horses, which was being administered by the Irish Horse Board, and in 1996 this scheme was extended to include

Doninga Bobby (G1322)

selected Connemara Pony Mares, and this section would be administered by the Connemara Pony Breeders' Society. The scheme was open to mares aged between six and ten years, and the 100 mares selected for the scheme would each receive £1000 for two live foals over three years, 1997 to 1999. A full veterinary examination was required before applying for the scheme, and each applicant owner was limited to two mares. The scheme was officially announced at the Clifden Show 1996 by the Minister of Agriculture, Food and Forestry, Mr Ivan Yates, and during the autumn the mares were inspected throughout the country at centres by the inspection team. There were 144 applications, and 104 mares were accepted for the scheme. This was a more selective scheme than the previous one when every foal was eligible for a grant without inspection, and it was hoped that better quality foals would result.

The Fifth Stallion Performance Test

A fifth group of twelve Connemara pony stallions was selected on 30th August 1996, once again the trainer was Padraig Foy at Drummindoo Equestrian Centre, Westport, and the course was completed with a demonstration on the final day by all the stallions on Sunday 1st December 1996. The stallions were assessed twice during the course by Ms. Sinead Slattery and Mr Edward Doyle, and after the final assessment, the stallion who gained the highest points was *Gun Smoke (986)*, s. Smokey Duncan (871) d. Brown Lady (7157) owned by Mr Dermot Gordon, Ballina Co. Mayo, and bred by Malachy Sweeney, Ballyconneely. This 4 year old stallion won his class at Clifden as a two year old, and he became the first stallion to complete the performance test whose sire had also been performance tested.

Stallion Custodian Retires

At the end of the 1996 season, Josie Conroy retired after 33 years of service to the Society as a stallion custodian. He and his father, the late Michael Conroy, had given 59 years acting as stallion custodians, and a Society stallion had been standing at the Conroy's home at Bunowen since 1937. *Adventure (11)* was the first of ten stallions to stand at Bunowen when Michael was custodian, and he was followed by *Clough Rebel (33), Keehaune Laddie (52), Gil (43), Clough Droighneann (67), Creganna Winter (63), Innishgoill Laddie (21) Calla Rebel (38), Dun Lorenzo (55)* and *Clonkeehan Auratum (104).*

Josie took over from his father in 1963 and his first stallion was *Carna Dun (89).* He was followed by *Rebel Wind (127), MacDara (91), Toombeola (221), Killyreagh Kim (308), Thundercloud (459), Dun Aengus (120), Abbeyleix Owen (496), Skryne Bright Cloud (622), Ashfield Alex (771).*

At the end of the 1984 season, Josie ceased to travel the stallion on his regular route of Roundstone, Toombeola and Cashel on Wednesdays, and Clifden and Recess on Saturdays, which was the same route his father had travelled since 1937, and in future he travelled the stallion out to mares by arrangement. *Seafield Silver Rogue (823)* came to Josie in 1986, and was followed by *Mervyn Kingsmill (762)* for two seasons. His last stallion was *Smokey Duncan (871)* who came to him in 1990, the year he won the Supreme Championship, and he remained with Josie until 1996 when Josie decided to resign as a custodian. His long service to the Society is remembered with gratitude by breeders, not only in Connemara, but also by his many friends who have known him over the years.

Judges Training
A training course for Junior Judges was held on three consecutive Sundays during January and February 1997. The course was held at Mr John Enda Feeney's Indoor Arena, at Spiddal, and eight Junior Judges took part in the course. There were lectures in the mornings and practical sessions in the afternoons. Mr John Enda Feeney's death after a short illness on 21st February came as a great shock, as he had been enthusiastic in his support of the Junior Judges course held at his yard, and had attended the first session. John Enda Feeney had served as a Council member since 1989, he was an inspector and judge, and had been a member of the Society for many years. He provided his yard as the centre at Spiddal for the Annual Inspections, and he was also a successful breeder using the Aran prefix.

AGM 9th March 1997
A large gathering of over two hundred members attended the AGM on 9th March 1997, and the two Council members elected were Mr Henry Whyte, who was re-elected, and Mr Sean Feeney, Spiddal who was elected to take his father's place on the Council. At the next meeting of the Council Mrs Joan Hawkins was re-elected, and Mr Seamus O'Neill, Co. Offaly was elected to the Council for the first time.

Annual Inspections
New regulations were introduced for the inspections in 1997 with all ponies being marked by each individual inspector, and the average result was sent to the owner by post, with no results being given at the time of inspection. An average mark of 128 was required for a filly or gelding to pass, while stallions needed a pass mark of 155. During the Spring inspections 580 ponies were registered and there was a very large increase in the number of fillies, with 409 accepted for registration. There were 25 stallions passed from the 67 presented, and 135 geldings. 6 ponies were entered in the Sports Section, and 5 in the Sports Register.

The same five stallions remained on the Society's stallion list for Connemara in 1997, with Paddy Folan taking over the care of *Smokey Duncan (871)* at Rosmuck.

Abbeyleix Owen (496) ....aged 26 ....Jimmy Canavan, Moycullen.
Smokey Duncan (871) ....aged 10 ....Paddy Folan, Turlough, Rosmuck.
Moy Hazy Cove (888) ....aged 9 ....Jimmy Canavan, Moycullen.
Village Boy (927) ....aged 8 ....Tommy O'Brien, Canal Stage.
Moy Johnny's Pride (938)..............aged 7 ....Bartley O'Malley, Carraroe.

More than 100 Registered Connemara Pony stallions were also standing throughout Ireland, and a list of these sires was provided by the Society's office.

Death of Canon Moran

The death took place on 5th July 1997 of the Very Reverend Canon Moran, at the age of ninety-two. Canon Willie as he was affectionately known by everyone, was made a Vice-President of the Society in 1953 and he held that office for life. Born in Carna in 1905, he was ordained in Maynooth in 1931, and served in several parishes before being appointed as Parish priest in Rosmuck in 1947. He always had a great love of Connemara and its ponies, and a yearling filly owned by his nephew, Miceal og Morain was one of the early exports to England, who later won many prizes for her new owner, and was named Carna Countess. Canon Willie was a keen sportsman and loved racing and coursing, he was also a fisherman and a supporter of Gaelic football. He became a member of the Council of the Connemara Pony Breeders' Society in 1947, and maintained his interest in the work of the Society all his long life, and his wise counsel was valued by members of the Council.

Very Rev. Canon Moran

ECPS Golden Jubilee

The English Connemara Pony Society celebrated its Golden Jubilee in 1997, having been formed fifty years earlier in 1947 and it was the first Connemara Pony Society to be established outside Ireland.

The Golden Jubilee Two Day Show was held at the Three Counties Showground at Malvern, on 15th and 16th July 1997, and two Irish Judges were invited, Mr Jimmy Canavan for the breeding section, and Lady Maria Levinge as Conformation judge for the Ridden Show. At the Show Dinner held in a marquee in the Showgrounds, Mr Eamonn Hannan presented a Galway Crystal Chalice to the English Connemara Pony Society on behalf of the Connemara Pony Breeders' Society to mark the occasion. Many breeders from other overseas societies also attended the Show which was held on two beautiful sunny days, and the Champion Pony of the Show was Sliabh na mBan Cailin (8500) owned by Mr and Mrs J. Cotterell.

74th Annual Pony Show, Clifden – 21st August 1997

Clifden Show day dawned bright and sunny, and this year a second ring had been made, and the youngstock classes were divided between the two rings. The main ring had three judges, Mrs Birgit Jorgensen from Denmark, Mrs Sarah Miller, and Ms. Emer Murphy, who judged the fillies in the morning, while the colt classes were judged in Ring Two by Mrs Nicola Musgrave, Mr Michael Casey and Mrs Phyllida Collier. The Junior Champion for the second year running was Henry O'Toole's 3 year old colt *Castle Comet (1026)* s. Abbeyleix Owen (496) d. Castle Dame (8640), with Padraig Hynes' two year old filly Bunowen Beauty (10782) s. Abbeyleix Owen (496) d. Irishtown Beauty (9447) in Reserve. The Stallion Class was won by *Garryhinch Finn (974)* s. Abbeyleix Fionn (810) d. Kilbracken Queen (7221), and he went on to be Reserve Champion of the Show, but the Supreme Champion of the Show was the winner of the Senior Mares class, Coral Misty (8642)

*Henry O'Toole with
Castle Comet (1026) Youngstock Champion.*

Padraig Hynes with Bunowen Beauty (10762)

owned by Bobby Bolger and bred by Pat Mullen, Roundstone. This was the second time Coral Misty had been made Champion, and Bobby Bolger's fourth time to win the Supreme Championship in five years. The Champion foal was Joe Cunniffe's colt foal by Moy Hazy Cove (888) dam Lishin Liath (9722), and the Champion Ridden Pony was the stallion *Callowfeenish Buachaill (1002)* also by Moy Hazy Cove (888), owned by Ms Barbara Hoffmann, Ballinafad.

In 1987 Alexander and Clive Evans rode their ponies from Donegal to Clifden to the Show, and ten years later it was their parents Mr and Mrs Clive Evans who drove their stallion *Drumclounish Davog (879)* from their home at Bruckless, Co. Donegal to Clifden, completing the 275km journey in seven days. They were met by members of the Connemara Pony Club when they arrived the evening before the Show, and were escorted into the town of Clifden and did two full circuits before trotting into the Showgrounds. En route they collected over £500 for the Riding for Disabled Association.

Another special feature of the 1997 Show was a presentation made to Mr Peadar O'Scanaill MRCVS to mark his 50 years as a Council member, and the presentation was made by Mr Padraig Flynn, E. U. Commissioner, who was Guest of Honour at the Show.

An interesting link between the first Show at Roundstone in 1924 and the 74th Show at Clifden in 1997 was the winner of the two year old filly class and Reserve Junior Champion. Bunowen Beauty (10782) was bred by Noel Sweeney, Bunowen, Ballyconneely, and won her class at Clifden as a foal in 1995. She has the same name as a mare foaled in 1917, who was registered at the first show at Roundstone in 1924, and was entered as Bunowen Beauty (37) in Volume I of the Stud Book. Bunowen Beauty (37) won the class for non-registered mares at the first Show which had 108 entries, with 90 present on the day, and 15 out of the class were selected for registration. The owner of the first Bunowen Beauty (37) was John Sweeney, Bunowen, Ballyconneely, father of Noel Sweeney, and Tom O'Malley of Ballyconneely can still remember the day that young John Sweeney rode proudly home on his mare having won his class at the first Show at Roundstone. The two ponies are not related, but the owners are, and Noel and Malachy Sweeney carry on their father's love of the ponies today and are enthusiastic breeders.

EGM 16th November 1997

With a greatly increased membership of the Society, there was a growing feeling amongst the members that they should have a greater say in the running of the Society, and pressure was brought to bear on the Council to alter the situation. On 16th November 1997, an EGM was called by 98 members, the meeting was attended by over 300 members of the Society, and many of the members present expressed their views. The two main issues arising from the meeting were that the Memorandum and Articles of Association needed to be reviewed again and the rules for electing members to the Council changed, and the second concerned the Inspections. Both these important issues were subsequently addressed by the Council, a further review of the Memorandum and Articles of Association was initiated, and a new inspection committee was set up under the Chairmanship of Mr Joe Gorham.

Sixth Stallion Performance Test

In September 1997 the sixth group of ten Registered Connemara Pony Stallions was selected to take part in the performance testing programme which was held at Drummindoo Equestrian Centre, Westport, under the trainer Padraig Foy, and the course was completed on 21st December 1997 with the usual passing out parade. The stallion who gained the highest points in the assessment was *Kingstown Boy (1011)* s. Village Boy (927) d. Kingstown Molly (7604) owned by Mr Joe McGlinchey, Stranorlar, Co. Donegal, and he was bred by Joe Gorham, Clifden. Sixty stallions had now completed the performance test which was first introduced in January 1992, and many have gone on to compete regularly in show-jumping and other performance fields.

Custodian for 35 Years

Tommy O'Brien became a stallion custodian in 1963, and the first stallion to stand with him at Canal Stage was *Ben Lettery (133)*, then *Mervyn Storm (140)* and *Ardilaun (261)*, each for three years, *Clonjoy (117)* and *Roundstone Oscar (337)* for one year each, and *Rebel Wind (127)* for three years. He stood *Ormond Oliver (653)* for three years followed by *Maam Hill*

J. Petch

Tommy O'Brien

(728), and then *Killyreagh Kim (308)*, *Abbeyleix Owen (496)*, *Ashfield Festy (859)*, and finally *Village Boy (927)* who has remained at Canal Stage since 1993. Three of the stallions have won the Open Stallion class while in his care, and *Killyreagh Kim (381)* was Supreme Champion in 1984 shown by his daughter Ann. Tommy O'Brien still keeps the stallion *Village Boy (927)*, and in 1998 he will have been a custodian for thirty-five years, which is a fine record in the history of the Society.

Dermot Power Leaves Council

In January 1998 Mr Dermot Power retired from the Council, having served as a member of the Council for twenty years, and as Vice- President of the Society since 1990. Dermot Power came from a farming family near Tramore, Co. Waterford and he first got to know Connemara ponies when he was at school in Dublin, and he used to help Stanislaus Lynch showing his ponies at the Spring Show. In 1972 he came to Galway as an Inspector for the Department of Agriculture, and first visited the Clifden Show that year. In 1978 he was elected a member of the Council and was also appointed a member of the Inspection Committee. He was a Society judge and judged both nationally and internationally. He acted as the chief ring steward at Clifden Show for nineteen years, and as Chairman of the Inspection Committee, he had the unenviable task of informing the owner when a pony failed to pass. He worked on many committees within the Council, including the Inspection

Michael Connaughton
Dermot Power

Committee, the International Committee and the Review Committee, and was the most hardworking member of the Council. Now for the first time since the Society was founded there was no representative of the Department of Agriculture on the Council. At a Council meeting held on 5th February 1998, many tributes were paid to Dermot Power, and he was thanked for all his work on behalf of the Society.

President Retires

At this meeting Mr Eamonn Hannan told the Council that he was retiring as President of the Society. He said he had enjoyed his term of office as President, and thanked the Council and its officers for their help and work over the last eight years. Since he became President in 1990 Eamonn Hannan had achieved many changes in the Society. A much larger membership and increased sponsorship had improved the state of the Society's finances, and State grants had helped to increase the number of breeding ponies. Full blood-typing was introduced in 1991, and the computerisation of the office was completed in 1995. Between January 1992 and December 1997, sixty registered Connemara pony stallions had completed the Stallion Performance Test. Eamonn Hannan had been a most energetic President, and he was thanked by members of the Council for the tremendous work he had done for the Society during his term of office.

Michael Connaughton
Eamonn Hannan

New President and Vice President

Mr John Luskin was then unanimously elected as President of the Connemara Pony Breeders' Society, and he became the ninth person to hold the office since the formation of the Society in 1923.

John Luskin was first elected to the Council in 1976, and became a member of the Stallion Committee in 1984 and the Inspection Committee in 1988. John lives in Cong, Co. Mayo and has a small herd of mares at his Doon Stud. He produced three winning stallions in the seventies, and his latest stallion *Ard Ri Cunga (946)* is now in Finland. He has been a Society judge for many years and has judged at Clifden and Dublin on many occasions as well as overseas.

Mr Willie Diamond was elected as Vice-President and joined Mr Peadar O'Scannaill MRCVS who had already been returned to that office. Willie Diamond

John Luskin

has been involved with ponies all his life, and can remember back to the very early days of the Society when his cousin Michael Diamond first stood the Society stallions at Letterfrack. One of his first mares was Fanny Bunty (635) by Silver Pearl (18) who was great-grand-dam of *Abbeyleix Owen (496)*, and another, Ace of Diamonds (3152), who traces back to May Day (322) by Rebel (7), was the foundation mare of his breeding line. Over the years he has had many successes in the Show ring including *Kimble (227)* who was Supreme Champion at Clifden in 1971. Willie Diamond has been a supporter of the Connemara pony all his life, is a Society Judge, became a member of the Council in 1976, and was made a Vice-President of the Connemara Pony Breeders' Society in its 75th year.

Abbeyleix Own (496), one of the best known stallions in the breed, came from Willie Diamond's breeding. His sire was *Kimble (227)* and his dam Queen of Diamonds (1934) was a Carna Bobby (79) mare who Willie sold to Lady de Vesci. *Abbeyleix Owen* was foaled at Abbeyleix in 1971, and later Lady de Vesci presented him as a gift to the Society. He joined the Society's stallion list in 1975 and was placed with Josie Conroy for his first four seasons in Connemara and stood in all the districts in Connemara before moving to Jimmy Canavan in Moycullen in 1991. *Abbeyleix Owen (496)* had a big influence on the breed in the twenty-two years he was on the Society's stallion list and sired many outstanding ponies including five Dublin or Clifden Champions, Silver Sparrow (6898), Cailin Ciuin (8785). Grey Rock Star (6947), Owen's Lady (8066) and Sliabh na mBan Cailín (8500).

Many of his daughters have become good broodmares, and include Village Grey (6951, Errisbeg Dolly (6940), Miss Logan

J. Petch

Jimmy Canavan with Abbeyleix Owen (496)

(7385), Brown Lady (7157), Castle Park (7385), Grey Molly (8789), Belcarra Rose (8853). Another of his daughters, Amaryllis Cuckoo (9261) owned by Tom McWilliams, Ballyconneely, produced twin foals by Coral Prince (934) in 1995, only the second set of twins found in the records of the Society.

Among his sons are the stallions *Cuchulainn (789)*, *Callowfeenish Martin (846)* and *Cloonisle Cashel (980)*, and his three year old colt *Castle Comet (1026)* was Junior Champion at Clifden in 1996 and 1997. His stock have also been successful in the performance field, and many have gone to new breeders overseas.

Abbeyleix Owen (496) carried the Red Line into the sixth generation from *Connemara Boy (9)*, and on his dam's side he traces back through her sire *Carna Bobby (79)* to the Blue Line and *Rebel (7)*, so that he combines the two earliest blood lines of the breed. He has passed on his strength and substance to his progeny, and as he retires in 1998 aged 27 years he has left a sound base of breeding stock in Connemara.

Seventy-five Years

Many changes have taken place in Connemara since 1923 when the Connemara Pony Breeders' Society was founded. Slowly the mechanisation of rural Ireland reached Connemara, and the tractor and the motor car gradually took over the role of the Connemara pony as a work pony. The pony had to adapt to the change, it found a new role and a new market as a riding pony, with buyers coming from all over the world, and the Connemara pony became an international success as a performance pony. Tourism has brought a new prosperity to Connemara, but with the increased traffic on narrow roads, it is no longer safe for ponies to graze by roadsides unprotected by fences. The stallions now travel by trailer, and the old way of travelling the stallion on his weekly route led from a bicycle belongs to history.

In the past the pony races provided great days out for the enjoyment of all, but the races have gone, and so have the fairs, and Maam Cross remains the only foal fair to have survived the changing times. However the pony still remains central to the way of life of many people in Connemara, and there is a new generation of enthusiastic breeders who travel to a pony show held in some part of Connemara, Galway or Mayo every Sunday from June to September. The shows provide an opportunity for the pony breeders to meet and compete against one another, although the emphasis at these shows is on in-hand showing rather than performance.

The work of the Connemara Pony Breeders' Society has greatly increased over the years, and although its primary function is still to preserve the Connemara pony as a distinct breed, by inspecting all ponies for registration and maintaining the Stud Book, it also has the added responsibility of being the Parent Society to the overseas societies in seventeen different countries worldwide where Connemara ponies are now bred, England, USA, Canada, Denmark, Sweden, Holland, Australia, France, Germany, Finland, New Zealand, Belgium, Austria, Norway, South Africa, Italy, Switzerland. The International Committee of Connemara Pony Societies meets annually at Clifden to review the rules governing the movement of ponies between the Stud Books and the rules and regulations for registration, and to ensure that all the societies have a common breeding policy.

Since 1990 membership of the Society has grown dramatically, and with 900 members and many new breeders from all over Ireland, the Society has become a much larger organisation. The introduction of tighter regulations for the registration of ponies has brought increased pressures on the members of the Inspection

Committee whose services have always been provided voluntarily, and the inspections are now carried out over a three week period each spring throughout the whole of Ireland. The list of Society-owned stallions standing in Connemara has dropped to four in 1998, with many more privately owned stallions in Connemara than during the foundation years of the Society. There are now 250 registered Connemara pony stallions standing throughout Ireland, and although some breeders travel long distances to the stallion of their choice, the Society-owned stallions remain in Connemara to cater for the small breeder who cannot travel his mare, but who is still an essential part of the future of the breed.

75th Anniversary

In 1998 the Connemara Pony Breeders' Society celebrates the 75th anniversary of its foundation, and we can be proud of what has been achieved during those years. In 1923 the Connemara pony was threatened with extinction, but since the Society began its work seventy-five years ago with a grant of £100 from the Department of Agriculture, the Connemara pony has been developed from the hardy working pony renowned for its good temperament, easy paces, stamina and endurance, into the high-class riding pony of today. The aim of the Society was to improve the breed by selecting the best stock from within the breed as the foundation for the Stud Book, and all the ponies being bred today trace back to those early ponies who were selected by the first inspection team. During the early years of the Society one of its greatest strengths was the long years of committed service given by its officers which provided continuity and stability in the formative years. The selection of suitable stock for the foundation of the Stud Book was slow and painstaking work, especially when set against the economic background of the day, and the breeders of today can look back with gratitude to what was achieved by that small group of dedicated men.

Twenty volumes of the Stud Book have been published, and almost 15,000 ponies have been registered, while many more Connemara ponies have gone overseas to become the foundation stock for new breeders in other countries. Today there is a new generation of Connemara pony breeders, and they will have the responsibility of guarding the old blood-lines, and ensuring the future of the breed.

We have been handed down a unique heritage by those who have fostered and developed the breed for the past seventy-five years, and in the introduction to Volume I of the Stud Book, published in 1926, Bartley O'Sullivan wrote these words which are still relevant today.

> "The Society looks to breeders throughout Ireland for support and co-operation. Good foundation stock is available. Careful selection and intelligent breeding are all that are needed to ensure success."

The fame of the Connemara pony has spread far and wide, and it is now established in many different countries, but the pony is essentially a product of its own native environment, and it is for today's breeders, the future custodians of the breed, to ensure that ponies will long continue to be bred and reared under natural conditions in their native Connemara.

BIBLIOGRAPHY AND MAJOR SOURCES

Records of the Connemara Pony Breeders' Society including:
Minute Books, Stallion Records, Annual Reports from 1963, Stud Books Vol I to XX and Show Catalogues.
Records of RDS Show results – RDS Library.

The Ponies of Connemara – Professor J.C. Ewart, 1900

Environment of the Ponies – Professor J.C. Ewart, 1901

Ponies Past and Present – Sir Walter Gilbey, 1900

Connemara – J. Harris Stone MA, 1906

Connemara Ponies – compiled by Michael O'Malley, 1913 (reprinted 1986)

The Connemara Pony – Bartley O'Sullivan, 1939

The Basotho Pony Project – Donal Kenny, 1976

Horse Breeding in Ireland – Colin Lewis, 1980

Shrouded in Mist – Pat Lyne, 1984

Beyond the Twelve Bens – Kathleen Villiers Tuthill, 1986

The Royal Horses of Europe – Sylvia Loch, 1986

A History of British Native Ponies – Anthony Dent and Daphne Machin Goodall, 1988

Out of the Mist – Pat Lyne, 1989

The History of Connemara – Patricia Kilroy, 1989

Reflections Through the Mist – Pat Lyne, 1994

Connemara After the Famine – Thomas Colville Scott, 1995

Letters from the Irish Highlands (reprint) – The Blake Family, 1995

Patient Endurance – Kathleen Villiers Tuthill, 1997

NEWSPAPERS
Connacht Tribune, Irish Independent, Irish Times, Irish Farmers Journal, Irish Field.

THE AUTHOR

Elizabeth Petch was born and educated in Co. Dublin, and she and her husband John farm in Kilbrittain, Co. Cork. She became a member of the Connemara Pony Breeders' Society in 1960 when she started breeding Connemara Ponies, and was made an inspector for the breed in 1972. She served on the Council from 1974 to 1990 and has been a national and international judge for twenty-six years, during which time she has visited ten Connemara Societies overseas.

LIST OF STALLIONS AND CUSTODIANS 1924-1998

Stallions approved for the service of nominated registered mares in Connemara.

(p) = private ownership

1924

1.	Rebel (7)	Gilbert Ryan, Rosshill, Galway (p)
2.	Cannon Ball (1)	Henri Toole, Leam, Oughterard (p)
3.	Gold Digger (5)	George Lyons, Bunakill, Maam Cross
4.	Connemara Dan (3)	Val Keaney, Gowla, Cashel
5.	Mount Gabel (6)	Martin Walsh, Finney, Clonbur (p)

1925

1.	Rebel (7)	Gilbert Ryan, Rosshill, Galway (p)
2.	Cannon Ball (1)	Henry Toole, Leam, Oughterard (p)
3.	Gold Digger (5)	George Lyons, Bunakill, Maam Cross
4.	Connemara Dan (3)	James O'Toole, Faulkeera, Clifden

5.	Mount Gable (6)	Martin Walsh, Finney, Clonbur (p)
6.	Galway Grey (4)	Colman Conneely, Ballinahown, Galway (p)
7.	Charlie (2)	Val Keaney, Gowla, Cashel

1926

1.	Rebel (7)	Gilbert Ryan, Rosshill, Galway (p)
2.	Mount Gable (6)	Martin Walsh, Finney, Clonbur (p)
3.	Galway Grey (4)	Colman Conneely, Ballinahown, Galway (p)
4.	Charlie (2)	Val Keaney, Gowla, Cashel
5.	Black Paddy (8).	Mark Geoghegan, Oughterard
6.	Connemara Boy (9)	Michael O'Neill, Clifden (p)
7.	Gold Digger (5)	George Lyons, Bunakill, Maam Cross

Cannon Ball (1) died March 1926. Connemara Dan (3) castrated and struck off register 1926. Mount Gable (6) died 1926. Galway Grey (4) taken off stallion list 1926 sold later. Rebel (7) bought by CPBS Spring 1927 for £25. Connemara Boy (9) bought by Val Mannion, Toombeola 1926.

1927

1.	Rebel (7)	Mark Geoghegan, Oughterard
2.	Bryan (10)	Owen Naughton, Inverin (p)
3.	Charlie (2)	Val Keaney, Gowla, Cashel
4.	Connemara Boy (9)	Val Mannion, Toombeola (p)
5.	Black Paddy (8)	Michael Diamond, Letterfrack
6.	Gold Digger (5)	George Lyons, Bunakill, Maam Cross

Connemara Boy (9) bought by CPBS Spring 1928 for £25

1928

1.	Rebel (7)	Val Keaney, Gowla, Cashel
2.	Bryan (10)	Owen Naughton, Inverin (p)
3.	Adventure (11)	Mark Geoghegan, Oughterard
4.	Charlie (2)	Ed.Conneely, Glentrasna, Rosmuck
5.	Black Paddy (8)	Michael Diamond, Letterfrack
6.	Connemara Boy (9)	Thomas de Courcey, Roundstone
7.	Gold Digger (5)	George Lyons, Bunakill, Maam Cross

Gold Digger (5) sold at end of 1928 season.

1929

1.	Rebel (7)	Val Keaney, Gowla, Cashel
2.	Bryan (10)	Owen Naughton, Inverin (p)
3.	Adventure (11)	Mark Geoghegan, Oughterard
4.	Charlie (2)	Ed Conneely, Glentrasna, Rosmuck
5.	Black Paddy (8)	Michael Diamond, Letterfrack
6.	Connemara Boy (9)	Thomas de Courcey, Roundstone

1930

1.	Rebel (7)	Val Keaney, Gowla, Cashel
2.	Bryan (10)	Owen Naughton, Inverin (p)
3.	Adventure (11)	Mark Geoghegan, Oughterard
4.	Charlie (2)	Ed.Conneely, Glentrasna, Rosmuck
5.	John Quirke (13)	Michael Diamond, Letterfrack
6.	Connemara Boy (9)	Thomas de Courcey, Roundstone

John Quirke bought from Michael O'Neill May 1930, and Black Paddy sold to Michael O'Neill, later castrated 1930

1931

1.	Rebel (7)	Val Keaney, Gowla, Cashel
2.	Bryan (10)	Owen Naughton, Inverin (p)
3.	Adventure (11)	Mark Geoghegan, Oughterard
4.	Charlie (2)	Ed.Conneely, Glentrasna, Rosmuck
5.	John Quirke (13)	Michael Diamond, Letterfrack
6.	Connemara Boy (9)	Thomas de Courcey, Roundstone
7.	Tommy (14)	Comyn Naughton, Costello (p)

1932

1.	Rebel (7)	Val Keaney, Gowla, Cashel
2.	Bryan (10)	Owen Naughton, Inverin (p)
3.	Charlie (2)	Ed.Conneely, Glentrasna, Rosmuck
4.	John Quirke (13)	Michael Diamond, Letterfrack
5.	Adventure (11)	Thomas de Courcey, Roundstone
6.	Tommy (14)	Comyn Naughton, Costello (p)
7.	Connemara Boy (9)	John Walsh, Kylesalia, Kilkerrin
8.	Noble Star (17)	Jack Bolger, Oughterard
9.	Heather Bell (15)	Michael Nee, Shinninagh, Clifden
10.	Heather Grey (16)	Michael O'Brien, Derrough, Maam Cross (p)

Bryan sold 1932, left Connemara, no registered progeny.

1933

1.	Rebel (7)	Val Keaney, Gowla, Cashel
2.	John Quirke (13)	Ed.Conneely, Glentrasna, Rosmuck
3.	Charlie (2)	Michael Diamond, Letterfrack
4.	Adventure (11)	Thomas de Courcey, Roundstone
5.	Tommy (14)	Comyn Naughton, Costello (p)
6.	Connemara Boy (9)	John Walsh, Kylesalia, Kilkerrin
7.	Noble Star (17)	Jack Bolger, Oughterard
8.	Heather Bell (15)	Festus King, Cushatrough, Clifden
9.	Heather Grey (16)	Michael O'Brien, Finny, Clonbur (p)

1934

1.	Rebel (7)	Val Keaney, Gowla, Cashel
2.	John Quirke (13)	Ed.Conneely, Glentrasna, Rosmuck
3.	Charlie (2)	Michael Diamond, Letterfrack

4. Adventure (11)   Thomas de Courcey, Roundstone
5. Tommy (14)   Comyn Naughton, Costello (p)
6. Connemara Boy (9)   John Walsh, Kylesalia, Kilkerrin
7. Noble Star (17)   Jack Bolger, Oughterard
8. Heather Bell (15)   Festus King, Cushatrough, Clifden
9. Heather Grey (16)   Michael O'Brien, Finny, Clonbur (p)

1935

1. Rebel (7)   Val Keaney, Gowla, Cashel
2. John Quirke (13)   Ed.Conneely, Glentrasna, Rosmuck
3. Charlie (2)   Michael Diamond, Letterfrack
4. Adventure (11)   Thomas de Courcey, Roundstone
5. Tommy (14)   Comyn Naughton, Costello (p)
6. Connemara Boy (9)   John Walsh, Kylesalia, Kilkerrin
7. Noble Star (17)   Jack Bolger, Oughterard
8. Heather Bell (15)   Michael O'Neill, Clifden
9. Silver Pearl (18)   Stephen Walsh, Keelkyle, Letterfrack (p)

Heather Grey sold to Ml.Hennelly, Corrandulla Dec 1934. Tommy sold out of Connemara 1935, 2 registered progeny. Charlie died of colic August 1935, 8 registered progeny

1936

1. Rebel (7)   Val Keaney, Gowla, Cashel
2. John Quirke (13)   Ed.Conneely, Glentrasna, Rosmuck
3. Adventure (11)   Thomas de Courcey, Roundstone
4. Connemara Boy (9)   John Walsh, Kylesalia, Kilkerrin
5. Noble Star (17)   Jack Bolger, Oughterard
6. Heather Bell (15)   Michael O'Neill.Clifden
7. Silver Pearl (18)   Stephen Walsh, Keelkyle, Letterfrack (p)

1937

1. Rebel (7)   Val Keaney, Gowla, Cashel
2. John Quirke (13)   Ed.Conneely, Glentrasna, Rosmuck
3. Adventure (11)   Michael Conroy, Ballyconneely
4. Connemara Boy (9)   John Walsh, Kylesalia, Kilkerrin
5. Noble Star (17)   Jack Bolger, Oughterard
6. Heather Bell (15)   Michael O'Neill, Clifden
7. Silver Pearl (18)   Stephen Walsh, Keelkyle, Letterfrack (p)
8. Innishgoill Hero (19) Thomas McDonagh, Derrylea, Clifden
9. Innishgoill Star (20) Michael Diamond, Letterfrack

10. Innishgoill Laddie (21)   Jack Bolger, Oughterard
Innishgoill Hero sold spring 1938. Rebel put down May 1938, heart and lungs destroyed aged 16, 10 years on CPBS list.

1938

1. Heather Bell (15)   Ed.Conneely, Glentrasna,Rosmuck
2. Connemara Boy (9)   Colman McDonagh, Tooreen, Bealadangan
3. Adventure (11)   Michael Conroy, Ballyconneely
4. John Quirke (13)   Val Keaney, Gowla, Cashel
5. Noble Star (17)   Thomas McDonagh, Derrylea, Clifden
6. Silver Pearl (18)   Stephen Walsh, Keelkyle, Letterfrack (p)
7. Innishgoill Star (20) Michael Diamond, Letterfrack
8. Innishgoill Laddie (21) Jack Bolger, Oughterard
9. Lavalley Noble (23)   Jack Bolger, Oughterard
10. Lavalley Rebel (24)   John Costello, Spiddal
11. Lavalley Star (25)   John Walsh, Kylesalia, Kilkerrin
12. Lavalley Con (26)   Thomas de Courcey, Roundstone
13. Paddy (28)   Bartley Naughton, Costello (p)

NON-REGISTERED STALLIONS
allowed to cover nominated mares for 1938 season

Mountain Lad   Michael Wallace, Tully (p)
(standing at Tully)
Finnane Hero   Michael Wallace, Tully (p)
(standing at Finnane, Oughterard)

John Quirke taken off register Dec 1938 and left with Val Keaney in settlement of original deposit of £5 paid in 1924

1939

1. Connemara Boy (9)   Patrick McMahon, Cartron, Kinvara
2. Adventure (11)   Michael Conroy, Ballyconneely
3. Heather Bell (15)   Ed.Conneely, Glentrasna, Rosmuck
4. Noble Star (17)   Thomas McDonagh, Derrylea, Clifden
5. Silver Pearl (18)   Stephen Walsh, Keelkyle, Letterfrack (p)
6. Innishgoill Star (20) Michael Diamond, Letterfrack
7. Innishgoill Laddie (21) Jack Bolger, Oughterard
8. Lavalley Rebel (24)   Val Keaney, Gowla, Cashel
9. Lavalley Star (25)   John Walsh, Kylesalia, Kilkerrin
10. Lavalley Con (26)   Jack Bolger, Oughterard
11. Paddy (28)   Bartley Naughton, Costello (p)

12. Curra Noble (29)   Thomas de Courcey, Roundstone
13. Derry Boy (30)   John Costello, Spiddal
14. Dun Heath (31)   Mortimer Davoren, Moycullen

NON-REGISTERED STALLIONS
approved to cover nominated mares for 1939 season.

Cloonisle Star.   John McDonagh, Rossaveel, Costello (p)
Mountain Lad.   Michael Wallace, Tully, Inverin (p)
Rainbow   P.K. Joyce, Clifden (p)

Mountain Lad (32) registered in 1939 but remained with Michael Wallace, Tully, died Winter 1939. Adventure (11) removed from list at end of season and sold to Ballina November 1939.

1940

1. Connemara Boy (9)   Patrick McMahon, Kinvara
2. Heather Bell (15)   Ed.Conneely, Glentrasna, Rosmuck
3. Noble Star (17)   Tommy McDonagh, Derrylea, Clifden
4. Silver Pearl (18)   Stephen Walsh, Keelkyle, Letterfrack (p)
5. Innishgoill Star (20)   Michael Diamond, Letterfrack
6. Innishgoill Laddie (21)   Jack Bolger, Oughterard
7. Lavalley Rebel (24)   Martin Ridge, Costello
8. Lavalley Star (25)   John Walsh, Kylesalia, Kilkerrin
9. Lavalley Con (26)   Jack Bolger, Oughterard
10. Paddy (28)   Bartley Naughton, Costello (p)
11. Curra Noble (29)   John de Courcey, Errisbeg, Roundstone
12. Derry Boy (30)   John Costello, Spiddal
13. Dun Heath (31)   Val Keaney, Gowla, Cashel
14. Clough Rebel (33)   Michael Conroy, Ballyconneely
15. Clough Con (37)   Tommy McDonagh, Derrylea, Clifden

Connemara Boy died of tetanus 1940 with P.McMahon Kinvara. Silver Pearl sold to Jack Bolger in Spring 1941 following fatal accident of owner Stephen Walsh at Carna Show 1940. Curra Noble sold to Maryborough 1940. Dun Heath sold Sept 1940 to Mr Leese, Castlecomer

1941

1. Heather Bell (15)   Ed.Conneely, Glentrasna, Rosmuck
2. Noble Star (17)   Tommy McDonagh, Derrylea, Clifden
3. Silver Pearl (18)   Jack Bolger, Oughterard (p)
4. Innishgoill Star (20)   Michael Diamond, Letterfrack
5. Innishgoill Laddie (21)   Jack Bolger, Oughterard

6. Lavalley Rebel (24)   Martin Ridge, Costello
7. Lavalley Star (25)   John Walsh, Kylesalia, Kilkerrin
8. Lavalley Con (26)   Jack Bolger, Oughterard
9. Paddy (28)   Bartley Naughton, Costello (p)
10. Derry Boy (30)   John Costello, Spiddal
11. Clough Rebel (33)   Michael Conroy, Ballyconneely
12. Clough Con (37)   Tommy McDonagh, Derrylea, Clifden
13. Calla Rebel (38)   John Fahy, Drumacoo, Kilcolgan

NON-REGISTERED STALLION
approved for service of registered Connemara mares

Dynamite   Patrick Mogan, Oughterard (p)
grey cob s. Heather Grey (16)

Lavalley Con castrated 1941 and sold as a gelding. Heather Bell sold Jan 1942 to Mr Gallagher, Co.Leitrim

1942

1. Noble Star (17)   Tommy McDonagh, Derrylea, Clifden
2. Silver Pearl (18)   Jack Bolger, Oughterard
3. Innishgoill Star (20)   Stephen Mannion, Ballinafad
4. Innishgoill Laddie (21)   Jack Bolger, Oughterard
5. Lavalley Rebel (24)   Martin Ridge, Costello
6. Lavalley Star (25)   John de Courcey, Roundstone
7. Paddy (28)   Bartley Naughton, Costello (p)
8. Derry Boy (30)   John Costello, Spiddal
9. Clough Rebel (33)   Michael Conroy, Ballyconneely
10. Clough Con (37)   Michael Diamond, Letterfrack
11. Calla Rebel (38)   John Fahy, Drumacoo, Kilcolgan
12. Gil (43)   John Walsh, Kylesalia, Kilkerrin
13. Airgead (45)   Ed.Conneely, Glentrasna, Rosmuck

NON-REGISTERED STALLIONS
approved for service of Registered Connemara Pony Mares

Dynamite.   Patrick Mogan, Oughterard (p)
grey cob, s. Heather Grey (16)
Skibbereen.I.D.   Jack Bolger, Oughterard.

Innishgoill Star was removed from list and sold to Kildare

1943

1. Noble Star (17)   John Costello, Spiddal
2. Silver Pearl (18)   Jack Bolger, Oughterard

3. Innishgoill Laddie (21)   T.J. McDonagh, Derrylea, Clifden
4. Lavalley Rebel (24)   Martin Ridge, Costello
5. Lavalley Star (25)   John de Courcey, Roundstone
6. Paddy (28)   Bartley Naughton, Costello (p)
7. Derry Boy (30)   Ed.Conneely, Glentrasna, Rosmuck
8. Clough Rebel (33)   Michael Conroy, Ballyconneely
9. Clough Con (37)   Michael Diamond, Letterfrack
10. Calla Rebel (38)   John Fahy, Drumacoo, Kilcolgan
11. Gil (43)   John Walsh, Kylesalia, Kilkerrin
12. Airgead (45)   T.J.McDonagh, Derrylea, Clifden
13. Tully Lad (48)   Michael Wallace, Tully, Inverin (p)

NON-REGISTERED STALLIONS
approved for service of Registered Connemara Pony Mares.

Dynamite.   Patrick Mogan, Oughterard (p)
grey cob, s. Heather Grey (16)
Skibbereen I.D.   Jack Bolger, Oughterard
Winter T.B.   Jack Bolger, Oughterard
(limited)

Winter was given to the CPBS by Mr Ussher, Swords, but he died suddenly in Nov. 1943 of ruptured liver. Lavalley Star sold Sept 1943 to Co. Offaly. Clough Rebel sold Dec 1943 to Co. Longford. Airgead sold 1943 to Co.Donegal

1944

1. Noble Star (17)   John Costello, Spiddal
2. Silver Pearl (18)   Jack Bolger, Oughterard
3. Innishgoill Laddie (21)   Michael Diamond, Letterfrack
4. Lavalley Rebel (24)   Peter Connolly, Bealadangan
5. Paddy (28)   Bartley Naughton, Costello (p)
6. Derry Boy (30)   Ed.Conneely, Glentrasna, Rosmuck
8. Clough Con (37)   Frank McDonagh, Derrylea, Clifden
9. Calla Rebel (38)   John Fahy, Drumacoo, Kilcolgan
10. Gil (43)   John Walsh, Kylesalia, Kilkerrin
11. Finnane Rover (47)   John Kyne, Leagaun, Moycullen
12. Tully Lad (48)   Michael Wallace, Tully, Inverin (p)
13. Kylesalia Star (49)   Patrick Keane, Cluggan, Maam
14. Keehaune Laddie (52)   Michael Conroy, Ballyconneely
15. Dun Lorenzo (55)   John de Courcey, Roundstone

NON REGISTERED STALLIONS
approved for service of Registered Connemara Pony Mares

Dynamite.   Patrick Mogan, Oughterard (p)
grey cob, s. Heather Grey (16)
Skibbereen I.D.   Jack Bolger, Oughterard

Noble Star sold Dec 1944 to M.J.Henigan Listowel. Silver Pearl sold in winter 1944 to Co.Wexford. Clough Con sold Sept 1944 to Castlerea.

1945

1. Innishgoill Laddie (21)   Michael Diamond, Letterfrack
2. Lavalley Rebel (24)   Peter Connolly, Bealadangan
3. Paddy (28)   Bartley Naughton, Costello (p)
4. Derry Boy (30)   Ed.Conneely, Glentrasna, Rosmuck
5. Calla Rebel (38)   John Fahy, Drumacoo, Kilcolgan
6. Gil (43)   John Walsh, Kylesalia, Kilkerrin
7. Finnane Rover (47)   John Kyne, Leagaun, Moycullen
8. Keehaune Laddie (52)   Michael Conroy, Ballyconneely
9. Tully Lad (48)   Michael Wallace, Tully, Inverin (p)
10. Dun Lorenzo (55)   Jack Bolger, Oughterard
11. Rusheen Heather (56)   Frank McDonagh, Derrylea

NON-REGISTERED STALLIONS
approved for service of registered Connemara mares

Dynamite.   Patrick Mogan, Oughterard (p)
grey cob, s. Heather Grey (16)
Skibbereen (I.D.)   John Costello, Spiddal
Hillside Rover (I.D.)   John de Courcey, Roundstone
May Boy (I.D.)   Jack Bolger, Oughterard (p)

Rusheen Heather sold to Co. Donegal Oct.1945. Dynamite removed from list at end of 1945 season

1946

1. Innishgoill Laddie (21)   Michael Diamond, Letterfrack
2. Lavalley Rebel (24)   Jack Bolger, Oughterard
3. Paddy (28)   Bartley Naughton, Costello (p)
4. Derry Boy (30)   Ed.Conneely, Glentrasna, Rosmuck
5. Calla Rebel (38)   John Fahy, Drumacoo, Kilcolgan
6. Gil (43)   Peter Connolly, Bealadangan
7. Finnane Rover (47)   John Kyne, Leagaun, Moycullen
8. Keehaune Laddie (52)   Michael Conroy, Ballyconneely

9. Tully Lad (48)   Michael Wallace, Tully, Inverin (p)
10. Dun Lorenzo (55)   John de Courcey, Roundstone
11. Dooyeher Con (59)   Frank McDonagh, Derrylea
12. Creganna Winter (63)   John Walsh, Kylesalia, Kilkerrin

APPROVED IRISH DRAUGHT SIRES

Skibbereen I.D.   John Costello, Spiddal
Hillside Rover I.D.   Michael Conroy, Ballyconneely
May Boy I.D.   Jack Bolger, Oughterard (p)

Paddy sold Nov.1946 to Miss Spotiswoode, Devon, registered in UK as Cama of Calla. Keehaune Laddie showed slight stringhalt, castrated and sold to Cahirciveen August 1946. Skibbereen I.D. removed from list end of 1946, castrated, and sold to Matt Healy, Oughterard 1947. Little Heaven T.B. purchased Dec 1946 for £100.

1947

1. Innishgoill Laddie (21)   Michael Diamond, Letterfrack
2. Lavalley Rebel (24)   Ed.Conneely, Glentrasna, Rosmuck
3. Derry Boy (30)   Bartley Naughton, Costello
4. Calla Rebel (38)   John Fahy, Drumacoo, Kilcolgan
5. Gil (43)   Michael Conroy, Ballyconneely
6. Finnane Rover (47)   Brendan Burke, Patches, Claddaghduff
7. Tully Lad (48)   Michael Wallace, Tully, Inverin (p)
8. Dun Lorenzo (55)   John de Courcey, Roundstone
9. Dooyeher Con (59)   Peter Connolly, Bealadangan
10. Creganna Winter (63)   John Walsh, Kylesalia, Kilkerrin
11. Clough Droighneann (67)   John Kyne, Leagaun, Moycullen
12. Tiger Gill (68)   Jack Bolger, Oughterard

APPROVED IRISH DRAUGHT SIRES

Hillside Rover I.D.   Michael Conroy, Ballyconneely
May Boy I.D.   Jack Bolger, Oughterard (p)

THOROUGHBRED STALLION

Little Heaven.   Jack Bolger, Oughterard
limited to 40 mares

1948

1. Innishgoill Laddie (21)   Peter Connolly, Bealadangan
2. Lavalley Rebel (24)   Ed.Conneely, Glentrasna, Rosmuck
3. Derry Boy (30)   Bartley Naughton, Costello
4. Calla Rebel (38)   John Walsh, Kylesalia, Kilkerrin

5. Gil (43)   Anthony Faherty, Roscrea, Moyard
6. Finnane Rover (47)   Andrew McGrath, Ballyconree, Clifden
7. Tully Lad (48)   Michael Wallace, Tully, Inverin (p)
8. Dun Lorenzo (55)   John de Courcey, Roundstone
9. Dooyeher Con (59)   John Fahy, Drumacoo, Kilcolgan
10. Creganna Winter (63)   Jack Bolger, Oughterard
11. Clough Droighneann (67)   Michael Conroy, Ballyconneely
12. Tiger Gill (68)   John Keaney, Gowla, Cashel
13. Farravane Boy (71)   Brendan Burke, Patches, Claddaghduff

APPROVED IRISH DRAUGHT SIRES

Hillside Rover I.D.   Michael Conroy, Ballyconneely
May Boy I.D.   Jack Bolger, Oughterard (p)

THOROUGHBRED STALLION

Little Heaven.T.B.   Jack Bolger, Oughterard
limited to 40 mares.

Finnane Rover removed from list and sold 1949. Tully Lad sold to Jack Bolger June 1949, and resold to CPBS Dec 1949, not on 1949 list. Dooyeher Con removed from list end of 1948 season, castrated 1949 (whistling) and sold.

1949

1. Innishgoill Laddie (21)   Peter Connolly, Bealadangan
2. Lavalley Rebel (24)   Ed.Conneely, Glentrasna, Rosmuck
3. Derry Boy (30)   John Fahy, Drumacoo, Kilcolgan
4. Calla Rebel (38)   John Walsh, Kylesalia, Kilkerrin
5. Gil (43)   Anthony Faherty, Roscrea, Moyard
6. Dun Lorenzo (55)   John de Courcey, Roundstone
7. Creganna Winter (63)   Michael Conroy, Bunowen, Ballyconneely
8. Tiger Gill (68)   John Keaney, Gowla, Cashel
9. Farravane Boy (71)   Brendan Burke, Patches, Claddaghduff
10. Man of Barna (73)   Joseph Hoade, Barna
11. Dun Orphan (77)   Ed.Conneely, Glentrasna, Rosmuck
12. Cilciarain (78)   Bartley Naughton, Costello
13. Carna Bobby (79)   Jack Bolger, Oughterard
14. Coill Ruadh (80)   Joe McGrath, Faulkeera, Clifden
15. Tully Nigger (81)   George Kyne, Loughwell, Moycullen

APPROVED IRISH DRAUGHT SIRES

Hillside Rover I.D.   Michael Conroy, Ballyconneely
May Boy I.D.   Jack Bolger, Oughterard (p)

THOROUGHBRED STALLION

Little Heaven.T.B.   Jack Bolger, Oughterard
will stand at Clifden Saturdays.

Lavalley Rebel sold Aug.1949 to John O'Mahony Meade, Chepstow, Wales, price £40. Derry Boy taken off list 1950 and sold to P.Treacy, Gort. Tully Nigger taken off list sold to Michael O'Malley who exported him to America 1950. Hillside Rover taken off list Jan 1950 and sold for £20

1950

1.	Innishgoill Laddie (21)	Michael Conroy, Ballyconneely
2.	Calla Rebel (38)	John Walsh, Kylesalia, Kilkerrin
3.	Gil (43)	Anthony Faherty, Roscrea, Moyard
4.	Tully Lad (48)	Jack Bolger, Oughterard
5.	Dun Lorenzo (55)	John de Courcey, Roundstone
6.	Creganna Winter (63)	Peter Connolly, Bealadangan
7.	Tiger Gill (68)	Michael Keane, Glynsk, Cashel
8.	Farravane Boy (71)	Brendan Burke, Patches, Claddaghduff
9.	Man of Barna (73)	Joseph Hoade, Barna (p)
10.	Dun Orphan (77)	Ed.Conneely, Glentrasna, Rosmuck
11.	Cilciarain (78)	Bartley Naughton, Costello
12.	Carna Bobby (79)	Jack Bolger, Oughterard
13.	Coill Ruadh (80)	Joe McGrath, Faulkeera, Clifden
14.	Creg Coneera (82)	John Hoban, Minna, Inverin
15.	Creg Usheen (85)	George Kyne, Loughwell, Moycullen
16.	Tooreen Laddie (86)	John Conneely, Glentrasna, Rosmuck

APPROVED SIRES

May Boy I.D.   Jack Bolger, Oughterard (p)
Little Heaven T.B.   Jack Bolger, Oughterard
will travel to Cashel and Carna.

Creg Usheen (85) died June 1950 of pneumonia. May Boy I.D. sold at end of 1950 season.

1951

1.	Innishgoill Laddie (21)	Michael Conroy, Ballyconneely
2.	Calla Rebel (38)	Jack Bolger, Oughterard
3.	Gil (43)	Anthony Faherty, Roscrea, Moyard
4.	Dun Lorenzo (55)	John Conneely, Glentrasna, Rosmuck
5.	Creganna Winter (63)	Peter Connolly, Bealadangan
6.	Tiger Gill (68)	Michael Keane, Glynsk, Cashel

7.	Farravane Boy (71)	John de Courcey, Roundstone
8.	Man of Barna (73)	Joseph Hoade, Barna (p)
9.	Dun Orphan (77)	John Walsh, Kylesalia, Kilkerrin
10.	Cilciarain (78)	Bartley Naughton, Costello
11.	Carna Bobby (79)	Jack Bolger, Oughterard
12.	Coill Ruadh (80)	Joe McGrath, Faulkeera, Clifden
13.	Creg Coneera (82)	John Hoban, Minna, Inverin
15.	Carna Dun (89)	Brendan Burke, Patches, Claddaghduff

THOROUGHBRED STALLION

Little Heaven T.B.   Jack Bolger, Oughterard
will travel to Clifden, Carna, and Cashel Saturdays

Tully Lad and Tooreen Laddie both taken back at end of 1950 season and spent 1951 season at grass at Killola.

1952

1.	Innishgoill Laddie (21)	Thomas Fahy, Drumacoo, Kilcolgan
2.	Calla Rebel (38)	Michael Conroy, Ballyconneely
3.	Dun Lorenzo (55)	John Conneely, Glentrasna, Rosmuck
4.	Creganna Winter (63)	Peter Connolly, Bealadangan
5.	Tiger Gill (68)	Michael Keane, Glynsk, Cashel
6.	Farravane Boy (71)	John de Courcey, Roundstone
7.	Dun Orphan (77)	John Walsh, Kylesalia, Kilkerrin
8.	Cilciarain (78)	Bartley Naughton, Costello
9.	Carna Bobby (79)	Murt Joyce, Ardnasilla, Oughterard
10.	Coill Ruadh (80)	Andrew McGrath, Faulkeera, Clifden
11.	Creg Coneera (82)	John Hoban, Minna, Inverin
12.	Tooreen Laddie (86)	Paddy Joyce, Knockilaree, Oughterard
13.	Carna Dun (89)	John de Courcey, Roundstone
14.	MacDara (91)	Anthony Faherty, Roscrea, Moyard

Gil (43) taken off list and sold to Kilorglin May 1952. Little Heaven T.B. found to be unsound with cataract and was castrated and sold 1952.

1953

1.	Innishgoill Laddie (21)	Thomas Fahy, Drumacoo, Kilcolgan
2.	Calla Rebel (38)	Michael Conroy, Ballyconneely
3.	Tully Lad (48)	James Grealish (Roger), Oranmore
4.	Dun Lorenzo (55)	Patrick Joyce, (MI) Shanakeela, Recess
5.	Creganna Winter (63)	Martin Walsh (Pat), Snabo, Rosmuck
6.	Tiger Gill (68)	Charles Lynch, Annavane, Bealadangan

7. Farravane Boy (71)   Mark Geoghegan, Oughterard
8. Dun Orphan (77)   John Walsh, Kylesalia, Kilkerrin
9. Cilciarain (78)   Bartley Naughton, Costello
10. Carna Bobby (79)   Peter Kyne, Knockranny, Moycullen
11. Coill Ruadh (80)   Joe Little, Bunowen, Ballyconneely
12. Creg Coneera (82)   John Hoban, Minna, Inverin
13. Tooreen Laddie (86)   Paddy Joyce, Knockilaree, Oughterard
14. Carna Dun (89)   John de Courcey, Roundstone
15. MacDara (91)   Anthony Faherty, Roscrea, Moyard

Creganna Winter taken back at end of 1953 season and sent to Oranmore. Farravane Boy removed from approved list at end of 1953 season. Coill Ruadh rejected for unsoundness at Connemara Show 53, and castrated, sold to Joe Little for £15.

1954

1. Innishgoill Laddie (21)   Festy King, Claddaghduff
2. Calla Rebel (38)   Michael Conroy, Ballyconneely
3. Tully Lad (48)   James Grealish (Roger), Oranmore
4. Dun Lorenzo (55)   Martin Walsh (Pat), Snabo, Rosmuck
5. Tiger Gill (68)   Charles Lynch, Annavane, Bealadangan
6. Dun Orphan (77)   John Walsh, Kylesalia, Kilkerrin
7. Cilciarain (78)   Bartley Naughton, Costello
8. Carna Bobby (79)   Peter Kyne, Knockranny, Moycullen
9. Creg Coneera (82)   John Hoban, Minna, Inverin
10. Tooreen Laddie (86)   Paddy Joyce, Knockilaree, Oughterard
11. Carna Dun (89)   John de Courcey, Roundstone
12. MacDara (91)   Anthony Faherty, Roscrea, Moyard
13. Inver Rebel (93)   Joe Little, Bunowen, Ballyconneely

Innishgoill Laddie became unsound in his wind and was destroyed in August 1954, aged 20. Left 58 progeny. Tooreen Laddie sold to Col. J.Hume Dudgeon exported to USA

1955

1. Calla Rebel (38)   Michael Conroy, Ballyconneely
2. Tully Lad (48)   John de Courcey, Roundstone
3. Dun Lorenzo (55)   Martin Walsh (Pat), Snabo, Rosmuck
4. Creganna Winter (63)   Paddy Joyce, Knockilaree, Oughterard
5. Tiger Gill (68)   Bartley Naughton, Costello
6. Dun Orphan (77)   James Grealish (Roger), Oranmore

7. Cilciarain (78)   Peter Kyne, Knockranny, Moycullen
8. Carna Bobby (79)   Festus King, Claddaghduff
9. Creg Coneera (82)   John Hoban, Minna, Inverin
10. Carna Dun (89)   John Walsh, Kylesalia, Kilkerrin
11. MacDara (91)   Anthony Faherty, Roscrea, Moyard
12. Inver Rebel (93)   Joe Little, Bunowen, Ballyconneely
13. Camlin Cirrus (94)   Charles Lynch, Bealdangan

Dun Orphan sold to James Grealish £25 at end of season

1956

1. Calla Rebel (38)   Thomas Fahy, Drumacoo, Kilcolgan
2. Tully Lad (48)   Martin Walsh (Pat), Snabo, Rosmuck
3. Dun Lorenzo (55)   Michael Conroy, Ballyconneely
4. Creganna Winter (63)   James Grealish (Roger), Oranmore
5. Tiger Gill (68)   Bartley Naughton, Costello
6. Cilciarain (78)   Peter Kyne, Knockranny, Moycullen
7. Carna Bobby (79)   Festus King, Claddaghduff
8. Creg Coneera (82)   John Hoban, Minna, Inverin
9. Carna Dun (89)   John Walsh, Kylesalia, Kilkerrin
10 MacDara (91)   Anthony Faherty, Roscrea, Moyard
11. Inver Rebel (93)   Joe Little, Bunowen, Ballyconneely
12. Camlin Cirrus (94)   Charles Lynch, Bealadangan
13. Doon Paddy (95)   Paddy Joyce, Knockilaree, Oughterard

(ARAB X CONNEMARA)

Clonkeehan Auratum   Jo Hoade, Barna.
This stallion limited to 20 mares selected by the CPBS.

Inver Rebel taken to Galway end of 1956 season and not located for 1957 season. Tully Lad sold Dec 1956 to P.Treacy, Gort, and purchased by Paddy Lally, Gort, Nov 1957. Calla Rebel sold to Thos Fahy, Kilcolgan, Dec 1956 for £15

1957

1. Calla Rebel (38)   Thomas Fahy, Drumacoo, Kilcolgan
2. Dun Lorenzo (55)   Michael Conroy, Ballyconneely
3. Creganna Winter (63)   James Grealish (Roger), Oranmore
4. Tiger Gill (68)   Bartley Naughton, Costello
5. Cilciarain (78)   Peter Kyne, Knockranny, Moycullen
6. Carna Bobby (79)   Festus King, Claddaghduff
7. Creg Coneera (82)   Martin Walsh (Pat), Snabo, Rosmuck

8. Carna Dun (89)   John Walsh, Kylesalia, Kilkerrin
9. MacDara (91)   Joe Little, Bunowen, Ballyconneely
10. Camlin Cirrus (94)   Charles Lynch, Bealadangan
12. Doon Paddy (95)   Paddy Joyce, Knockilaree, Oughterard

(ARAB X CONNEMARA)

Clonkeehan Auratum   Anthony Faherty, Roscrea, Moyard

Creganna Winter 63 was destroyed 23/7/57 having broken both hind legs.

1958

1. Dun Lorenzo (55)   Michael Conroy,Bunowen, Ballyconneely
2. Tiger Gill (68)   John Mulkerrins, Knockerasser, Moycullen
3. Cilciarain (78)   Peter Kyne, Knockranny, Moycullen
4. Carna Bobby (79)   Festy King, Claddaghduff
5. Carna Dun (89)   Paddy Joyce, Knockilaree, Oughterard
6. Inver Rebel (93)   Martin Walsh (Pat), Snabo, Rosmuck
7. MacDara (91)   Joseph Little, Bunowen,Ballyconneely
9. Doon Paddy (95)   John Walsh, Kylesalia, Kilkerrin
10. Tooreen Ross (99)   James Grealish (Roger) Carnmore, Oranmore
11. Gael Linn (103)   Thomas McDonagh, Roundstone (p)
12. Clonkeehan Auratum (104)   Anthony Faherty, Roscrea,Moyard.
Fees for this stallion. Nominated mares free with ticket.
Reg.mares from outside district 3 guineas, others 5 guineas
Camlin Cirrus (94) sold in 1959 to J.O'Mahony Meade.

1959

1. Dun Lorenzo (55)   Michael Conroy, Bunowen, Ballyconneely
2. Tiger Gill (68)   John Mulkerrins, Knockerasser, Moycullen
3. Cilciarain (78)   Peter Kyne, Knockranny, Moycullen
4. Carna Bobby (79)   John Walsh, Kylesalia, Kilkerrin
5. Carna Dun (89)   Paddy Joyce, Knockilaree, Oughterard
6. Inver Rebel (93)   Martin Walsh (Pat), Snabo, Rosmuck
7. MacDara (91)   Joseph Little, Bunowen, Ballyconneely
8. Doon Paddy (95)   James Grealish (Roger) Carnmore, Oranmore
9. Tooreen Ross (99),   Michael King, Cushatrough, Claddaghduff
10. Gael Linn (103)   Thomas McDonagh, Roundstone (p)
11. Clonkeehan Auratum (104)   Anthony Faherty, Roscrea, Moyard
Fees for this stallion. Nominated mares free with ticket.
Reg.mares from outside district 3 guineas, others 5 guineas

Gael Linn (103) sold August 1959 to Stanislaus Lynch and exported to USA to Hon O C Fisher, Congress of USA.

1960

1. Tiger Gill (68)   John Mulkerrins, Knockerasser, Moycullen.
2. Cilciarain (78)   Anthony Faherty, Roscrea, Moyard, Clifden
3. Carna Bobby (79)   John Walsh, Kyesalia, Kilkerrin, Carna.
4. Carna Dun (89)   Patrick Joyce, Knockilaree, Oughterard
5. Mac Dara (91)   Peter Kyne, Knockranny, Moycullen.
6. Inver Rebel (93)   Martin Walsh (Pat), Snabo, Rosmuck.
7. Doon Paddy (95)   James Grealish (Roger), Oranmore.
8. Tooreen Ross (99)   Michael King, Cushatrough, Claddaghduff.
9. Clonkeehan Auratum (104)   Michael Conroy, Bunowen, Ballyconeely.

Cilciarain (78) left Connemara end of 1960, sold to Mrs Duff, Scotland.

1961

1. Tiger Gill (68)   John Mulkerrins, Knockerasser, Moycullen.
2. Carna Bobby (79)   John Walsh, Kyesalia, Kilkerrin, Carna.
3. Carna Dun (89)   Patrick Joyce, Knockilaree, Oughterard
4. Mac Dara (91)   Peter Kyne, Knockranny, Moycullen
5. Inver Rebel (93)   Martin Walsh (Pat), Snabo, Rosmuck
6. Doon Paddy (95)   Michael Little, Bunowen, Ballyconneely
7. Tooreen Ross (99)   Michael King, Cushatrough, Claddaghduff.
8. Clonkeehan Auratum (104)   Michael Conroy, Bunowen, Ballyconeely
9. Clonjoy (117)   James Grealish (Roger), Oranmore.

Carna Bobby (79) left Connemara end of season, sold to Paddy Lally, Gort for £35.

1962

1. Tiger Gill (68)   Michael O'Brien Glenhoghen, Recess.
2. Carna Dun (89)   Patrick Joyce, Knockilaree, Oughterard
3. Mac Dara (91)   Peter Kyne, Knockranny, Moycullen
4. Inver Rebel (93)   Martin Walsh (Pat), Snabo, Rosmuck
5. Doon Paddy (95)   Michael Little, Bunowen, Ballyconneely
6. Tooreen Ross (99)   Michael King, Cushatrough, Claddaghduff.
7. Clonkeehan Auratum (104)   Michael Conroy, Bunowen, Ballyconeely
8. Clonjoy (117)   John Mulkerrins, Knockerasser, Moycullen
9. Dun Aengus (120)   John Walsh, Kylesalia, Kilkerrin, Carna.
10. Aura Dun (123)   James Grealish (Roger), Oranmore.

Tiger Gill (68) left Connemara end of season, sold to Malahide, Co. Dublin 1963.

1963

1. Carna Dun (89)   Joseph Conroy, Bunowen, Ballyconneely.
2. Mac Dara (91)   Michael Little, Bunowen, Ballyconneely
3. Inver Rebel (93)   Michael King, Cushatrough, Claddaghduff.
4. Doon Paddy (95)   Patrick Joyce, Aughanure, Oughterard
5. Clonkeehan Auratum (104)   Peter Kyne, Knockranny, Moycullen
6. Clonjoy (117)   John Mulkerrins, Knockerasser, Moycullen
7. Dun Aengus (120)   John Walsh, Kylesalia, Kilkerrin, Carna.
8. Aura Dun (123)   Martin Walsh (Pat), Snabo, Rosmuck.
9. Tooreen Ross (99)   James Grealish (Roger), Oranmore.
10. Ben Lettery (133)   Thomas O'Brien, Canal Stage, Ballinafad.
11. Bridge Boy (124)   Patrick Geoghegan, Oughterard (p)

Tooreen Ross (9) left list end of season, sold to Mrs Duff Scotland Jan 1965.
Inver Rebel (93) left list end of season, sold to J. Bermingham, Kinvara.

1964

1. Carna Dun (89)   Joseph Conroy, Bunowen, Ballyconneely.
2. Mac Dara (91)   Michael Little, Bunowen, Ballyconneely
3. Dun Aengus (120)   Michael King, Cushatrough, Claddaghduff
4. Doon Paddy (95)   Patrick Joyce, Aughanure, Oughterard
5. Clonkeehan Auratum (104)   Peter Kyne, Knockranny, Moycullen
6. Knockranny Ruby (134)   Peter Kyne, Knockranny, Moycullen.
7. Clonjoy (117)   John Mulkerrins, Knockerasser, Moycullen
8. Rebel Wind (127)   John Walsh, Kylesalia, Kilkerrin, Carna.
9. Mervyn Storm (140)   Martin Walsh (Pat), Snabo, Rosmuck.
10. Aura Dun (123)   James Grealish (Roger), Oranmore.
11 Ben Lettery (133)   Thomas O'Brien, Canal Stage, Ballinafad.
12. Bridge Boy (124)   Patrick Geoghegan, Oughterard (p)
13. Atlantic Storm (139)   Tom Feeney, Clynagh, Carraroe.

Clonkeehan Auratum (014) retired from list end of season moved to Tom
Whelan, Ardrahan. Aura Dun (123) removed from list end of season.

1965

1. Carna Dun (89)   Joseph Conroy, Bunowen, Ballyconneely.
2. Mac Dara (91)   Michael Little, Bunowen, Ballyconneely
3. Errigal Prince (159)   Michael King, Cushatrough, Claddaghduff
4. Doon Paddy (95)   Patrick Joyce, Aughanure, Oughterard
5. Knockranny Ruby (134)   Peter Kyne, Knockranny, Moycullen.
6. Clonjoy (117)   John Mulkerrins, Knockerasser, Moycullen

7. Rebel Wind (127)   John Walsh, Kylesalia, Kilkerrin, Carna.
8. Mervyn Storm (140)   Martin Walsh (Pat), Snabo, Rosmuck.
9. Ben Lettery (133)   Thomas O'Brien, Canal Stage, Ballinafad.
10. Bridge Boy (124)   Patrick Geoghegan, Oughterard (p)
11. Atlantic Storm (139)   Tom Feeney, Clynagh, Carraroe.

1966

1. Rebel Wind (127)   Joseph Conroy, Bunowen, Ballyconneely.
2. Mac Dara (91)   Michael Little, Bunowen, Ballyconneely
3. Errigal Prince (159)   Michael King, Cushatrough, Claddaghduff
4. Doon Paddy (95)   Patrick Joyce, Aughanure, Oughterard
5. Knockranny Ruby (134)   Peter Kyne, Knockranny, Moycullen.
6. Ben Lettery (133)   John Mulkerrins, Knockerasser, Moycullen
7. Clonjoy (117)   Martin Walsh (Pat), Snabo, Rosmuck.
8. Mervyn Storm (140)   Thomas O'Brien, Canal Stage, Ballinafad.
9. Carna Dun (89)   James Palmer, Glenlo Abbey, Bushypark (p)
10. Dun Aengus (120)   John Bolger, Cashel, Connemara.
11. Bridge Boy (124)   Patrick Geoghegan, Oughterard (p)
12. Atlantic Storm (139)   Tom Feeney, Clynagh, Carraroe.

Errigal Prince (159) left list end of season, sold December 1966 to Michael
Connolly, Ballyglunin.

1967

1. Rebel Wind (127)   Joseph Conroy, Bunowen, Ballyconneely.
2. Mac Dara (91)   John Curran, Kilkerrin, Connemara.
3. Dun Aengus (120)   Michael King, Cushatrough, Claddaghduff
4. Doon Paddy (95)   Patrick Joyce, Aughanure, Oughterard
5. Knockranny Ruby (134)   Peter Kyne, Knockranny, Moycullen.
6. Ben Lettery (133)   John Mulkerrins, Knockerasser, Moycullen
7. Clonjoy (117)   Pat Murphy, Snabo, Rosmuck.
8. Mervyn Storm (140)   Thomas O'Brien, Canal Stage, Ballinafad.
9. Carna Dun (89)   James Palmer, Glenlo Abbey, Bushypark (p)
10. Bridge Boy (124)   Patrick Geoghegan, Oughterard (p)
11. Atlantic Storm (139)   Tom Feeney, Clynagh, Carraroe.
12. Clonkeehan Auratum (104)   John Brennan, Fort Lorenzo, Taylors Hill.

1968

1. Mac Dara (91)   Joseph Conroy, Bunowen, Ballyconneely.
2. Rebel Wind (127)   Joseph Conroy, Bunowen, Ballyconneely
3. Doon Paddy (95)   John Curran, Kilkerrin, Connemara.

4. Dun Aengus (120)   Michael King, Cushatrough, Claddaghduff
5. Atlantic Storm (139)   Patrick Joyce, Aughanure, Oughterard
6. Knockranny Ruby (134)   Peter Kyne, Knockranny, Moycullen.
7. Ben Lettery (133)   John Mulkerrins, Knockerasser, Moycullen
8. Clonjoy (117)   Pat Murphy, Snabo, Rosmuck.
9. Mervyn Storm (140)   Thomas O'Brien, Canal Stage, Ballinafad.
10. Carna Dun (89)   James Palmer, Glenlo Abbey, Bushypark.
11. Bridge Boy (124)   Patrick Geoghegan, Oughterard.
12. Toombeola (211)   Tom Feeney, Clynagh, Carraroe.

Knockranny Ruby (134) sold to Sweden.

1969

1. Toombeola (211)   Joseph Conroy, Bunowen, Ballyconneely.
2. Rebel Wind (127)   Joseph Conroy, Bunowen, Ballyconneely
3. Doon Paddy (95)   John Curran, Kilkerrin, Connemara.
4. Thunderbolt (178)   Michael King, Cushatrough, Claddaghduff
5. Atlantic Storm (139)   Patrick Joyce, Aughanure, Oughterard
6. Mac Dara (91)   Peter Kyne, Knockranny, Moycullen.
7. Dun Aengus (120)   John Mulkerrins, Knockerasser, Moycullen
8. Clonjoy (117)   Pat Murphy, Snabo, Rosmuck.
9. Ardilaun (261)   Thomas O'Brien, Canal Stage, Ballinafad.
10. Carna Dun (89)   James Palmer, Glenlo Abbey, Bushypark (p)
11. Bridge Boy (124)   Patrick Geoghegan, Oughterard (p)
12. Paddy's Boy (183)   Patrick Geoghegan, Oughterard (p)
13. Kimble (227)   W.J.Diamond, Tully, Renvyle, Dun.
14. Ben Lettery (133)   Tom Feeney, Clynagh, Carraroe.

Toombeola (211) left Connemara end of season.

1970

1. Killyreagh Kim (308)   Joseph Conroy, Bunowen, Ballyconneely
2. Rebel Wind (127)   Joseph Conroy, Bunowen, Ballyconneely
3. Thunderbolt (178)   Stephen Curran, Kilkerrin, Connemara.
4. Doon Paddy (95)   Michael King, Cushatrough, Claddaghduff
5. Atlantic Storm (139)   Patrick Joyce, Aughanure, Oughterard
6. Mac Dara (91)   Peter Kyne, Knockranny, Moycullen.
7. Clonjoy (117)   Paddy Folan, Knockadave, Camus.
8. Ardilaun (261)   Thomas O'Brien, Canal Stage, Ballinafad.
9. Carna Dun (89)   James Palmer, Glenlo Abbey, Bushypark (p)
10. Bridge Boy (124)   Patrick Geoghegan, Oughterard (p)

11. Paddy's Boy (183)   Patrick Geoghegan, Oughterard (p)
12. Kimble (227)   W.J. Diamond, Tully, Renvyle.
13. Ben Lettery (133)   Tom Feeney, Clynagh, Carraroe.
14. Dun Aengus (120)   John Mulkerrins, Knockerasser, Moycullen.

Paddy's Boy (183) removed from list end of season. Doon Paddy (95) retired end of season, moved to Joe MacNamara, Craughwell.

1971

1. Killyreagh Kim (308)   Joseph Conroy, Bunowen, Ballyconneely
2. Rebel Wind (127)   Paddy Folan, Knockadave, Camus.
3. Thunderbolt (178)   Stephen Curran, Kilkerrin, Connemara.
4. Doon Paddy (95)   Michael King, Cushatrough, Claddaghduff
5. Atlantic Storm (139)   Patrick Mulkerrins, Knockerasser, Moycullen.
6. Mac Dara (91)   Peter Kyne, Knockranny, Moycullen.
7. Ardilaun (261)   Thomas O'Brien, Canal Stage, Ballinafad.
8. Carna Dun (89)   James Palmer, Glenlo Abbey, Bushypark (p)
9. Bridge Boy (124)   Patrick Geoghegan, Oughterard (p)
10. Kimble (227)   W.J.Diamond, Tully, Renvyle.
11. Ben Lettery (133)   Tom Feeney, Clynagh, Carraroe.
12. Dun Aengus (120)   Patrick Joyce, Aughanure, Oughterard

Thunderbolt (178) removed from list end of season.

1972

1. Killyreagh Kim (308)   Joseph Conroy, Bunowen, Ballyconneely
2. Rebel Wind (127)   Paddy Folan, Knockadave, Camus.
3. Ben Lettery (133)   Stephen Curran, Kilkerrin, Connemara.
4. Lough Easkey (133)   Michael King, Cushatrough, Claddaghduff
5. Atlantic Storm (139)   Patrick Mulkerrins, Knockerasser, Moycullen.
6. Mac Dara (91)   Peter Kyne, Knockranny, Moycullen.
7. Clonjoy (117)   Thomas O'Brien, Canal Stage, Ballinafad.
8. Carna Dun (89)   James Palmer, Glenlo Abbey, Bushypark (p)
9. Bridge Boy (124)   Patrick Geoghegan, Oughterard (p)
10. Kimble (227)   W.J.Diamond, Tully, Renvyle.
11. Ardilaun (261)   Tom Feeney, Clynagh, Carraroe.
12. Dun Aengus (120)   Patrick Joyce, Aughanure, Oughterard

MacDara (91) retired end of season, went to Jimmy Jones, Carlow. Clonjoy (117) retired end of season, went to Frank Quinn.

1973

1. Thunder Cloud (459) — Joseph Conroy, Bunowen, Ballyconneely
2. Killyreagh Kim (308) — Joseph Conroy, Bunowen, Ballyconneely
3. Rebel Wind (127) — Paddy Folan, Knockadave, Camus.
4. Ben Lettery (133) — Stephen Curran, Kilkerrin, Connemara.
5. Atlantic Storm (139) — Michael King, Cushatrough, Claddaghduff
6. Rosmuck Master (340) — Patrick Mulkerrins, Knockerasser, Moycullen.
7. Roundstone Oscar (337) — Thomas O'Brien, Canal Stage, Ballinafad.
8. Carna Dun (89) — James Palmer, Glenlo Abbey, Bushypark (p)
9. Bridge Boy (124) — Patrick Geoghegan, Oughterard (p)
10. Kimble (227) — W.J.Diamond, Tully, Renvyle.
11. Ardilaun (261) — Tom Feeney, Clynagh, Carraroe.
12. Dun Aengus (120) — Patrick Joyce, Aughanure, Oughterard

Carna Dun (89) died winter of 1973. Kimble (227) removed from list, sold to Sweden.

1974

1. Thunder Cloud (459) — Paddy Folan, Knockadave, Camus.
2. Killyreagh Kim (308) — Paddy Folan, Knockadave, Camus.
3. Rebel Wind (127) — Thomas O'Brien, Canal Stage, Ballinafad.
4. Roundstone Oscar (337) — Patrick Joyce, Aughanure, Oughterard
5. Dun Aengus (120) — Joseph Conroy, Bunowen, Ballyconneely
6. Ben Lettery (133) — Stephen Curran, Kilkerrin, Connemara.
7. Atlantic Storm (139) — Michael King, Cushatrough, Claddaghduff
8. Rosmuck Master (340) — Patrick Mulkerrins, Knockerasser, Moycullen.
9. Bridge Boy (124) — Patrick Geoghegan, Oughterard (p)
10. Ardilaun (261) — Tom Feeney, Clynagh, Carraroe.

Ben Lettery (133) removed from list end of season. Ardilaun (261) removed from list end of season.

1975

1. Abbeyleix Owen (496) — Joseph Conroy, Bunowen, Ballyconneely
2. Thunder Cloud (459) — Martin O'Reilly, Old Town, Moycullen.
3. Killyreagh Kim (308) — Paddy Folan, Knockadave, Camus.
4. Rebel Wind (127) — Thomas O'Brien, Canal Stage, Ballinafad.
5. Roundstone Oscar (337) — W.J.Diamond, Tully, Renvyle.
6. Dun Aengus (120) — Stephen Curran, Kilkerrin, Connemara.
7. Atlantic Storm (139) — Michael King, Cushatrough, Claddaghduff
8. Rosmuck Master (340) — Patrick Mulkerrins, Knockerasser, Moycullen.

9. Bridge Boy (124) — Patrick Geoghegan, Oughterard (p)
10. Tulira Snowball (561) — Tom Feeney, Clynagh, Carraroe.

Bridge Boy (124) left list end of season, sold to Denmark.

1976

1. Abbeyleix Owen (496) — Joseph Conroy, Bunowen, Ballyconneely
2. Thunder Cloud (459) — Martin O'Reilly, Old Town, Moycullen.
3. Killyreagh Kim (308) — Paddy Folan, Knockadave, Camus.
4. Rebel Wind (127) — Thomas O'Brien, Canal Stage, Ballinafad.
5. Roundstone Oscar (337) — W.J.Diamond, Tully, Renvyle.
6. Dun Aengus (120) — Stephen Curran, Kilkerrin, Connemara.
7. Sarsfield (579) — Michael King, Cushatrough, Claddaghduff
8. Ardnasillagh Magnus (547) — Patrick Geoghegan, Canrower, Oughterard (p)
9. Atlantic Storm (139) — Tom Feeney, Clynagh, Carraroe.
10. Tulira Snowball (561) — Liam O'Toole, Spiddal.

Thundercloud (459) removed from list. Tulira Snowball (561) removed from list.

1977

1. Abbeyleix Owen (496) — Joseph Conroy, Bunowen, Ballyconneely
2. Killyreagh Kim (308) — Martin O'Reilly, Old Town, Moycullen.
3. Rebel Wind (127) — Tom Feeney, Clynagh, Carraroe.
4. Roundstone Oscar (337) — W.J.Diamond, Tully, Renvyle.
5. Dun Aengus (120) — Paddy Folan, Knockadave, Camus.
6. Atlantic Storm (139) — Festy Mulkerrin, Callowfeenish, Carna.
7. Skryne Bright Cloud (622) — Paddy Folan, Knockadave, Camus.
8. Ormond Oliver (653) — Thomas O'Brien, Canal Stage, Ballinafad.
9. Sarsfield (579) — Michael King, Cushatrough, Claddaghduff
10. Ardnasillagh Magnus (547) — Patrick Geoghegan, Canrower, Oughterard (p)

Atlantic Storm (139) retired end of season to Jimmy Jones, Carlow. Dun Aengus (127) died during season. Roundstone Oscar (337) removed from list end of season. Rebel Wind (127) died spring 1978.

1978

1. Abbeyleix Owen (496) — Joseph Conroy, Bunowen, Ballyconneely
2. Killyreagh Kim (308) — Martin O'Reilly, Old Town, Moycullen.
3. Rebel Wind (127) — Tom Feeney, Clynagh, Carraroe.
4. Davy D (671) — W.J.Diamond, Tully, Renvyle (p)
5. Ardnasillagh Casey (654) — Paddy Folan, Knockadave, Camus.
6. Ballinaboy Barry (655) — Festy Mulkerrin, Callowfeenish, Carna.

7. Greaney Rebel (186)   Henry Whyte, Knocknacarra, Salthill.
8. Skryne Bright Cloud (622)   Paddy Folan, Knockadave, Camus.
9. Ormond Oliver (653)   Thomas O'Brien, Canal Stage, Ballinafad.
10. Sarsfield (579)   Michael King, Cushatrough, Claddaghduff
11. Ardnasillagh Magnus (547)   Patrick Geoghegan,Canrower, Oughterard (p)

Ardnasillagh Casey (654) died. Ardnasillagh Magnus (547) removed from list.

1979

1. Skryne Bright Cloud (622)   Joseph Conroy, Bunowen, Ballyconneely
2. Killyreagh Kim (308)   Martin O'Reilly, Old Town, Moycullen.
3. Davy D (671)   W.J. Diamond, Tully, Renvyle (p)
4. Ballinaboy Barry (655)   Festy Mulkerrin, Callowfeenish, Carna.
5. Greaney Rebel (186)   Henry Whyte, Knocknacarra, Salthill (p)
6. Ormond Oliver (653)   Thomas O'Brien, Canal Stage, Ballinafad.
7. Sarsfield (579)   Paddy Folan, Knockadave, Camus.
8. Slyne Head (710)   Michael King, Cushatrough, Claddaghduff
9. Abbeyleix Owen (496)   Bartley O'Malley, Derrarthabeg, Carraroe.
10. Ashfield Alex (711)   Joe Nee, Tullybrick, Oughterard.

Ballinaboy Barry (655) removed from list. Slyne Head (710) removed from list.

1980

1. Skryne Bright Cloud (622)   Joseph Conroy, Bunowen, Ballyconneely.
2. Davy D (671)   W.J.Diamond, Tully, Renvyle (p)
3. Killyreagh Kim (308)   Festy Mulkerrin, Callowfeenish, Carna.
4. Ormond Oliver (653)   Thomas O'Brien, Canal Stage, Ballinafad.
5. Thunderbolt (178)   Michael King, Cushatrough, Claddaghduff.
6. Sarsfield (579)   Paddy Folan, Knockadave, Camus.
7. Greaney Rebel (186)   Henry Whyte, Knocknacarra, Salthill (p)
8. Abbeyleix Owen (496)   Bartley O'Malley, Derrarthabeg, Carraroe.
9. Ashfield Alex (711)   Joe Nee, Tullybrick, Oughterard.

Sarsfield (579) removed from list end of season.

1981

1. Skryne Bright Cloud (622)   Joseph Conroy, Bunowen, Ballyconneely
2. Davy D (671)   W.J.Diamond, Tully, Renvyle.
3. Killyreagh Kim (308)   Festy Mulkerrin, Callowfeenish, Carna.
4. Maam Hill (728)   Thomas O'Brien, Canal Stage, Ballinafad.
5. Thunderbolt (178)   Michael King, Cushatrough, Claddaghduff
6. Ormond Oliver (653)   Paddy Folan, Knockadave, Camus

7. Greaney Rebel (186)   Henry Whyte, Knocknacarra, Salthill (p)
8. Abbeyleix Owen (496)   Bartley O'Malley, Derrarthabeg, Carraroe.
9. Ashfield Alex (711)   Joe Nee, Tullybrick, Oughterard.

Skryne Bright Cloud (622) removed from list end of season.

1982

1. Ashfield Alex (711)   Joseph Conroy, Bunowen, Ballyconneely.
2. Davy D (671)   W.J.Diamond, Tully, Renvyle (p)
3. Killyreagh Kim (308)   Festy Mulkerrin, Callowfeenish, Carna.
4. Maam Hill (728)   Thomas O'Brien, Canal Stage, Ballinafad.
5. Thunderbolt (178)   Michael King, Cushatrough, Claddaghduff
6. Ormond Oliver (653)   Paddy Folan, Knockadave, Camus
7. Greaney Rebel (186)   Henry Whyte, Knocknacarra, Salthill (p)
8. Abbeyleix Owen (496)   Bartley O'Malley, Derrarthabeg, Carraroe.
9. Murphy Rebel (696)   Stephen Heanue, Bridge Street, Clifden (p)
10. Fort Boffin (759)   Joe Nee, Tullybrick, Oughterard (p)

Davy D. (671) removed from list end of season. Greaney Rebel (186) removed from list end of season.

1983

1. Ashfield Alex (711)   Joseph Conroy, Bunowen, Ballyconneely.
2. Thunderbolt (178)   Festy Mulkerrin, Callowfeenish, Carna.
3. Killyreagh Kim (308)   Thomas O'Brien, Canal Stage, Ballinafad
4. Mervyn Kingsmill (762)   Michael King, Cushatrough, Claddaghduff
5. Maam Hill (728)   Bartley O'Malley, Derrarthabeg, Carraroe.
6. Abbeyleix Owen (496)   Bartley O'Malley, Derrarthabeg, Carraroe.
7. Ormond Oliver (653)   Paddy Folan, Knockadave, Camus
8. Murphy Rebel (696)   Stephen Heanue, Bridge Street, Clifden (p)
9. Fort Boffin (759)   Joe Nee, Tullybrick, Oughterard (p)

Thunderbolt (178) removed from list end of season, sold to England. Fort Boffin (759) removed from list end of season.

1984

1. Ashfield Alex (711)   Joseph Conroy, Bunowen, Ballyconneely.
2. Abbeyleix Owen (496)   Festy Mulkerrin, Callowfeenish, Carna.
3. Killyreagh Kim (308)   Thomas O'Brien, Canal Stage, Ballinafad
4. Mervyn Kingsmill (762)   Michael King, Cushatrough, Claddaghduff
5. Maam Hill (728)   Bartley O'Malley, Derrarthabeg, Carraroe.
6. Loobeen Larry (670)   Bartley O'Malley, Derrarthabeg, Carraroe (p)

7. Ormond Oliver (653)   Paddy Folan, Knockadave, Camus
8. Murphy Rebel (696)   Stephen Heanue, Bridge Street, Clifden (p)

1985

1. Ashfield Alex (711)   Joseph Conroy, Bunowen, Ballyconneely.
2. Abbeyleix Owen (496)   Festy Mulkerrin, Callowfeenish, Carna.
3. Killyreagh Kim (308)   Thomas O'Brien, Canal Stage, Ballinafad
4. Mervyn Kingsmill (762)   Michael King, Cushatrough, Claddaghduff
5. Maam Hill (728)   Bartley O'Malley, Derrarthabeg, Carraroe.
6. Loobeen Larry (670)   Bartley O'Malley, Derrarthabeg, Carraroe (p)
7. Ormond Oliver (653)   Paddy Folan, Knockadave, Camus
8. Murphy Rebel (696)   Stephen Heanue, Bridge Street, Clifden (p)

Ashfield Alex (711) removed from list end of season.

1986

1. Seafield Silver Rogue (823)   Joseph Conroy, Bunowen, Ballyconneely
2. Abbeyleix Owen (496)   Festy Mulkerrin, Callowfeenish, Carna.
3. Killyreagh Kim (308)   Thomas O'Brien, Canal Stage, Ballinafad
4. Mervyn Kingsmill (762)   Michael King, Cushatrough, Claddaghduff
5. Thunder Storm (796)   Michael King, Cushatrough, Claddaghduff
6. Maam Hill (728)   Bartley O'Malley, Derrarthabeg, Carraroe.
7. Loobeen Larry (670)   Graham Tulloch, Moyard (p)
8. Ormond Oliver (653)   Paddy Folan, Knockadave, Camus
9. Murphy Rebel (696)   Stephen Heanue, Bridge Street, Clifden (p)

Killyreagh Kim (308) retired at end of season. Maam Hill (728) removed from list end of season.

1987

1. Seafield Silver Rogue (823)   Joseph Conroy, Bunowen, Ballyconneely
2. Ormond Oliver (653)   Festy Mulkerrin, Callowfeenish, Carna
3. Abbeyleix Owen (496)   Thomas O'Brien, Canal Stage, Ballinafad
4. Mervyn Kingsmill (762)   Michael King, Cushatrough, Claddaghduff
5. Fort Dara (718)   Bartley O'Malley, Derrarthabeg, Carraroe.
6. Loobeen Larry (670)   Graham Tulloch, Moyard (p)
7. Canal Cormac (848)   Dudley Nee, Camus.
8. Murphy Rebel (696)   Stephen Heanue, Bridge Street, Clifden (p)
9. Cuchulainn (789)   James de Courcey, Errisbeg, Roundstone (p)

Ormond Oliver (653) retired at end of season to Jimmy Jones, Carlow. Fort Dara (718) removed from list.

1988

1. Mervyn Kingsmill (762)   Joseph Conroy, Bunowen, Ballyconneely
2. Abbeyleix Owen (496)   Thomas O'Brien, Canal Stage, Ballinafad
3. Granard Storm (737)   Michael King, Cushatrough, Claddaghduff (p)
4. Seafield Silver Rogue (823)   Bartley O'Malley, Derrarthabeg, Carraroe.
5. Loobeen Larry (670)   Graham Tulloch, Moyard (p)
6. Canal Cormac (848)   Dudley Nee, Camus.
7. Murphy Rebel (696)   Stephen Heanue, Bridge Street, Clifden (p)
8. Cuchulainn (789)   James de Courcey, Errisbeg, Roundstone (p)

Canal Cormac (848) removed from list end of season and sold. Granard Storm (737) removed from list end of season.

1989

1. Mervyn Kingsmill (762)   Joseph Conroy, Bunowen, Ballyconneely
2. Abbeyleix Owen (496)   Dudley Nee, Camus.
3. Ashfield Festy (859)   Thomas O'Brien, Canal Stage, Ballinafad (p)
4. Seafield Silver Rogue (823)   Bartley O'Malley, Derrarthabeg, Carraroe.
5. Loobeen Larry (670)   Graham Tulloch, Moyard (p)
6. Ashfield Alex (711)   Graham Tulloch, Moyard.
7. Murphy Rebel (696)   Stephen Heanue, Bridge Street, Clifden (p)

Murphy Rebel (696) removed from list end of season, sold to Philip McMahon.

1990

1. Mervyn Kingsmill (762)   Dudley Nee, Camus.
2. Abbeyleix Owen (496)   Johnny Lee, Moycullen.
3. Ashfield Festy (859)   Thomas O'Brien, Canal Stage, Ballinafad (p)
4. Seafield Silver Rogue (823)   Bartley O'Malley, Derrarthabeg, Carraroe.
5. Loobeen Larry (670)   Graham Tulloch, Moyard (p)
6. Smokey Duncan (871)   Joseph Conroy, Bunowen, Ballyconneely.

Smokey Duncan (871) bequeathed to the Society by executors of the late Graham Tulloch. Mervyn Kingsmill (762) removed from list end of season, sold to England.

1991

1. Abbeyleix Owen (496)   Jimmy Canavan, Moycullen.
2. Seafield Silver Rogue (823)   Bartley O"Malley, Derrarthabeg, Carraroe.
3. Smokey Duncan (871)   Josie Conroy, Ballyconneely.
4. Ashfield Festy (859)   Tommy O'Brien, Canal Stage (p)
5. Moy Hazy Cove (888)   Dudley Nee, Camus.

1992

1. Abbeyleix Owen (496)   Jimmy Canavan, Moycullen.
2. Seafield Silver Rogue (823)   Bartley O'Malley, Derrarthabeg, Carraroe.
3. Smokey Duncan (871)   Josie Conroy, Ballyconneely.
4. Village Boy (927)   Joe Gorham, Clifden
5. Ashfield Festy (859)   Tommy O'Brien, Canal Stage (p)
6. Moy Hazy Cove (888)   Dudley Nee, Camus.
7. Matchmaker's Lad (937)   Tommy O'Brien, Canal Stage.

Ashfield Festy (859) removed from list at end of season and returned to owner Jimmy Jones. Seafield Silver Rogue (823) removed from list end of season, sold to Joe McGlinchey, Co. Donegal.

1993

1. Abbeyleix Owen (496)   Jimmy Canavan, Moycullen.
2. Smokey Duncan (871)   Josie Conroy, Ballyconneely.
3. Village Boy (927)   Tommy O'Brien, Canal Stage.
5. Moy Johnny's Pride (938)   Bartley O'Malley, Carraroe.
6. Moy Hazy Cove (888)   Dudley Nee, Camus.
7. Matchmaker's Lad (937)   Tommy O'Brien, Canal Stage.

Matchmaker's Lad (937) removed from list end of season.

1994

1. Abbeyleix Owen (496)   Jimmy Canavan, Moycullen.
2. Smokey Duncan (871)   Josie Conroy, Ballyconneely.
3. Village Boy (927)   Tommy O'Brien, Canal Stage.
5. Moy Johnny's Pride (938)   Bartley O'Malley, Carraroe.
6. Moy Hazy Cove (888)   Dudley Nee, Camus.

1995

1. Abbeyleix Owen (496)   Jimmy Canavan, Moycullen.
2. Smokey Duncan (871)   Josie Conroy, Ballyconneely.
3. Village Boy (927)   Tommy O'Brien, Canal Stage.
5. Moy Johnny's Pride (938)   Bartley O'Malley, Carraroe.
6. Moy Hazy Cove (888)   Joe Gorham, Clifden.

1996

1. Abbeyleix Owen (496)   Jimmy Canavan, Moycullen.
2. Smokey Duncan (871)   Josie Conroy, Ballyconneely.
3. Village Boy (927)   Tommy O'Brien, Canal Stage.
5. Moy Johnny's Pride (938)   Bartley O'Malley, Carraroe.
6. Moy Hazy Cove (888)   Joe Gorham, Clifden.

Josie Conroy retired at end of season having served as a custodian for 33 years.

1997

1. Abbeyleix Owen (496)   Jimmy Canavan, Moycullen.
2. Smokey Duncan (871)   Paddy Folan, Turlough, Rosmuck.
3. Village Boy (927)   Tommy O'Brien, Canal Stage.
5. Moy Johnny's Pride (938)   Bartley O'Malley, Carraroe.
6. Moy Hazy Cove (888)   Jimmy Canavan, Moycullen

Abbeyleix Owen (496) retired, but remained with Jimmy Canavan.

1998

1. Smokey Duncan (871)   Paddy Folan, Turlough, Rosmuck.
2. Village Boy (927)   Tommy O'Brien, Canal Stage.
3. Moy Johnny's Pride (938)   Bartley O'Malley, Carraroe.
4. Moy Hazy Cove (888)   Jimmy Canavan, Moycullen

BLUE LINE

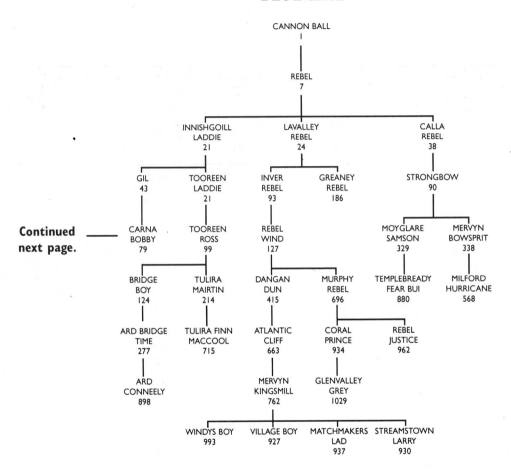

CANNON BALL
1

REBEL
7

INNISHGOILL
LADDIE
21

LAVALLEY
REBEL
24

CALLA
REBEL
38

GIL
43

TOOREEN
LADDIE
21

INVER
REBEL
93

GREANEY
REBEL
186

STRONGBOW
90

Continued next page.

CARNA
BOBBY
79

TOOREEN
ROSS
99

REBEL
WIND
127

MOYGLARE
SAMSON
329

MERVYN
BOWSPRIT
338

BRIDGE
BOY
124

TULIRA
MAIRTIN
214

DANGAN
DUN
415

MURPHY
REBEL
696

TEMPLEBREADY
FEAR BUI
880

MILFORD
HURRICANE
568

ARD BRIDGE
TIME
277

TULIRA FINN
MACCOOL
715

ATLANTIC
CLIFF
663

CORAL
PRINCE
934

REBEL
JUSTICE
962

ARD
CONNEELY
898

MERVYN
KINGSMILL
762

GLENVALLEY
GREY
1029

WINDYS BOY
993

VILLAGE BOY
927

MATCHMAKERS
LAD
937

STREAMSTOWN
LARRY
930

BLUE LINE Continued

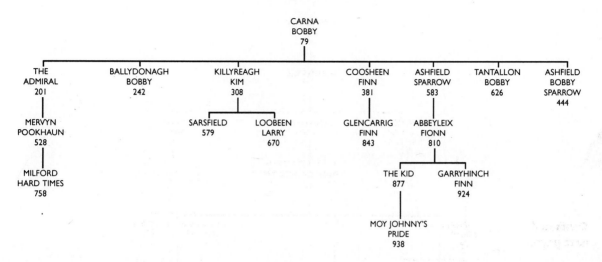

CARNA
BOBBY
79

THE
ADMIRAL
201

BALLYDONAGH
BOBBY
242

KILLYREAGH
KIM
308

COOSHEEN
FINN
381

ASHFIELD
SPARROW
583

TANTALLON
BOBBY
626

ASHFIELD
BOBBY
SPARROW
444

MERVYN
POOKHAUN
528

SARSFIELD
579

LOOBEEN
LARRY
670

GLENCARRIG
FINN
843

ABBEYLEIX
FIONN
810

MILFORD
HARD TIMES
758

THE KID
877

GARRYHINCH
FINN
924

MOY JOHNNY'S
PRIDE
938

RED LINE

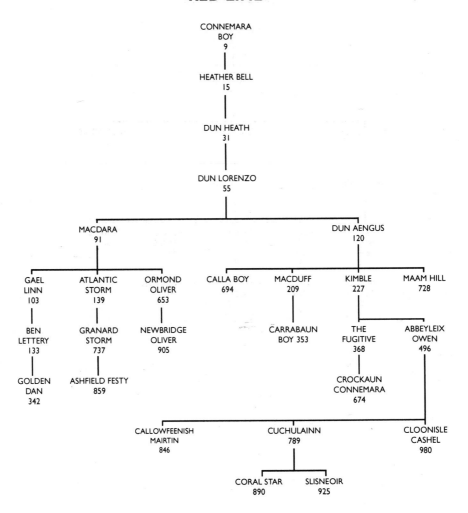

CONNEMARA
BOY
9

HEATHER BELL
15

DUN HEATH
31

DUN LORENZO
55

MACDARA
91

DUN AENGUS
120

GAEL
LINN
103

ATLANTIC
STORM
139

ORMOND
OLIVER
653

CALLA BOY
694

MACDUFF
209

KIMBLE
227

MAAM HILL
728

BEN
LETTERY
133

GRANARD
STORM
737

NEWBRIDGE
OLIVER
905

CARRABAUN
BOY 353

THE
FUGITIVE
368

ABBEYLEIX
OWEN
496

GOLDEN
DAN
342

ASHFIELD FESTY
859

CROCKAUN
CONNEMARA
674

CALLOWFEENISH
MAIRTIN
846

CUCHULAINN
789

CLOONISLE
CASHEL
980

CORAL STAR
890

SLISNEOIR
925

GREEN LINE

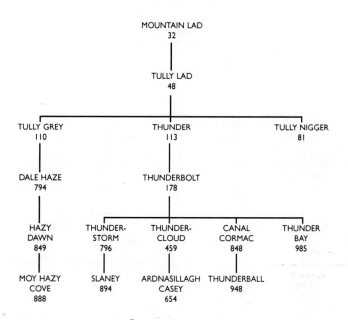

MOUNTAIN LAD
32

TULLY LAD
48

TULLY GREY   THUNDER   TULLY NIGGER
110   113   81

DALE HAZE   THUNDERBOLT
794   178

HAZY   THUNDER-   THUNDER-   CANAL   THUNDER
DAWN   STORM   CLOUD   CORMAC   BAY
849   796   459   848   985

MOY HAZY   SLANEY   ARDNASILLAGH THUNDERBALL
COVE   894   CASEY   948
888   654

PURPLE LINE

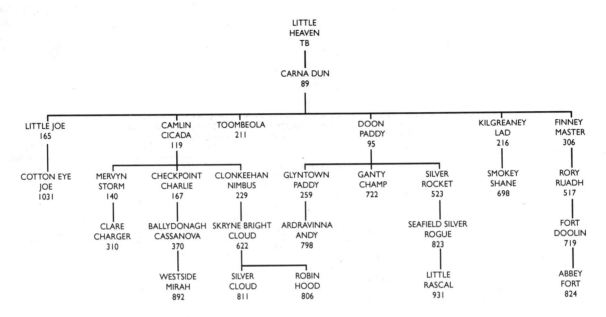

LITTLE
HEAVEN
TB

CARNA DUN
89

LITTLE JOE
165

CAMLIN
CICADA
119

TOOMBEOLA
211

DOON
PADDY
95

KILGREANEY
LAD
216

FINNEY
MASTER
306

COTTON EYE
JOE
1031

MERVYN
STORM
140

CHECKPOINT
CHARLIE
167

CLONKEEHAN
NIMBUS
229

GLYNTOWN
PADDY
259

GANTY
CHAMP
722

SILVER
ROCKET
523

SMOKEY
SHANE
698

RORY
RUADH
517

CLARE
CHARGER
310

BALLYDONAGH
CASSANOVA
370

SKRYNE BRIGHT
CLOUD
622

ARDRAVINNA
ANDY
798

SEAFIELD SILVER
ROGUE
823

FORT
DOOLIN
719

WESTSIDE
MIRAH
892

SILVER
CLOUD
811

ROBIN
HOOD
806

LITTLE
RASCAL
931

ABBEY
FORT
824

ORANGE LINE

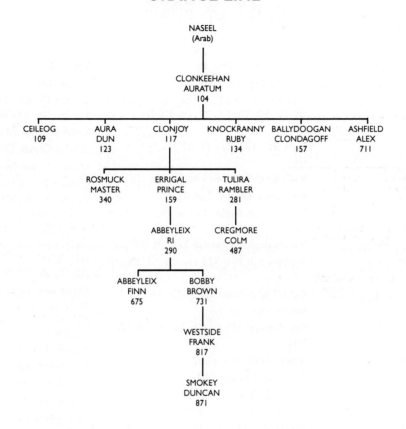

NASEEL
(Arab)

CLONKEEHAN
AURATUM
104

CEILEOG
109

AURA
DUN
123

CLONJOY
117

KNOCKRANNY
RUBY
134

BALLYDOOGAN
CLONDAGOFF
157

ASHFIELD
ALEX
711

ROSMUCK
MASTER
340

ERRIGAL
PRINCE
159

TULIRA
RAMBLER
281

ABBEYLEIX
RI
290

CREGMORE
COLM
487

ABBEYLEIX
FINN
675

BOBBY
BROWN
731

WESTSIDE
FRANK
817

SMOKEY
DUNCAN
871

INDEX OF PONIES

GELDINGS

MARE INDEX